37

Virtual Reality

Virtual Reality
Through the New Looking Glass
2nd Edition

Ken Pimentel
Kevin Teixeira

1026102

intel® / McGraw-Hill

New York   San Francisco   Washington, D.C.   Auckland   Bogotá
Caracas   Lisbon   London   Madrid   Mexico City   Milan
Montreal   New Delhi   San Juan   Singapore
Sydney   Tokyo   Toronto

©1995 by **McGraw-Hill, Inc.**

Printed in the United States of America. All rights reserved. The publisher takes
no responsibility for the use of any materials or methods described in this book,
nor for the products thereof.

pbk   1 2 3 4 5 6 7 8 9 0 FGR/FGR 9 9 8 7 6 5 4
hc   1 2 3 4 5 6 7 8 9 0 FGR/FGR 9 9 8 7 6 5 4

Library of Congress Cataloging-in-Publication Data
Pimentel, Ken.
    Virtual reality : through the new looking glass / by Ken Pimentel
& Kevin Teixeira.—2nd ed.
        p.   cm.
    Includes bibliographical references and index.
    ISBN 0-07-050167-X   ISBN 0-07-050168-8 (pbk.)
    1. Human-computer interaction.   2. Virtual reality.   I. Teixeira,
Kevin– II. Title.
QA76.9.H85P56   1994
006—dc20   94-3440
                                                      CIP

Editorial team: Brad J. Shepp, Acquisitions Editor
                Kellie Hagan, Book Editor
                Robert E. Ostrander, Executive Editor
Production team: Katherine G. Brown, Director
                Susan E. Hansford, Coding
                Ollie Harmon, Coding
                Brenda M. Plasterer, Desktop Operator
                Nancy K. Mickley, Proofreading
                Jodi L. Tyler, Indexer
Design team: Jaclyn J. Boone, Designer   WK2
                Brian Allison, Associate Designer   0501688

This book would never have been possible without the love and support of our best friends—our wives, Patty and Terri. They not only believed in the book when it was still an idea in our heads, but they provided encouragement and ideas through all the long weekends and nights. Even more importantly, they reduced our weekend chores so we could finish the book.

"Let's pretend the glass has got all soft like gauze, so that we can get through. Why, it's turning into a sort of mist now, I declare! It'll be easy enough to get through—"

She was up on the chimney-piece while she said this, though she hardly knew how she had got there. And certainly the glass *was* beginning to melt away, just like a bright silvery mist.

In another moment Alice was through the glass, and had jumped lightly down into the looking-glass room. The very first thing she did was to look whether there was a fire in the fireplace, and she was quite pleased to find that there was a real one, blazing away as brightly as the one she had left behind.

Lewis Carroll, *Through the Looking Glass*

Contents

Part 3
Brave new worlds

Acknowledgments

A special thanks needs to go to the members of the VR community who opened their doors and provided valuable input and support to this project. People such as Brenda Laurel of Interval Research, Steve Ellis of NASA-Ames, Randy Walser formerly of Autodesk, Walter Greenleaf of Greenleaf Medical Systems, Mark Bolas of Fake Space Labs, Bruce Bassett from Virtual Research, Brian Blau from IST, Dr. Nomura from Matsushita, Pete Tinker from Xtensory, Suzanne Weghorst from the HIT Lab, and dozens of others. Included also is the entire cast at Sense8, specially Tom Coull, Pat Gelband, and Ben Discoe, along with Eric Gullichsen formerly of Sense8. Lisa Johnson deserves a special mention for her persistence in obtaining all the pictures used in this book, along with Ken's mom, Marie Pimentel, who wasn't pleased to learn she wasn't mentioned in the first edition of the book.

There's no way this book could have been made without the enthusiastic support of Vince Thomas, Janet Brownstone, and Pauline Albert. We hope the final results vindicate their faith in the project. A special thanks to Dennis Carter and Jim Jarrett for their support of the ongoing Intel VR program.

Acknowledgments

The Computer Museum in Boston, the Guggenheim Museum in New York, the Jack Tilton Gallery in New York, the Banff Center for the Arts, Thomas Dolby, and Jenny Holzer were instrumental in providing background information and access to new communities hungry to learn about VR. We look forward to working with all of them in the future.

Foreword

The human being is an intensely visual animal. Most of our information comes from visual images that are interpreted by an extremely efficient image-processing computer—the human brain. On the other hand, computers have typically responded only to implements such as keyboards and mice.

Now with virtual reality, computers and the human mind are entering a realm where communication between the two can proceed at a much more intimate level. This qualitatively new capability promises to extend the range of computer-assisted human experience in completely new directions. Certainly, we're only at the beginning of a major new extension of the use of computer technology.

Simulation has been an important use for computers from the beginning. Originally, just being able to calculate in more detail allowed better prediction of physical phenomena—starting with artillery ballistics. As computer capability and availability has grown, however, simulations have become more complex. Flight simulators are used to train pilots, contributing both increased safety and economy to the process. Increasingly, graphical data presentations are replacing tables of numbers as the output of computations. The result is a greatly enhanced ability to interpret results.

VR is the next major step in making the results of computer manipulation easy for the human brain to interpret. *Virtual Reality: Through the New Looking Glass* outlines the current thinking and future directions of this fascinating technology that sits at the foundation of "humanized" computing.

Gordon E. Moore, Chairman, Intel Corporation

Introduction

"Cyberspace. Reality isn't enough anymore!"
John Walker, Autodesk

Virtual reality is a breakthrough technology that allows you to step through the computer screen into a 3-D simulated world. You can look around, move around, and interact within computer worlds every bit as fantastic as the wonderland Alice found down the rabbit hole. All you have to do is put on the special video goggles, and then almost anything is possible—you can fly, visit exotic lands, play with molecules, swim through the stock market, or paint with 3-D sound and color.

Since the first edition of this book two years ago, virtual reality (VR) has gone from being an obscure scientific toy to being touted as the future of computing. Dozens of VR conferences and companies have appeared overnight in England, Germany, France, the U.S., and Japan. VR entertainment centers are springing up in almost every major city. The word on the street is that VR is something special, just maybe one of those rare concepts that come along and change everything else.

Figure I-1

Ken and Kevin on the set of "CBS Morning News" introducing TV viewers to a VR system.

We wrote this book to answer the kind of questions we had when we started working in VR. Where did VR come from? Who first thought it up and how is it accomplished? What are people really doing with it today? And where can I get one?

Since the first edition, we've received many letters and Internet messages from readers asking for more information. You are holding our response. We have gone through the book and updated it with the latest technology, applications, and ideas. We've included new

photos and a completely revised resource section listing companies, newsletters, and universities offering VR courses.

When this book was first published in 1992, only a few VR books were available, while today there are dozens crowding the shelves. Even with all these additional publications, this book retains several unique qualities. It is still the only book with a detailed history, explanation of the technology, review of its applications, and comprehensive list of the products and companies involved in VR. It's also one of the only books written by authors with any experience in the industry. We've been told by our readers that this book contains information on VR that they couldn't find anywhere else. We hope you discover the same thing.

For many people, the first time they heard about flying through data in a computer-generated world was in William Gibson's science-fiction novel, *Neuromancer*. Published in 1984, it became an inspiration to young VR builders. It describes life in the next century when the world's telephone system has been superseded by the Matrix, the interconnected sum total of all the world's computer networks.

Cyberspace is Gibson's term for this alternative computer universe in which data exists like cities of light. Information workers (and corporate data bandits) use a special virtual reality system, called a *deck*, to jump into the Matrix and travel its data highways. The deck gives them the experience of being physically free to go anywhere in cyberspace.

"Cyberspace. A consensual hallucination experienced daily by billions of legitimate operators, in every nation, by children being taught mathematical concepts . . . a graphic representation of data abstracted from the banks of every computer in the human system. Unthinkable complexity. Lines of light ranged in the nonspace of the mind, clusters and constellations of data. Like city lights, receding . . ."

No longer science fiction, virtual reality products exist. In Europe, the U.S., and Japan, there are programs going on at places like NASA, Tokyo University, Banff Center for the Arts, and the Human-Interface

Lab in Seattle, Washington. It's being pursued inside companies like Boeing, IBM, NEC, DEC, Intel, Fujitsu, Sun Microsystems, and Autodesk.

But the real innovation is happening at the grass-roots level. The Silicon Valley myth of starting a business out of a garage and growing it into a successful company is still alive and well at Sense8, Fake Space Labs, Greenleaf Medical Systems, Virtual Research, and many others.

We've based the book on our combined years of experience developing, designing, and teaching about virtual reality and computer technology. We've written articles, built worlds, and given speeches as well as hundreds of public VR demonstrations—including events at The Boston Computer Museum, the Guggenheim Museum, and the "CBS Morning News" show.

With support from the Intel Corporation, we've explored the conceptual frontier of what VR can do by working with leading artists and educators like Jenny Holzer, Thomas Dolby, and Carl Loeffler at Carnegie Mellon University. Working with Intel and the Guggenheim Museum in New York, we were able to bring these projects together for the world's first VR presentation at a major art museum, Virtual Reality: An Emerging Medium.

This book is your tour guide to virtual reality. Think of it as a guidebook to Bali, a gateway to adventure. We're going to give you the local history, describe transportation requirements, and tell you what to bring with you and what to do when you get there. We'll even suggest side trips to some exotic islands no one has visited yet.

Each section is filled with photographs and illustrations. And there are interviews and reports from the adventurous virtual explorers who have gone ahead of you—the people who are turning virtual dreams into real products and applications.

How this book is organized

This book is organized into three parts. Actually, it's three books in one, so you can find the information you want and skip what you

don't want. Our objective is to provide you with the kind of resource we wish we had when we first stepped through the new looking glass.

⇨ Stepping through the new looking glass

What is virtual reality and where did it come from? The name has become a media buzzword, cut loose from its original intentions and caught up in the cultural excitement over potential and imagined uses of the technology.

The term *virtual reality* was coined by Jaron Lanier, founder of VPL Research, to distinguish between the immersive digital worlds he was trying to create and traditional computer simulations. The history of virtual reality and what makes virtual worlds different from other simulations is what the first part of this book, *Stepping through the new looking glass*, is all about.

There are several different methods for providing virtual realities and variations of them. VR is more than a computer technology that places the user inside a 3-D world; it's the artificial world itself and a new kind of experience. It's also a method of communicating ideas. Inside a virtual world, everything is potentially alive because the laws of reality are up to the designer. The computer can just as easily bring to life the world of atoms as it can let you fly through space.

Chapter 1 gives an overview of what's happening in the field and describes the varieties of virtual experience, while explaining what kind of methods are being used. With this overview it's possible to journey into the land of VR with some sense of what's going on.

Given the suddenness with which virtual reality has burst on the public scene, it would seem to have been born overnight. But the desire for immersive experiences, the ticket to enter another world, is an age-old desire. From Renaissance art to motion pictures, modern civilization has been moving steadily towards more participation in imaginative worlds.

Today's movie industry is a worldwide phenomenon. For an industry so large, it's amazing that there's almost no research and development effort. The basic technology has remained stuck at the level of color introduced in the 1940s. There have been dreamers, however, who saw the potential of providing richer, more realistic experiences. They attempted to create them with innovations such as Cinerama and Sensorama. Their efforts foreshadowed what would finally be possible with the new technology of computers.

Chapters 2, 3, and 4 track the historical development of virtual realities. While artists and the movies understand realism, the computer industry understands interaction. It was left to computer pioneers, therefore, to finally step through the looking glass into dynamic, responsive, artificial worlds.

The early pioneers in this area were looking for the ultimate display technology, one in which the computer would disappear and allow users to navigate naturally with their eyes, ears, feet, and hands. Over the last 30 years, developments at NASA and elsewhere have finally led to the emergence of a commercial virtual reality industry.

⇨ 21st-century tools

The history of virtual reality is made up of false starts, inventive dead ends, and a lot of hard work. Today, it's a fledgling industry based on computers and a wide range of exotic technology. What makes it all work? What is a wired glove and how do VR goggles create a virtual world?

Part 2: 21st-century tools is a layman's guide to VR technology. It steps behind the magician's curtain to explain how the tricks are accomplished. It takes you inside the structure and components that make up reality engines, wands, and worlds.

Chapter 5 provides an overview of the technology behind virtual reality. It explains the science and language for creating virtual worlds, which is a new form of communications that encompasses not only the visual, but the auditory and tactile as well. For each sensory effect there are a range of technologies for supplying the information.

The technology for providing VR is no longer limited to scientific research centers. Chapter 7, *Desktop VR*, presents the basic building blocks for designing a virtual reality system using a desktop personal computer. The most common image people have of virtual reality is somebody sitting in a chair with what looks like a scuba mask strapped to his face, with a metal box over his eyes. VR technology, however, has already gone a long way beyond this.

Chapter 8, *Gloves, goggles, and wands*, goes into detail about the input and navigation tools for working in a virtual environment. It explains what goes into a set of goggles and how the two tiny LCD screens inside them create a sense of 3-D space.

Beyond a basic description of the hardware, this section explores the way a virtual world is built. A virtual world is part animation, part computer-aided design, and lots of imagination. There are special software tricks that give a virtual world greater levels of realism without bogging down the computer. The goal of this section is to remove the mystery of how virtual reality works and explain what's involved in building a VR system of your own.

 Brave new worlds

After learning about what VR is, where it came from, and how it works, you're bound to be wondering "What can I do with it?" *Part 3: Brave new worlds* is a tour through all the wonderlands and practical applications being developed using virtual reality.

Our brains do some pretty sophisticated image processing to present us with the 3-D view of the world we call reality. Chapter 9 looks at the psychological, philosophical, and artistic reasons for creating virtual experiences. It includes ideas and suggestions from designers who have been building worlds and suggests that they can find inspiration from theatrical and artistic practices.

Chapter 10 is called *Education as simulation*. Every virtual reality experience is an educational experience. With VR, you see things in new ways and learn by using multiple senses: hearing, sight, movement, sensation. While all the following chapters touch on VR

as a way of learning, here we explore it from the classroom level. What happens when children can do more than just read about ancient Egypt or the human body? Beyond the cutting edge of education theory are new ideas about blending computer simulations and computer game theory into a new kind of thrilling learning.

Chapter 11, *Business enters the cyberage*, explores the design, manufacturing, and business uses of VR. Developers at Boeing, Lockheed, Matsushita, and NASA have shared with us some of the ways they're using VR technology. Virtual reality is more than a new design tool, however; it's also a method of managing information so money managers and business executives can make faster, more effective decisions.

Chapter 12 discusses how the American medical industry is already a very high-tech realm, and one for which VR tools are being developed. This chapter looks into how doctors will combine these VR tools with CAT scans, MRIs, X-rays, and a host of other procedures to explore and heal our bodies.

Chapter 13, *The new entertainment economy*, might be the most fun to read. The technology of VR has already reached the level where the quality is good enough for arcades and theater systems. Hollywood and amusement parks are embracing VR in a big way. These simulation theaters and VR arcades move you past the discussion of how-to technology and into the question of content. What does it mean when you can enter strange new worlds, ride a bike around Paris, or battle monsters over lunch—and then return to the everyday world?

In chapter 14, the uses of virtual reality in the arts bring us to the edge of where VR might take us. The role of the artist is not only to express ideas and emotions through various media, but also to provide insight into the nature of perception and consciousness. As a culture, we look to artists not only to champion new ideas but also to challenge them. Virtual reality is a field in need of such examination.

Beyond debating its merits, virtual reality might create a completely new category of art—a nonmaterial, interactive art form of the mind. One where there's no longer a separation between art object and art

viewer. Through the computer's ability to control and manipulate our senses, the visual experience can now be given the same properties as music. Will this become a new kind of drug as some people fear, or a means for new and insightful experiences?

The final chapter, *The next generation*, pulls the curtain aside to reveal technology advances both just over the horizon and imagined for the future. What is the potential for hyper-realistic virtual worlds? When will cyberspace be possible and what will be the social impact when VR becomes widely available? What kind of world will tomorrow be?

Television has already warned us that there's a need for a new kind of literacy, a visual literacy of experience. What is real and what is truth when what we know is no longer played out on a screen, but acted out inside of a favorite world? The future is no longer approaching; it's here.

Are you ready? Turn the page to begin your travels into virtual reality country. One thing we should warn you of, however—this trip doesn't include a return ticket. Like the steam engine, telephone, and television, virtual reality is a technology that will keep moving ahead, causing other changes around it. This book is one trip you won't be coming back from.

The interface is the application

"I like John's one-sentence definition of cyberspace: 'The place you are when you're on the phone.'"

Mitch Kapor, Founder of Lotus, quoting John Perry Barlow, President of the Electronic Frontier Foundation and lyrist for the Grateful Dead

THIS morning, at the NASA Ames Research Center in Mountain View, California, Dr. Lew Hitchner explores the surface of Mars. He's wearing virtual reality (VR) goggles with two tiny liquid crystal display (LCD) screens inside. They give him a realistic, 3-D view of the rocky Martian landscape, Utopia Planitia (see Figs. 1-2 and 1-3), which was reconstructed from satellite data sent back by a Viking spacecraft stationed on Mars. With a change of software, he'll be flying across the sprawling canyons of Valles Marineris later this afternoon.

Just down the hallway in the "view lab," Dr. Stephen Ellis is remotely controlling robots, wearing VR goggles and a wired glove. The glove senses the movements of his hand and fingers, and a computer interprets and transmits them as commands for a robot arm. Ellis sees what the robot sees and the robot mimics his movements, even though he and the robot are in different rooms and can't see each other. Someday, using VR, robots will act as human eyes, arms, and ears on other planets, allowing many people to visit space as virtual astronauts.

In San Diego, California, another Virtual World center has opened in a shopping mall. The first in a coming wave of location-based virtual

Figure 1-1

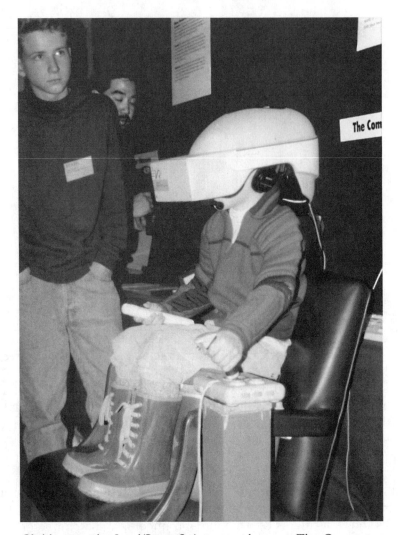

Child using the Intel/Sense8 Artroom demo at The Computer Museum in Boston.

reality entertainment companies, it's a mixture of Disney theme ride, video arcade, and sci-fi novel, with a decor that spans Victorian England and colonized Mars. Sipping cappuccino in the Explorer's Lounge, visitors await their turn to compete against each other while strapped inside space-age pods.

Figure 1-2

NASA Ames Research Center

Virtual visit to the Martian surface. Photographs collected by NASA's Viking 2 lander are instantly reassembled by computer to generate appropriate views, depending on where the participant is looking.

Figure 1-3

NASA Ames Research Center

340-degree panoramic view of the Utopia Planitia region of Mars, captured by the Viking 2 lander. The outlined box shows the view depicted in Fig. 1-2.

All the pods are networked and customers compete in teams. The interior of each pod resembles a jet fighter cockpit with joystick, foot controls, and dozens of buttons. But instead of windows there are big computer screens that show you the other robot warriors, called

BattleMechs, you're fighting in the interactive arcade cyberspace called BattleTech.

To think of BattleTech as a giant video game doesn't do it justice. "We have to make a game, adventures, of such depth that there is almost limitless room for you to grow in your capability and experience," says Jordan Weisman, president of Virtual World Entertainment.

In Seattle, Washington, Chris Esposito runs the Computer Interface Group at Boeing Corporation. The company has committed to completely developing its next generation of commercial aircraft using computers. "We've already identified three dozen applications for virtual reality, spanning the entire range of a product's life-cycle. From concept development to manufacturing and maintenance operations, even in-flight uses. And the list is getting longer."

At the Center for Creative Inquiry at Carnegie Mellon University, Carl Loeffler's team has been homesteading cyberspace. They've built a virtual museum with several galleries and even the first block of a virtual city that simultaneously welcomes networked visitors from Tokyo, Vienna, and CMU.

Together with Professor Lynn Holden (an Egyptologist), Loeffler is now trying to start a revolution in education. Wearing VR goggles with 3-D headphones, visitors tour a mockup of the ancient Temple of Horus. Photographs of actual carvings and re-creations of real murals cover the 60-foot-high walls. Moving through the many rooms of the temple, past huge pillars, your presence brings murals to life by triggering embedded animations. When you reach the innermost shrine, a statue becomes your guide, explaining the secrets of the chamber, while ancient Egyptian chanting fills the background.

Lynn Holden sees the virtual temple as the first module in an entire ancient virtual world. He wants to blend computer game theory and role-playing with VR to experientially teach about ancient cultures. As in a video game, a student would advance to different levels (from peasant to warrior to pharaoh) by living in each character's private, professional, and religious world (a farm, village, fort, city, temple, or palace).

At a grand old cathedral in San Francisco that has been converted into a theater, on Saturday night a full-house audience puts on 3-D glasses to visit *Invisible Site*, a George Coates Performance Works (GCPW) multimedia play that uses actors, 3-D projections, film, real-time animated computer graphics, and some sophisticated theater tricks to give people a taste of "virtual virtual reality."

"It's a way of evoking the sense of awe that immersing yourself in virtual reality produces," George Coates says, and adds with a chuckle, "Someday we'll be handing out VR goggles instead of 3-D glasses."

On stage, characters enter a store of the future, called Invisible Site, that sells virtual reality experiences. Once inside, as customers, they dress in goggles and gloves. Then they enter cyberspace through a computer network, where they visit new worlds and assume completely new identities.

After the show, some of the audience heads towards San Francisco's nightclub dance district, where Toon Town is getting ready to open its doors. Like George Coates, Toon Town has found an audience hungry for new media concepts—using computers to visit, simulate, create, and control new worlds. In a corner of the club, dozens of people line up to pay for a chance to sit down, put on goggles, and fly around in a virtual world. "They all expect to be using one at home in a couple of years," says Vince Thomas, one of the club's owners.

A second group of people in the club is gathered to use the Mandala Machine, where a Toon Town patron is dancing and playing imaginary musical instruments. Her image is captured by a video camera and fed into a computer, where it's combined with interactive video and animation, and projected onto the wall in front of her. She controls the animation through her movements as she watches herself on the wall in the scene—with synthesized notes erupting as she slaps the virtual drums (see Fig. 1-4).

This is a very small sample of what's going on in the exploding realm of virtual reality. Don't worry if at first you feel a bit confused. VR is both a new technology and a set of ideas—concepts that are spreading faster than the hardware and software that produce them. There are several different approaches that fall under the label of

Figure 1-4

Using real-time image-processing techniques, a video camera captures a person's outline and combines it with a 2-D graphic of musical instruments. Hand movements, detected by the computer, can activate each instrument in turn.

virtual reality, though they don't all use the same effects to achieve the same results.

VR is happening worldwide—inside giant corporations, universities, and small entrepreneurial start-ups; in Europe and Japan; and especially in the San Francisco Bay Area. VR has spawned a new interaction between musicians, artists, entrepreneurs, and electronic tinkerers. A rare excitement is in the air, an excitement that comes from breaking through to something new. Computers are about to take the next big step—out of the lab and into the street—and the street can't wait.

⇨ Experiential computing

"As long as you can see the screen, you're not in virtual reality.
When the screen disappears, and you see an imaginary scene . . .
then you are in virtual reality."

**Gabriel D. Ofeisch, Emeritus Professor of Educational
Technology at Howard University**

Virtual reality is all about illusion. It's about computer graphics in the
theater of the mind. It's about the use of high technology to convince
yourself that you're in another reality, experiencing some event that
doesn't physically exist in the world in front of you. Virtual reality is
also a new media for getting your hands on information, getting inside
information, and representing ideas in ways not previously possible.

Virtual reality is where the computer disappears and you become "the
ghost in the machine." There's no little screen of symbols you must
manipulate nor type commands into to get the computer to do
something. Instead, the computer retreats behind the scenes and
becomes invisible, leaving you free to concentrate on tasks, ideas,
problems, and communications.

For three generations, people have experienced a type of virtual reality
using the telephone. It has now been over 100 years since the
introduction of the telephone, and today it's so deeply embedded in our
cultural consciousness that we give it as much thought as a doorknob.
As a society, we've forgotten what a shock the telephone was when it
was first introduced—the strangeness of listening to a ghostly,
disembodied voice. Today we rely on the telephone not only to
communicate, but to give us the sense of someone else's presence,
even though in reality we're listening to an electromechanical re-
creation of a human voice. We've learned to ignore the telephone and
concentrate on the conversation; the interactivity makes the difference.

Alan Kay, computer pioneer and Apple Computer fellow, has thought
a long time about the way humans and computers could work
together. Part of his concept of a Dynabook (a mobile, networked,
multimedia, clipboard-sized computer), conceived more than 20 years
ago, is coming to fruition today in small notebook computers and in
machines like Apple's Newton.

What's still missing is the point-of-view simulations he included in his Dynabook vision, the kind of simulations VR now makes possible. His product was people-oriented, not hardware-oriented. He was interested in the way technologies could be used by people, and the way they disappeared when their ease of use and functionality crossed a certain threshold.

"I read McLuhan's *Understanding Media* and understood that the most important thing about any communications medium is that message receipt is really message recovery; anyone who wishes to receive a message embedded in a medium must first have internalized the medium so it can be subtracted out to leave the message behind." (Kay, 1990)

Media is the plural form of *medium*. *Webster's Ninth New Collegiate Dictionary* describes *medium* as ". . . a means of affecting or conveying something . . . a channel or system of communication, information, or entertainment." Computers are a medium, a means or agency for doing something. What Kay suggests is that for the computer to really work, the way we use it has to become so comfortable, familiar, and effortless (like the television, telephone, and light switch) that we can unconsciously subtract it out and focus only on its function—the communication, information, and entertainment it provides.

Like the telephone, computers are a communications medium. Like the telescope and microscope, computers are a tool for revealing new ways of looking at information. With virtual reality, the computer equipment disappears; it gets subtracted out. VR gives users an efficient and effortless flow of data, details, and information in the most natural format possible—vision, sound, and sensations presented as an environment, part of the natural data forms of human experience and thought.

The first 21st-century tool

"The primary defining characteristic of VR is inclusion, being surrounded by an environment. VR places the participant inside information."

Dr. William Bricken, Human Interface Technologies Lab

New inventions are rarely appreciated for what they are when they first arise. Around the turn of the century, when the automobile first appeared on city streets, it was called a *horseless carriage*. Built like a buggy, it moved about as fast as a horse and was considered an expensive novelty. Nobody could imagine then that we would become so dependent on them, that they would change our way of life, the face of the land, the economy, and the quality of the air we breathe.

Often inventors can't foresee what their discoveries will actually be used for, or the side effects they might cause. Alexander Graham Bell thought the telephone would be useful as a way to pipe music to people. The developers of radio (and later television) imagined that their devices would launch a world of two-way communications to replace the telephone.

How then are we to understand this new method of using computers? Is virtual reality new, or just another form of television? Is it similar to or different from multimedia, the other new way of using computers to get at information? Can VR let us see things we've never seen before? If so, how?

The first great wave of the computer revolution was hardware based; mainframes, mini-computers, and personal computers automated the workplace. Then computers became office rolodexes, electronic filing cabinets, typewriters, accounting ledgers, drafting tables, and the company mail. They changed the way individuals work, providing them with access to more information and new forms of communications, but people have had to struggle with the computer to get at the information—often alone.

Now, as an increasing amount of media is converted into the digital language of computers, computers are beginning to adapt to people. Digitizing analog signals translates the media of sound, video, text, and graphic images into machine language, a mixture of ones and zeros (bits) that can be decoded and shared by other computers. With digitization, all media and information can be intertwined and blended together—sometimes even transformed into each other.

The older media of television and radio deluge the viewer in a continuous stream of information that cannot be customized. Television and radio are passive experiences, with users as viewers or

listeners. Information control is limited to an on/off switch and channel surfing. Computers give the consumer more control over the information, over their experience. Control now means mixing, matching, and blending information and media. Multimedia and virtual reality are the two best examples of this change.

"Being able to mix together existing [media] forms, such as photos, images, sound, and books, and then come up with something new is what multimedia is all about," says Sandra Morris, multimedia developer and author of the book *Multimedia Applications Development Using DVI Technology*. "The difference between virtual reality and multimedia is that VR is about creation, while multimedia is about bringing the old media forms together into the computer. They don't change so much as they get combined in new ways. VR is about creating something completely new."

Multimedia and virtual reality both benefit from digital technology developments. However, as Morris points out, a large distinction between virtual reality and multimedia is the creation of environments ("worlds"), versus the juxtaposition of existing media.

Multimedia allows someone to watch a famous play on half of a computer screen while following along in the script, or with a video lecture by the playwright, on the other half. In another application, a person can study the image of an ancient stone tablet while hearing what it says in the simulated voices of ancient Egyptians. At the same time the hieroglyphics on the tablet light up in synchronization with the spoken words, accompanied by English subtitles at the bottom of the screen that reveal grammar and syntax differences.

In virtual reality, the smallest details of sensory experience, the building blocks of human reality, are used to create environments. The location, tone, tempo, and pitch of each sound is a creative choice in VR. The entire visual range of experience—color, hue, brightness, saturation, the location and behavior of shapes—is under the VR developer's control. A virtual world might contain forms of old media, or multimedia, but it's used to populate the complete environments it creates.

Virtual reality allows a person using a computer to assemble complex three-dimensional star fields of the galaxy and fly around in the data to understand how the universe is structured. Different types of stars can be given appropriate colors reflecting their size and age. This research is being performed by astronomers at the National Supercomputing Center in Ohio, using Cray supercomputers. As a result, the astronomers are now seeing things in the data they couldn't experience when it was just numbers on a page. One surprise was the way vast numbers of galaxies are clumped together in threads, ribbons, and clusters, leaving tremendous, empty voids between them. By speeding up the movement of all these galaxies, you could sit among the stars and see what an expanding universe looks like.

 # The various forms of virtual reality

There are a variety of different formats and systems calling themselves *virtual reality*. Throughout this book, we'll try to carefully categorize what we mean by virtual reality, and use more specific labels to separate the various forms.

As a guideline, a virtual reality system should have the three following characteristics: response to user actions, real-time 3-D graphics, and a sense of immersion. It isn't enough to have just one or two of these properties; all three should be present.

Because immersion is such a key aspect of a virtual reality system, it's important to explore it a little before venturing on. An immersive experience is one so absorbing that you cease to notice your surroundings or "how you got there." Current immersive systems stimulate your visual and aural senses in such a way that you find yourself immersed in a computer-generated experience.

Though it's possible for sensory immersion to someday be so complete that the mind is convinced it's really in another world, current implementations fall far short of this. Total sensory immersion would theoretically include temperature, tactile sensations, bodily movement, sounds, images, and even odors. Few of these

senses are understood well enough to allow a computer to re-create them, despite Hollywood's many imaginings to the contrary.

Keeping the three characteristics of a virtual environment in mind, let's now review existing attempts at creating immersive environments.

Cab simulators

Flight simulators for airplane pilots are the original virtual reality experience and the most familiar example of cab-based simulation. A user is seated inside a box that resembles the interior of a car, the cockpit of a jet, or a Star Wars' starfighter. The windows of the pod have been replaced with high-resolution computer screens. In some cases the entire pod is bolted onto a moving platform. As the user drives or flies the pod, the images on the "windows" and the tilt and angle of the cabin change in response. With the addition of surround-sound effects, a very realistic and thrilling interactive experience is created.

The BattleTech game at the Virtual World center mentioned at the beginning of the chapter is an example of cab-based simulation. So is FighterTown, where you can fly an F-16 jet fighter simulator and shoot down enemy aircraft.

Projected reality

VIDEOPLACE by Myron Krueger is an example of a projected environment that Krueger calls *artificial reality*. VIDEOPLACE, first developed in the 1970s, uses two rooms, each with wall-sized video screens, a computer, and a video camera. Unlike a videophone, which displays only the other person on the screen, VIDEOPLACE displays colorized silhouettes of users onto the screen. In essence, users watch themselves as they're projected into a virtual world, as opposed to seeing the world through the eyes of a computer. This is also referred to as a "mirrorworld."

Krueger can enhance the experiences of people using VIDEOPLACE by adding effects not ordinarily found in day-to-day reality; for example, users can "fingerpaint" colored designs and messages to each other in the air.

Another example of projected reality is the Mandala Machine, created by the Vivid Group (mentioned earlier in the chapter). This system overlays the real video images of users onto an artificial world of computer-graphic images (see Fig. 1-5). The system perceives users' images in motion, analyzes them, makes sense of what it sees, and responds instantly with graphics, video effects, and synthesized sound.

Figure 1-5

Vincent John Vincent, The Vivid Group

Video cameras capture the motion of performers in front of a specially colored screen. The computer can then combine the performers' images with that of any computer-generated world.

Augmented reality

Augmented reality uses special transparent head-mounted displays onto which data, diagrams, animation, and 3-D graphics can be projected to aid people who need to simultaneously be in the real world and also be able to access additional data to do their jobs. These transparent displays are also known as heads-up-displays

(HUDs) because the outside world is visible along with the computer-generated graphics. This provides an augmented or enhanced view of the world.

Boeing is exploring the possibilities of such a system for use by aircraft engine mechanics. In this case, the mechanic's glasses would display schematic diagrams, parts lists, and text without blocking out the image of a real-world engine. Someday, a structural layout of a jet engine assembly, positioned accurately over an actual engine, could provide a simulated form of x-ray vision for a mechanic actively performing repairs. Even those parts of the engine reachable only with hands out of view could become visible.

⇨ Telepresence

Telepresence uses video cameras and remote microphones to immerse users so deeply as to project them into a different place, as shown in Fig. 1-6. Robotic control, such as the planetary exploration work at NASA Ames, is the most immediate example under research, but there are also potential medical uses for telepresence. In surgical procedures, doctors already use video cameras and fiberoptic cables to view patients' bodies. With VR, they could actually "go inside" patients to direct their work or inspect the work of others.

⇨ Desktop VR

Desktop VR is a subset of traditional virtual reality systems. Instead of a head-mounted display, a large computer monitor or projection system is used to present the virtual world. This is a popular choice for business users due to the inadequacies of existing head-mounted displays. Some systems allow users to see a 3-D image on their monitor by using lightweight glasses and LCD shutters.

⇨ Visually coupled displays

Finally, there's the class of immersive systems most often associated with virtual reality. These are all based on placing a display directly in

Figure 1-6

Liquid Image

One method of immersion is based on using a head-mounted display device, such as the Liquid Image MRG2, to view a virtual world. Sensors track the participant's head movements, allowing the computer to generate the appropriate image.

front of the user's eyes and coupling head movements with the displayed image.

In most visually coupled systems, immersion is achieved through the use of a head-mounted display (HMD) and stereophonic headphones, as shown in Fig. 1-7. Special head-tracking sensors monitor the position and orientation of the viewer's head. This information is used by the computer to update the viewer's 3-D image of the world. By tracking where the viewer is looking, it's possible to create a computer-generated virtual world, or virtual reality.

In general, then, the term *virtual reality* refers to an immersive, interactive experience based on real-time 3-D graphic images generated by a computer. Although the press plays up future

Figure 1-7

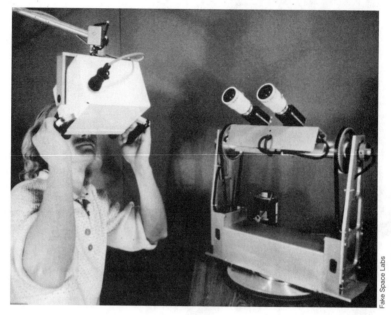

A remotely controlled platform uses stereoptic cameras to transmit real-time images back to a stereoptic display. When viewed through the two suspended displays, the operator sees a 3-D, or stereo, view of the remote scene.

scenarios of high-resolution systems capable of replacing reality, current systems are restricted to fairly simplistic environments that are highly unlikely to be mistaken for the rich sensory experience we call "reality."

⇨ The interface is the application

Like any tool, the hardware to create virtual reality isn't the experience itself. The methods are simply ways of putting the user into the application.

> "An interface is a 'contact surface.' It reflects the physical properties of the interactors, functions to be performed, and the balance of power and control . . . We naturally visualize an interface as the place where contact between two entities occurs.

The less alike those two entities are, the more obvious the need
for a well-designed interface becomes."
Brenda Laurel, *The Art of the Human-Computer Interface*

Virtual reality is the place where humans and computers make
contact. Just as the steering wheel, brake, clutch, stick-shift, and
dashboard instruments are the interface between a driver and a car,
virtual reality is an interface between humans and computers. In both
cases, these interfaces act as contact points where human
movements are translated into commands that direct the machine's
operation, and also where the machine's condition is communicated
to the user.

The shape and function of each interactive contact point is designed to
meet the needs of both the machine and the user. In the case of a car,
although we think of ourselves as controlling the machine, when the
gas gauge nears empty or red lights on the car's dashboard flash, it
would appear that the car is actually commanding us. Similar reactions
could be expected from interactive virtual reality contact points.

The car, like the telephone, has been with us for so long that we tend
to ignore it when we use it. It functions as a bodily extension,
allowing us to expand our physical capabilities. Similarly, computers
allow us to extend the capabilities of our minds. Like car engines,
computers are useless by themselves; they require an operator and an
interface to transfer their power into useful functions. In the case of
virtual reality, the interface hides the computer engine from the
operator. It guides and both extends and limits what we can do with a
computer.

The evolution of human-computer interfaces has been an ongoing
trade-off between the limits of the equipment, the creativity of the
programmers, and users' willingness to put up with the results.
Historically, the interface has been designed to leverage human
capabilities to the advantage of computers, not humans. All too
often, it would seem that the interface has been as much a way for
the programmer to control the behavior of the user as a way for the
user to control the behavior of the computer. In turn, this often
places great limitations on a human's ability to use a computer.

In the 1940s, the first computers were built using vacuum tubes, and required plug boards, dials, and switches to operate. Controlling the computer required dozens of trained technicians to service the machine; setting up the unit to solve a problem could take days. And the results were a cryptic series of printed mathematical codes.

During the Eisenhower years, computer interfacing evolved slightly, with the use of punch-card stacks to run software programs. The results, however, were still cryptic printouts of mathematical codes. Access to the information was restricted to an elite group of people who typically wore white jackets and met in restricted rooms to emerge after several days with answers to problems.

In the 1960s and 1970s, users began to have direct access to computers through workstations and PCs, instead of working through intermediaries in corporate computing centers. Gradually, computers became more efficient; tubes were replaced by transistors, which were replaced by integrated circuits.

Fast, alphanumeric terminals made it possible to present large amounts of information to the user electronically. This allowed the computer to interface with a user through a "menu" of choices. The user could make selections from the menu by simply pressing one or two keys. Menus and data entry, modeled on filling in forms, became the standard for applications intended to be used by nonspecialists (almost everyone).

The microprocessor, introduced in 1971, made the personal computer possible and provided a hardware interface platform for modern graphical software interfaces. These graphical interfaces (GUIs), which were developed at Xerox PARC and later gained public notice when used for the Apple Macintosh, have transformed our conversational interactions with computers.

In the past, you typed commands into the computer to receive alphanumeric key responses. But now you can graphically select the objects displayed on a screen and receive graphic representations of information, sometimes in full color. It's no longer necessary to read lists of filenames that scroll down the entire length of a screen; computer software and application files are symbolized by icons that

act as representations for the ways we organize our offices. Icons can appear as books, folders, and trash cans. Using a cursor, you can manipulate symbols on a computer screen to accomplish various tasks, without even touching a computer keyboard.

Now, with virtual reality, the window of the GUI that has kept us outside the screen looking in has dissolved, and we can step through the glass—replacing the desktop metaphor with a complete environment. How is this unique? Virtual reality is a human-computer interface in which the computer creates a three-dimensional, sensory-immersing environment that interactively responds to and is controlled by the behavior of the user.

The two key words here are *sensory-immersing* and *interactively*. The creation of an environment requires the immersion of your senses in a computer-generated world to create the experience of "being there." The question isn't whether the created virtual world is as real as the physical world, but whether the created world is real enough for you to suspend your disbelief for a period of time. This is the same mental shift that happens when you get wrapped up in a good novel or become absorbed in playing a computer game. You stop considering the quality of the interface media and accept the computer-generated world as a viable one (just as you might accept the voice on a phone as real, even with a bad connection).

⇨ Immersion

What is the value of immersion? One powerful effect is its ability to focus your attention. It's common to say that people immerse themselves in their work. *Immersion* means to block out distractions and focus selectively on just the information with which you want to work. The power to concentrate on work seems to be a prerequisite for highly creative and intelligent people.

While Picasso's creativity was as much a mystery to him as to everyone else, one easily verifiable behavior was the intense way he did everything—even signing his name. He would bend over, place his face very close to the page, and nothing else existed for him for the moment but that act.

Another key attribute of immersion is that it can act as a powerful lens for extracting knowledge from data by turning it into experience. This capability is the chief reason so many industries are exploring the use of virtual environments. The potential exists for uncovering secrets long buried in an avalanche of data.

Howard Rheingold suggests that the use of immersion can be traced as far back as the ceremonial caves of prehistoric humans. Youngsters were brought into the darkness of painted caves, where stories were told, images and songs were revealed in precise sequence, and the youths became immersed in their coming-of-age ceremonies.

Only by shutting out the rest of the world and immersing themselves in this separate space could the learning occur that changed a child into an adult. Brenda Laurel draws parallels between the immersive qualities of virtual reality and theater, itself a descendant of religious ceremony.

In the theater, your attention is focused on the actors' performances. Through lights, setting, drama, and music you're invited to lose yourself in their story. When it works, theater has the power to engage you, focus you, and hold your attention. This immersive, ritualized experience can convince, teach, and inspire you. It might even provide you with a kind of emotional catharsis.

Interactivity

Interactivity, like immersion, is a crucial aspect of VR. There are two unique aspects of interactivity in a virtual world: navigation within the world and the dynamics of the environment. *Navigation* is simply a user's ability to move around independently, as if inside an environment (see Fig. 1-8). Constraints can be set by the software developer for access into certain virtual areas, allowing various degrees of freedom—you can fly, move through walls, walk around, or swim.

Another aspect of navigation is the positioning of a user's point of view. Controlling point of view might mean watching yourself from a distance, viewing a scene through someone else's eyes, or moving

Figure 1-8

Human Interface Lab, Fujitsu Lab Ltd.

Users of Fujitsu's VR system navigate through a fanciful aquarium world full of interesting creatures. Virtual worlds can be either abstract or realistic in nature.

through the design of a new building as if in a wheelchair, waist-high, to test if it really will be wheelchair accessible.

The dynamics of an environment are the rules for how its contents (people, rocks, doors, everything) interact in order to exchange energy or information. A simple example of dynamic rules are the Newtonian laws used to describe the behavior of billiard balls reacting to the impact of a cue ball. A medical simulation would be based on the dynamics of the human body. Alice's looking-glass wonderland would follow the wacky laws that Lewis Carroll created, based partially on the game of chess (he was a Cambridge mathematician as well as a writer).

Every object and its relationship to every other object (including the user) is a design element at the discretion of the developer. Among these elements are the location, color, shape, and size of the environment; the plasticity of walls; the laws of gravity; and the capabilities and functions of objects and actors in the environment. As a result, virtual reality is the experience of *being in another world*—a world governed by selected laws, and inhabited by objects (and actors) with whatever properties the creator chooses to assign.

It's this flexibility for creating and representing responsive environments that has created the excitement about virtual reality. 3-D movies have come and gone, and Disneyland provides simulation rides like Star Tours, which passively immerse people in other worlds. But to go into a world that responds to you and uniquely to you, that has its own independent life—that is virtual reality.

Because a computer fitted with the right equipment can control and manipulate the complete human range of visual, auditory, and someday even kinesthetic sensations, almost any form of "reality" a developer can think up can be simulated. Instead of using a computer interface to manipulate data, with VR the interface is the application, as the computer disappears and we immerse ourselves in the experience. Ultimately, it means that a time will come when there's nothing you can imagine that can't be shared with someone else.

The language of experience

> "Language serves not only to express thoughts, but to make possible thoughts which could not exist without it."
> **Bertrand Russell**

Language, writing, and mathematics are symbol systems with vast powers to communicate meaning, allowing people to construct and communicate mental representations. They are tools that have made science possible, thinking tools for making thinking tools. But they're also abstracts, or stand-ins, for the real thing—the inner experience of the imagination. Virtual reality is a new thinking tool, a way of directly representing what we think.

Down through the centuries, great leaders, artists, scientists, and thinkers in every field have struggled with the gap between their inner visions and how little of it they were able to communicate. In a letter to a friend, Einstein revealed that his primary mode of thought was not abstract words or mathematical symbols, but rather a kind of mental "play" he used in order to come up with his great theories:

"The psychic entities which seem to serve as elements in thought are certain signs and more or less clear images which can be 'voluntarily' reproduced and combined . . .. The above mentioned elements are, in my case, of visual and some of the muscular type. Conventional words or other signs have to be sought for laboriously only in a secondary stage, when the mentioned associative play is sufficiently established and can be reproduced at will."

While he is usually described as a visual thinker, it's important to note here that Einstein refers to both his visual and muscular thinking modes, and calls them *entities* (which suggests dynamic properties). It was this combination of internal experiences, an internal sensory language of experience, that led to his theories and writings. Virtual reality can be used to translate information (mental or symbolic) into experiences that people can explore in the same kind of purposeful play that Einstein experienced in his thoughts.

Simply, virtual reality, like writing and mathematics, is a way to represent and communicate what you can imagine with your mind. But it can be more powerful because it doesn't require you to convert your ideas into abstract symbols with restrictive semantic and syntactic rules, and it can be shared with other people.

VR can reveal processes that are invisible because they're distant in time and space, occur too fast or too slow, or are too large or too small for human physical senses. Because VR can incorporate events, symbols, and media from other forms of communications in addition to recreating what's in your mind, virtual reality mirrors back how your mind works.

Like the inventions of writing several thousands years ago, and more recently film, virtual reality will make possible the expression and construction of ideas never before dreamed possible. Virtual reality might not only change the way we communicate, it might also change the way we think.

"When [Marshal McLuhan] said 'the medium is the message,' he meant that you have to become the medium if you use it . . .. That's pretty scary. It means that even though humans are the

animals that shape tools, it is in the nature of tools and man that learning to use tools reshapes us."
Alan Kay, 1990

More than a "fantasy machine," virtual reality is the lifting of the curtain on one of the unique uses of computers—the creation of a universal metalanguage. This metalanguage, like mathematics, allows us to share ideas and thoughts across cultures and languages by communicating in the most natural human data form of all—the human sensory language of reality.

The evolution of cyberspace

"Reality has always been too small for human imagination. The impulse to create an 'interactive fantasy machine' is only the most recent manifestation of the age-old desire to make our fantasies palpable—our insatiable need to exercise our imagination, judgment, and spirits in worlds, situations, and personae that are different from those of our everyday lives."

Brenda Laurel, *Computers As Theater*

THROUGHOUT history, attempts have been made to capture the essence of an experience and distill it in order to make it available for us to enjoy and analyze. Through the direct experience of theater, music, and paintings, people have been able to perceive both the real and imaginary expressions of other worlds, other times, new ideas, and new perspectives on old ideas. Computers and virtual reality aren't the first tools to change the way people absorb, debate, and relate to knowledge.

The Greeks of the 4th and 5th centuries B.C. used the theater, public debate, and storytellers as tools for thought. They discovered and invented a new world order of science, art, and society. The theater was a way to engage and focus the public's attention, to take them to the distant shores of Troy or the halls of Olympus while simultaneously involving them in the great philosophical debates, acted out in the emotions and decisions of dramatized events.

These carefully constructed simulations gave spectators new points of view by putting them in the shoes of people not unlike themselves who were faced with difficult decisions. The power of these

simulations can be attested to by the fact that over 2,000 years after their creation they're still performed and are still engaging, entertaining, and speaking to audiences about the human condition.

Not only did these simulations entertain and educate, they created a sense of community among the attendees. Men and women went together to a special place (the shows were held during the annual spring religious festivals) and shared a unique experience. The plays communicated and shaped the virtual community of thought among ancient Greeks. By engaging the audience's attention and immersing them in the sights and sounds of a performance, these creative simulations weren't unlike the way we use computers today, or envision using them in the not-too-distant future.

In the 1400s, the Florentine artist Giotto intuitively stumbled upon a method of projecting three-dimensional perspective onto a flat, two-dimensional canvas. This method of organizing objects and relationships on the canvas as if there was a single point of view created a sense of depth, of stereoscopic vision. Within a few years Giotto's discovery was copied and became one of the foundations of art for the next 500 years.

Through changing styles of art, the basic assumption of 3-D perspective has been a constant. Even today, the notion of perspective has such a powerful grip on the consciousness of society that modern art that doesn't use perspective (cubist and abstract art, for example) has gone largely unaccepted by the general public.

In 1455, the invention of the printing press and the subsequent development of the mass-produced book changed people's sense of community and their relationship to knowledge. Unlike the medieval Christian era, where knowledge, as represented by the church and marketplace politics, was experienced within a group setting, books strengthened the idea of private thought and opinion, of individuality. The right to study ideas and knowledge was no longer limited to special people, places, or times, or the accident of birth, but became commodities to be shared. The rise of democracy and the printing press went hand in hand.

Through reading, the experience of being immersed in a special imaginative and contemplative state of mind, similar to the absorbing engagement that good theater evoked, could be experienced alone. Writers developed the skills and techniques for debate and story-telling on the printed page to produce a sense of realism and presence in the virtual simulations they created within people's minds.

The printed page became a way of creating a shared community of ideas and experiences, even though the individuals might have never met. The printed book became a magic carpet ride, taking readers on journeys down rabbit holes, stranding them on desert islands, and involving them in the emotional life of fictional characters and the great intellectual debates of their times (*Gulliver's Travels* is one of the greatest and earliest examples).

Books were the first mass-produced commodity, a means of idea production and distribution that made other ideas and inventions possible. More than painting, music, or theater, the printed page allowed people to develop an idea, an attitude, and a state of mind that could be shared with others. Concepts became something that could be examined repeatedly, shared, and debated by everyone.

The use of perspective in art created a bias in the public for viewing images in a stereoscopic viewpoint. Painting was supposed to be about transporting the viewer into the presence of the scene, the painting acting as a window into another place or time. The success of books also helped fuel this hunger among the public for the experience of being somewhere else, not just in their imagination. As the industrial revolution began to unfold, new inventions and techniques began to appear that fed this hunger and allowed people to immerse themselves in new experiences.

Panorama paintings

In 1788, the Scottish painter Robert Barker painted a 360-degree view of the city of Edinburgh. He displayed the 10-foot tall canvas in a circular room 60 feet across. Viewers could enter into the center of the specially constructed room and be surrounded by the scene. He called it a *panorama*. He succeeded at providing a new level of realism because the image filled more than 180 degrees of the viewer's horizontal field of view (it would be another 150 years before Hollywood rediscovered this technique and named it Cinerama). These created environments soon became a popular form of entertainment throughout Europe and North America.

Sometimes, in order to increase the sense of realism, actual objects would be cleverly blended into the foreground of the picture so that it was difficult to tell where the real object ended and the painting began. Clever use of indirect lighting was also used to suggest light emanating from the painting.

Panoramas were created of London and of various battle scenes (see Fig. 2-1). In 1883, *The Battle of Gettysburg* was exhibited by Paul Philippoteaux in several American cities and can still be seen today at the Gettysburg National Military Park in Pennsylvania. These were the first early experiments at providing a sense of immersion in a virtual experience. Their popularity was based on the reaction of the audience to feeling that it was getting a first-hand experience of another place and time. Their weakness was that scenes were static and devoid of movement.

Figure

Panorama painting in which real objects in the foreground are "blended" into the painting to achieve additional realism.

At the end of the 19th century, the fledgling motion-picture industry quickly distracted audiences away from the static panoramas. Within a few years, they were rolled up, stored away, and mostly forgotten.

⇨ Stereoscopic pictures

In the mid-1800s, the new technology of photography became popular. For the first time, people were able to take and reproduce accurate images of real places, people, and events. Almost as soon as photography was introduced, a viewing technique was developed to further enhance the sense of realism. In 1833, Wheatstone invented the *stereoscopic display*, allowing individuals to use a simple device to view stereo images with a strong sense of depth (see Fig. 2-2). At the height of its popularity, Wheatstone's invention could be considered the 1800s' version of a video game. Every home had to have one.

Figure 2-2

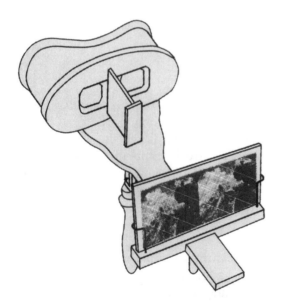

Late 19th-century stereoscope based on David Brewster's invention. This was the predecessor of the more modern Viewmaster. Webster's Third New International Dictionary, 1971

You created stereoscopic images by either taking a picture of a scene, shifting the camera a couple of inches to the side, and taking another picture, or using a special camera with two lens and two sets of negatives. This essentially duplicated the pair of images as seen by both eyes. When the two images were viewed so that the left eye

received only the left image and the right eye only the right image, a sense of depth and realism was achieved.

This invention was further refined by David Brewster in 1844 and evolved into the mass-produced Viewmaster of the mid-1900s. Unfortunately, the stereoscopic viewers suffered from the same limitation as the panorama painting. They were both incapable of displaying moving images.

The success of the stereoscopic viewer was based on its inexpensive ability to provide an entertaining illusion of reality. It enjoyed a long reign of popularity before the increasing availability of dynamic images on film and TV proved too irresistible for consumers. Yet another entertainment form was swept aside by the growing dominance of the new visual medium of film and TV.

 # The movies

> "Film is truth at 24 frames per second."
> **Jean-Luc Godard**

Using static scenes or pictures to re-create a previous event or to provide a sense of being somewhere else was only partially successful. Within minutes the participant would have explored the visual information provided and be ready for fresh stimulation. Because visual perception focuses on movement in an image, your attention will wander when movement is missing. Realizing that you're looking at only a picture, no matter how artfully created, you quickly lose your suspension of disbelief.

Another weakness of static images is their limited ability to tell a story. It's the difference between reading a detailed paragraph describing a hilltop scene, and reading a novel about the events and personalities that shaped the scene. A medium that could not only keep your attention using moving images but also tell a complex story would have great potential.

Edison's invention of the Kinetoscope in 1889 and the first public demonstration in 1894 was the birth of that medium, although Edison didn't realize it at the time. He was primarily interested in developing a visual accompaniment for his very successful phonograph. Edison intended the Kinetoscope to become a home-entertainment machine capable of illustrating the sound from the phonograph.

The Kinetoscope was based on a loop of film, guided through a complicated series of rollers, and contained in a chest-high viewing enclosure. After depositing a nickel (initially 25 cents, until the novelty wore off), you could look through a small window on top of the device, turn a handle, and watch a three- to five-minute film.

Almost overnight, parlors sprang up all over the country, catering to the public's demand for this new experience. Edison rejected the notion of using his device to project images for a large audience; instead, he believed that the future belonged to individual experiences.

Hollywood would prove otherwise. In 1895, two brothers, Auguste and Louis Lumiere, projected their first film (*La sortie des ouvriers de l'usine Lumiere*) to a private audience in Paris. Film historians designate this as the world's first moving picture. They called their system Cinematographe, which eventually became the name of the new medium.

The business of synthesizing reality was born. Now life could be captured on film as it occurred, historical events re-created, and fictional stories brought to life. Inexpensive to duplicate, the resulting experience could be widely distributed. Almost immediately, a rapidly expanding industry was formed around the new medium, providing audiences with new visual experiences for a fee.

> "Initially the image quality was grainy and poor. The frame rate varied from 14–24 frames per second and the equipment was cumbersome and expensive. In the first few years, technologists and experimenters controlled the medium and created productions with little or no dramatic or narrative content."
> **Cook, 1981 (A description of the film industry in 1896)**

It's interesting to note that this depiction is equally valid of today's virtual reality industry and indicates the many parallels between these two industries.

 # Development of narrative

Initially, film was used to simply document the staged plays of the time. Everything was filmed from a static perspective with no camera movement. (The concept of a "camera shot" wasn't introduced until much later, with D. W. Griffith's work in 1908.) It wasn't until 1902 that Melies' film, *A Trip to the Moon*, clearly exhibited the changing role of film, from documentary to narrative.

> "One afternoon in the fall of 1896, while Melies was filming a Parisian street scene, his camera jammed in the process of recording an omnibus as it emerged from a tunnel. When he got the machine working again, a funeral hearse had replaced the omnibus, so that in projection the omnibus seemed to change into a hearse. By this accident, Melies came to recognize the possibilities for the manipulation of real time and real space inherent in the editing of exposed film. He had discovered that film need not obey the laws of empirical reality, as his predecessors had supposed, because film was in some sense a separate reality with structural laws of its own."
> **David A. Cook, 1981**

From this start, it would take 19 years before the camera and editing innovations of D. W. Griffith would appear in the monumental film *The Birth of a Nation* (1915). Griffith single-handedly created most of the camera work and editing techniques still in use today. He revolutionized the use of film to narrate a story. He introduced the concept of the camera shot, where the camera cuts to a close-up of a scene to provide more dramatic effect or simply to allow the actors to more easily articulate emotion.

In addition, he invented the idea of cutting between different scenes of action to depict parallel events, such as a woman inside a house and the action taking place outside the building by burglars attempting to break in. Griffith rapidly cut between these parallel events, thereby creating a sense of tension. These new techniques were at first regarded suspiciously by the executives at Biograph, where Griffith worked. His wife, Linda Arvidson Griffith, reported the following encounter:

> "When Mr. Griffith suggested a scene showing Annie Lee waiting for her husband's return to be followed by a scene of Enoch cast away on a desert island, it was altogether distracting.
>
> 'How can you tell a story jumping about like that? The people won't know what it's about.''
>
> 'Well,' said Mr. Griffith, 'doesn't Dickens write that way?'
>
> 'Yes, but that's Dickens; that's novel writing; that's different.'
>
> 'Oh, not so much, these are picture stories; not so different.'"
>
> **Linda A. Griffith, 1969**

Griffith exploited the freedom of the new medium and explored its many possibilities. He's considered perhaps the greatest cinematic genius in history. Today, similar geniuses are among us—those who are conceptualizing how the new medium of virtual reality can be used as a medium of expression. What new techniques will they invent? What revolutions will they lead?

During the early 1900s, technology kept refining the cinematic experience. Sound made its debut in 1923 as the first sound-on-film Phonofilm was shown in New York City. For the first time since the Kinetoscope, sound was synchronized to the film action. The success of Warner Brothers' *The Jazz Singer* (1927) signaled the end of the silent era and ushered in "the talkies."

Within two years almost all American theaters had converted to sound at the staggering cost of $300 million dollars (more than several billion in today's dollars), and audiences began pouring into theaters. Sound's popularity ensured the survival of the major studios during the difficult years of the Depression.

Right on its heel, the three-color Technicolor process was introduced in 1932, but the difficulties and expense of working with it limited its use to major features. By 1946, two-thirds of the entire U.S. population (100 million people) went to the cinema weekly. It became a fixture in every community.

People went there to get news, learn about the world, be entertained, and escape to exotic locations. Viewers imagined themselves through the eyes of their favorite actors and actresses, vicariously experiencing what transpired on the silver screen. For them, film represented more than just photons striking a screen; it became part of their lives. The film industry was never again to enjoy such immense popularity.

From Edison's first flickering images, the desire to improve the cinematic experience led to increasing levels of realism. The introduction of color, multichannel sound, wider screens, and even stereoscopic images (more commonly known as 3-D), all contributed to enhancing the illusion of reality.

Initially, the film industry treated many of these technological advancements as mere gimmicks designed to lure people into the theater. As the novelty wore off, however, a greater reliance on story-telling occurred and the emphasis shifted from technology to content. Along the way, some of the gimmicks that couldn't contribute to the story were dropped (such as 3-D effects).

Today, most virtual experiences are also based on gimmicks. As the entertainment industry begins to recognize the enormous potential of cyberspace experiences, there will probably be a proliferation of gimmicks until storytellers master the new art. It might take a few years, but it should be worth waiting for.

Television

Technology once again provided a new medium (and the cinema's great rival) as regular broadcasts of television signals began in 1941. It's interesting to compare the introduction of television to the introduction of virtual experiences. Here was a technology fascinating to view, though limited in content and image quality. Crowds formed wherever it was initially demonstrated. Ideas abounded for possible applications, but predictions fell far short of actual uses. Sound familiar?

Television provided a mass distribution system, bringing much of the impact of movies into everyone's home. No longer did people have to go to the theater—now the theater was delivered to the home. Much as VCRs later drew viewers away from network broadcasting, television sets drew people away from the movies.

In addition, television could do what movies could never do; it could put viewers on the scene live, or in *real time*. It introduced the concept of *telepresence*, the sense of being there through the eyes of the camera. The 1991 war in the Persian Gulf illustrates this ability, but it was the Kennedy assassination that first truly drove the point home as the entire nation participated in the disaster and mourning.

Over the years, television's potential for escapism and distorting the nation's moral fabric has been debated, much as similar debates swirl over the role of virtual reality today. Few adults are fully comfortable with the role television plays in our lives. Fifty years after its introduction, we're still trying to understand the impact and influence of television on our lives.

⇨ Cinerama

Using television and film to create a sense of realism had one important drawback; the audience felt as if they were watching the action through a large window or frame. All the drama was out there beyond the window; nothing ventured inside the theater. The audience was isolated from directly experiencing the events shown on the screen. 3-D movies were marginally successful at breaking through this barrier and bringing the action inside, but they didn't succeed because they were too gimmicky.

To allow a more direct experience, a larger image would have to be captured and displayed so it would fill the audience's entire field of view. Our eyes can see about 180 degrees horizontally and about 150 degrees vertically. Depending on where someone sits in a theater, a 35mm-film screen could be as small as 50 degrees horizontally and 38 degrees vertically. This is about 5 percent of our visual field. Television is much worse. Various approaches tried to expand the view, and in the early 1950s Fred Waller convinced producer Mike Todd to invest $10 million in a new process called Cinerama (see Fig. 2-3).

Figure 2-3

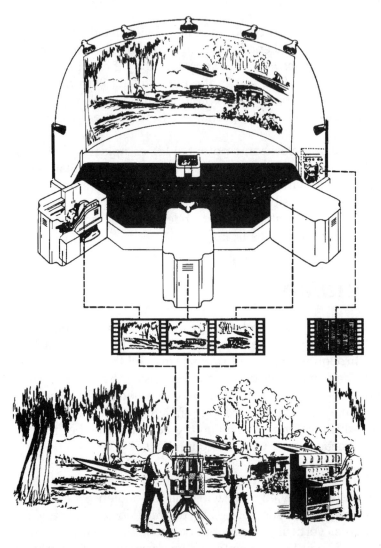

Cinerama illustration depicting the use of three separate cameras to record the action, which is later played back by three film projectors onto a very wide screen.

Three synchronized 35mm-film cameras recorded each scene from slightly different views. In the theater, three projectors displayed the separate images onto a specially built screen that curved around the audience and provided almost an entire 180 degrees of horizontal view. The image was now three times as wide and nearly twice as tall (it used a taller film format). With six times the visual image and six-track stereophonic sound, it dramatically increased the perception of experiencing a movie rather than looking through a window.

Narrative movies such as *How the West was Won* (1962) and *The Wonderful World of the Brothers Grimm* (1962) were shot using this process. Though popular, the cost of outfitting theaters and difficulties in synchronizing and producing films using three cameras instead of one proved too formidable. *How the West was Won*, for example, required the services of three directors (John Ford, Henry Hathaway, and George Marshall) and four cinematographers, and cost over $14 million to shoot.

At the height of its popularity, only 100 theaters in the world were equipped to show Cinerama films. After 1963, movies were no longer produced using the Cinerama format, but it's credited with bringing audiences back to cinemas in numbers unseen since 1946. It proved that audiences would respond to experiences that had a greater sense of presence—of "being there."

Hollywood, threatened by the popularity of television in 1950, recognized the value of the wide-screen experience and began searching for other solutions. In 1953, simpler processes such as Cinemascope and later 70mm Panavision were developed for the wide screen and are still in use today (in addition to Omnimax, which is the ultimate wide-screen experience, with almost a total field of view horizontally and vertically). People were willing to pay for the experience of being immersed in a movie. Fortunately, Morton Heilig (a young cinematographer from Hollywood) had a chance to experience Cinerama in the early 1950s prior to its demise.

> "I became fascinated by Cinerama after reading about it. I was already involved with cameras and film and the technological influences in film. On a visit back to New York I went down to see Cinerama. This was a pivotal experience in my life. The

37

narrator described the scene, the curtain swept back, revealing a
screen four times bigger than normal and they showed a roller
coaster ride. You no longer identified with some actor who was
having your experience, you had the experience yourself. I
subsequently went to see all the Cinerama films."
Morton Heilig

 # Sensorama

Realizing its potential to reduce the barrier of the screen and to
transport the audience through the window into the movie itself,
Morton Heilig proposed a radical idea. He decided that the logical
future of the film industry would be that of supplying highly realistic
experiences to large audiences. His goal was the complete elimination
of all barriers that kept people from accepting the cinematic illusion.

Methodically, he studied the sensory signals used to distinguish
illusion from reality. He isolated sight, sound, touch, and smell as the
primary senses needed for stimulation. Next, he analyzed what
current technology could provide for sensory stimulation. This
resulted in a clear understanding of the pieces missing to complete his
concept of the "experience theater."

Stereophonic sound and stereoscopic images were already
commercially available. If Heilig could combine them with a full field
of view better than Cinerama, and figure out how to stimulate the
nose and provide tactile sensations, his goal would be achieved. With
little more than simple faith in his ideas, Heilig attempted to
revolutionize Hollywood.

Unfortunately, Hollywood wasn't listening. Despite repeated attempts
to communicate his call to revolution, he didn't find any support in
the film industry. After moving to Mexico in 1954 and receiving
financial backing for some initial research, his backer was killed in an
accident, forcing Heilig to return to New York.

By 1960 he and a partner created a personal version of the
experience theater as a way to demonstrate his concepts. Similar to
an arcade machine, and called Sensorama (shown in Fig. 2-4), it was

Figure 2-4

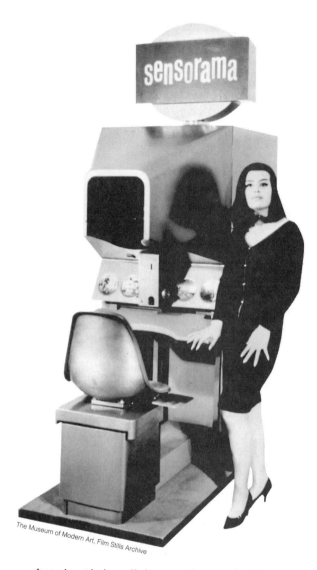

The Museum of Modern Art, Film Stills Archive

Early promotional picture showing one of the Sensorama prototypes.

outfitted with handlebars, a binocular-like viewing device, a vibrating seat, and small vents that could blow air when commanded. In addition, stereophonic speakers were mounted near the ears, and a device for generating odors specific to the events viewed stereoscopically was located close to the nose.

One of the recorded "experiences" was a motorcycle ride through Brooklyn. The seat vibrated, you felt the wind against your face, and

you even smelled different odors as you passed along the street—a full sensory experience that hasn't been duplicated since, even with today's $250,000 computerized virtual experiences.

Of course, you couldn't direct the motorcycle to turn down your favorite street (it wasn't interactive), but you received a very direct experience as a passive observer. This was the logical evolution in the search for realistic, immersive experiences, but the film industry didn't realize it.

They also had problems with the economics of Heilig's ideas. Films absorb very high production values that either must be amortized over time or across a mass market to get the necessary return on investment. Movies are very expensive to produce, but relatively easy to reproduce and distribute. And they can be experienced by large groups so that costs can be spread out over repeated viewings by large audiences. Heilig's stand-alone ride would require thousands of "rides" to pay back its cost, or otherwise the cost of each ride would be prohibitively expensive.

Of course, Hollywood would also miss the significance of the video-game craze of the 1980s and the multi-billion-dollar revenues it generated. Video games provided personal entertainment through dedicated hardware. The film industry is one of few industries that is successful despite spending an insignificant amount on research and development on new technologies.

After a few more unsuccessful attempts at marketing Sensorama and the development of another prototype for a different backer, Heilig had to accept the inability of the industry to recognize Sensorama's potential. Finally, the first cyberspace machine was covered up and rolled away to storage. Things could have turned out quite a bit different.

Pioneers in cyberspace

"'. . . Computers are a lot worse than real life. You have to be hit over the head with that before you realize how true it is.'

'Why bother, then?' [Brand] asked. 'Why not stick with real life?' Strassman didn't hesitate: 'Because you can't automate real life. I can't get this shrimp to swim if I draw it on real paper with a real brush.'

Junior deities, we want to be. Reality is mostly given. Virtual reality is creatable."

Stewart Brand, *The Media Lab*

AS Morton Heilig struggled to convince a reluctant entertainment business to back his ideas, the first minicomputer based on transistors rather than tubes became available in 1960. The Digital Equipment Corporation's (DEC) PDP-1 was a harbinger of the technology that would, more than 25 years later, succeed at popularizing virtual experiences where Sensorama failed.

The PDP-1 represented a revolution in computer affordability and performance. Based on the new silicon technology, computers began spreading out to universities and research institutes across America.

Interacting with these early computers was difficult because they weren't designed from a user point of view. Punchcards and batch processing required the user to adapt to the needs of the computer instead of the other way around. Time sharing and interactive video screens didn't exist in 1960, and it would be almost 20 years before

the first personal computer would appear. Using one of these early computers was a frustrating experience—there had to be a better way.

In the early 1950s, an engineer in Mountain View, California, Douglas Engelbart, decided to figure out a way to turn computers into a powerful problem-solving tool that anyone could use. With a background in working with radar systems for the Navy, Engelbart realized that video screens could be used instead of paper to display the computer's output.

His next breakthrough was realizing that they could also be used to control the computer, to provide it with input. This was a revolutionary idea, given that both video screens and computers were relatively rare and inaccessible.

Engelbart spent the next several years organizing his thoughts and trying to gain access to the few computers available at the time. While working at SRI in Menlo Park in the mid-1960s, the Advanced Research Projects Agency (ARPA, forerunner to DARPA and sponsored by the U.S. Defense Department) provided funding for Engelbart to pursue his ideas.

He finally had the resources to build the mind-augmentation devices he had been dreaming of for the last decade. His lab, the Augmentation Research Center (ARC), was responsible for some of the key computer-human interface developments we use today.

In 1968, he gave an amazing demonstration at the Fall Joint Computer Conference. Using a crude pointing device (the first mouse), he selected a document to read from an iconic representation on a video display. This opened up and displayed the contents of the document on the screen. Still using the mouse, he cut and pasted a section of text elsewhere in the document. Remember, almost everyone used punched cards to talk to computers at the time. This was a radically new way to use computers. Alan Kay had this to say about the performance:

> "We thought of Douglas as Moses opening the Red Sea. You know he was like a biblical prophet . . . they were actually doing the kinds of things that people still dream about today . . . I think

of it as the vision of what we today call personal computing or desktop computing."
Alan Kay (Palfreman and Swade, 1991)

Not only did Engelbart invent word processing, but he also demonstrated the rudiments of a hypertext environment. This was a real breakthrough—now people could interact with computers in a more direct and natural way. While Cinerama and Sensorama struggled to break down barriers in the film experience, Engelbart was breaking down the same barriers with computers.

⇨ The ultimate display

Back on the East Coast, Ivan Sutherland was also busy changing the way people interacted with computers. He realized the enormous importance of getting computers to conform to the way people worked and thought, instead of people conforming to computers. Credited with being the "father of computer graphics" by the industry he helped found, he pioneered many of the basic methods of using computers to represent 2-D and 3-D images.

His Sketchpad program in 1962 demonstrated the use of a light-pen to draw images on a computer screen, and was the precursor to the multi-billion-dollar computer-aided design (CAD) industry of today. In 1965, Sutherland published an article entitled *The Ultimate Display*, in which he described the following:

> "We live in a physical world whose properties we have come to know well through long familiarity. We sense an involvement with this physical world which gives us the ability to predict its properties well. For example, we can predict where objects will fall, how well-known shapes look from other angles, and how much force is required to push objects against friction. We lack corresponding familiarity with the forces on charged particles, forces in nonuniform fields, the effects of nonprojective geometric transformations, and high-inertia, low-friction motion. A display connected to a digital computer gives us a chance to gain familiarity with concepts not realizable in the physical world. It is a looking glass into a mathematical wonderland."
> **Ivan Sutherland, 1965**

Another example of Sutherland's creativity was his development of the first computer-based head-mounted display (HMD) in 1966 at the MIT Lincoln Laboratory and later at the University of Utah. He had to invent from scratch most of the technology that 20 years later NASA would use to assemble the modern virtual environment.

⇨ The sword of Damocles

Sutherland's head-mounted display earned the nickname *the sword of Damocles* due to the mass of hardware that was supported from the ceiling above the user's head. The weight of the HMD was too much to bear without some additional support. A mechanical apparatus determined where the viewer was looking, and monoscopic wire-frame images were generated using two small cathode-ray tubes (CRTs) mounted alongside each ear.

Optics focused the image onto half-silvered mirrors placed directly in front of the eyes. The mirrors allowed the computer-generated images to overlay the view of the world (in contrast, most of today's VR systems obscure the view of the outside world). Users of the system viewed a wire-frame cube floating in space in the middle of the lab. By moving their head around they could see different aspects of the glowing cube and determine its size and placement (see Fig. 3-1).

When Sutherland joined the University of Utah, he continued to refine the hardware and software until, in 1970, the first fully functional HMD was completed. His final system consisted of several hardware accelerators to improve the performance of the graphics system and the generation of stereoscopic images instead of monoscopic.

In general terms, there's no difference between this system and the system that was to emerge from NASA Ames almost 20 years later. The long search for a synthesized reality had finally lead to a system capable of generating virtual objects. Finally, the visions of Sutherland and Engelbart were realized. The barrier between the computer and the user had finally been eliminated; the user was now inside the computer.

Figure 3-1

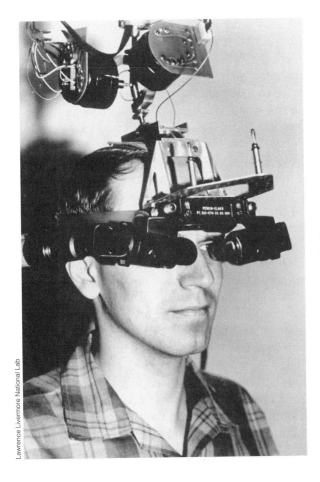

Lawrence Livermore National Lab

Sutherland's head-mounted display worn by Donald L. Vickers at the University of Utah.

Early reality simulators

During World War II, the military discovered the value of training pilots in flight simulators. A pilot's chances of coming back from a mission jumped up to 95 percent if he made it through his first five missions. And anything that increased his chances of surviving those first missions was crucial to saving his life.

As early as 1929, the Link corporation was building flight simulators. A full-sized mock-up of a fighter cockpit was constructed and mounted on a motion platform. The cockpit physically pitched, rolled, and yawed based on the pilot's actions. Results from the

simple Link trainer showed that a pilot's training could be successfully simulated on an earth-bound platform.

Decades later, as aviation became more complex, spending thousands of dollars on a flight simulator that saved millions of dollars in operating a real fighter or replacing a lost one made sense. These economics were the driving force behind an entire industry committed to the realistic simulation of airplanes, helicopters, tanks, and even ships.

Early simulators, however, had one major limitation. Real-time visual feedback was impossible. The pilot couldn't view the outside world or watch it change by moving the control stick. Without visual feedback, training was limited to instrument flying.

This all changed in the early 1950s, as commercial video cameras became available. Cameras were mounted on movable platforms suspended over scale models of airports. Motion of the camera platform was controlled by the pilot. If he pulled back on the control stick, the camera tilted back, projecting a new image on the front window. The camera "flew" over the model, controlled by the pilot.

This improvement in reality increased the simulation's effectiveness. Soon, multiple cameras were combined to project additional perspectives, allowing left and right views along with forward views. Over the next 20 years, video cameras continued to shrink in size as models grew in complexity. The advent of sophisticated computers capable of generating similar images slowly replaced the cameras and models. However, this technique is still widely used in movies by Hollywood's special-effects wizards.

Scene generators

While working on the first electronic head-mounted display, Ivan Sutherland recognized the potential for computers to generate the images for flight simulators instead of video cameras and scale models. Sutherland teamed up with David Evans in 1968 to create electronic "scene generators." Later that year, they formed Evans and Sutherland to sell these systems.

Instead of constructing scale models from paint, foam, and glue, the computer constructed images with stored data. Any 3-D object could be digitized and entered into the computer. For example, an airport could be represented as a large number of 3-D points with lines connecting each point. After a series of calculations, a view from any vantage point could be constructed.

Custom hardware accelerated the calculations so that each scene was drawn in a fraction of a second, in less time than you could blink. This process of calculating and drawing images is called *rendering*. A rapid sequence of scenes rendered by the computer appears movielike to the pilot. Controlling the computer like a movable camera platform creates the same sense of flying around the model.

The number of scenes rendered in a fixed amount of time is called the *update rate*, and is measured in frames per second (fps) or hertz (Hz). Early scene generators (circa 1973) achieved around 20 fps with simple 3-D models (200–400 polygons). Studies showed that pilot training performance suffered below this update rate.

Scene complexity is the crucial factor controlling update rates. A 3-D image of a cube might be drawn at 60 fps, but a 3-D image of an airport, with buildings, hangars, and other aircraft might bring a computer to its knees—drawing only a single frame every second. With complexity and speed, a balance must be struck. As computers become faster, either model complexity or update rates can increase, but rarely both. This constant tension won't be resolved soon.

One of the first flight simulators to use computers was built by General Electric Company's Electronics Laboratory for the Navy in 1972. Their Advanced Development Model was used as an instrument to measure the effectiveness of computer-generated images for pilot training. Consisting of three independent rendering channels, images were projected onto three screens that surrounded the physical mockup of the cockpit. This provided the pilot with a realistic 180-degree field of view (see Fig. 3-2).

This early simulator revealed many of the demands of simulating reality. The Navy discovered that the complexity of a scene (determined by the number of polygons) and texturing (each polygon

Figure 3-2

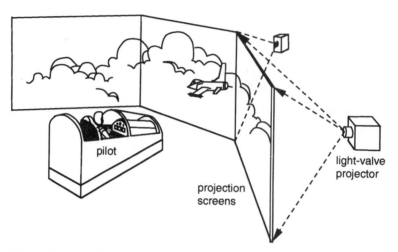

The Advanced Development Model (ADM), one of the first flight simulators using computer-generated graphics. Computer Image Generation
Schachter

is "painted" with an image) was crucial in providing adequate velocity and attitude cues for line ups and landings on both airfields and aircraft carriers. The advanced development model also showed that simulation of haze significantly contributed to the realism of the experience. Generally, the more realistic the image, the better the training.

And just to prove that there's an exception to any rule, they also noticed that pilots were having difficulties orienting themselves with respect to the featureless surface of the ocean. Their solution was to draw a checkerboard pattern on it to provide additional perspective cues—a good example of how decreasing realism can sometimes improve training effectiveness.

As early as 1979, the military was experimenting with head-mounted displays. If an effective one could be built, it would significantly reduce the expense and physical size of the simulation system. By projecting the image directly into the pilot's eyes, bulky screens and projection systems could be eliminated.

One of the first of these, McDonnell Douglas's VITAL helmet (see Fig. 3-3), used an electromagnetic head tracker to sense where the pilot was looking. Dual monochromatic cathode-ray tubes were mounted

Figure 3-3

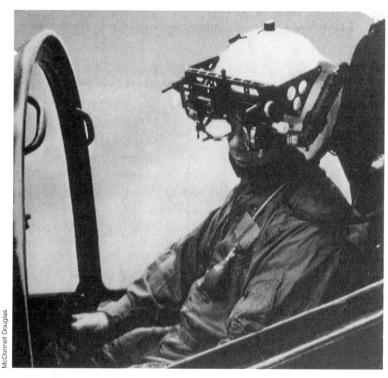

McDonnell Douglas

VITAL helmet, one of the first commercially available head-mounted displays.

next to the pilot's ears, projecting the image onto beam splitters in front of his eyes.

This allowed the pilot to view and manipulate mechanical controls in the cockpit, while seeing the computer-generated image of the outside world. Problems with bulky headgear and the unnaturalness of viewing through beam splitters, however, limited the acceptance of these early head-mounted displays.

For over 20 years, America's armed forces have been manufacturing realities in order to improve the effectiveness of their personnel. It has proven conclusively the usefulness and cost-effectiveness of simulation training. In addition, these same simulators have become standard training tools for commercial aircraft. Better qualified pilots mean safer planes.

Without the initial investment by NASA and the Defense Department, many of these technologies would have taken much longer to evolve. It's likely that virtual reality would not exist in its present form if not for this initial investment. It's one of many valuable spin-offs of military research.

⇨ Artificial reality

At the same time Sutherland was donning his new head-mounted display at the University of Utah, Myron Krueger was experimenting with combining computers and video systems to create *artificial realities* (a term he later coined to describe this new experience) at the University of Wisconsin.

Krueger had the same driving passion as Engelbart and others to use computers to establish natural dialogs with people. The computer would be taught about people instead of people having to learn the computer. Krueger established simple interactive demonstrations that allowed users to walk up and immediately start interacting with computer-generated images.

In his most famous work, *VIDEOPLACE* (1976), the user's body image is captured by a video camera in real time and represented as a silhouette on a large video projection screen in a darkened room. It's like watching your shadow projected on a video screen. Using image processing techniques to detect edges of the silhouette, users can "fingerpaint" by holding up a finger and moving it. A trail of colored paint will appear on the video screen following the movements of the finger. Holding up five fingers will erase the image.

In addition, an animated creature named CRITTER can be introduced into the image (see Fig. 3-4). This synthesized being appears to chase your image and attempts to climb your silhouette to reach the top of your head. CRITTER can also be directed to dangle from a finger, where an abrupt movement will cause it to fall to the bottom of the screen.

Figure 3-4

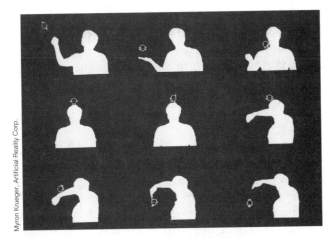

Myron Krueger, Artificial Reality Corp.

Sequence of frames showing Myron Krueger's CRITTER interacting with the outline of the participant.

Krueger was doing something new here. He had changed the definition of what a computer could do and how it interacted with people. The computer had almost disappeared, to be replaced with a friendly and benign sprite. Krueger's mix of video image processing and computer graphics took him into a new realm where the computer allowed for artistic expression in the form of these artificial realities. He pioneered a unique form of nonintrusive virtual environments. It wasn't necessary for the participants to don special clothing or wear a cumbersome viewing apparatus (Krueger considered such technology, but dismissed it as being too intrusive).

Artificial reality has come to represent an experience similar to but different than what is commonly called virtual reality. We've coined the term *projected reality* to help differentiate the two approaches. In Krueger's application, you see yourself projected into the action happening on a screen instead of directly experiencing yourself in an environment. This is a crucial difference.

In VIDEOPLACE and Krueger's related efforts, participants are aware that they're in a darkened room and interacting with computers through a "window" in front of them. Virtual reality, on the other

hand, like Sensorama and Sutherland's head-mounted display, takes you through this window and into a new experience.

Both intrusive and nonintrusive technologies will continue to develop and hopefully combine to provide us with the best of both worlds. Krueger makes an important point about the influence of computers and our interaction with them in an essay about future interfaces:

> "When judging user interfaces, our usual standard of goodness is the efficiency with which one can progress from point A to point B using the application. At some point we must recognize that our lives are spent in between. As more of our commercial and personal transactions are accomplished through computers, the quality of the experience provided by the computer interface has bearing on the quality of life itself. Therefore, the aesthetics of interaction will be as important as the efficiency."
> **Krueger, 1991**

One way to improve the quality of our interaction with computers is to learn Hollywood's techniques of entertainment. Hollywood understands realism and narrative—what it takes to involve the audience and create compelling experiences. Hollywood has had almost 100 years to learn about keeping the audience's attention and providing a pleasant experience. No one ever had to go back to the movies once the novelty wore off; the movies had to create attractive experiences to keep bringing people back. Of course, this need to appeal to the masses can lead to mediocrity, the rule of the lowest common denominator.

If Hollywood understands narrative and realism, computer people understand interactivity. They know how to use computers to create a form of conversation with the user, exchanging data and responding back and forth. They have traditionally not worried much about realism or the attractiveness of screens, but the computer industry can learn from the movie moguls. And vice versa.

 Super cockpit

Interaction with computers became a life-or-death experience for pilots in the 1970s, as the capabilities of advanced jet fighters began

to exceed that of the humans to control them. Imagine the cognitive hurdle of learning the F15. It has nine different buttons on the control stick and seven more on the throttle. In the stress and confusion of battle, pilots always had to pick the correct one. Mistakes could be fatal.

As anyone who has peeked into the cockpit of a modern airplane can attest, the complexity and quantity of dials, gauges, and switches is staggering. Fighter pilots must manage this bewildering barrage of information even as they suffer from brief blackouts during high-G turns. Realizing the need to manage the quantity of information presented to pilots, the United States Air Force started looking for new technologies and research candidates.

With a background in creating visual displays for the military since 1966 and extensive research in the field of visual perception, Thomas Furness III had the experience the Air Force needed. After years of fighting for funding, Furness finally got the go-ahead to prototype a state-of-the-art control system at Wright-Patterson Air Force Base in Ohio. In 1982, he demonstrated a working model of the Visually Coupled Airborne Systems Simulator, or VCASS (see Fig. 3-5). It resembled Darth Vader's helmet in the movie *Star Wars*. Test pilots wore the oversized helmet and sat in a cockpit mock-up.

Instead of a normal view, pilots saw only an abstract or symbolic representation of the world outside (see Fig. 3-6). These synthetic images were projected onto screens in the helmet, masking off the view outside. Seeing only symbolic representations of landmarks, flight paths, and potential hazards reduced the distraction caused by an overload of visual information.

We use the same principle when pulling a map rather than an aerial photograph out of the glove box of a car. Symbolic information on the map is much easier to decipher than detailed aerial pictures. Information is reduced to the minimum that's necessary for achieving a goal—navigation in this case.

The VCASS used a 6D position and orientation tracker, from a company called Polhemus, to monitor where the pilot was looking. Electromagnetic pulses, emitted by a transmitter, were picked up by a small sensor mounted on the helmet. Processing the signal yielded an

Figure 3-5

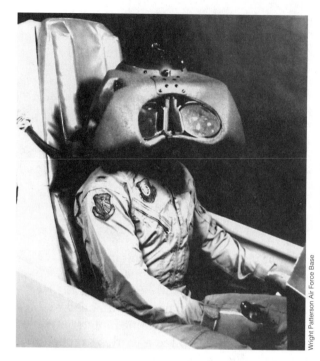

Pilot wearing "Darth Vader" helmet as part of the Super Cockpit project directed by Tom Furness.

Wright Patterson Air Force Base

accurate reading of the current position and orientation of the helmet. Using this information, the computer rendered the appropriate view. By obscuring images from outside the cockpit, immersion in a symbolic world was achieved.

Technology and funding allowed Furness to render images more complex than Sutherland's simple wire-frame cubes. In addition, custom one-inch-diameter CRTs with 2,000 scan lines projected the images, almost four times the resolution of a typical TV set. Virtual environments could be viewed in much more detail than anything commercially available, even today.

The Air Force saw enough promise in VCASS that a second phase was funded, known as Super Cockpit. An article in *Air & Space* magazine described how future pilots would use this technology:

> "When he climbed into his F-16SC, the young fighter jock of 1998 simply plugged in his helmet and flipped down his visor to activate his Super Cockpit system. The virtual world he saw

Figure 3-6

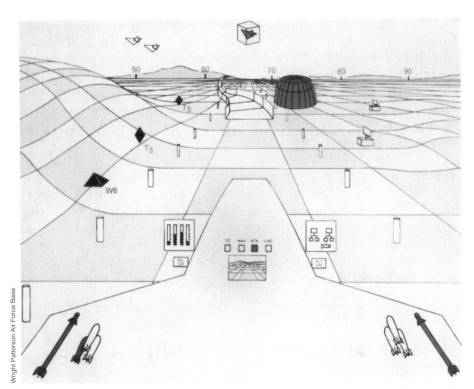

Wright Patterson Air Force Base

Super Cockpit view in which an abstract world is generated to reduce and simplify information presented to the pilot.

exactly mimicked the world outside. Salient terrain features were outlined and rendered in three dimensions by the two tiny cathode ray tubes focused at his personal viewing distance. Using voice commands, the pilot told the associate to start the engine and run through the checklist . . .

Once he was airborne, solid clouds obscured everything outside the canopy. But inside the helmet, the pilot 'saw' the horizon and terrain clearly, as if it were a clear day. His compass heading was displayed as a large band of numbers on the horizon line, his projected flight path a shimmering highway leading out toward infinity.

A faint whine above and behind him to the left told the pilot even before the associate announced it that his 'enemy' . . . was closing in . . ."

Thompson, 1987

55

By rethinking the entire process of flying a jet fighter, Furness created a powerful yet natural method of interacting with and controlling an aircraft's complex machinery. His tools were a computer and head-mounted display. They allowed him to construct a virtual world that gathered the storm of navigation, radar, weapons, and flight-control data into a single manageable form. Symbolic representations of the outside world and sensor data provided a filtered view of reality, thus simplifying the operation of the aircraft.

VCASS, one of the most advanced simulators developed, demonstrated the effectiveness of virtual reality techniques. Furness joined Engelbart, Sutherland, and Krueger in tearing down the barrier separating computers from their users. Removing this barrier allowed pilots to enter a strange new world carved out of the silicon of the computer. Radar became their eyes and ears, servos and electromechanical linkages were their muscles, and the plane obeyed their spoken commands. Flying would never be the same.

⇨ Reach out and touch with UNC

So far, researchers probing the man-machine interface had focused primarily on the simulation of sights and sounds, from Sutherland's initial experiments with head-mounted-displays to Krueger's playful interaction using video cameras and projection systems to Furness's integrated HMD and 3-D sound environment. All three researchers explored the visual and audio dimensions of the human perceptual system. Not since Heilig and his Sensorama had anyone focused much attention on re-creating tactile or force-feedback cues.

Even without sight, our sense of touch allows us to construct a detailed model of the world around us. The roughness of concrete, the smoothness of glass, and the pliability of rubber communicate detailed cues about our environment. Theoretically, computers could create a virtual world using tactile feedback just as they had with sights and sounds. Frederick Brooks at the University of North Carolina (UNC) set out to chart this unexplored territory.

Ivan Sutherland's vision, defined in his 1965 paper "The Ultimate Display," became the basis for Brooks' research in the early 1970s. Realizing that little work was being done with force or tactile feedback, he decided to pursue combining computer graphics to force-feedback devices. Not only did he agree with Sutherland and Engelbart that computers could be mind- or intelligence-amplification devices, but he set out to show how it could be done.

One early project by Brooks, called GROPE-II, proposed a unique molecular docking tool for chemists. Detecting allowable and forbidden docking sites between a drug and a protein or nucleic acid is crucial in designing effective drugs. Because both drug and nucleic acid molecules are complex 3-D structures, locating effective docking sites is a daunting task.

Imagine two complex tinker-toy structures two to three feet high. Your job is to manipulate each model, examining how well a knob or groove on one model docks with those on another. There might be hundreds of potential sites to test. Brooks wanted to create a tool capable of simulating the physical feel of docking a molecule. He reasoned that chemists could work more effectively if they could get their hands on a molecule and actually feel the tug and pull of docking forces.

Tinker-toy representations of two molecules were rendered by the computer, and chemists used a special device to grab one of the molecules and attempt to dock it with the other. An Argonne remote manipulator (ARM) was modified for this purpose. Originally used for handling radioactive materials, they were operated by a mechanical hand-grip that controlled a remote robotic arm.

UNC acquired a surplus ARM and modified it for their purposes by adding extra motors to resist the motion of moving the hand-grip. Controlled by a computer, the ARM exerted physical force against the operator's hand.

After assembling a system in 1971, Brooks and his students were disappointed to learn that available computer technology wasn't up to the task. They couldn't simulate anything more complex than simple building blocks, let alone the intricacies of molecular docking. So the

GROPE-II system was moved into storage, awaiting the arrival of more powerful computers.

⇨ GROPE-III

It wasn't until 1986 that computing power had increased sufficiently to justify dusting off the system and having another go at the problem. A simulation of a drug with over 1,500 atoms and a protein of 21 atoms was modeled on the new GROPE-III system.

Wearing polarized eyeglasses, a chemist could view a stereoscopic image of the molecules. This provides a sense of depth as she tries to manipulate the molecule using the ARM, shown in Fig. 3-7. Even with 100 times the computing power of the original GROPE-II, the simulation was so complex that it took a third of a second to render each image (3 fps), resulting in jerky, noncontinuous motion. For realistic modeling, closer to 20 frames per second is required.

Despite the limited performance, Brooks' researchers learned that the system could still be effective for studying docking problems. By reducing the complexity of the model, they increased the update rate to 10 frames per second.

Now docking the model felt like holding a six-inch bar magnet in your hand and moving it closer to an identical magnet fixed in place. Identically charged surfaces repelled each other, pushing your hand away. Oppositely charged surfaces attracted, pulling your hand closer. You could feel the force field surrounding the molecules.

At UNC, chemists could feel forces impossible to directly experience without the aid of the computer. The researchers also noted an important warning in their 1988 paper: "Unlike a computer system, the manipulator arms, if used improperly, have the physical capability of destroying themselves and their environment. Therefore, follow the instructions carefully and exactly." Computers can generate incorrect images or sounds without harming the operator. However, incorrect forces in a system like GROPE could have unhealthy consequences.

Figure 3-7

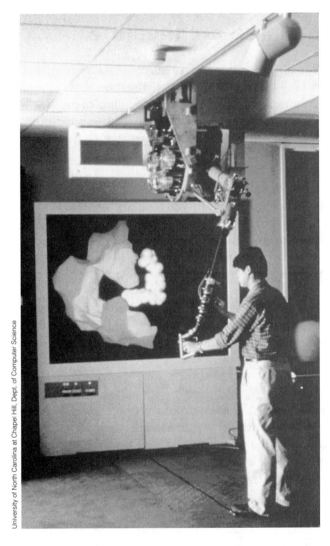

University of North Carolina at Chapel Hill, Dept. of Computer Science

UNC's Grope III system allows you to "feel" the forces involved in finding the appropriate docking site between two molecules.

Chemists weren't the only ones to have their minds amplified at UNC. Architects were also among the chosen few. For centuries, they had struggled with communicating their vision to those around them. Using scale models and perspective drawings helped, but they were inflexible. If the customer wanted changes, the model would have to be rebuilt or the drawing redone. This was both expensive and time-consuming. Architects and their clients would benefit tremendously from a tool that allowed them to visit the design and walk around it before it was even constructed.

 # Computer-simulated architecture

In the mid '80s, UNC decided to construct a new multi-million-dollar building called Sitterson Hall. This was to be the new home of Brooks' group of researchers. As they would be spending many hours within its walls, the researchers were very interested in the building's design. They decided to create a simulation of the structure using the technology they had spent years developing.

With blueprints as a guide, they modeled the structure in 3-D using the computer instead of building a scale model in foam or wood. Using a powerful graphics computer, they were able to position the viewpoint anywhere in the model and quickly render the scene. By controlling the direction and speed of the viewpoint, they were able to generate a consecutive series of images of the interior or exterior.

It was like watching a film that someone had shot while walking down a hallway of the yet-to-be constructed building. But, unlike a movie, you could interactively decide which hallway or room to explore. No limits were imposed on where you might wander.

Taking this a step further, they hooked up a treadmill and movable handlebars to the computer. This allowed you to physically walk down hallways while steering yourself by turning the handlebars. The image of the hallway was projected on a screen in front of you, although in later demonstrations they used a simple head-mounted device based on LCD screens.

The experience was realistic enough that they determined that a certain partition in the lobby caused a cramped feeling. Once the architects experienced the simulation, they agreed and the partition was moved.

This computer simulation provided valuable knowledge that was then used to improve the environment. Architects could now directly experience their design and improve upon it based on what they learned from their virtual explorations. Clients exposed to the simulation could provide valuable feedback long before the first concrete was poured. Architecture, perhaps more than any other field, is poised to reap the benefits of virtual reality.

UNC's research through the mid-1980s explored the boundaries of force-feedback simulations. They proved the potential for virtual environments to provide useful tools for both chemists and architects. Much of this work took advantage of the growing sophistication and power of computer systems. In fact, without the order-of-magnitude increase in computing power that was occurring every four to five years, UNC researchers couldn't have achieved what they did.

By the mid-1980s, all the important components of today's virtual reality systems existed in one form or another, awaiting an inventive mind to bring all the pieces together and the exploration of virtual worlds to begin in earnest.

Putting it all together at NASA

In 1981, Michael McGreevy, who was studying for a Ph.D. in cognitive engineering, and Dr. Stephen Ellis, a cognitive scientist, began a program of research in spatial information transfer at NASA Ames, emphasizing the interpretation of 3-D displays. Aware of the pioneering work by Sutherland and Furness in using head-mounted displays, McGreevy put forth a proposal in 1984 to craft a similar system for NASA called a *virtual workstation*.

Based on the ideas and applications mentioned in the report, McGreevy obtained a small amount of seed money ($10,000) from division management to build a prototype display system. He had followed with interest the work done at Wright-Patterson Air Force Base by Thomas Furness III on the state-of-the-art VCASS for pilots.

VCASS had the necessary qualities of high resolution and the ability to quickly render complex images that McGreevy needed to pursue his research in the simulation of virtual environments. But VCASS had one problem: it would cost a million dollars just for the helmet. This was a limitation that overshadowed the system's qualities. McGreevy would simply have to build his own.

The most expensive part of the VCASS helmet was the use of custom CRTs to generate the high-resolution images seen by the pilot. If these could be replaced with a less-expensive display and combined with special lenses that allowed a much wider field of view, McGreevy would have his helmet. He sought the help of contractors Jim Humphries, Saim Eriskin, and Joe Deardon to develop his low-cost alternative to VCASS.

Fortunately, a consumer product had recently appeared on the scene that solved their most important problem—a small inexpensive display that could be worn on the head. Black-and-white hand-held TVs, based on LCD technology (Sony called theirs a Watchman), had recently become available. A quick trip to Radio Shack netted two such devices. The early LCD displays had limited resolution of 100×100 elements (contrasted to the millions of pixels in the VCASS displays), but they were a start and the price was right.

Next, the LCD displays were mounted on a frame similar to a scuba mask that was then strapped on your face. Special optics in front of the displays focused and expanded the image so it could be viewed without effort. McGreevy dubbed the odd-looking device the Virtual Visual Environment Display (VIVED, pronounced *vivid*). It was the only $2,000 head-mounted display on the planet.

To test their novel display, they needed to create independent left- and right-eye images, or *stereo pairs*. Without a computer to do this, they turned to a different source. Two video cameras, mounted side by side, were wheeled up and down the hallway to create stereo videotapes. Their first production was a walking tour from NASA's human factors lab, through the offices of the division, and on to the hangar where the XV-15 Tilt-Rotor aircraft was being developed. When users watched the videos through the VIVED system, they had a sense of "being there."

McGreevy and Amy Wu, his support programmer, proceeded to develop the hardware and software necessary to create the rest of the virtual workstation. They patched together a Picture System 2 graphics computer from Evans and Sutherland, two 19-inch display monitors, a DEC PDP-11/40 host computer, and the same Polhemus head-tracker used by Furness.

The Evans and Sutherland graphics system generated separate (stereo) wide-angle perspective images on each of the two display monitors. To convert the video signal into the proper format for the head-mounted display, two video cameras were mounted so that each pointed directly at one of the 19-inch displays.

Next, the Polhemus head-tracking sensor was mounted on top of the VIVED display, communicating the position and orientation of the wearer's head movements to the PDP-11/40. Users who strapped the odd contraption onto their face suddenly found themselves immersed in a computer-generated world (see Fig. 3-8).

Figure 3-8

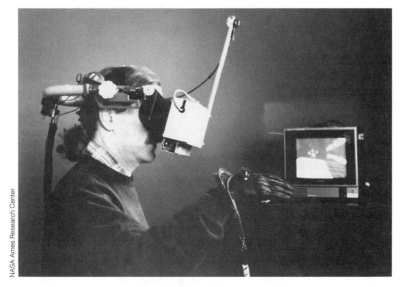

Original head-mounted display built by Michael McGreevy and James Humphries for NASA Ames VIVED project.

Data from one of McGreevy's earlier projects to study air-traffic-control issues was used for this first virtual environment. Users felt as if they were standing on a horizontal computer-generated grid that stretched out to the horizon. Turning their head, they saw the grid extending to infinity in all directions. Simple 3-D wire-frame models of tiny aircraft hung suspended in mid-air.

Users could walk around and inspect each aircraft in turn. The aircraft were fixed in space but, with a little programming, you might find yourself at the center of a swirling confusion of planes busily landing and taking off again.

As word got out of McGreevy's achievements, a steady stream of visitors from industry, academia, and the military made their way to the small cluttered lab where a revolution was taking place. By 1985, McGreevy and crew had created history's first example of a practical head-mounted stereoscopic display system. Unlike previous examples, this one would eventually capture the attention of the public and trigger a small industry.

Scott Fisher joined NASA's VIVED project the same year, 1985, that Michael McGreevy headed East for a two-year training stint in Washington D.C. Fisher's background at the Architecture Machine Group at MIT and his more recent tenure at Atari's Research Center (ARC) gave him valuable insight in directing the research at NASA.

Fisher was interested in extending the initial system by including a wired glove, voice recognition, 3-D sound synthesis, and tactile feedback devices. His objective was to develop a system that could be the foundation for many different forms of research into virtual environments. While Fisher conceptualized, McGreevy fought the necessary funding battles to keep the program alive at NASA.

Wired gloves

While at ARC, Fisher had met Thomas Zimmerman, the developer of a new kind of glove that could be used to measure the degree of bend or flex in each finger joint. Zimmerman had originally developed the glove with the intent of using it as an instrument to create music. By hooking it up to a computer that controlled a music synthesizer, wearers could play invisible instruments simply by moving their fingers. It was designed to be the ultimate "air guitar."

Because it accurately tracked finger movements, Fisher realized that it could be used as an input device to create a virtual hand that would appear in the computer-generated worlds being developed at NASA.

If you were wearing the glove and the NASA helmet, and looked at your hand, you would see a caricature of it generated by the computer. If you wiggled your fingers, the image would wiggle its fingers. For the first time, a representation of a person's physical body could become part of the simulation.

In 1983, Zimmerman teamed up with Jaron Lanier (who had also recently left Atari) to wed the glove technology to Lanier's ideas of a virtual programming interface for nonprogrammers. This collaboration evolved into a company, VPL Research, which was officially founded in 1985. They called their first product a DataGlove. That same year, Fisher ordered one of the unique gloves for his work at NASA.

By the time the glove arrived in 1986, NASA's VIVED group had grown to include Warren Robinett (an Atari video-game programmer and creator of Rocky's Boots and the popular Atari game, Adventure) and later Douglas Kerr, another programmer. Robinett used his programming skills to create dramatic demonstrations of the versatility of this new visualization tool.

He was, however, somewhat constrained by the less than state-of-the-art equipment McGreevy had assembled on his shoestring budget. Just as Ivan Sutherland was limited to rendering worlds in glowing green vectors back in 1968, Robinett was limited to stick-figure and wire-frame representations of real-world objects. Making the most of the available tools, Robinett created simulations of architectural structures, hemoglobin molecules, the space shuttle, and turbulent flow patterns.

⇨ Exploring cyberspace

By the end of 1986, the NASA team had assembled a virtual environment that allowed users to issue voice commands, hear synthesized speech and 3-D sound sources, and manipulate virtual objects directly by grasping them with their hand. No longer was the computer this separate thing you sat in front of and stared at; you were now completely inside. You communicated with it by talking and gesturing instead of typing and swearing.

Probably the most important thing NASA achieved was demonstrating that all this was possible by assembling an assortment of commercially available technologies that didn't cost a fortune to acquire or develop. Pandora's box had been sitting around for awhile—others had peeked into it, but NASA threw it wide open.

Cybernauts venturing into NASA's virtual worlds had to outfit themselves with a collection of gear that a scuba diver might recognize, particularly because the original design used a scuba-mask frame to mount the LCD displays. Instead of a glass window into the undersea world, the displays were glass windows into the virtual world.

The goal of the NASA design was to completely isolate the user from the outside world. Furness had pioneered this same approach with his Darth Vader helmet. NASA also added headphones that further contributed to the isolation. Reality no longer intruded. The virtual world commanded all the user's attention.

The cybernaut's lifeline was a series of cables that led from the headgear and DataGlove to an array of computers and control boxes. Just as early divers used compressor pumps and air hoses to provide access to their new world, virtual explorers were similarly connected to their reality-generating machines. In their exploration of these new virtual environments, cybernauts were like divers descending alone into the undersea realm.

Sticking your head into one of these early NASA HMDs, you would first notice the grainy or low-resolution image. It was like looking through a magnifying glass at a TV screen; you could see how the image was composed of individual points or picture elements. Because of this, the image quality was a great deal worse than anything usually seen on a computer monitor.

Normally, you don't notice that images on your TV or computer screen are composed of tiny dots. With the NASA display, it was glaringly obvious. As Myron Krueger has so aptly pointed out, the image quality was so poor that you would be declared legally blind in most states if you had similar vision.

After adjusting to the low resolution, the next thing you would notice was that, by moving your head, the stick-figure representation of the world would also move. A sensor attached to the top of the HMD registered the position and orientation of your head. As you moved, the computer would query the sensor (every 60th of a second) and redraw the image.

You would also notice that the image noticeably lagged behind your head movements. If you quickly moved your head it would take about one-fifth of a second or 200 milliseconds for the computer to catch up. You soon learned to make slower head movements. It's not fun being out of sync with reality.

Holding up your gloved hand in front of you, you would see a simple, blocky, wire-frame representation of a hand. You could turn it and move your fingers, and the disembodied hand would mimic the motion. Using fiberoptic sensors to measure the flex of each finger joint and an additional position and orientation sensor, the computer knew exactly where your hand was and what movements your fingers made.

Seeing the representation of your hand suddenly changes your perspective. You now have a perceptual anchor in the virtual world. You're actually inside the computer because you can see your hand in there.

Imagine sitting a foot away from your television screen while watching a commercial for detergents. Now imagine that you're wearing a special glove, like the one in Fig. 3-9, that allows your hand to pass unimpeded through the glass screen. Your hand is now part of the commercial and you can see it just as if you had recorded it with a video camera. Move your hand and the video image of your hand moves. Finally, imagine using your gloved hand to grasp the box of detergent in the commercial and change its position. NASA had achieved something similar to this. Of course, you couldn't feel your hand touching the box; that would come later.

To move about the tinker-toy world, you simply point with one gloved finger in the appropriate direction and the angle of your thumb controls the speed of your flight. The computer had been taught to

Figure 3-9

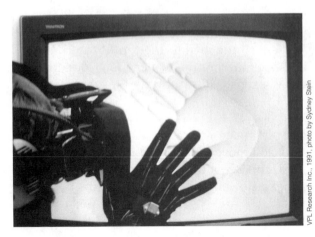

Close-up of VPL's DataGlove. Fiberoptic sensors, running across the knuckles, detect bent fingers. The participant sees the computer-generated image of his hand in the display.

VPL Research Inc., 1991, photo by Sydney Stein

recognize that gesture as the desire for movement. Other gestures were possible; for example, closing your fist caused you to grab any object that your hand intersected. As long as you kept your hand closed, the object stayed stuck to it. This allowed you to move objects around. Opening your hand released the object.

Attached to the HMD was a small mike that allowed you to give simple voice commands to the computer. Fisher had simply purchased a commercially available voice-recognition package and had it connected to the system. Voice input was important because, once you put the HMD on, you could no longer use the keyboard or find any buttons to control your environment. A voice-synthesis package had also been connected into the system. If you spoke a command, after a slight pause a robotic voice would echo it back to you.

⇨ 3-D sound

Fisher was also familiar with another new technology—3-D or *binaural* sound. Just as stereoscopic images produce a strong sense of depth when viewed correctly, binaural recordings generate the same sense of depth when using headphones. This shouldn't be confused with either *stereo* or *quadraphonic* sound, which are lesser attempts to achieve a binaural effect.

In a perfect 3-D sound system, you wouldn't be able to distinguish between reality and the simulation if you closed your eyes and just listened to the sounds. When you listen to a stereo recording, the musical sources appear somewhere in a flat plane facing you. Listening to a 3-D recording allows the musical sources to appear anywhere in a sphere surrounding your head. In other words, sounds appear above your head, behind it, or in front of your nose.

Based on Elizabeth Wenzel's work in the perceptual psychology of sound and the engineering talents of Scott Foster, president of Crystal River Engineering, Fisher contracted for the development of a system capable of creating 3-D sounds in the virtual world. Fisher wanted to attach sounds to virtual objects and have the sound follow the object if it moved.

Imagine you've just entered a virtual room. In the middle of the room you can see a small radio that appears to be playing music. You go over and pick up the virtual radio with your gloved hand. Moving the radio around, you notice that the sound follows the location of the wire-frame radio, just as you would expect from a real radio. If this is done correctly, you should be able to close your eyes and pinpoint where the sound is coming from.

Wenzel and Foster were able to create such an effect. When the hardware was completed, it was capable of manipulating up to four sound sources at once. They called it a Convolvotron. You could now have four different radios, each playing a different tune simultaneously. More importantly, instead of hearing all four tunes hopelessly fused together, you could distinguish each sound source if you focused your attention on each one. This is the same ability that allows us to distinguish different voices in a crowded room where everyone appears to be talking at once.

NASA's efforts resulted in the first computer-synthesized reality that combined computer-generated stereoscopic images, 3-D sound, voice recognition, voice synthesis, and a device for manipulating virtual objects, as seen by the scientist in Fig. 3-10 who holds an object only he can see. They had mounted a major expedition into the virtual world on a shoestring budget.

Figure 3-10

A NASA scientist holds a virtual object in his hands that only he can see. Special gloves allow him to reach into the virtual world and grab or manipulate objects.

NASA Ames Research Center

Scientific American published James Foley's article entitled "Interfaces for Advanced Computing" in October 1987, and VPL's DataGlove made the front cover. The public had finally became aware of NASA's work. The realization that NASA's achievements were based on commercially available equipment and that devices like the HMD could be built for around $2,000 triggered new research programs throughout the world.

The same year, McGreevy returned from his two-year stint on the East Coast and resumed control of the project. By 1988, the VIVED project had become the VIEW project (Virtual Interface Environment Workstation). Robinett had left the project to set sail for foreign shores, and Douglas Kerr had ported the original software to a new Hewlett-Packard 9000 that had sufficient computing power to draw virtual worlds with shaded surfaces instead of wire-frame outlines (see Fig. 3-11).

You no longer viewed stick-figure representations, and walls finally had surfaces instead of just outlines. Additional improvements were also made to the display resolution of the HMD and to other aspects of the simulation.

By the time Scott Fisher left NASA in 1990 to form Telepresence Research in Palo Alto, California with Brenda Laurel, the research

Figure 3-11

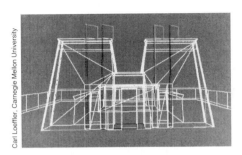

Carl Loeffler, Carnegie Mellon University

The virtual world on the left is rendered as a wire-frame model. The one of the right is rendered using flat-shaded surfaces.

had spread into other departments at NASA. There were ongoing projects to research telepresence and telerobotics, a virtual wind-tunnel project, and a virtual planetary exploration group. The initial seed planted by McGreevy, Fisher, and the pioneers before them had taken root and was beginning to spread. The commercialization of virtual reality would not be far behind.

Cyberspace for sale

⇨ VPL Research

VPL Research, founded in 1985 in Redwood City, California, was the first company to focus on the manufacture and development of products for virtual environments. Any discussion of VPL Research always starts with a profile of its founder and chief scientist, Jaron Lanier. His distinctive physical presence—John Barlow's *Mondo 2000* article succinctly describes him as "amiable, round, and dread-locked . . . a Rastafarian hobbit"—and provocative visions of virtual reality created a magnet for the media. Lanier quickly became the *de facto* spokesperson for virtual reality (to the chagrin of several earlier pioneers).

At the height of the video-game craze in 1983, Lanier created a popular game called Moondust for Atari. The success of the game and the royalties it generated gave Lanier the freedom to pursue the Silicon Valley ethos of entrepreneur.

Lanier wasn't satisfied with using just words to program and control computers. He imagined a computer that could be programmed visually through the use of images. Pursuit of this goal led to him teaming up with Thomas Zimmerman in 1984. Zimmerman's wired glove interested Lanier as a new method of communicating with the computer.

A year later, VPL Research was officially founded and Scott Fisher from NASA came knocking. At the same time, Jean-Jacques Grimaud joined VPL as president and Lanier became Chief Executive Officer. Grimaud's management background and conservative business

approach was an important counterpoint to Lanier's eclectic style. Conservative companies had difficulty accepting Lanier's unorthodox appearance and radical image—a big problem if you're trying to sell a $250,000 system.

A team comprised of Zimmerman, Lanier, and Young Harvill reengineered the existing glove to improve its accuracy and usefulness. Fiberoptics for sensing finger flex and a Polhemus sensor for measuring position and orientation of the hand were added, and improvements were made to the supporting software and control electronics.

After delivering the first glove to NASA in 1986, VPL continued work on creating software tools for producing virtual worlds much like the ones developed at NASA. Up to this point, VPL was only a supplier of the wired glove.

Because NASA's work was in the public domain, VPL was well positioned to adopt many of the ideas from NASA, improve their design, and begin marketing them. For example, the facemask with LCD screens that McGreevy prototyped was used as the basis for VPL's EyePhones, the first commercially available head-mounted display that cost less than $10,000.

VR vendor

VPL entered the business of selling complete solutions for virtual reality in 1988. In fact, Lanier is credited with coining the popular term for these synthetic experiences (*virtual reality*). To sell a system for immersive experiences, you need display devices to reproduce sight and sound, graphics hardware, interaction devices, and software to make everything run.

For display devices, VPL developed one based on NASA's design, and then integrated Scott Foster's Convolvotron 3-D sound processor for an aural display. VPL's DataGlove served as a general-purpose interaction device. By combining all this with a Macintosh computer and two Silicon Graphics workstations, VPL created RB2, or Reality Built for Two—the first commercial VR system. This new form of

reality wasn't cheap; it cost $225,000 for a single user or $430,000 for two. In a 1989 product handout, VPL poetically defined the quarter-million-dollar experience:

> "VR is shared and objectively present like the physical world, composable like a work of art and as unlimited and harmless as a dream. When VR becomes widely available, it will not be seen as a medium used within physical reality, but rather as an additional reality. VR opens up a new continent of ideas and possibilities."
> **VPL product brochure**

VPL began a booming business in selling DataGloves and EyePhones to researchers cobbling together their own systems. Within several years, hundreds of both devices were spread all over the world. By 1990, VPL claimed 500 customers worldwide. Customers for VPL's RB2 system included premier labs in Japan, Europe, and the U.S. that were tackling problems in human-factor simulation and visualization.

Interesting software tools have also evolved for creating virtual environments. Young Harvill came up with Swivel 3-D as a tool for creating or modeling 3-D worlds and objects, which has since become one of the more popular 3-D modeling packages for the Macintosh.

In addition to Swivel 3-D, Chuck Blanchard designed Body Electric to control the dynamics of a virtual environment. Information from Swivel and Body Electric is passed to a rendering program called Isaac, which draws the final images. Swivel and Body Electric run on a Macintosh, while Isaac runs on Silicon Graphics workstations.

To understand how it all works, follow the process of creating a simple world with a spinning banana. First, sitting in front of a Macintosh, you use a mouse and Swivel 3-D to create a 3-D model of a yellow banana. With Body Electric, you describe how fast the banana should spin, the direction it spins, and what happens if a DataGlove touches it. Finally, the information is passed to the Silicon Graphics workstation and Isaac renders the image.

Body Electric, running on the Macintosh, controls the simulation and the Silicon Graphics machine. If EyePhones and a DataGlove are connected, the banana's stereoscopic image would appear to float in front of your face as it slowly spun about. With the glove on, you could reach out and grab the banana. With a lot more work, you could peel it.

⇨ Shared worlds

One of the more important concepts demonstrated by VPL was the ability of two people to enter into the same virtual environment and interact. One of the early demonstrations of this involved two people represented as lobsters in the virtual world.

Climbing into a full-body version of the DataGlove called a DataSuit brought their entire body into the simulation instead of just their hands. They could choose how their bodies were represented from a collection of stored images—lobsters were one of the choices on the menu.

The two systems were networked together, each running the same simulation. Any change in the state of one simulation would be communicated to the other system. If one participant moved his clawed hand, the other person would see the movement.

VPL proved that virtual reality didn't have to be an individual experience, that it could be shared. This represents one of the most provocative concepts that has evolved in this new field. Shared VR opens new worlds of research and entertainment possibilities. As a medium of communication, it might represent what the telephone was to the telegraph.

With the telephone, communication improved because the nuances of spoken language were transmitted, contrasted to the impersonality of Morse code. With virtual environments, you can not only talk but also gesture. Because of this improvement in communication, shared virtual reality might make the world a smaller place and at the same time provide an unlimited world to explore—a curious contradiction.

⇨ VPL the rise and fall

After reaching a peak employment of 35 people and moving into expansive new headquarters in early 1992, the tight knot holding VPL together began to unravel. With over one million dollars in loans from Thompson CSF, a French electronics company, VPL had launched a costly product design and development effort. While this resulted in eye-catching prototypes of a new DataGlove, EyePhone, workstations, and other equipment, it came at a price that VPL learned it could ill afford. As the cash began to run out, VPL scrambled to convince customers to pay for products it was unable to deliver. As word spread of VPL's difficulties and customer problems, pressure steadily mounted for change.

In mid-1992, Lanier announced he was removing himself from day-to-day operations with VPL to pursue his interests in the artistic and technological challenges of VR. Walt Fisher, formerly an executive at Hewlett-Packard, was brought in as CEO to help direct an attempt to rescue the company. Unfortunately, Fisher had only a few months prior to a total implosion at VPL.

By the end of November 1992, VPL was officially out of business and all employees, including Lanier, were laid off. As the dust settled, news leaked out that they had desperately signed over all their intellectual property to Thompson CSF as collateral for a series of loans. Several of these patents were considered potentially valuable since they covered using a computer and wired glove to control computer-generated images. Unlike many other creditors, Thompson CSF emerged from the wreckage with something of tangible value.

VPL's passing from the scene had little impact on the emerging VR industry. Ex-customers of VPL sought out other sources of software and hardware, while new start-ups emerged on the scene almost weekly. Those closely associated with the VR industry were not surprised to learn of VPL's failure because reports of quality, reliability, and customer problems had been circulating for over a year. VPL's inability to deal with these problems doomed them to the same fate as any other company who disregards such ominous signals.

By early 1994, Lanier had moved to Sausalito and pretty much disappeared from the VR scene. Others at VPL were pursuing careers with companies working in related fields. VPL's rise and fall became part of the long history of the development of virtual environments.

Before VPL emerged on the scene, VR was the province of obscure research projects at universities and labs in the U.S. Sutherland's wire-frame cubes, the military's training simulators, and Furness's Super Cockpit all eventually led to NASA Ames' assembly of commercially available tools to explore virtual environments.

NASA had proven it could be done and VPL set out to prove a market existed. In this, they initially succeeded where Heilig had failed; manufacturing "realities" became a business. Even though VPL had little to do with inventing VR, their contribution is important because it finally made the technology accessible to the public and industry in general.

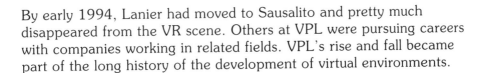 Autodesk

John Walker, the reclusive, brilliant programmer and former Chief Executive Officer of Autodesk, read with growing interest of VPL's and NASA's efforts in 1987–1988. An intensely private man and one of the founders of Autodesk in 1982, Walker immediately understood the potential of this new technology to revolutionize computer-aided design (CAD).

Six years after its founding, Autodesk had grown into a large company with over $100 million per year in revenues. Started with a single vision of developing an inexpensive CAD program for the PC, Autodesk had become one of the most successful software companies around. Customers included architects and other designers who previously used expensive analysis and drawing tools running only on mainframes and minicomputers. Autodesk's product, AutoCAD, became a run-away success with over 500,000 users in the U.S. at the end of 1991.

As the demands of running Autodesk grew too onerous, Walker withdrew from day-to-day management to focus on programming and working on his famous internal manifestos. Walker used these eloquent documents to convey his vision to others. In September 1988, "Through the Looking Glass: Beyond User Interfaces" began making the rounds within Autodesk. It documented the progress of computer interfaces from punchcards to virtual worlds, and challenged Autodesk to develop its own cyberspace tools.

Just as Autodesk had taken mainframe CAD tools and brought them to PCs, Walker realized that VPL's quarter-million-dollar system could be inexpensively re-created on the PC. He defined his vision:

> "Now we're at the threshold of the next revolution in user-computer interaction: a technology that will take the user through the screen into the world 'inside' the computer—a world in which the user can interact with three-dimensional objects whose fidelity will grow as computing power increases and display technology progresses. This virtual world can be whatever the designer makes it. As designers and users explore entirely new experiences and modes of interaction, they will be jointly defining the next generation of user interaction with computers."
> **John Walker, *Through the Looking Glass*, 1988**

Walker documented how each new interface paradigm evolved and the limitations or barriers it created for the user. Table 4-1 lists these "generations."

Table 4-1   **User interface generations**

Generation	Description	Barrier
First	Plugboards, dedicated set-up	Front panel
Second	Punched card batch, RJE	Countertop
Third	Teletype timesharing	Terminal
Fourth	Menu systems	Menu hierarchy
Fifth	Graphical controls, windows	Screen
Sixth	Cyberspace	?

Source: John Walker, Through the Looking Glass, internal Autodesk memo

Each succeeding generation opened up new applications and markets and made computers easier to use. As they became easier, more people used them to solve more kinds of problems. Markets rapidly expanded to support new demands for hardware and software. We're in the midst of moving to the sixth generation and, if previous generations are any guide, we have much to look forward to.

⇨ Desktop cyberspace

Based on the strength of Walker's vision, the "Autodesk cyberspace initiative" began in the latter part of 1988. Walker chose William Gibson's cyberspace novel *Neuromancer* as the inspiration for naming the project. Initial project members included William Bricken, Eric Gullichsen, Eric Lyons, and Randal Walser. They were later joined by Pat Gelband, Meredith Bricken, Gary Wells, and Christopher Allis.

Leading the project, William Bricken had an eclectic background in statistics, psychology, artificial intelligence programming, and education. Meredith's qualifications were also in education and curriculum design for schools. Eric Gullichsen, a Canadian transplant who epitomizes the tinkerer-hacker, along with Pat Gelband and Randy Walser, became the programmers responsible for crafting the vision. The rest of the crew filled supporting roles.

Posting a sign labeled *Cyberia* on their work area, the team began assembling a Gibsonian "deck." Duplicating NASA's assembly of a head-mounted display from scrounged parts and purchasing VPL's DataGlove gave them the tools of the VR trade—gloves and goggles. Two special Matrox graphics boards installed in a Compaq/386 PC provided the rendering horsepower to draw the worlds.

For under $25,000 they replicated VPL's quarter-million-dollar system. Now for virtual reality to fulfill its many promises, a larger pool of researchers, developers, and artists needed access. Autodesk's project demonstrated that day was rapidly approaching.

⇨ Inventing reality

It arrived in March, 1989 with the demonstration of the first PC-based virtual-reality system. The Autodesk cyberspace team was catapulted into the spotlight as word spread of its achievement. People took notice when a company like Autodesk demonstrated its interest in this new and unproven technology.

Over the course of the next several months, additional demos were created that explored possible sports-related applications. One of them, a virtual bicycle ride, used a stationary exercise bike as an input device. As you pedaled the bike wearing an HMD, virtual landscapes rolled past you. If you pedaled fast enough, it appeared that you left the ground and flew off into the sky. A boring exercise turned into an exciting trip into a new world.

Pat Gelband used her background in physics to develop the first virtual-reality racquetball game, shown in Fig. 4-1. She knew she was following historical precedent; the first video arcade game, Pong, also involved bouncing a ball off paddles and walls. Figure 4-1 shows a player holding a modified racquet and wearing an HMD, using the racquet to send a computer-generated ball bouncing off the walls and back to her.

All that was missing was the shock of contact between the synthesized ball and the wooden racquet. You simply took swipes at the air, only your eyes discerning the impact of ball and racquet. With further refinements, sound and tactile feedback might approximate the actual feel of hitting the ball.

Bending the rules of reality slightly, Gelband programmed the ball to automatically return to the location of the racquet. This lessened the likelihood of someone being hurt in a desperate maneuver to reach the ball. It also lessened the possibility of whacking an innocent onlooker.

Despite the fun and games of cyberspace, the research program at Autodesk began falling apart in August of 1989 as William and Meredith Bricken left the company in a dispute over the project's

Figure 4-1

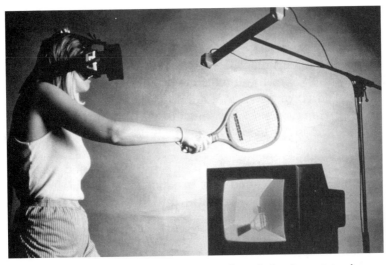

While at Autodesk, Pat Gelband developed the first virtual racquetball game, a demonstration of the Autodesk cyberspace system.

future direction. Frustrated by the glacial pace of turning their research into real products, Gullichsen and Gelband decided to do it themselves. By Thanksgiving, they had departed to form Sense8.

Randy Walser became project leader and continued demonstrations, but real development ground to a halt. Even John Walker withdrew from Autodesk to pursue his interests from a redoubt in Switzerland.

It wasn't until mid-1990 that Autodesk woke from its slumber and began actively restaffing the project. Rudy Rucker, science-fiction writer and programmer, joined the group along with others. It seemed that Autodesk was again serious about commercializing cyberspace. By the end of the year, Randy Walser provided the first peek at TRIX, an interactive language for cyberspace that John Walker was developing.

Following this were rumors of a Cyberspace Development Toolkit (CDK) in early 1991. CDK would allow AutoCAD owners to bring wire-frame images to life as solid, 3-D objects they could manipulate and view from different angles. By early 1992, none of these projects had quite made it out the door, though CDK was promised by the end of 1992.

Carol Bartz, a former executive of Sun Microsystems, became CEO of Autodesk in April of 1993. This led to a new focus on results and bottom-line contributions, which spelled the end of innovative research in the Cyberia lab. CDK was transferred to Autodesk's multimedia group with the intent of finally releasing it as a product. It wasn't until March of 1993 that CDK finally appeared on the scene. By this time, Randy Walser and most of the development team had either left Autodesk or were assigned to other jobs inside Autodesk.

Autodesk's Cyberspace Development Kit was designed as a programmer's toolkit instead of a product for those less technically inclined. It was well integrated with Autodesk's main product, AutoCAD, and contained powerful features that simulated physical properties such as mass, momentum, and gravity. You could even use its solid-modeling features to create a virtual drill or slice objects into sections.

Unfortunately, in the rush to get the product released, the initial release had inaccurate documentation and annoying bugs. These problems were further compounded by a technical support system consisting mainly of Autodesk dealers who hadn't a clue how to create a software program—especially something as complicated as CDK. While these "teething" problems diminished CDK's initial value, they will likely be resolved given enough time and Autodesk's commitment to the product.

Autodesk's impact on the virtual reality field shouldn't be underestimated. Whether they revolutionize virtual reality as they did CAD won't be decided for a few more years. More importantly, Autodesk risked money and effort in proving that practical VR systems could be developed with desktop systems. In addition, the seed of Walker's vision was firmly planted in many of those who participated in the original cyberspace group. As they scattered across the country, Walker's seed took root in various fertile grounds.

 Sense8

In the four months after leaving Autodesk's Cyberspace Initiative, Gullichsen and Gelband spent 14-hour days, seven days a week,

creating the core of a new object-oriented 3-D simulation language. Starting from scratch, but retaining lessons learned at Autodesk, a tool for rapid prototyping of complex 3-D simulations evolved. Driving them was a vision of a development tool that programmers could easily use to create complex virtual environments.

Working out of an office in Sausalito, California, they built their first VR system out of two Amigas and two Sony Watchmans. Following in the grand tradition of John Hewlett and David Packard, who started their multi-billion-dollar business from a simple garage in Palo Alto, Gullichsen and Gelband set out to build revolutionary simulation tools.

Gullichsen, an inveterate tinkerer and high-tech wizard, made the Amiga do things it simply wasn't designed to do. Working long nights in an espresso-induced frenzy, Gullichsen became a highly kinetic coding machine. Accompanied by Gelband on her well-worn keyboard, they gave form to the structure of the new product.

Gelband not only developed the advanced rendering technology at the core of the product, her rigorous background in math and physics provided new insights into efficient techniques for representing 3-D objects. In her spare time, she managed the practical details of running the small start-up.

With their synergistic talents, they crafted a powerful and flexible tool. In January of 1990, Sense8 was founded. Gelband derived the name from the adjective *sensate*, or perceiving through the senses— appropriate for their new line of work.

Showing the Amiga prototype to contacts at Sun Microsystems led to a contract and loan of workstations to port their software to the Sun system. Recognizing that Gullichsen and Gelband were on to something, Sun hoped to demonstrate technology leadership in this emerging field, and counter Silicon Graphics' lock on the 3-D graphics market.

The founders survived by obtaining various contracts from the military. One of these involved the development of a low-cost HMD helicopter training simulator. Another contract provided the incentive for developing an IBM PC version of their original system using Texas

Instruments' TIGA-based graphics boards. Within a single year, they had moved their core technology to three dissimilar platforms.

⇨ Texturing reality

In the spring of 1990, Gullichsen and Gelband brought one of the few VR systems in the world to Intel for a demonstration. After setting up the system, everyone in attendance had a chance to explore Sense8's strange new worlds. By carefully lowering a hand-tooled HMD over your face, you suddenly found yourself in a fuzzy checkerboard world. Dual Amiga computers, encased in surplus ammo canisters, generated cartoonlike images of buildings and a large sphere hanging in space.

As you moved your head to look around, more of this strange world was revealed. Grabbing a baseball-sized device mounted on a small platform and pushing it in the appropriate direction sent you flying through the virtual world. After learning to drive with the odd, rubber-coated ball, you could fly into a hangarlike structure that abruptly transported you to yet another intriguing world.

Intel was interested in finding a partner to collaborate on the development of a VR system based on Intel's DVI (Digital Video Interactive) technology. After presentations by other VR companies and research efforts, Sense8 was selected because of their ability to deliver a prototype within the project's six-month deadline and their previously demonstrated ability to support various hardware platforms.

Intel's DVI chip set was the offshoot of research by Sarnoff Labs in the late 1980s. Not only could the chips decompress moving images, allowing 72 minutes of full-screen, full-motion video from a 3½-inch compact disc, but the chips could also be programmed to draw graphics and perform texture mapping.

Texture mapping is particularly important. A photograph is first scanned into the computer and loaded into the DVI graphics board. Next, the digital image is "mapped" or reshaped to a perspectively correct position on the screen. Utilizing this in a real-time 3-D rendering turns the normally cartoonish world into a realistic model (see Fig. 4-2).

Figure 4-2

The picture on the left shows a computer-generated view of only flat-shaded polygons. The picture on the right shows the same view with texture-mapped polygons.

For example, a furniture maker might use this to show a customer a textured 3-D model of a couch. After selecting a scanned swatch of fabric, the swatch could be texture-mapped onto the entire surface of the couch. With DVI, you didn't have to wait minutes to view the result; the new image was drawn instantly. Other controls allowed the customer to walk around or spin the couch to view it from any angle.

Because 20–30 scanned images could be stored in the DVI board, you could create a 3-D world rich in detail. Wooden floors, stone fireplaces, pictures on the walls, and rugs on the floor were all possible. Architects could have an interactive rendering tool that represented the world the way it really is, with complex images and textures wherever you look.

Interested in the potential of DVI products to add a completely new level of realism to virtual worlds, Intel approved funding to pursue research into a PC-based VR system. Working with DVI microcode experts back in Princeton on rendering optimizations resulted in significant performance gains. Many more months were spent integrating the new texturing capabilities with Sense8's code.

Finally, at the San Francisco Meckler VR conference in late 1990, Sense8 and Intel unveiled the result of their collaboration. Participants were treated to a virtual trip through a garden with realistic trees and a lawn. Passing through a portal, you suddenly dropped into an art museum with scanned images of art hanging on the walls. Another portal gave you a 360-degree, panoramic view of a Mayan temple. Looking in any direction revealed more of the temple surroundings or the sky above.

For two days, attendees waited hours in line for an opportunity to try it. The demonstration represented a breakthrough in PC realism and rendering performance for virtual worlds. Sense8 was clearly on to something.

WorldToolKit

Based on this initial success, Sense8 developed plans for marketing a product based on the DVI chip set's capabilities. At this point, Gullichsen and Gelband had created an impressive set of core technologies that could be accessed through an elegant and powerful set of programming function calls.

In June 1991, WorldToolKit became commercially available. Intended for programmers, it contains a C library of over 400 functions and a powerful simulation manager that allows rapid prototyping of custom applications. 3-D models created with Autodesk software such as AutoCAD or 3D Studio can be read in as discrete objects and then manipulated.

The commercial availability of WorldToolKit in 1991 represented a dramatic reduction in the cost of VR. Now it was possible to assemble a complete system for less than $25,000, or a third of the cost of other existing platforms.

This also brought the technology within the reach of many research budgets, as evidenced by the initial customers. They ranged from Rockwell, NASA Ames, and Sandia Labs to the Computer Museum in Boston and the Banff Center for the Arts. (Many of these applications are covered elsewhere in this book.) Within a few months, distributors were signed up in England, Italy, Germany, and Japan. WorldToolKit had gone worldwide.

The diversity of Sense8's customer base portends the widespread use of VR and its significance as an enabling technology. To encourage this, Sense8 adapted WorldToolKit to run on Silicon Graphics, Sun, and DEC/Kubota workstations in addition to the PC.

In March of 1994, Sense8 (with Intel's help) released WorldToolKit for Windows, bringing the first true VR product to the Windows operating system. This inexpensive product further opened the door to engineers and scientists interested in exploring the fabric and nature of virtual environments. Any computer capable of running Windows could now be enlisted in the battle of extracting knowledge from an overwhelming sea of information.

Sense8 is but one of several successful companies that have emerged from the chaos of the nascent VR industry's formation. As in any industry, a focused, customer-driven approach is necessary just to stay in business.

 Virtual Reality, Inc.

There are literally dozens of small start-ups all over the world busily attempting to carve a future out of virtual reality. They're so numerous, in fact, that it's impossible to cover all their efforts and origins. They include suppliers of head-mounted displays, gloves, head-trackers, and many other devices. Consider them the outfitters of VR.

Many of these small start-ups, like Virtual Research, Fake Space Labs, and VREAM have emerged from their garages and are rapidly growing by producing the quality products demanded by customers. Others, like VPL, Ono Sendai, VRontier, and Spectrum Dynamics, struggled unsuccessfully for survival and have since faded from the scene. The rules of survival are no less harsh in the VR business than in any other.

In addition, research projects at universities in Japan, the U.S., and Europe are attempting to provide conceptual frameworks and practical advice in the construction and habitation of virtual worlds. Many of these companies, products, and universities are listed in the resource guide in appendix A of this book.

We singled out the individuals and efforts documented in this chapter for either their foresight, contributions, or advancement of this new technology. Virtual reality didn't spring forth fully formed. It emerged slowly, in fits and starts, over the last 40 years. Only recently has it been rapidly thrust into the public eye.

What you've seen so far is just a glimpse of what will be. VR represents a fundamentally revolutionary way of interacting with computers. It also presents us with a powerful new medium of expression that's still evolving and changing. What the technology has promised, however, is rapidly outpacing its capabilities. Understanding how VR works and the technologies driving it are the subject of the next chapter. One of our hopes is that this will help separate fact from fiction.

Reality simulators

PICTURE a virtual environment where gradually rolling hills, covered with grass, lead to a rustic house perched high on a ridge. Below the ridge, a river winds its way through a broad open valley. By controlling your point of view, you can fly across the hills and up to the house's entrance. As you pick up speed, the rush of wind becomes louder.

As you near it, the front door automatically swings open—beckoning you inside. You move through the hallway and into the living room, where low-slung couches and comfortable chairs surround a stone fireplace. A lamp glows on a table next to the wall. Hearing the sound of a radio, you turn your head to locate it perched on a tabletop. As you turn, you notice that flames appear to dance and cavort among the logs in the fireplace. Moving over to a large bay window, you see trees dotting the hillsides and the river far below.

Facing back into the living room, you decide to move the lamp away from the wall. While looking directly at the lamp, you press a trigger button on a joystick, causing a ray to leap out and touch the lamp. A box appears around the lamp signifying its selection, and as you begin to move the joystick the lamp moves also. Moving the lamp around the room, you notice how it causes the shading of furniture and wall surfaces to brighten and darken. You set it down by a chair. Pleased with the result, you fly back out the front door and leave the simulation.

As we near the end of the 20th century, virtual realities like the one described provide examples of the kinds of tools we'll be working with in the next century. This part of the book describes how to get a jump on these 21st-century tools—today.

The previous description of a virtual environment is just one example of the kinds of realities manufacturable by today's VR systems. At the heart of these systems are *reality simulators*, which continuously churn out sensory information, like the images of a flickering fireplace or the sound of wind rushing by, in order to keep the virtual illusion alive. VR exists in the interplay or dance of the user and computer as they respond to each other.

It begins when participants react to what they're seeing and hearing by turning their heads, gesturing with their hands, or moving their joysticks. These input signals are processed by the computer to create yet another set of sights and sounds.

Referring to the description at the beginning of this chapter, the participant reacts to hearing sounds from a radio by turning to look at the radio. As he turns his head, input sensors capture this action and instruct the computer to generate new image and sound signals. This continuous feedback cycle powers the illusion of reality (see Fig. 5-1).

Figure 5-1

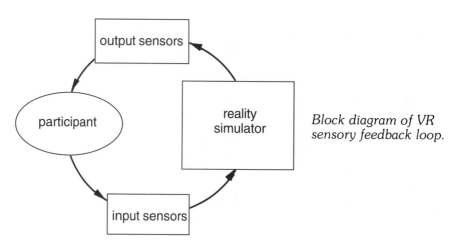

Block diagram of VR sensory feedback loop.

Feedback is crucial to VR. It represents the interactivity of the medium. If reality simulators are the heart of virtual reality, then interactivity is its soul. VR represents the first fully interactive medium.

Movies, for example, are completely noninteractive—you passively watch what's presented. Television, on the other hand, began

evolving from noninteractive to interactive when remote controls became available. After all, continuously switching channels, or "channel surfing," is a simple form of interactivity (and rumored to be dominated by the male of the species).

In addition to television, other forms of media are becoming interactive. Hypertext, computer games, and multimedia are all part of this trend—fueled by access to inexpensive computing power and the digitization of media. Virtual reality is a logical result of mixing media with interactivity. You finally enter into the media and become part of it.

At its simplest, VR is a tool for enabling the user's immersion into a sensory-rich, interactive experience. Using input and output sensors, a virtual world is fabricated under the control of both the reality simulator and the participant.

But how is interactivity and sensory information created, sustained, and managed? What's the "magic" behind the technology? This chapter explores the hardware and software tools required for the creation of virtual environments, and issues and limitations surrounding their use. Step by step, we'll break down a VR system into its basic components and explain each one, revealing what's behind the new looking glass.

⇨ Components of a VR system

The term *virtual reality* is widely used and might mean different things to different people. If anything, its meaning will continue to evolve with the technology. Our preferred definition is an immersive experience in which participants wear visually-coupled displays, view stereoscopic or biocular images, listen to 3-D sounds, and are free to explore and interact within a 3-D world. Based on this definition, all VR systems can be broken into the following four separate parts, as shown in the illustration in Fig. 5-2:

Effectors Effectors are any type of interface device that provides access to a virtual environment. This includes output devices that

Figure 5-2

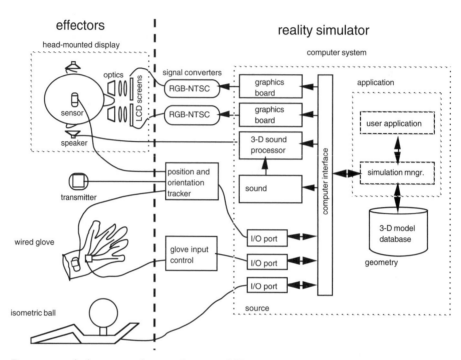

Diagram of elements that make up a VR system.

stimulate the senses to create a sense of presence in the virtual world, like head-mounted displays (HMDs) or stereo headphones, and input devices that register where you're looking or the direction you're pointing, like head-trackers and wired gloves.

Reality simulator The "heart" of a VR system, the reality simulator comprises the computer system and external hardware, such as graphics and sound synthesizing equipment, that supply effectors with the necessary sensory information.

Application An application is software that describes the context of the simulation, its dynamics, structure, and the laws of interaction between objects and the user. It determines if the virtual world is for designing kitchens or flying B2 bombers.

Geometry Geometry is the information that describes the physical attributes of objects (shape, color, placement, etc.). In the example at the beginning of this chapter, geometry would describe the shape of the rolling hills, along with the placement, construction, and color of the house. This information is processed by the application to build the virtual world.

⇨ Effectors

Stepping through the barrier of the computer screen, to travel or interact in a virtual world, is the primary goal of a VR system. To do this, sufficient sensory input must be provided for the participants to become immersed in the experience—temporarily suspending their disbelief and becoming engaged with the application. In other words, they accept the synthetic world as a place in which they're currently present.

Think of the wrap-around, 360-degree movie at Disneyland. You know you're standing in the middle of a large theater, but as the camera flies through the clouds or across the landscape, you briefly experience a sense of presence. You become the camera as it swoops through mountain passes.

Virtual reality generates a similar sense of presence and requires less sensory input to achieve it than you might think. Our sensory processors (eyes, ears, etc.) have been reliably constructing realities over millions of years of evolution. Just provide a minimum of sensory cues and the brain fills in the gaps.

Effectors deliver these cues to our senses. They're specialized devices, like the HMD or wired glove that engage the user in the simulation—just as movie projectors and screen images are effectors in the cinema.

Currently, most efforts are focused on immersing the visual and aural senses, while research continues with tactile and force feedback. Taste and odors remain largely unexplored. Though we've made our first faltering steps, we're still a long way from total sensory immersion. The promises (or threats) of Hollywood, as depicted in movies like *Total Recall* or *Wild Palms*, remain to be realized.

 # Visual cues

Generating the required visual cues is currently the greatest challenge to a VR system. Image rendering is a key component of the overall system expense and forces compromises between cost, performance, complexity, and quality.

However, drawing or rendering is only part of the problem. For people to believe they're really flying over rolling hills of grass or are inside a house looking around, the movement of their head must be tracked so that the proper image is always in front of them.

The following are a few of the factors controlling visual immersion:

Field of view How much does an image fill your field of view? Remember the discussion of Cinerama earlier in the book? Using three movie screens instead of one gave audiences a much wider field of view and stronger sense of presence. Special optics can create this same effect in a head-mounted display. While VR displays vary from 20 to 140 degrees, humans have a 180-degree horizontal field of view (see Fig. 5-3).

Figure 5-3

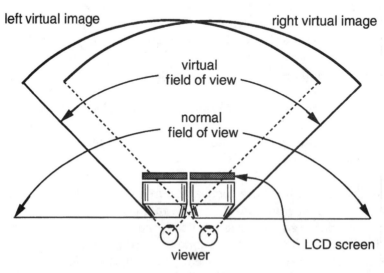

Special optics are used to create an enhanced field of view of the LCD display screens. It's the same effect as looking at a large projection TV from one to two feet away. LEEP Systems Inc.

Resolution When you wear an HMD, how grainy does the image look? A by-product of using wide field-of-view optics with current low-resolution LCD displays is that the image quality is drastically affected. LCD displays typically have between 86,000 and 110,000 colored elements, but it takes three elements (1 red, 1 blue, and 1 green) to make a single pixel or triad. This means that the eye receives only 30,000–40,000 pixels of color information. PCs and workstations commonly have about 1,000,000 pixels of information, or 30 times as many, as shown in Fig. 5-4.

Figure 5-4

NASA Ames Research Center

The larger image is a picture of the computer display monitor showing a robotic hand. The smaller, inset image is a picture of the same view taken through wide field-of-view optics.

Complexity What is the visual complexity of an image (textures, polygons, etc.)? The world described earlier in the chapter might contain 1,000–1,500 different 3-D shapes or polygons. For performance reasons, fewer and smaller polygons are better. Rendering or shading styles also determine overall image complexity. The more detailed the scene, the more pleasing and informationally rich it is. However, the additional complexity takes longer for the computer to process, slowing down the frame rate (speed).

Rendering speed How long does it take to render one complete image or frame? Drawing the image of the house on top of the rolling hills must occur within a blink of an eye to be useful for VR. Anything longer will result in the loss of presence. Remember from the discussion of flight simulators that drawing speed is typically measured in frames per second (fps) or hertz. To achieve a sense of presence, about 10–12 fps is a good target, while greater than 30 fps has diminishing returns.

Perceptual lag How long does it take to register changes in head orientation or other sensor input? Studies have shown that lags greater than 50 milliseconds affect performance. Lag is primarily composed of sensor lag and the time spent drawing the new image. Sensor lag can vary from three to more than 100 milliseconds, and drawing a 10-fps image adds an additional 100 milliseconds. In a worst-case scenario, this can add up to a noticeable lag of over a quarter second.

Engagement How interesting is the application? Does it capture your interest? This is one of the most difficult factors to judge, but it can have a tremendous effect on the sense of presence in the virtual world. A simple VR application that allows you to float through a building while looking around is less engaging than a "hands-on" VR application where you struggle to find an appropriate docking site for two molecules.

Different applications place different emphasis on these factors. In the example at the beginning of this chapter, sense of presence is more important than image detail. So resolution can be traded for more field of view. A medical system might do the opposite, choosing resolution over field of view. Until both are available at a reasonable cost, trade-offs will be required.

Most visual effectors or HMDs work on a simple principle of viewing a small color or monochrome display through a set of wide field-of-view optics (see Fig. 5-5). The optics not only allow you to comfortably focus on a display placed three inches from your eyes, they also exaggerate the size of the image. Because of this, the picture fills your view and creates a sense of immersion.

Figure 5-5

head-mounted display

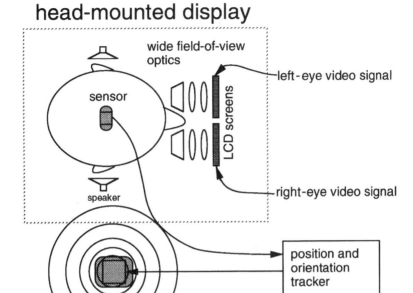

Diagram showing the components of a head-tracked HMD.

While images are displayed, the outside world is typically masked off from sight. This allows total immersion in the virtual world and is popular for entertainment, architectural visualization, and applications where the only focus is the virtual world. This is the kind of immersion used in the example at the beginning of the chapter. The goal is to have people believe they're in a different place, surrounded by blue sky and rolling hills.

Another approach is to use transparent lenses with half-silvered mirrors to overlay the virtual image over the real world. Known as heads-up display (HUD) or augmented reality, surgeons could use it to view virtual diagnostic screens while performing surgery. Vital signs could be displayed where the surgeon might easily glance at them while operating.

HMDs remain the greatest stumbling block in a VR system. The availability of a low-cost, high-resolution, lightweight design will

revolutionize the industry. Several new approaches are covered in chapter 8, *Gloves, goggles, and wands*, that stand a good chance of triggering this revolution.

Because of these new designs, VR might become more practical and affordable sooner than anyone anticipated. However, current technology is marginally effective for anything other than entertainment. Remember Myron Krueger's point that if a person had the kind of vision seen in some of the earlier HMDs, he would be declared legally blind!

Sound cues

"After silence, that which comes nearest to expressing the inexpressible is music."
Aldous Huxley, *Music at Night*, 1931

After sight, sound is the next most important sensory channel for virtual experiences. It has the advantage of being a channel of communication that can be processed parallel to visual information without being distracting. This same capability allows you to read a book without being distracted by music played at the same time.

In chapter 8, you'll learn about the *preconscious* power of the visual system that allows you to process information without conscious effort. To a lesser extent, aural processing works in much the same way.

Imagine a virtual representation of the stock market, where each stock is represented by a small colored square in an immense grid. The color of the square represents its trading volume, while its volatility is represented by the varying pitch of a flute.

As you fly over each square, you hear the stock's volatility while you watch its trading volume. Instead of trying to combine all the variables into a complicated visual image and thereby overloading the visual system, you can use other sensory cues.

Sound provides valuable feedback about the nature of the environment. If you drop a brick on a hard surface, it makes a different noise than if you drop it on a soft surface.

Sound can also be used as a substitute for tactile sensory cues. If you bump into a virtual object, you might hear a sound informing you of the contact. If you move an object, it might make a sound when it comes in contact with other surfaces. Or if you wore a wired glove and moved your hand across a virtual surface, you might hear a modulated sound based on the smoothness or roughness of the surface. After some initial learning, you might even begin to believe that you actually felt something through your fingertips.

Voice synthesis is an additional form of feedback first demonstrated at NASA Ames. It too has many uses: echoing a command, prompting for input, or warning of a dangerous condition.

Because text is nearly impossible to read in a low-resolution HMD, voice synthesis can be used to read textual information out loud in the virtual world. When combined with voice-recognition techniques, it allows simple verbal communication with the computer—an important feature if your hands are busy performing other tasks.

In yet another area, sound can contribute to visual experiences. Studies at MIT's Media Lab demonstrated that simply improving the quality of sound can influence the perception of image quality. When people were shown identical images on two side-by-side TV sets, the one with CD-quality sound was consistently rated as having a better image over the one with standard monaural sound. This same effect can be used to improve the perceived quality of virtual images—especially when current HMD resolution and image quality is so poor to begin with.

NASA Ames pioneered the use of 3-D sounds that can be positioned in the virtual world. 3-D sounds provide important distance and position cues of objects with respect to the participant. In a simulator experiment at NASA Ames, pilots could hear the 3-D sounds of approaching aircraft. Normally, the Traffic Collision Avoidance System (TCAS) alerts pilots to aircraft that have approached too close. By linking the out-the-window position of the approaching aircraft with the virtual sound of the aircraft, pilots were able to more quickly locate the possible threat and take evasive action.

Sound is yet another powerful tool of expression for a world builder. It has the ability to draw you much further into the virtual

environment. Can you remember a particularly moving musical piece that gave you chills just listening to it?

Now imagine coupling that song with compelling virtual images and you get some idea of the potential for expression in this new medium. Of course, few of today's virtual environments generate such a strong emotional reaction. Artists are just beginning to use these untapped powers of expression to create powerful new experiences.

⇨ Haptic cues

Tactile and force feedback are the other senses being actively researched today. Both are part of our *haptic* perceptions. *Tactile feedback* refers to our sense of touch, or pressure applied to the skin. Forces acting on muscles, tendons, and joints are called *force feedback*. When you pick up a baseball, tactile feedback communicates the smoothness of the leather and the roughness of the stitches, and force feedback describes the ball's weight and firmness.

Unfortunately, due to the complexities in accurately simulating and reproducing these forces, a useful device to representing them might never exist. Recently, products have emerged that generate a limited sense of force feedback. One of these is a glove with miniature air capillaries that can be pressurized under control of a computer.

First, a special glove is used to record the feel of picking up an object. It measures the amount of pressure at various bent angles of the fingers and hand, thereby creating a force map of the object. After recording the forces, the computer plays them back by controlling the pressure in the glove's capillaries. Though not as solid as the real object, the effect is quite entertaining. It is, however, of limited practical use.

Additional work in developing effective tactile sensors using minute fingertip vibrators is also being researched. These promise to duplicate varying sensations of smoothness, roughness, and simple feedback that something has been touched in the virtual world. This could help counter one of the biggest problems with using a wired glove.

When wearing a glove, you can't easily tell when you've touched an object. Everything being ghostly and insubstantial leads to major difficulties in interaction. You watch your virtual hand pass right through the virtual baseball. Sound feedback could help, but a slight sense of touch in every finger would enhance the experience significantly.

New technologies and materials might revolutionize the development of effective tools for duplicating our haptic senses. But it's more likely to be a few years before you can just "reach out and touch" with a VR system.

Allowing interaction

Because a myriad of devices exist for interacting in a virtual world, choosing the correct one can be difficult. Each one has strengths and weaknesses that need to be considered. For example, grabbing a virtual object with a wired glove might be intuitive, but flying or gesturing requires learning a strange form of sign language that isn't as easy to grasp.

Over the last ten years, the mouse has been the only new computer interface device to become widely accepted on desktops. This kind of dominance doesn't exist yet for VR and probably won't for many years. New interaction devices are being researched, developed, and reengineered continuously. Some prove useful; others don't. But lessons are being learned as various approaches are tried and tested.

Eventually, a set of tools optimized for virtual explorations will rise from this cauldron of creativity. In fact, ten years from now current devices will seem practically prehistoric in comparison. This constant flux of ideas and approaches will keep users busy sorting useful techniques from evolutionary dead-ends for some time to come.

Before reviewing various devices, however, it's important to consider types of interactive tasks performed in a virtual environment. These can be broken down into the following categories:

Navigation Navigation means moving your point of view through 3-D space. Examples are moving through a corridor and into another

room, flying over a landscape, rotating about, or moving straight up and down. Movement can be constrained or unconstrained.

Selection Selection involves picking a particular element in the 3-D world with the intent of performing an action on it. Examples are selecting a lamp in a living room in order to reorient it, picking a wall to change its color or dimensions, selecting an object with your hand in order to pick it up, or selecting a particular person to talk to.

Interaction After selecting an object, how easy is it to interact with? Some common forms of interaction are moving, deforming, or scaling objects. Once the lamp in the living room has been selected, how you move it to a different location is based on interaction.

Command Some method of controlling or issuing commands to the simulation is required. For example, after selecting an object, you must issue a command to change its color by pressing a button or turning a knob. Remember that wearing HMDs effectively blindfolds you, making the keyboard useless as an input device.

Each device's performance can be evaluated against these four basic tasks. Doing so reveals weaknesses in all current devices. Not one device is successful at all tasks in any kind of simulation. Just as you wouldn't use a hammer to open a window, you need to use the correct tool with VR.

Remember, too, that a device's weakness might simply be a function of the software controlling it. Using a mouse can be a good or bad experience depending on how the software controls the interaction. By modifying the interaction, weaknesses can be turned into strengths. Indeed, a rich vein of research is waiting to be mined in the analysis and development of better interaction techniques. It's likely that a whole generation of graduate students will be kept busy researching many of these ideas.

For now, research lags behind the commercialization of many of these devices. We hope that, in coming years, a better balance will be struck to prevent immature technologies from being dropped in the laps of unsuspecting users. Some of the current VR input devices are:

Wired gloves Wired gloves are composed of fiberoptic, resistive, or mechanical sensors that measure the bend and flex of fingers and the hand (see Fig. 5-6). They usually include a sensor for measuring overall hand orientation and position, known as a six-degree-of-freedom (6 DOF) sensor because it measures a total of six values that define an object's unique position and orientation. Commands are communicated through hand gestures.

Figure 5-6

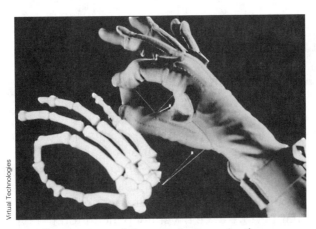

Virtual Technologies

Another version of the wired glove. As the person bends and flexes his hand, the computer depicts the motion on the display monitor.

The strength of gloves is that they provide intuitive interaction with objects. They also reinforce the sense of presence by allowing you to see your own hand in the virtual world. Their weaknesses are the lack of tactile feedback, difficulty in precisely navigating 3-D space, and the training required to learn an extensive set of gestures.

Isometric devices These devices use electromechanical methods to measure the multiple forces or torques applied to different shapes of actuators (see Fig. 5-7). They usually include several buttons for user-defined commands. Their strength is that they allow for simultaneous input of multiple degrees of freedom, which makes them useful for flight control or object manipulation. Their weakness is that they're not always intuitive to use.

Figure 5-7

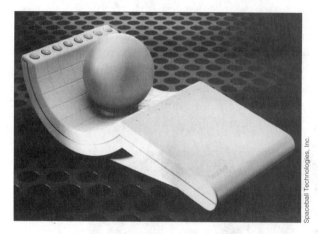

Spaceball Technologies, Inc.

An example of an isometric device. The rubber-coated ball measures forces and torques applied to it.

6 DOF wands and mice A mouse or wand can be combined with a 6-DOF tracking system. Some of these designs allow the mouse to be used in normal 2-D mode and then automatically switched to 6 DOF once it's lifted off the desk (see Fig. 5-8). Usually one to four switches are available for commands. Its strength is that it provides a simple method of navigating, selecting, and interacting with objects. Its weakness is that performance is very dependent on the type of tracking system used.

Voice recognition VR systems can effectively use voice-recognition techniques based on speaker independence and discrete commands. Each word can control an action. Its strength is in providing a "hands-off" means of controlling the simulation. Its weakness is that it isn't very effective at navigation or directing movement. Due to the computational effort required for recognition, an independent processing system is usually required to operate in parallel with the rest of the VR system.

The next group of devices are either being researched or developed and therefore aren't commonly available; however, they offer other intriguing methods of interaction:

Biosensors These are special glasses or bracelets containing electrodes that must be worn. Dermal electrodes monitor muscle electrical activity, and are capable of tracking gross eye movements by measuring muscle movements. There isn't enough data yet to

Figure 5-8

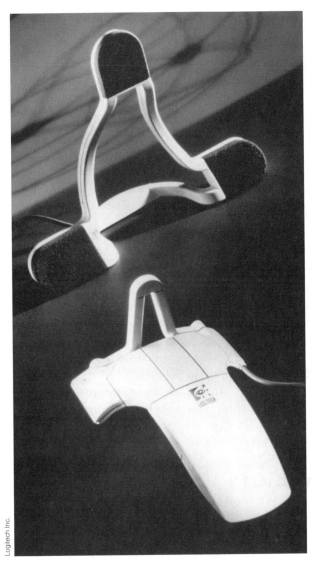

Logitech Inc.

Ultrasonic tracking allows the Logitech 3-D mouse's position and orientation to be monitored as it moves through space.

evaluate strengths or weaknesses, but they have the potential to be a natural interface.

Eye tracking Infrared or other optical means are used to track where the eye is currently looking. This technique could be used like biosensors to control view or motion, and could provide a possible

interface for those who have lost use of their hands or other motor skills. Again, there isn't yet enough data to evaluate strengths or weaknesses.

This list is a single snapshot in time of a few current devices and their effectiveness. Because they're all being continually improved, expect many of the weaknesses to be resolved by new materials or interaction modes.

On the far fringe of VR interaction are devices like pivotable surfboards, MIDI (musical-instrument digital interface) devices, and a full-body DataSuit. Though interesting, they haven't been readily adopted.

But just imagine surfing through a 3-D representation of the stock market in search of overlooked market opportunities while playing an electronic flute to select particular industry segments. Brightly colored cubes flash by as you maneuver through a checkerboard landscape of dynamically changing shapes.

Playing a rapid sequence of notes on your flute causes the world to suddenly shift as new stocks are summoned up to replace those previously displayed. Your search continues. Somewhere in that endless digital landscape exists the opportunity you've been looking for. As strange as it might seem, the technology exists today to create this.

⇨ Reality simulators

Whether they're images, 3-D sounds, or tactile vibrations, all aspects of VR must be coordinated and precisely delivered or confusion will result. Think of a symphony and its conductor. The reality simulator represents the orchestra, the instruments the effectors, and the application or simulation manager the conductor.

Working in concert, a virtual experience is constructed from the interplay of the different instruments. Bringing an orchestra to life requires physical power supplied by musicians; bringing a reality simulator to life requires significant computing power supplied by complex microprocessors and related hardware.

Only within the last ten years has the required processing power become widely available and affordable. This is an outgrowth of efforts from companies like Intel, Silicon Graphics, Sun, and Motorola to deliver ever more powerful computer chips. Virtual reality is just one of many technologies, like cursive handwriting recognition and speech recognition, that have been waiting in the wings for the right combination of silicon and software.

A peek under the hood of a virtual reality system reveals an engine that an average PC user would quickly recognize. In fact, at the heart of most commercially available VR machines is an Intel-based personal computer. Special devices and software turn ordinary PCs from word processors into reality generators. If you were to simplify a VR system, focusing only on the reality simulator, you'd wind up with the illustration in Fig. 5-9.

Figure 5-9

reality simulator

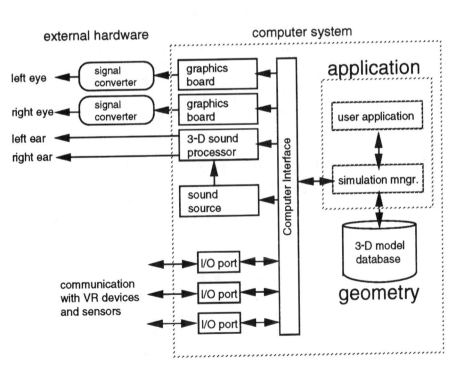

Diagram showing the major components of a reality simulator. Fake Space Labs

To create a virtual-reality system, you'd start with a personal computer or workstation and probably add hardware to supplement sound and graphics creation. If a stereoscopic image is important, then separate video signals for each eye must be generated, which requires twice the graphics hardware. Alternatively, two separate computers can be used, as long as some method of keeping them synchronized exists (without this, it becomes distracting if your left eye is in one world and your right eye is in a different one).

Before the video output from the graphics boards can be used by the head-mounted display, it usually has to be converted to the same kind of signal your VCR accepts (NTSC), though some HMDs accept the computer's video signal directly.

If 3-D sound is used, special boards are required, along with some method of creating synthesized sounds or playing back sampled ones. Communication with other VR devices, like head-trackers, wired gloves, and isometric devices, is done through standard input/output ports found on the back of every computer.

All these pieces taken together represent quite a number of additions to the original system. This is why some VR vendors provide complete system integration to minimize the confusion of assembling such a Gordian knot of cables, connectors, and boards. Table 5-1 summarizes some of the different hardware approaches major VR vendors are currently offering.

As you can see, quite a mix of hardware is represented. Generating complex 3-D images in a fraction of a second determines, more than anything else, whether certain hardware can be used for a virtual reality system. If smooth, 3-D images can't be generated in real time, then the computer can't be used for VR.

⇨ Real-time requirements

Our everyday sense of reality isn't experienced in discrete "chunks," nor does it pause before resuming. Virtual environments must be smooth and responsive to be useful. Human perceptual studies show that response times of under 100 milliseconds are generally

Hardware platforms used by major VR vendors

Table 5-1

Vendor	Platform	Graphics subsystem	Sound
Autodesk	Intel PC	VGA, i860, Division	MIDI, 2-D/3-D sound
Dimension	Intel PC	VGA	MIDI, 2-D sound
Division	SGI	All options	MIDI, 2-D/3-D sound
	Intel PC	Transputer/i860, custom	Custom
Sense8	Intel PC	i860 CPU, custom, VGA	MIDI, 2-D/3-D sound
	Sun Micro.	Sun ZX, E&S Freedom	MIDI
	DEC Alpha	Kubota Pacific Denali	MIDI, 2-D/3-D sound
	SGI	All options	MIDI, 2-D/3-D sound
VREAM	Intel PC	VGA	MIDI, 2-D sound
W. Industries	Amiga	TI 34020, custom	Custom
	Intel PC	Custom	Custom

considered interactive, or real-time. Response times slower than this become noticeable and affect performance.

Within this tiny slice of time, not much more than a blink of an eye, the reality simulator must process the entire cycle of retrieving user input (head or hand movements), performing calculations, and generating a new image for the head-mounted display. Most of the time is spent rendering the new image, or left and right images in the case of stereoscopic views. This is the reason why all commercial VR systems use powerful graphics hardware to accelerate the rendering process.

If it takes 100 milliseconds to make one pass through the event loop, then one frame is rendered every 0.1 seconds or 10 frames in one second. This doesn't sound very impressive when you consider that movies are shown at 24 fps and TVs display at 30 fps.

However, it's important to understand the difference between playback experiences like movies and interactive experiences like virtual reality. Movies and TV simply play back previously recorded images, while VR systems calculate new images from scratch every frame. Images aren't prestored or prerendered. This is a crucial

difference, because it allows interactive movement of your point of view to any location or orientation in the 3-D world.

Imagine generating the images of rolling hills and the house mentioned at the beginning of this chapter. One way would be to use an imaginary camera that could take a spherical picture of a scene from any vantage point. Using this camera and a 3-D rendering program, you could follow a path through the 3-D world, taking a picture every few steps. Replaying the correct images, you would appear to travel along a 3-D path and be able look all about you.

Storing all possible positions and views, however, would require quite a few gigabytes (1,000 megabytes) of space, so that isn't a very practical solution. Instead, VR systems interactively calculate what you would see depending on where you are in the 3-D world.

More importantly, you can now wander off the beaten path and perhaps discover some new sight previously missed, unlike the camera method, which restricts your movement to a predefined path. This level of interactivity sets virtual reality apart from other noninteractive forms of visualization.

Virtual-world building blocks

WHAT is the virtual world composed of? What are its basic building blocks? Answers to questions like these invariably depend on various implementations. However, most virtual environments share some fundamental aspects—which you can learn about by disassembling a virtual world into its component parts.

Basic building blocks

The following definitions are loosely based on Sense8's WorldToolKit development tools:

Objects

Objects are discrete 3-D shapes that can be independently interacted with. A movable lamp or sofa, a flying bird, and a swimming fish are all examples. They can be represented by visible, audible, or tactile cues. This can lead to interesting juxtapositions, where you can feel an object but not see it, or hear it but not see or feel it.

Objects are optionally subject to physical laws. If you drop an object, does it fall? Several objects can be assembled hierarchically into a single object—like a hand composed of fingers, which in turn are composed of finger segments. Moving the hand moves all the related pieces.

Objects are typically the movable elements in a virtual world. They can be *static*, which don't move until interacted with, or *dynamic*,

which move based on simulation control—like an automatic door that opens as you approach it, or a rotating carousel. Without objects, virtual environments would be static and lifeless—limited to simple walk-throughs.

⇨ Backdrop

Only a single stationary backdrop is present at one time. It can't be moved or broken into smaller elements. Typically, it's the underlying structure upon which the virtual environment is built. In the example from the previous chapter, the rolling green hills and structure of the house would be the stationary backdrop. This is a choice made by the world designer to prevent participants from moving the house, the hills, or the walls in the house—these capabilities might distract from the task at hand.

Though the backdrop remains fixed in place, it doesn't mean that it can't be interacted with; often, the colors and other physical properties can be modified. For example, a wall that's part of a backdrop can change color or appearance, but it can't be moved or resized.

⇨ Viewpoints

The viewpoint is the perspective, or point of view, of the observer in the virtual world. By controlling the viewpoint with a sensor like a joystick, the observer can navigate the virtual world. When a head-tracking sensor is attached to the viewpoint, the motion of the observer's head also controls the viewpoint, allowing him to look around naturally. Multiple viewpoints are possible; they can even be shown on the same display, allowing you to see ahead of and behind you at the same time.

⇨ Sensors

Sensors are all the physical devices, like head-tracking sensors, wired gloves, and isometric devices, that are used in a virtual world. Sensors can be attached to viewpoints or to objects. If attached to viewpoints,

then movement of the physical sensor moves the participant's point of view equivalently. If attached to an object, like attaching the 3-D model of a hand to wired-glove sensors, you can see the fingers wiggle on your virtual hand.

⇨ Lights

Multiple light sources can be positioned and oriented anywhere in the world. There are different forms, such as directed, spot, and ambient. Intensities and colors can be interactively modified. Light is dynamically calculated, so you can move a light around and watch different surfaces light up.

⇨ Universe

The universe is the current environment of the simulation. It includes objects and related entities: lights, sensors, viewpoints, and sound channels. The simulation manager is aware only of entities previously "added" to the universe. And only objects in the universe are actually drawn on the display.

Objects and entities that exist outside the universe are ignored until they're added to the simulation. This allows multiple objects to be loaded into an application, and added or removed as necessary. By keeping them part of the application and not deleting them, you can quickly put them back into the simulation. See Fig. 6-1 for a diagram of this process.

For example, several different models of sofas might be loaded into an application, but only one added to the universe. The user could step through the various sofa models by removing the old sofa and then adding the next model. This kind of flexibility is important in developing complex simulations.

This is only one type of model for conceptualizing a virtual world. Because of the malleable nature of VR, other representational models exist and are just as relevant. This is just one approach that has

Figure 6-1

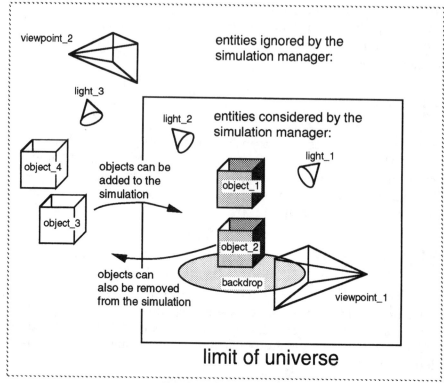

Logical components of a virtual simulation. Entities can be moved in and out of the simulation manager's consideration.

already been implemented and is being used to build virtual environments.

Keep in mind that current VR systems have only a vague understanding of real physical properties. Dropping a virtual glass onto a virtual floor of a kitchen doesn't cause it to shatter or make a sound unless the world designer specifically programmed it to do so.

Simple underlying physical principles like these are almost completely missing from current systems. Another magnitude increase in computing power will be required before complex dynamics or kinematics become standard aspects of a virtual environment. Simulating reality is no mean feat.

Simulation management

Orchestrating computational resources, interface devices, and system resources to manufacture a semblance of reality is the responsibility of the *simulation manager* and *application* in a virtual-reality system.

Think of the simulation manager as the core of a spreadsheet program (like Lotus 1-2-3 or Microsoft's Excel), and the VR application as the actual spreadsheet that appears on the computer screen. You use the spreadsheet's graphical interface to harness the power of the simulation engine at the core of the spreadsheet program. Through this interface, you determine the nature of your simulation. It could be a financial, scientific, or even a home diet simulator. The spreadsheet interface is a blank slate waiting for problems to solve.

In the same way, a VR application uses the capabilities of the simulation manager to rapidly construct and model visualization problems. Just as the user's spreadsheet defines what kind of problem is being analyzed, the VR application defines the kind of 3-D simulation being presented.

At the beginning of the previous chapter, a simulation of a landscape and house was described. Inside the house, a lamp was selected and moved from one position to another. The application defined how this interaction would occur and gave instructions to the simulation manager, which then directed the hardware to carry out the task.

Depending on your imagination and tools, you can create almost any kind of virtual environment. In fact, the many different VR applications covered in the third part of this book prove the flexibility of this new technology.

Simulation-management tools

Just as there are many issues to consider when looking at different spreadsheet programs, the same is true of the tools necessary for simulation management:

Interface to the simulation manager How are applications created? Do they require programming, or do they use graphical interfaces? This usually determines who can use the tool and the amount of flexibility.

Device support How many different interface devices can be used? It's too early in the development of VR to single out a single interface technology as the best one for all purposes. Support for multiple devices allows you to experiment and pick the correct one for an application.

Object control What can you do with an object once you've selected it? Can you interact with it or modify its shape, position, and appearance? Objects should have tasks that can be independently executed, like an automatic door that opens as you approach. Collision detection is another key feature. It constrains objects so they don't interpenetrate, or warns you when they do. Additionally, constraints and hierarchical behavior simplify creating links between objects, such as the fingers of a hand. If you move the hand, you want the fingers to automatically follow.

Simulation control Many different attributes control a simulation. Rendering style, lighting, viewing angle, communication with other programs, and databases are just a few. Support for modeling of mass, gravity, momentum, and other physical properties could also be useful. Advanced tools even allow networking of multiple simulations so that more than one participant can interact in the same virtual world.

Modeling support How are 3-D models created? Some tools provide a simple modeling capability or read common file formats. More powerful tools allow interactive creation of objects within the virtual environment itself.

⇨ Interface options

As you can see, someone investigating the development of a VR application must grapple with many issues. Other considerations of price, performance, and platform support are important, but our intent here is to focus on just capabilities. The first and probably most important consideration is the interface to the simulation manager. Three possibilities exist:

Compiled libraries A compiled library is also known as an API (application programming interface or toolkit). It typically provides the most flexibility in creating a virtual environment. The cost is that you generally have to be a programmer to use one and you usually need to compile your application every time you make a change. A compiled library is the tool of choice for those interested in developing complex, stand-alone virtual reality applications. Nonprogrammers should avoid using it.

Scripted language A scripted language allows for the fairly simple creation of simulations. Even nonprogrammers can pick up the language in a relatively short amount of time. It typically uses an interpretive environment, where changes are instantly incorporated into the simulation. It's similar to learning a database programming language. Scripting generally trades off some flexibility for a much simpler interface to the simulation manager.

Graphical This is the tool for the point-and-click crowd. If properly done, it provides a simple intuitive interface to the simulation manager, allowing you to quickly create and modify basic simulations. It's a very accessible tool for nonprogrammers, but might be more difficult to use for intricate simulations. VPL's *Body Electric* graphic interface is an example of this approach, as shown in Fig. 6-2.

Each of these interfaces allows different kinds of interaction with the simulation manager and its simulation event loop. This loop is the locus of control for a VR system, which means that the entire simulation depends on its consistent, rhythmic timing.

Performing a calculation in 0.1 second or even 10 seconds isn't important in a spreadsheet because the simulation is time-independent. But if the VR system's simulation event loop took 0.2 second instead of 0.1 second, you'd notice it because the world would suddenly become less interactive.

Figure 6-2

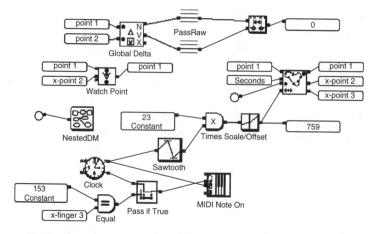

VPL's Body Electric is an example of a graphical method of describing the dynamics of a virtual environment. VPL Research Inc.

⇨ Event loop

When running a VR application, the computer repeatedly loops through a sequence of events until the simulation quits. This is known as the *simulation event loop*. A single pass through the loop is considered a *tick* and often occurs in a fraction of a second.

Unlike a clock where each tick represents a precise amount of time, a simulation manager's tick varies constantly because it depends on the complexity of the scene and how long it takes the computer to render it. The number of frames per second and the number of ticks per second is always identical.

In the example at the beginning of the previous chapter, the participant enters a virtual living room and proceeds to move a lamp that's incorrectly positioned. We can dissect the interaction so you'll better understand how the event loop functions (see Fig. 6-3). Most of the steps in the event loop are performed automatically by the simulation manager without the programmer's help. These steps are identified with an (SM).

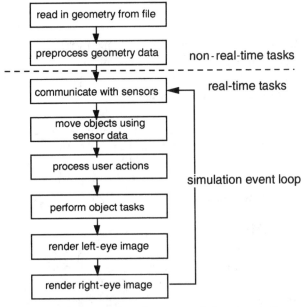

Figure 6-3

Diagram showing the elements of the simulation manager's event loop.

❋ Query sensors (SM)

Each input sensor attached to the computer has to be polled as to its current state. For example, the head-tracker has to communicate the current position or orientation of the participant's head. The simulation manager looks at its list of currently enabled input sensors, and questions each one in turn. The state of each sensor is stored away for later use.

❋ Update objects (SM)

At this point the stored information from the sensors is used to update the position and orientation of any objects the sensors are attached to. They can be attached to viewpoints, as in the case of head-tracking, or to other objects, as in the case of the lamp. Sometimes more than one sensor is attached to an object. For example, your viewpoint might be controlled by both a head-tracking sensor and a joystick. This would allow you to look around and, at the same time, fly over the rolling green hills.

✳ User actions

This is the world designer's chance to control and direct the simulation. User actions define the type of interaction that occurs between the participant and the virtual environment. This is the break or pause in the event loop where control is passed to the world designer's unique set of rules or specifications.

For example, based on an event like the lamp being selected, perhaps a bounding box is created around the lamp, "connecting" it to the sensor that controls movement. It could be a joystick, wired glove, or any other device. The next time through the event loop, if the sensor is moved the lamp will also move.

✳ Object tasks (SM)

Any object can have a task that's automatically executed every tick. This allows autonomous activity by objects in the simulation. In the earlier example, the front door automatically opened for the participant as he neared it. In this case, the distance between the door and the user is tracked and, if the user passes a certain point, it triggers an event causing the door to begin rotating open. Each successive tick the door opens slightly wider.

✳ Render (SM)

Once all activity has been registered for a single frame, the world is ready to be rendered (drawn). This is a complex operation all by itself, and is covered in greater detail in the next chapter. Basically, it involves examining the 3-D model or geometry information, and determining how to draw 3-D models on the 2-D screen of the display device.

VR systems capable of rendering stereoscopic views (left/right eye images) have to render each eye independently. Sometimes dual graphics hardware allows these images to be drawn simultaneously.

If the reality engine is the heart of a VR system, then the event loop is the portion of the brain that controls the beating of the heart. It endlessly cycles until the simulation is terminated.

Now that we've defined the building blocks and explained how the simulation manager supervises how the blocks are handled, it's time to examine how objects and backdrops are actually represented and understood by the computer.

⇨ Geometry

3-D structures, whether a house or a landscape, can be described as a series of 3-D coordinate values. A collection of such values is called *geometry* or *model* data. Remember how in the discussion of early scene generators, Sutherland and others discovered the technique of using computers to interactively draw scenes of airports and landscapes?

Prior to that discovery, video cameras had been mounted on movable platforms over detailed miniature models to generate similar views. Computers were found to be much more effective than video cameras, which eventually became obsolete for this purpose. VR systems use computers in the same way to image or render 3-D worlds.

Any point in space can be described using three coordinate values: X, Y, and Z. With three such points, you can define a flat triangular shape; with eight points, you can define a cube. The illustration in Fig. 6-4 shows how a cube would be viewed from a particular point in space.

Simple rules of perspective guide the computer in creating the 2-D image on the video screen, using 3-D information defining the size and placement of the cube. This is how 3-D graphics are generated—the tricky part is doing it quickly enough for VR.

More complex objects can easily be constructed with simple procedures like the triangular patch. The terrain and house described at the beginning of the previous chapter would require at least 1,000 of these basic shapes. To keep track of all this 3-D data, it's organized and stored in special geometry or model files. These files are usually distinct from the actual VR application, and are created with 3-D modeling tools like Autodesk's AutoCAD, 3D Studio, Paracomp's Swivel3-D, and Software Systems' Multigen.

Figure 6-4

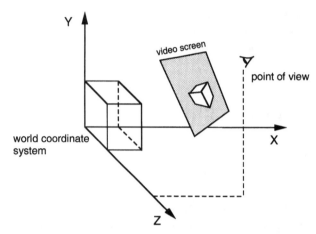

Any 3-D object can be represented on the 2-D computer screen using standard techniques of perspective.

To understand the process of modeling a virtual world, imagine trying to construct the earlier described terrain using simple paper shapes. Starting with the hills and valley, triangular shapes can fit together to approximate their surfaces, as shown in Fig. 6-5. By making the triangular pieces smaller, a more natural looking hillside can be created, as illustrated in Fig. 6-6.

Figure 6-5

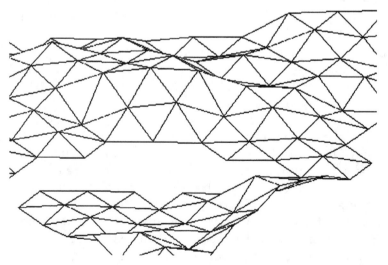

Simple terrain rendered by computer.

Figure 6-6

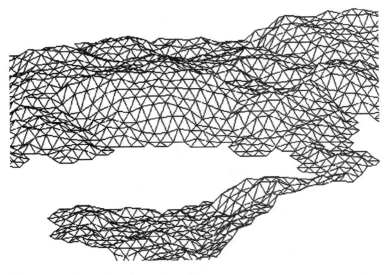

More complex terrain rendered by computer.

Unfortunately, if you use too many small triangular pieces (or polygons), it will take forever to assemble the world either by hand or by computer. Just to give you some idea, there are around 150 polygons in the first drawing and about 1,500 in the second one. The second image, therefore, would require at least ten times the processing power to be drawn as fast as the first image.

For now, let's stick with the first drawing. To make the landscape look more natural, you can simply color each triangle a different shade of green, based on how light strikes its surface, as seen in Fig. 6-7. This changes the original wire-frame image into one with shaded surfaces.

All VR systems render worlds with at least this quality of representation. Shading objects based on a light source helps you recognize outlines and orientations of objects. In this case, it helps distinguish the shape of the hills. Even with shading, however, the landscape still appears cartoonish and unnatural. To improve the realism, you can take a picture of a hillside and scan it into a computer (see Fig. 6-8).

Figure 6-7

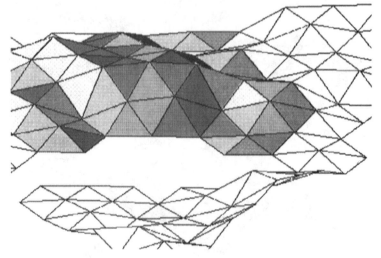

Simulation of lighting by the computer results in a shaded view of the terrain.

Figure 6-8

Scanned image of a portion of a hillside.

This rectangular image must then be cut and shaped to fit on the triangular patches. Doing this results in the final image of the terrain, showing real images mapped onto the surface of the triangles, as shown in Fig. 6-9.

Figure 6-9

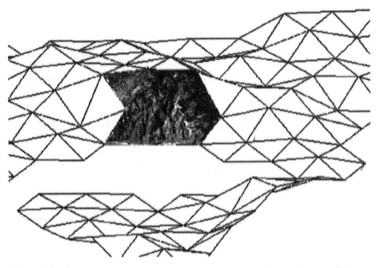

The hillside image is texture-mapped onto the surface of the terrain, creating a more realistic image.

Applying images in this manner is called *texture mapping*, and requires special hardware to process it quickly enough for a VR system. Texturing can dramatically improve the realism of the finished image, which is why all high-end flight simulators take advantage of this technique.

Satellite photos of terrain mapped onto 3-D models allow virtual trips to anywhere on Earth or beyond. You probably saw news clips of a simulated camera ride over the surface of Mars and Venus. It might have appeared to be produced by a real camera, but it was actually a synthetic view created frame by frame on a computer. It clearly demonstrated just how effective this technique can be.

Instead of building worlds out of pieces of cardboard and photographs, VR systems assemble them by calculating how each triangle or polygon (there can be thousands) would look if viewed

from a certain distance and direction. The next step is to perform *hidden-surface removal*. This ensures that polygons closest to the viewer are drawn last, obscuring polygons further away. In this way, the 3-D scene is built-up from layers of polygons drawn on the screen.

This entire process is repeated every time the viewpoint changes (in a head-tracked VR system, each time users move their head slightly). Don't forget that this all has to occur in a blink of an eye to be useful, which is why real-time 3-D graphics is so computationally intensive and why the number of polygons in the scene is so important.

The woes of world building

One of the greatest challenges facing a world designer lies in creating the 3-D models needed for building virtual experiences. Because of performance constraints (the update rate decreases as the number of polygons increases), world designers have to carefully construct their world—too many polygons and it becomes jerky and uninhabitable.

It's like telling a carpenter that he can use only a limited amount of wood to create a house. It forces the carpenter to use each piece of wood wisely and to the greatest effect. So too must a world builder craft his experience. Instead of wood and nails, shaded and textured polygons are cleverly assembled to provide the most effective environment with the fewest number of polygons.

This constraint will always exist, although the threshold or "polygon budget" will increase over time. In 1994, most mid-range VR systems are limited to worlds of roughly 1,000 to 3,000 polygons in size. When you consider that the average architectural model uses 6,000–20,000 polygons, you can see that we're still a couple years away from supporting the needs of architects who want to walk through the worlds they've already built without deleting a great deal of detail first.

One method around this restriction is the use of *texture mapping*. It's been said that a picture is worth a thousand words; well, in VR, a texture-mapped polygon is worth at least ten and sometimes even thousands of shaded polygons. Instead of using hundreds of polygons to model the complexity of a tree with its branches and leaves, a simple approximation can be made using just two polygons and a realistic image of a tree.

This image is edited with a paint program so that black paint is applied to all parts of the image except the tree. When drawn by the computer, the black paint becomes transparent and it appears that you can look through the branches of the tree. Using a trick developed by the flight-simulation industry, two intersecting polygons and the transparent texture of a tree can be combined to form a very realistic 3-D image of a tree, as illustrated in Fig. 6-10.

Figure 6-10

Realistic 3-D trees are created by combining two perpendicular tree images. When viewed transparently, they appear to be fully formed trees.

If you're building a virtual forest with hundreds of trees, tricks like this are crucial to creating a sense of realism with only a few polygons to go around. In fact, texture mapping is often the only way to achieve a sense of realism. Imagine trying to create a 3-D model of a lawn by drawing each blade of grass by hand—it's neither practical nor useful. Instead, a single texture-mapped polygon of a swatch of grass (used repeatedly) would achieve a far better effect. Because of its obvious advantages, texture mapping is certain to become a fundamental aspect of all virtual worlds.

This leads to the next problem. Although there are dozens of software tools for 3-D modeling, few provide the right combination of features for a virtual-world builder. Ideally you would want a paint program, 3-D modeler, real-time renderer, and interface to a hierarchical database all in a single package. The Multigen modeling tool is shown in Fig. 6-11.

Figure 6-11

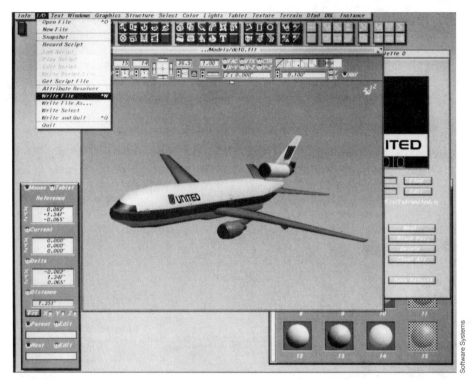

Software Systems

*Sophisticated modeling tools and hierarchical databases are needed to create
and manage virtual worlds. Powerful tools from the flight-simulator industry
will eventually become available for desktop systems.*

Few 3-D modeling tools understand the challenges of not only
building virtual worlds, but also efficiently managing a complex
database of objects and attributes. Except for some notable
exceptions from the flight-simulation industry, which cost tens of
thousands of dollars, our world-building tools are stuck in the Stone
Age. Hopefully, the Bronze Age is right around the corner.

One fundamental problem with all 3-D modeling tools is that they're
primarily concerned with only a visual representation of an object.
Though these tools might provide powerful capabilities to create
photorealistic scenes, visual information is just one of many different
object attributes a virtual-world builder must consider.

What are the object's physical properties? How much does it weigh? Where is its center of mass? What is it made of? What sound does it make on contact with another surface? Is its surface spongy or hard, rough or smooth?

These are just a few of the representational issues. What about the relationship between objects? How do you describe the mechanics of a chain link or all the interconnected parts of a piston engine? How do you define a fluid or a gas? What is its viscosity or color?

This entire book could be filled with all the facets of reality we can't represent. Imagine a carpenter being asked to build a 100-story skyscraper using only a stone axe. Today's virtual-world builders face a similar task in creating truly realistic experiences.

Of course, most technologically based media, like film and television, have battled initial limitations only to succeed through the determined efforts of those able to see beyond the limitations. There's much we can't do with the state of today's technology, but there's also much we *can* do.

At the beginning of chapter 5, *Reality engines*, a virtual experience of flying over green, rolling hills and visiting a house was detailed. This helped set the context for exploring the hardware, software, and perceptual issues involved in a VR system. It also revealed the complexity hidden behind the naturalness of the virtual experience.

Though a correctly designed virtual world can dramatically simplify our interaction with a computer, it's also one of the most complicated systems to build. No one said manufacturing reality would be easy— and it isn't. The next challenge is to take a descriptive virtual experience, and figure out how to turn an IBM PC from a word processor into a cyberspace machine.

Desktop VR

HOW can your average desktop word processor be transformed into a mythical magic carpet capable of flying through a virtual world of hills, trees, and wide rivers? How do you create such a world in the first place? The intent of this chapter is to answer some of the mechanical issues associated with duplicating the virtual experience described at the beginning of chapter 5.

By using an Intel-based personal computer, we'll demonstrate that VR isn't a technology restricted to those with multimillion-dollar budgets—it's well within reach of average-sized businesses.

A high-performance PC-based VR system

Since no standard definition exists for a *VR system*, we'll use one at the very beginning of chapter 5. Such a system should support an immersive experience in which participants wear visually-coupled displays, view stereoscopic images, listen to 3-D sounds, and are free to explore and interact within a 3-D world. Even with this narrow definition, a powerful PC-based system can be assembled for less than $15,000 in 1994 dollars. If you eliminate the need for a stereoscopic system and use a biocular (monoscopic) system instead, the system would cost quite a bit less.

When this book was originally written in mid-1992, we described how you could assemble a PC-based VR system for under $20,000. Comparing the system described two years ago with the $15,000 system described here, the new configuration is 25% cheaper and four times as powerful. You can expect this trend to continue for the next several years.

Though a $15,000 budget might seem like a lot of money, it still imposes many limits. If you examine appendix A at the back of this book, you'll see the vast assortment of hardware available for virtual environments. Because so many different hardware and software configurations can be assembled to create virtual experiences, we need some form of methodology in picking a particular configuration.

 # Making a shopping list

One approach is to first sit down and list the essential elements of the simulation. Next, you can match each requirement with appropriate hardware or software tools. The list in Table 7-1 is based on the requirements of creating the virtual world presented at the beginning of chapter 5.

VR application requirements and configuration Table 7-1

Requirement	Configuration
Stereoscopic view	Two graphics boards or two PCs
Grass-covered hillsides	Texture-mapping capability
Sense of "being there"	Head-mounted display, head-tracking
Locating sound of radio	3-D sound hardware
Changing pitch of wind sound	Sound synthesizer hardware
Selecting lamp	Interaction device
Movement of objects and viewpoint	Navigation device
Moving lamp	Separate objects in simulation
Lamp movement changes lighting	Dynamic lighting in simulation

We recommend a stereoscopic system because it provides important depth cues when manipulating objects in the virtual world. Though there's much debate over the value of stereoscopic visualization, in certain situations it's an important feature. However, the choice of a stereoscopic system restricts your options because only a couple VR solutions support this capability within the proposed budget. This requirement eliminates all the inexpensive VGA-based solutions and in addition requires the purchase of two special graphics boards.

Since texture-mapping is also one of the requirements, this narrows the software selection to Sense8's WorldToolKit-860. Since this product is designed for programmers, it also needs a C compiler. If you aren't a programmer, a product named VREAM offers support for almost everything we need (unfortunately, it can't generate stereoscopic images).

⇨ Choosing the reality simulator and output devices

Next, you'll want a powerful Intel Pentium microprocessor PC with a reasonable amount of memory (at least 8MB) as the computing platform. In addition, two SPEA Fire graphic boards are used to generate the left- and right-eye views of your virtual world. These boards contain an Intel i860 microprocessor, which provides additional computing power to create real-time texture-mapped images.

To create a sense of immersion you'll need a head-mounted display. As of mid-1994, over 20 different choices exist, but only a few fit the budget and can handle stereoscopic images. Displays with a wide field of view provide the best sense of immersion. Unfortunately, few inexpensive displays provide much above 40 degrees.

For this project, we'll use the Forte VXF1 head-mounted display because it's inexpensive and includes an integrated head-tracking system. Though the field of view is limited to 46 degrees and it uses relatively low-resolution LCD panels (428×244), it fits our other requirements. Because we're also using the Forte HMD with the SPEA Fire graphics boards, the video output of the Fire board needs to be converted to TV-formatted signals (NTSC), which requires a couple of NTSC signal encoders.

Re-creating the sound of the virtual radio playing in a corner of the virtual house on the hill requires a sound-convolving engine like Crystal River Engineering's Beachtron, which also happens to have sound-synthesizing capability (for the wind). The output of this device will be fed into headphones integrated into Forte's HMD.

Interaction and navigation choices

If you remember the description from chapter 5, one of the tasks the observer performed was selecting a virtual lamp and moving it to a different location within the virtual house. Since participants will be isolated from the real world (and the computer's keyboard) while wearing the HMD, they can't use the keyboard to control interaction. We can't have a wired glove because they're all too expensive except for the discontinued Mattel Power Glove (which has its own limitations), so the navigation device will have to do double duty.

To get around the virtual world, a common analog joystick will provide an inexpensive and intuitive solution. Moving objects around and changing lighting dynamically is a feature of Sense8's WorldToolKit, which also supports all the devices listed and described so far. In addition to the hardware and software, you'll also need a 3-D modeler, like Alias Upfront, 3D Studio, or AutoCAD, to construct the basic objects in the world, and an image or paint program to create custom textures.

By the time you read this, further developments have probably brought the cost of such a system down to an even lower level. For example, Sega is rumored to be working on a sub-$500 HMD with head-tracking that will be available late 1994. Table 7-2 reveals the relative expense of various system elements based on a total budget of $15,000.

Remember that this is just one of many ways a VR system can be configured. You could combine other devices, software, and hardware to re-create the necessary experience. This combination is driven primarily by cost—which forced you to make some trade-offs.

If cost isn't a factor, you could spend $100,000 on a Silicon Graphics Inc. (SGI) Reality Engine, $56,000 on an N-Vision HMD, $6,000 on a Polhemus FASTRAK, and $12,000 on a Virtual Technologies CyberGlove. You would be the envy of everyone in your neighborhood, though your electrical bills might be a bit excessive.

Table 7-2 | **Relative costs of a PC-based VR system**

Product	% of budget
(2) SPEA Fire Graphics boards	24
60-Mhz Pentium CPU-based PC with 8MB of RAM and a 200MB hard drive	20
Sense8 WorldToolKit-860	17
Crystal River Engineering Beachtron (3-D sound)	10
Forte VFX1 head-mounted display and tracker	7
(2) NTSC converters	5
C compiler	5
3-D modeling program	4
Image or paint program	3
Analog joystick	1

⇨ Some assembly required

We've already described the basic components of a VR system: *effectors*, *reality simulator*, *application*, and *geometry*. Using these terms, we can describe the system being built in Fig. 7-1.

In this chapter, we won't describe the technical details behind the HMD, head-tracker, and joystick because they're covered in the next chapter. Note, however, that putting together a VR system isn't a job for the technically challenged. If you haven't figured out how to program your VCR clock, you should avoid acquiring a VR system until they become more "plug and play."

After installing the two graphics boards, the 3-D sound board, the game-port board, and the special Forte head-tracking board, either you or your computer might be suffering from indigestion. Luckily they make computers with enough slots to stuff all this gear into. Next, you need to use cables to connect the HMD to the NTSC encoders, the joystick and the PC, the NTSC encoders and the graphics boards . . . well, you get the idea.

Figure 7-1

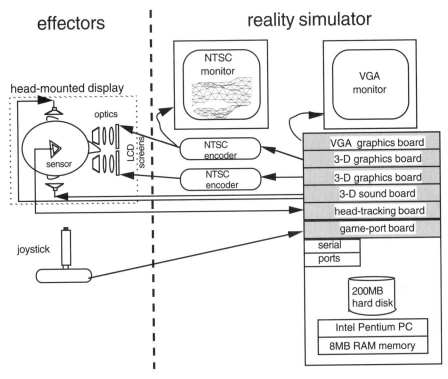

Components of an Intel PC-based virtual reality system.

Once the system is assembled and you've made some test flights, you need to start work on developing the particular application (described at the start of chapter 5). It's easiest to tackle this in the following order: first, modeling—constructing the physical representation of the rolling hills, house, and furniture—and second, application development—defining how the automatic front door works, how the lamp is moved, and how the sound of the radio is located.

⇨ Reality on a budget

All world designers have a "polygon budget" they must consider when developing a VR application. This is defined as the number of polygons available to build the virtual world at a particular update

rate. Designers need to understand how to juggle the conflicting demands of image complexity (measured in polygons) with performance (measured in frames per second).

Different combinations of hardware and software yield different polygon budgets. This is also strongly influenced by the expense of the system's graphics hardware. Performance varies from 17,000 polygons per second on the Intel Pentium/SPEA Fire board system to more than 300,000 polygons per second on the SGI Reality Engine.

Determining the polygon budget is about as simple as dividing the performance numbers by the required update or frame rate. Because the use of a head-tracking system requires a minimum of 10 frames per second in order to minimize lag effects, you wind up with a budget of about 1,700 polygons with which to build your world. (With the $20,000 PC-based system described two years ago in this book, your budget was a miserly 300–500 polygons.)

Depending on the system configuration, if both left- and right-eye images are being rendered to create stereo pairs, this polygon budget will be further reduced by 20 to 50 percent because of the additional computations for two views. If completely separate PCs or graphics channels were used to generate the view for each eye, then no degradation in performance would occur.

Because the system mentioned at the beginning of the chapter uses two graphics boards, the impact of stereo is about 20 percent, or a budget of about 1,400 polygons. This is then divided between the various objects in the world, such as the landscape, house, and furniture. Knowing how many polygons you can use to build the house determines how much complexity you can put into it.

Modeling

Now that you know your polygon budget, you can go to work creating the physical models of the landscape, house, and furniture described at the beginning of chapter 5.

Starting with the terrain and using a 3-D modeling package, you must painstakingly assemble dozens of small triangular patches to represent the hills and valleys—a somewhat tedious effort depending on your talents as a 3-D modeler.

You can either color each patch green to represent grass, or apply a picture of real grass to each segment of the terrain with texture mapping, described in the final section of chapter 6. When the WorldToolKit software reads the file containing the terrain's geometry information, it can automatically apply a picture of a swatch of grass onto every triangle in the terrain.

Instead of creating the terrain by hand, you could use WorldToolKit's built-in terrain-generation functions or a fractal algorithm (a random method based on chaos theory, heavily used in computer graphics to generate detailed, imaginary landscapes). The 3-D terrain shown in the section of chapter 6 called *Geometry*, for example, was created using fractal techniques.

Another possibility is using real-world data. There are several government sources of terrain information, like the Department of Defense's Mapping Agency. They have collected elevation data, photographs, and cultural data (objects like buildings, factories, etc.) from locations all over the world.

In the flight simulator business, automated tools read in this assortment of data and create a recognizable virtual world of just about any well-traveled location. And if you want to go off-planet, NASA has publicly accessible elevation and image data for Mars and other heavenly bodies.

Continuing with your world building, you can add trees to the terrain by using the method of two crossed polygons with an image of a tree transparently mapped onto each one (see the discussion at the end of the previous chapter). This allows you to populate the hillside with foliage, even on a limited budget.

You construct the house by assembling polygons into walls, floors, windows, sofas, and lamps. Where appropriate, images can be mapped onto surfaces like stone on the fireplace or wood paneling

on the floor or walls. Various companies sell computer disks with hundreds of prescanned and pattern-matched images of wood, stone, and other natural images. These can be a useful starting point, or you can scan photographs into a computer and modify them.

For example, you can create an animated sequence of flames by taking a scanned picture of a fireplace, modifying the flames with a paint program, and then saving the new image. After doing this four or five times, you'll create an animation where cycling quickly through the pictures gives the appearance of flickering flames.

For now, the first picture in the animation is applied to the opening in the fireplace. Later, using WorldToolKit's texture-flipping features, you'll animate the images to bring it to life. Figure 7-2 is an illustration of the textures created so far.

Figure 7-2

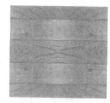

Grass, stone, wood, and fireplace images. These are examples of scanned photographs that can be used as textures and applied to surfaces of 3-D objects.

Using the same paint program, you can draw a large bay window and color all the glass pure black. A special WorldToolKit texture mapping mode turns the black color into transparent paint that you can see through. This creates the effect of looking through a framed window at the world outside, as shown in Fig. 7-3.

Figure 7-3

Using a special color, you can create transparent windows and "look through" the glass.

You'll have to create the movable lamp and automatic front door separately from the stationary world because there's no standard way to keep objects separate in AutoCAD DXF files (the most popular 3-D file format). You'll also need to create the radio separately in order to attach a 3-D sound source to it later in the application. This way, if you move the radio, the sound will move with it. At the end of the world building, the files listed in Table 7-3 have been created.

Files used to describe the virtual world Table 7-3

File	Type	Description
WORLD.DXF	Geometry	Contains terrain and house along with furniture
RADIO.DXF	Geometry	Single model of the radio
DOOR.DXF	Geometry	Single model of the front door
LAMP.DXF	Geometry	Single model of the lamp
WINDOW.TGA	Texture	Picture of bay window with glass blacked out
FIRE1-5.TGA	Texture	Five-file animated sequence of flames
GRASS.TGA	Texture	Scanned image of section of lawn
STONE.TGA	Texture	Scanned image of stonework
WOOD.TGA	Texture	Scanned image of wood paneling
TREE.TGA	Texture	Scanned image of tree with outline blacked out

The next task is to create an application that brings the world to life and opens it for exploration. If all you want to do is walk around the world just created, no additional work is needed—this is called a *walk-through* application. However, if you remember the original description of the virtual experience, it contained several features that required special attention. To bring these features to life means developing a unique application.

Application development

Starting with the standard walk-through application, you then must modify it to support the features unique to the particular virtual environment you're creating. Picking apart the description at the

beginning of chapter 5, *Reality simulators*, you'll find that it has the following unique features:

❋ **Object movement**

The front door needs to pivot open when the viewer nears it. Additionally, the viewer must be able to select the lamp and move it around the room.

❋ **3-D sound**

Music must appear to be physically located where the virtual radio object is positioned.

❋ **Dynamic sound**

Based on how fast the person is moving, the volume and pitch of the wind speed sound must increase or decrease.

❋ **Texture animation**

In order to make the fire appear to be flickering in the fireplace, the five textured files created earlier need to be sequentially mapped onto the correct place.

❋ **Dynamic lighting**

When the lamp is moved, it should appear that lights are actually being moved in the simulation.

⇨ Sample program outline

To avoid getting bogged down in the particular syntax of a programming language, we're going to document just an outline of the application. The actual WorldToolKit C programming code used to build a simple walk-through application can be found in appendix C.

Although some of the following outline is WorldToolKit-specific, most is general enough to cover other VR systems. Indentations are used to give a sense of nesting in the program's flow. Details that the WorldToolKit software handles without any intervention from the user are labeled with a (WTK).

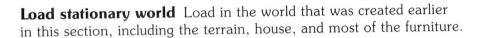

Load stationary world Load in the world that was created earlier in this section, including the terrain, house, and most of the furniture.

Load lamp Load in the lamp and correctly position it in the living room. Also position one of WorldToolKit's light sources so that it's at the correct height and orientation with respect to where the bulb would be in the lamp object.

Load door Load in the door and correctly position it in the front door opening. Set up the door so that it will pivot on one side. The door object is also assigned a special task to execute once every simulation tick.

Create sensors (WTK) Initialize sensors used for the built-in Forte head-tracker and analog joystick. This establishes communications and "wakes up" the devices.

Initialize 3-D sound Initialize Crystal River Engineering's Beachtron convolving engine with appropriate filters for spatializing the sound of the radio.

Initialize sound Initialize the Beachtron synthesizer to generate the sound of wind when required. Simple random noise generation will duplicate a windlike sound.

Attach sensors to viewpoint The viewpoint represents where the participant is in space. By attaching the sensor to the viewpoint, the view moves whenever the sensor does. This is how people fly in a virtual world.

Initialize viewpoint Move the viewpoint to a reasonable position and direction so that the participant has a chance to get oriented. In this simulation, it's moved so that it appears to be a few miles from the house on the hill.

Start simulation (WTK) This is where the previously discussed real-time event loop begins. Everything before this has been setting up the simulation. Everything following this is part of the simulation event loop and cycles continuously, executing each step in turn, until some action stops the program from running.

Query sensors (WTK) The Forte head-tracker is polled about the current orientation of the participant's head. At the same time, the analog joystick is queried about its current state (whether or not the user has moved it or pressed any buttons).

Update objects (WTK) Update the viewpoint with new position and orientation information from the joystick and the Forte head-tracker. If the joystick was used to select an object (like the lamp), then update the lamp's position based on the joystick's movement.

User actions This is an opportunity for the application or user to influence the simulation. Here is where most of the unique features of this application are implemented:

Animate fire Once every tick, the current fire texture-map is replaced with the next one in the sequence. Just like simple flip-book animations, this makes the fire appear to be flickering.

Control wind sound Using measurements of the viewer's speed, adjustments are made to the pitch and volume of the wind sound. The faster the movement, the louder and higher pitched the sound. This reinforces a sense of movement.

Test the joystick Test the joystick and see if the trigger button was pressed. Here is one scheme to select the lamp using only the joystick. The user looks directly at the lamp and presses the trigger button; doing so casts a visible ray that intersects with the lamp. A bounding box appears around the lamp to signify selection. Once the trigger is released, the beam disappears and the lamp remains selected. The next time the joystick is moved, the lamp moves instead of the person's viewpoint. This remains in effect until the lamp is deselected.

Move light If the lamp is in the process of being moved, the special light source must also move with it. This gives the effect of moving a lamp with the bulb turned on. The amount of shading on surfaces within the living room is recalculated as the lamp moves, just as it would with a real lamp.

End of user actions Return control back to WorldToolKit's simulation manager.

Object tasks Only the door has been assigned a special task. It checks the distance between the viewer and itself. If this distance is less than a certain amount, the door switches to an open state. If the door is in this state, it gradually rotates about its hinge point a little bit every tick. It might take 10 frames or ticks for the door to swing fully open. This emulates an door opening as the viewer approaches it.

Render (WTK) This is an internal function that simply assembles all the information about the state of the universe and renders the left- and right-eye views appropriately. The video signal is converted to an NTSC format and fed to the head-mounted display.

Loop (WTK) Go back to *Query sensors* and start the loop again.

End simulation The end of the simulation loop, and the simulation.

One way to estimate the complexity of developing an application like this one is to consider the number of lines of code needed to implement it. This example could be constructed with fewer than 500 lines of code, which also means that it could be easily assembled in a week or less by a typical programmer.

Within the next couple of years, direct manipulation, or point-and-click tools, will be available to allow nonprogrammers to quickly create similar demonstrations in an hour or two. Unlocking the true potential of using 3-D simulation awaits the development of such simple but powerful tools.

After starting up the previous application and using the joystick to fly into the living room of the house, the image in Fig. 7-4 would appear on the screen.

This application could easily be extended to provide control over the appearance of any object or surface in the scene, such as color or the particular texture applied to a surface. With a little more work, you could begin moving and reshaping walls, or creating brand-new walls

Figure 7-4

Sense8 Corp., 1992

Resulting view of a living room created by using the techniques discussed in this chapter.

in the environment. In the future, buildings will be constructed from inside of a virtual environment instead of as a separate external step. Tools like this are just beginning to be developed and deployed.

⇨ Conclusion

The point of this chapter was to remove some of the mystery involved in actually constructing a virtual environment. By applying concepts learned in previous chapters to a concrete example, you can clearly see how this technology works. It's important to experiment with VR tools to understand how they can be effectively applied to solve real problems.

Understanding the capabilities of current VR software tools and devices will help you evaluate future developments. With the principle "you need to know where you are to get to where you want" in mind, you hopefully now have a base camp for your explorations. And now that you know "where you are," where we're all headed is still an open question. A few interesting possibilities are explored in part 3, *Brave new worlds*.

Gloves, goggles, and wands

"The empires of the future are the empires of the mind."
Sir Winston Churchill, 1874-1965

FOR Alice to enter her strange, fanciful new world, she had to venture down a deep, dark, rabbit hole. Luckily, our explorations needn't involve following crazed rabbits or any subterranean wanderings. With the assistance of various sensors and devices, we can easily visit and interact with many new and interesting worlds (part 3 of this book describes several possible destinations).

This chapter focuses on various VR devices used for interfacing to the virtual world. While the previous chapters were a broad brushstroke, covering the basic hardware and software building blocks of VR, this chapter provides the fine detail on just how these tools and devices work.

An incredible assortment of sensors already exists for interacting with virtual worlds. All these various devices serve as tools for either creating sensory output or interfacing the user's actions to the computer. Head-mounted displays (HMDs) and 3-D sound boards are examples of output sensors, while wired gloves and isometric devices are examples of input or interaction sensors. Many of these devices represent the most interesting developments in the field of VR.

Output sensors

Currently, entering a virtual world typically requires the user to strap on fairly unwieldy equipment, like some deep-sea diver in search of Atlantis, and become isolated from the environment. This isolation is useful because it allows the substitution of a computer-realized alternative in place of the real world. Today, most VR experiences are based on sensory isolation, though other alternatives are also being explored.

As discussed in the previous chapter, sight, sound, and touch are the three main senses stimulated by current VR hardware. Most efforts have been directed at providing effective tools for sight and sound, while touch is only beginning to be explored.

Sight

A large portion of the brain is dedicated to processing and organizing visual input, more so than any other sense. In addition, the bandwidth of the visual system far exceeds that of other senses. Just think of the detail present in a single glimpse of your living room. The fidelity and resolution of that glimpse far surpasses that of any real-time computer-generated image. It has been suggested that it would take at least 80 million textured polygons to represent that same view using a computer. Since the fastest research computers (costing millions of dollars) can draw only 2 to 4 million shaded polygons per second, we're many years from replicating reality.

Our eyes channel this staggering amount of information into processing centers that filter and reduce the data into something we can use. Much of this processing occurs without conscious effort—it happens continuously without us being directly aware of it. Form, shape, color, and depth information is extracted from images without us recognizing the effort.

One of the challenges of virtual environments is to enlist the use of these *preconscious* visualization powers to understand complex issues.

By visualizing problems, we can quickly gain new insights or see new patterns revealed that were previously masked in the raw data. And most importantly, this processing occurs without conscious effort.

3-D perception

How a person's visual system converts a 2-D image, mapped on the retina, into the 3-D world we experience is still a subject of much research. Simply the fact you can still perceive depth with one eye closed implies a more complicated process than purely stereoscopic vision.

Monocular or *pictorial depth perception* works by first identifying the nature of an object before determining how far away it is. In other words, you need to know what an object is to know where it should be. Several depth cues contribute to the eye being able to establish the relationship of objects in a scene (Friedhoff, 1989):

Linear perspective This is the same effect that makes parallel railroad tracks converge in the distance. The foreshortening of a building communicates its depth in the same way. In addition, buildings are composed of right angles, which also helps us understand their relationship with other objects.

Occlusion Objects in the foreground occlude, or obscure, objects in the background.

Shadows Shadows help establish the interrelationships of objects with each other and with the background.

Detail perspective Objects become less distinct with distance. You see less and less detail, and objects become smoother.

Aerial perspective Haze washes out distant objects and makes them appear bluer than they really are.

Motion parallax As you move your viewpoint, say shifting your head two feet to the left, closer objects move more than distant ones.

Combining all these factors helps to establish the depth of objects within a scene. These are important factors to understand in a virtual environment because the world builder controls the virtual environment's sense of scale, or depth. If a completely abstract world is created where no object is readily identifiable or objects are represented so simply that you can't resolve them, then misunderstandings in depth perception can occur.

➡ Stereoscopic visualization

In addition to monocular or pictorial depth cues, several other processes are involved in depth perception. One of these, *stereopsis*, involves both eyes cooperating to identify depth. Unlike monocular depth perception, this isn't dependent on form recognition, as demonstrated by Bela Julesz in 1971. While doing perceptual research at Bell Laboratories, he created a series of random dot stereograms such as the one in Fig. 8-1.

Figure 8-1

By viewing this from about one foot away and letting your eyes relax so that you see a single image, a small L-shaped section should appear to float above the page (about 80 percent of the population can see this).

When viewed stereoptically, a small L-shaped section at the center of the pattern appears to float above the plane of the page. Because this floating section becomes apparent only when viewed stereoptically, Julesz proved that differences in horizontal positioning of objects in the left and right eyes is the basis for stereoscopic depth perception. This is also known as *disparity* or *binocular parallax*.

Previous to Julesz's work, it was believed that depth perception was based on first recognizing an object and then determining the angle between the eyes as they're focused on the object. Julesz also discovered that somewhere between 5 and 20 percent of the population has trouble seeing stereoptically, which is believed to be linked to astigmatism.

As you can see, many parameters influence our ability to distinguish depth of objects in the real world, which is why the value of stereopsis or stereoscopic displays continues to be discussed. This is an important (and expensive) consideration because generating individual images for the left and right eyes can take twice the computing power as for a single eye.

In a stereoscopic VR system, the left eye's image is rendered independently from the right eye's image. In a monoscopic or biocular VR system, only a single eye is rendered and the resulting video signal is then fed to both eyes at the same time. The two arrangements are shown in Fig. 8-2.

A virtual world designer has to decide how important stereoscopic depth perception is in the design of an application. Stereopsis simplifies the user's selection and interaction with objects in a virtual world.

Try closing one eye and picking a point on an object within two to three feet of you. Now, starting with your finger on the tip of your nose, try to touch the point on the object. Try doing the same thing with both eyes open. In the first case, it's difficult to judge if your finger has traveled far enough or not. In the second case, your finger moves rapidly to the spot without hesitation. The same holds true for similar tasks in the virtual world.

Another benefit of stereopsis is on the visual impact of the virtual world. Objects seem to leap out or hang in space. They also seem to be more solid and real, which can be a very compelling aspect of the simulation.

On the other hand, some VR applications work fine on monoscopic systems. These are usually walk-throughs or environments where little direct manipulation of objects occurs. As described earlier, many

Figure 8-2

stereoscopic VR system

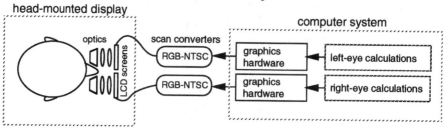

monoscopic VR system

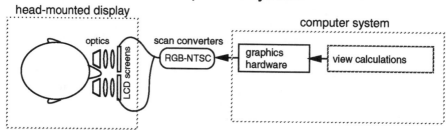

Diagram showing the difference between a stereoscopic VR system and a monoscopic system.

depth cues exist in even a monoscopic image, so stereopsis isn't crucial. When surveyed after playing a monoscopic VR game, most participants were surprised to find that it wasn't stereoscopic—they became too engrossed in the game to notice.

Remember that stereopsis is just one more factor to consider in a long list of features that control the sense of immersion. A VR system doesn't have to be stereoscopic if other aspects of the simulation provide the necessary depth cues. Learning to balance these factors is part of the art of being a virtual world builder.

⇨ Viewing parameters

There are several parameters that control how images are displayed or rendered in a VR system. Several of these can be interactively modified for different effects. They are all based on the viewing geometry shown in Fig. 8-3.

Figure 8-3

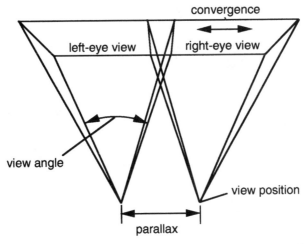

Viewing parameters under the control of the virtual world designer.

❈ Convergence

In a stereoscopic system, you achieve convergence when separate left- and right-eye images fuse into a single image. Because this varies depending on the viewer and optical design of the HMD, an adjustment to the horizontal position of the left- and right-eye images usually needs to be provided.

This is done either optically, mechanically, or by telling the computer to shift the displayed image to the left or to the right. It shouldn't be confused with parallax (see the next section). Convergence simply shifts the entire image within the frame without changing the geometry of either the left- or right-view positions.

❈ Parallax

Parallax represents the distance between the viewer's left and right eyes in the virtual world (see Fig. 8-4). It also determines the sense of depth of virtual objects. If you view a mountain from far away, both left and right eyes will see the same image because the two- to three-inch distance between your eyes means nothing when viewing an object miles away. However, if you look at a book from one to two feet away, each eye will see a slightly different perspective.

By alternately opening and closing your left and right eyes, you can see this difference for yourself. The closer an object is to your eyes,

Figure 8-4

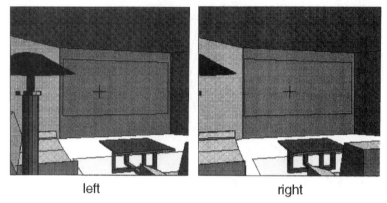

left   right

Left- and right-eye images differ when parallax is considered.
Not only is the image shifted slightly, but you see everything
from a different angle.

the more different it looks from each eye. By controlling this
parameter, you can have a building appear as either a tiny toy model
or as an immense structure. By switching between a large and small
value of parallax, a participant would first feel large and then small
relative to other objects in the virtual environment. This is another
powerful technique to consider when designing worlds.

There is some concern that improper use of parallax in a
stereoscopic system would place undue strain on a person's visual
system. Unnatural values of parallax cause the eyes to strain as they
attempt to converge the image. This is an area that requires
additional research before being resolved.

✳ View angle

Think of the view angle as the size of the camera lens through which
the virtual world is viewed. A zoom lens would have a small view
angle and a fish-eye lens would have a large view angle. The image in
Fig. 8-5 illustrates the effect of changing this parameter.

All these parameters provide a virtual world designer with incredible
flexibility in presenting virtual experiences. Think of how Hollywood
uses camera angles and effects to present a particular view. These
same techniques can be borrowed to help dramatize specific aspects
of a virtual simulation. A world builder can heighten or reduce

Illustration showing the effect of changing the viewing angle of a scene. The left image has a small viewing angle and the right image has a large viewing angle.

viewers' sense of reality by cleverly shifting these parameters as they experience a virtual environment.

✳ Immersion or sense of presence

Many virtual environments attempt to harness and exploit the visual system's innate capabilities, but there isn't a single "right" way to do it. This is one reason so many approaches have evolved to view virtual environments. Each approach can be ranked by the degree of *immersion*, or sense of presence, it provides.

For example, sitting in front of a computer screen and viewing an interactive 3-D simulation of a molecule is less immersive than donning a stereoscopic, head-mounted display and interacting with the molecule directly, but both techniques have advantages and disadvantages.

The sense of immersion is a product of several parameters related to visual stimulus and other simulation factors, as shown in Fig. 8-6. Many of these parameters are visual, stressing the crucial role that visual cues play in the creation of an immersive experience.

Figure 8-6

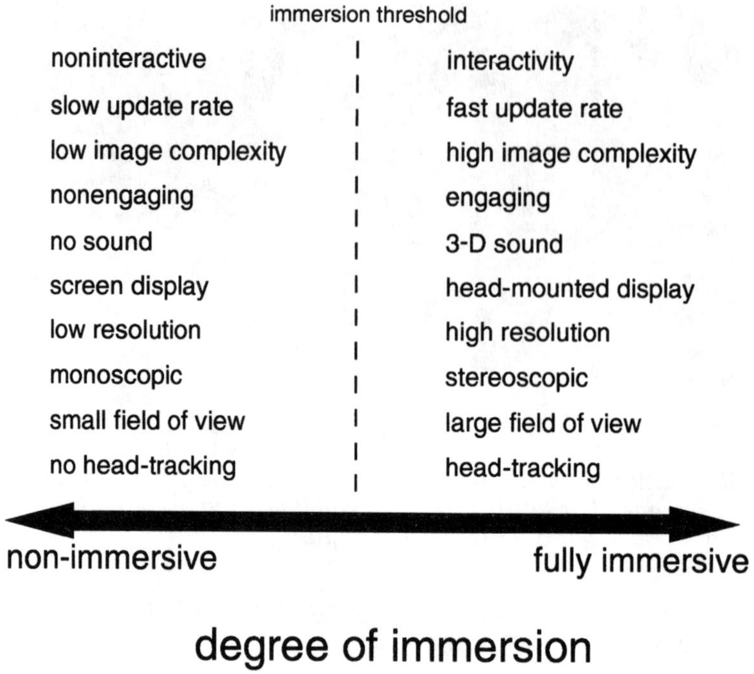

immersion threshold

noninteractive	interactivity
slow update rate	fast update rate
low image complexity	high image complexity
nonengaging	engaging
no sound	3-D sound
screen display	head-mounted display
low resolution	high resolution
monoscopic	stereoscopic
small field of view	large field of view
no head-tracking	head-tracking

non-immersive   fully immersive

degree of immersion

Diagram showing factors that govern the degree of visual immersion.

It's important to realize that we don't fully understand the role all these factors play in what is primarily a personal experience—what is immersive to one person might not be to another. Nor can science supply a simple formula for calculating the degree of immersion someone experiences.

Notice, too, the many different paths to achieving a sense of presence, or immersion. One approach might project a large, stereoscopic, high-resolution image on a wall that you view through stereo glasses, but movement of your head isn't tracked. Another approach could be the one most associated with VR, the use of a head-mounted display with 3-D sound and head-tracking.

The most important point is that you can't just focus on one factor while ignoring the others. An effective VR application balances all of them. Even a simple computer monitor can become a fascinating

window into another world if the application is interesting enough to engage the viewer (as many computer video games do).

⇨ Visually coupled displays

Virtual displays can be divided into those that are visually coupled and those that aren't. Head-mounted displays (HMDs), which you wear like a hat, or head-coupled displays, which use mechanical arms to suspend a video monitor in front of your face, are examples of visually coupled displays. Their chief characteristic is that, no matter which direction you turn your head, the display is always kept in front of your face.

Nonvisually coupled displays are typically computer monitors or video-projection systems capable of producing a stereoscopic image. These monitors don't move with the viewer, so the viewer must always face the video screen. Since the technical issues are fairly straightforward, they won't be covered in this book.

Most people associate virtual reality with head-mounted displays (someone wearing a goofy-looking head-piece). HMDs provide the most direct visual experience of virtual worlds. They do this by partially excluding the view of the real world and by enhancing the field of view of the computer-generated world.

In its simplest incarnation, an HMD is composed of optics and a pair of display screens, as shown in Fig. 8-7. The difficult part of HMD design is providing these two elements in a robust, low-weight, ergonomic, and hygienic package. At least 20 different HMD manufacturers are striving to create the ultimate display that Ivan Sutherland envisioned over two decades ago.

✳ Optics
Using the original NASA Ames HMD design as a guide, we can examine how optics and display screens interrelate. Optics do two things: they allow you to focus on a display screen two to three inches from your face, and they increase the field of view of the displayed image.

Figure 8-7

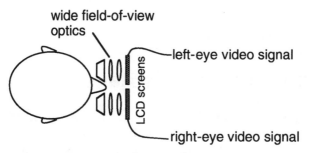

Basic components of an LCD-based head-mounted display.

The initial optics used by NASA Ames were produced by a small company called LEEP Systems in Waltham, Massachusetts. LEEP had been building special lenses for use with stereoscopic photography when NASA came along and ordered one for their prototype HMD. Because the optics were designed to view the stereoscopic, wide, field-of-view image of a large photographic slide, they were ideal for use with LCD displays salvaged from small portable TVs.

One of the unique characteristics of the LEEP optics is its anamorphic projection for creating a wide field of view. Anamorphic lenses are used by the film industry to squeeze a wide image from a camera onto the dimensions of a standard 35mm-film frame. A similar lens on the projector reverses the process and displays the wide image on the screen.

When used with computer-generated images, the computer is supposed to predeform the image before displaying it—though this isn't always done due to the computational effort of calculating the necessary distortion. This projection, represented by the diagram in Fig. 8-8, was designed to provide maximum detail in front of the eye, where it can be resolved, and minimum detail on the periphery, where detail isn't as important. Images viewed through these optics are distorted in a manner known as the "pincushion effect." Normally straight lines become curved, causing an object in the center of view to bend away from the viewer. If images aren't precorrected for this effect, distortion can become a problem.

Figure 8-8

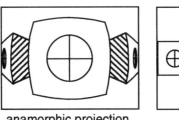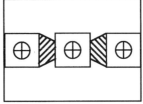

anamorphic projection   linear projection

Differences between anamorphic and linear projections. LEEP Systems Inc.

The degree of distortion varies with the lens' design. Early LEEP optics had a 90-degree field of view and minimal distortion. Later versions had a 140-degree field of view, which requires some form of correction. This can be done with either cameras and specially modified lenses or through digital or analog image processing.

LEEP optics found their way into almost all the early HMD designs. VPL used them in their first EyePhones before designing their own optics, and Virtual Research used them in their original Flight Helmets. LEEP's optics also addressed a couple of other issues with the designs of HMDs, as described in the following sections.

Interpupillary distance (IPD) Because the distance between a person's pupils varies across the population, the design of an HMD must account for differences in interpupillary distance (IPD). LEEP achieved this by providing a large-exit pupil diameter (see Fig. 8-9). This means that the focal diameter of the image near the eye is quite large, allowing room for a variety of IPDs without making a mechanical adjustment. Optical designs with small-exit pupil diameters require a mechanical IPD adjustment.

Another important consideration is the interaxial spacing of the optics. A value representing the average IPD likely to be found in the general population (95% of the adult population have IPDs from 50 to 71 millimeters) is used to ensure that the left- and right-eye visual axes converge instead of diverge when trying to merge two screen images.

While it's easy to cross your eyes inwards (converge), it's painful for each eye to try to look outwards (diverge). By using a smaller value

Figure 8-9

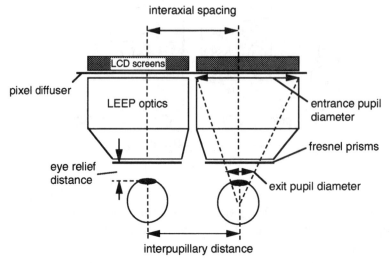

Key optical factors in the design of the LEEP wide-field-of-view optics. LEEP Systems Inc.

for the interaxial spacing, the majority of the population should experience convergence rather than divergence.

Spacing of the optics also places restrictions on the physical size of the LCD screens used in HMDs. If the LCDs are too large, they won't fit side by side in front of the optics, causing additional imaging problems.

Image overlap Image overlap is another important consideration. If an HMD is designed with 100% image overlap, it means that if you connected the left and right displays to the same video signal, you would see a single converged image. If an HMD has less than 100% convergence, this is no longer true. The same video signal being fed into the two separate eyes would result in seeing two offset images that your eyes might not be able to converge (depending on the degree of overlap and your eye's abilities).

This is a crucial issue for a monoscopic or biocular system since a single video image must be fed to both eye displays. In a stereoscopic system, two video images are created, so the computer can adjust each eye image until convergence occurs. It does this by "sliding" the appropriate image to the left or the right.

Another possible solution for adjusting overlap problems is to use a flexible fresnel prism placed over one or both of the exit pupil lenses. This optically shifts the image either left or right. Some VR systems that produce only monoscopic output use this technique when hooked up to HMDs designed with less than 100% overlap (like the original LEEP optics).

Field of view Field of view is one of the more crucial optical parameters. Much debate centers around how wide it should be for proper immersion. The wider the field of view, the more sense of presence is experienced. Unfortunately, it also worsens the perceived resolution of the LCD displays because the optics magnify the display screens. This is one reason why several HMD manufacturers use values as low as 30 to 60 degrees; they do so in order to increase the perceived resolution of their displays (with the additional advantage of greatly simplifying the optical design).

In some VR applications where detail or text needs to be read, resolution is more important than field of view. In other applications, like architectural walk-throughs, however, this is reversed and field of view becomes more important than resolution. Understanding how this parameter affects a VR experience is important to a virtual world designer.

HMD manufacturers have evolved many different optical approaches. One of the more interesting is an experimental holographic lens that resembles mirrored sunglasses. It's based on the same technology used in supermarket laser scanners. A complex set of optics can be duplicated with an appropriate hologram and re-created on inexpensive, lightweight plastic film.

In this prototype, an LCD display is positioned directly above the eye, pointing down into the lens. A half-silvered mirror reflects the LCD image onto the inner surface of the sunglasses, where the holographic film is applied. After passing through the holographic lens, the image is reflected back into the eye. If the inner surface of the sunglasses is only partially reflective, the viewer will see both the virtual world and the real world through the lens.

It's like wearing a set of dark sunglasses with the virtual world projected on the inside of the lens. Holographic lenses are one of several promising designs well suited for mass production and low cost.

✳ Display technology

A comprehensive examination of the visually coupled display market shows that it has split into three parts. One segment is pursuing low-cost, low-resolution, small-FOV designs based on liquid-crystal displays (LCDs) for the home and gaming systems, while another segment provides moderately expensive, medium-resolution, medium-FOV designs using either LCDs or monochrome CRTs with color shutters. A final segment is producing very expensive, high-resolution, wide-FOV designs using CRTs or light-valves for flight simulators and high-end research.

Along with the optics, the display system is an important issue in a visually coupled display. Two primary technologies exist: LCDs and CRTs. There are also some exotic variations on this theme that are being researched.

LCDs HMD builders have struggled to find LCD displays that are acceptable for their needs. Conflicting factors of screen size, housing size, price, availability, image quality, and drive circuitry all have to be carefully considered. One of the more frustrating factors is screen size. A display of 2.5 to 3.5 inches (diagonal measurement) works well with LEEP optics, but LCD manufacturers are intent on producing sizes either larger than this for the portable computer and TV markets or smaller than this for camera viewfinders.

Housing size is also a consideration because two LCD displays must fit edge to edge in front of the optics, or imaging problems will result. To keep costs down, HMD manufacturers initially used off-the-shelf Sony Watchman 2.7-inch color LCD displays. They purchased these consumer products wholesale, and then proceeded to dismantle and use them in their high-tech VR goggles. Unfortunately, in late 1991 Sony retired the design that worked best with HMDs, forcing HMD manufacturers to search for other solutions.

Several groups have explored the use of custom-designed LCDs. NASA Ames worked with Casio to develop a single, wide,

monochrome LCD panel that would cover both eyes. Unfortunately, out of Casio's initial shipment of prototypes, only two worked, which was one reason the project didn't go any further.

VPL's HRX head-mounted display also utilized a custom-designed LCD with considerably higher resolution than anything else on the market at the time (720×480 elements). Not only was this an expensive solution (it cost $49,000), but VPL began telling customers in mid-1992 that due to reliability problems with the LCDs the HRX had been pulled from the market.

The biggest problem with most color LCDs is their limited resolution—typical ones have 440 horizontal and 240 vertical elements. To make matters worse, it takes a combination of three elements (red, green, and blue) to make a single triad, or pixel.

So the entire display represents only 35,000 pixels compared to a standard Apple Macintosh 9-inch display with 175,000 pixels, or a PC VGA display with 307,000 pixels. This limited resolution doesn't matter when you're watching a Sony Watchman from one to two feet away, but viewing it from two to three inches away through wide field-of-view optics is far less acceptable.

Another problem with low resolution is that, when you're looking through the optics, each LCD element is clearly visible and becomes distracting. This is partially due to the eye's attraction to edge detail and sharp boundaries. The illustration in Fig. 8-10 mimics the degradation in image quality due to low-resolution LCD displays. As you can see, the image on the right is clearly divided into individual elements. It's like looking at the world through a screen door—the pixel boundaries become a barrier between you and the virtual world.

VPL developed a clever method of countering this distraction. They experimented with various filters, like wax paper, to diffuse or blur the image slightly. They found that a soft blur was enough to stop the eye from focusing on the harsh boundaries of the pixels.

In a further refinement, VPL added a small dot pattern on top of the diffuser to counter the fuzziness caused by the diffuser. It was intended to fool the eye into believing that the image was more

Figure 8-10

Resolution of the left image is typical of what you might see on a 640×480 computer monitor. On the right is the same image as it might appear in a low-resolution LCD display through wide-field-of-view optics.

detailed than it was. Today, almost all LCD HMD manufacturers use some form of diffusion filter or depixelator to improve the quality of the displayed image.

LCDs have proven to be an inexpensive method of displaying virtual worlds. Because the displays go into consumer products, their costs can be driven quite low. However, the resolution needs to improve by a factor of ten before they become effective for anything other than entertainment. This kind of dramatic improvement will take a few years to achieve in a low-cost package. In the two years since this book was originally written, little progress has been made as 770×234 color LCD panels (twice the resolution) are only just becoming available to HMD manufacturers.

CRTs One approach to solving the resolution problem is to use commercially available miniature CRTs, with approximately 500- to 1,000-line resolution. These monochrome displays are typically mounted near the ear and the image is reflected into the viewer's eyes. The military uses this approach because the resolution and brightness of the CRTs allow them to be used as heads-up displays (HUDs), even in bright daylight.

These CRTs are very similar in principle to the inexpensive low-resolution versions found in any video-camera viewfinder. Their biggest limitation is that the displays are mostly monochrome and the HMD manufacturer must properly shield users from the 800 to several thousand volts positioned near their head (of course, there's very little electrical current involved so the danger is much less than might be expected).

In one implementation, the CRT image is projected onto a complex set of optics that reflects it into the viewer's eyes (see Fig. 8-11). Sutherland pioneered this technique back in 1968 and it continues to be in use today. One of its key advantages is that the optics in front of the person's eyes can be semireflective so that the outside world remains in view. This is crucially important if the person wearing the HMD is also operating an aircraft.

Figure 8-11

Kaiser Electronics

Prototype of a CRT-based, advanced HUD display helmet designed for helicopter pilots.

Color is the biggest problem facing CRT displays. Creating a high-resolution miniature color CRT is beyond the capabilities of even today's high-tech wizardry. It simply isn't possible to manufacture a

shadowmask (a metal screen placed just behind the glass face) with the required mechanical dimensions.

However, a color display can be created with a single monochrome CRT that has a rapidly switching LCD color filter placed in front of it. By quickly displaying a single scan line or field in first red, then green, and then blue, the eye perceives only the combined color and not the discrete elements.

This technique gives a high-resolution color display without much additional hardware, but it does require a scan frequency of three times the normal rate. A standard workstation monitor with a 1,000×1,000-pixel display is scanned at least once every 60th of a second, which means that it has about a 60-MHz bandwidth. To avoid flickering, a filtered CRT at the same resolution would have to run three times faster (or at 180 MHz), which requires customized high-speed electronics.

Even with this limitation, various designs based on this technique are commercially available. Tektronix, based in Oregon, sells a version of a VGA-resolution (640×480), one-inch monochrome CRT with an LCD color shutter for around $16,000 a pair. This is used by N-Vision, a high-end HMD manufacturer. Virtual Research found a less expensive supplier of monochrome CRTs with a spinning color wheel capable of 493×250 resolution and used them in their Eyegen3 product. CRT-based designs are currently the highest resolution on the market.

Fiberoptics Using bundled fiberoptic cables, companies like Polhemus Labs and CAE-Link have created a simple, high-resolution, head-mounted display (see Fig. 8-12). Doctors have used similar, smaller-diameter bundles called *endoscopes* to explore a patient's internal structure without using surgery.

For HMDs, a color light-valve projects a bright, high-resolution image onto one end of a fiberoptic cable about one inch thick that contains at least one million fibers. The image that emerges from the other end is then reflected into the viewer's eyes.

Figure 8-12

Example of using fiberoptic cables in a lightweight head-mounted display. Polhemus Labs

Though the idea is very simple, manufacturing a pair of optically correct cables like this is very expensive (depending on the number of fibers). The expense of this approach has restricted its use to only the most advanced HMDs where cost isn't a significant factor but resolution and light weight is.

Fiberoptics, CRTs, and LCD displays represent the bulk of commercially available techniques for building head-mounted displays. The LCD approach dominates the field, due to its low cost and ease of integration.

Light-emitting diodes (LEDs) An interesting challenge to LCDs is a low-cost monochrome display developed by Reflection Technology. Rapidly vibrating mirrors scan a single column of red LEDs across the user's visual field. As long as everything is carefully synchronized, a full-screen image (720×280) can be created with just a single column of LEDs.

This is all mounted in a small, lightweight package and placed about four inches from the user's face. A mechanical adjustment is provided for focusing the image. A 1,000×1,000 monochrome prototype of this is rumored to exist, but production plans seem to be several years off. Reflection Technology will succeed with this technology only if they can produce a color display.

Head-coupled displays Several companies now produce display systems based on mounting a color CRT or LCD display at one end of a mechanical arm. The arm is either counterbalanced or sprung so that the display has "zero weight." This design was first pioneered by Fake Space Labs in Palo Alto, California. The illustration in Fig. 8-13 shows an example of their BOOM product.

Figure 8-13

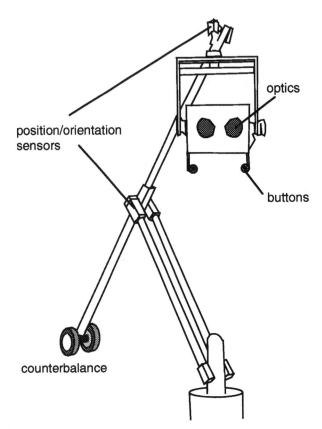

Diagram showing the key elements of a suspended-display system.

By using a counterweighted design, problems with optic and display weight along with display size are eliminated. This also allows much higher-resolution CRT devices to be used instead of low-resolution LCD displays. Six shaft encoders measure the position and

orientation of the display device, providing complete 6-DOF sensing. The shaft encoders almost eliminate the delay between physically changing your view and seeing it change in the display.

The design provides an easy transition from peeking into a virtual world and interacting with a keyboard and monitor to control the simulation, which is one reason it's very popular in the research community.

Back in 1989, only a single LCD-based HMD was on the market. By the end of 1992, at least six different vendors were supplying various forms of visually coupled displays. This increased to over 20 different vendors by mid-1994. As you can see, this is one of the highest-growth areas of VR investment and development. Hopefully, we'll achieve Sutherland's "ultimate display" sooner than anyone predicted.

⇨ Sound

Close your eyes and listen closely to the activity around you. Notice how you can easily identify where sounds are coming from. By measuring the signal delay between your left and right ears, in addition to other factors, your brain can quickly locate the source of a sound. This delay is the *interaural time difference* (ITD) and is part of the study of psycho-acoustics.

Sound reflections off walls and ceilings communicate not only room size, but also whether surfaces are hard or soft. The shift in sound of an approaching vehicle, due to the Doppler effect, helps us to estimate its speed. Listening to sounds when objects interact helps us identify material properties.

The sharp ringing of glass, the knock of wood, and the rustle of paper are all valuable cues about our environment. Including these cues in a virtual reality system will dramatically enhance what can be learned from the simulation.

⇨ Directional sounds

The pursuit of realistic 3-D sound has revealed interesting insights into how sounds are received and processed by the brain. Several factors control this ability (Begault, 1987 and Greuel, 1991):

Interaural time difference The interaural time difference is the time disparity between each ear receiving the same sound. Our ears can distinguish differences as small as 70 microseconds.

Interaural amplitude difference The interaural amplitude difference is the difference in sound pressure (loudness) of the ear closest to the sound.

Frequency difference As sounds bend around the head, much of the higher frequencies are impaired. High-frequency sounds are less likely to bend than low-frequency sounds because they're more directional. This results in one ear hearing a "brighter" sound than the other.

Head-related transfer functions (HRTFs) The convolutions of the pinnae, or outer ear, not only gather sounds, they also reinforce certain sound frequencies. The HRTFs are a summed measure of the pinnae's response to varying frequencies of sound.

Of all these factors, HRTFs are the most complex to model. Measurements are first gathered by placing small probe microphones inside each ear of a dummy head in an anechoic chamber. A speaker emits a sound at a known frequency while the microphones record the received signal, as shown in Fig. 8-14.

About 150 finite impulse responses (FIRs) are measured while the speaker is moved to different locations around each ear. This builds a map of listener-specific "location filters," which are then loaded into a powerful digital signal processor (DSP). Any monaural sound source can then be *convolved* by the DSP to generate separate left and right signals that a listener, wearing headphones, would be able to accurately locate in space.

Figure 8-14

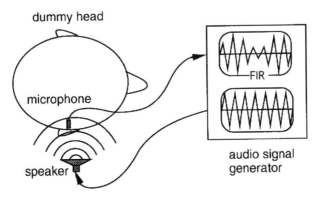

dummy head

microphone

speaker

FIR

audio signal generator

Diagram that shows the process of collecting finite impulse responses (FIRs) in order to acoustically model the pinnae, or outer ear.

Because this process occurs in real time, sounds can be interactively moved or can appear fixed in space as listeners move their head. This is how, in the example at the beginning of chapter 5, the person visiting the virtual living room heard a radio playing from a corner of the room. Even as he moved through the living room, the sound of the radio always appeared fixed in the same location.

All these factors help locate the direction of a sound. To determine its distance, environmental reflections surrounding the sound and the listener become important—especially relationships between direct sound and reflected sound.

Though direct sound levels decrease with distance, reflected sounds tend to remain constant. Additionally, high-frequency sounds are attenuated more by distance than low frequencies. Our brains examine these differences along with the delay between reflected and direct sounds to calculate distances.

Because HRTFs are created in an anechoic chamber, they're incapable of mimicking environmental reflections. This means you wouldn't hear any difference between a radio playing in a large virtual room and one playing in a small virtual room. Nor would it matter if the virtual walls were made of a hard or soft surface.

Obviously, this is a poor representation of the way sounds really work. But the same process of convolving sounds can be used to create simple reflective models of rooms and surfaces. Research efforts have already demonstrated the ability to model a cube-shaped room with four different sound sources in each corner. Reflections from each source are modeled by creating a sound source behind each wall that generates the reflected sounds.

To understand how this works, think of yourself standing in the middle of an empty room. Previously, you stationed a friend behind each wall of the same room. When you shout out any word, they have been told to echo the same word back to you. In the same way, sound sources are positioned and programmed to provide echoes of the main source.

Controlling this allows diverse acoustical environments to be re-created. Acoustical parameters such as room size or shape, along with reflective properties such as hard, soft, or metallic walls, can be quickly changed.

To do all this requires a staggering amount of computing power— 1,200 MFLOPS (megaflops), or million of floating-point operations per second; PCs vary from 0.5 to 4 MFLOPS. Continuing improvements in processing power will bring ever more accurate simulations of sounds.

⇨ Ambient sounds

The uses of sound were covered in chapter 5, *Reality simulators*. In this next section we'll examine the different methods of ambient (nondirectional) sound generation and some of their unique limitations.

By borrowing the same tools musicians use to create sounds, a virtual world designer has almost unlimited flexibility in dealing with sounds. The most popular method of controlling and generating sounds is the MIDI (musical instrument digital interface) standard. Sounds are first digitally sampled, or converted from analog to digital form (like the data on a CD-ROM), then played back using a sequencer.

Any kind of sound can be sampled: voices, musical instruments, and special effects. As they're played back, further modifications can be made, like changes in pitch or the sound envelope, or reverberations (echoes). Depending on the complexity of the sequencer, you can simultaneously generate multiple outputs (typically four or more), with each output handling up to 16 notes at a time. Some sequencers can be connected, doubling the number of sound sources.

In the virtual world, the designer simply sends a command like "play note 14 on channel 1" or "increase pitch by 25 percent on channel 2, note 16." Additional commands control the volume and timing of all notes and channels. One limitation of using an external MIDI sequencer is that you have to preload all the sounds necessary for the simulation.

Using the MIDI standard, the computer can control hundreds of different kinds of musical devices. Almost all electronic music devices speak the MIDI language. In addition, many different tools exist for sampling and creating unique sound effects.

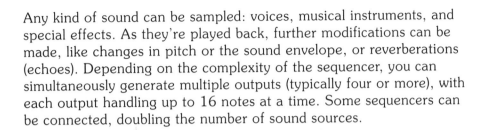 # Sound limitations

Sound differs from visual information in at least one important regard—it requires a rigidly fixed playback speed. If you start playing back a sampled sound, nothing can interrupt it until it's finished, or the sound will be noticeably distorted.

The same isn't true for visual signals. You can speed up, slow down, and even pause a movie on your VCR and still easily understand what you're watching. You can't pause a sound recording, however, and if you fast-forward or reverse it all you'll hear is something unintelligible.

This difference is important because in virtual environments the frame rate usually varies from instant to instant depending on what the participant is looking at. If sound was synchronized to the frame rate, it would be continuously shifting, like playing back a cassette tape in a badly worn-out tape player. Obviously, sounds used in

virtual environments have to be designed to be independent of the frame rate.

In addition to variations in the visual frame rate, the operating systems used by most VR systems are not based on real time. This means there's no fixed schedule as to when any event occurs, and events can be preempted by other events. This wreaks havoc when attempting to generate sounds note by note instead of playing back prerecorded samples.

This also means that movielike musical soundtracks, where visual action is synchronized to a prerecorded audio signal, are difficult in a virtual environment because there's no easy way to maintain synchronization. Instead, sounds are generally keyed to activities or events in the virtual world, like playing back a presampled sound of a thud when a door is shut, or musical notes when someone presses a particular button.

One solution to this problem is for virtual environments to run at fixed frame rates. Multimillion-dollar scene generators have this capability, but it will be a few years before it's available on lower-cost systems.

Despite all these problems, you might be surprised to learn that we're far closer to accurately modeling sound than we are to generating realistic images. It might be just a few more years when, closing your eyes, you won't be able to tell the difference between what's real and what isn't.

⇨ Haptic

Unlike sight and sound output devices, which deal with easily reproducible forces, tactile or force-feedback devices require complex electromechanical interaction with the human body. It's one thing to slip headphones and a display device on your head, but it's much different to insert your arm and hand into an enclosing structure capable of measuring and reflecting the forces of virtual objects.

It doesn't seem likely that we'll ever be able to achieve the same level of realism with tactile senses that we will with visual and aural senses.

The complexity of generating the necessary sensations to clearly recognize the difference between a felt-covered and cloth-covered virtual surface without restricting body movement is far beyond today's technology.

It isn't only a problem of building the appropriate mechanical devices to generate the feedback, it's also a problem of understanding and simulating the correct forces. In fact, representational models for describing these haptic forces barely exist.

How do you explain "a felt-covered surface" to a computer? What parameters help you distinguish between a felt- and a cloth-covered surface? These issues have only recently been tackled, and they're far from being part of today's 3-D CAD systems.

As mentioned earlier, tactile and force feedback are two different forms of haptic perception. Tactile feedback represents the forces acting on your skin, while force feedback represents the forces acting on your muscles, joints, and tendons.

 Tactile feedback

Wearing a special glove developed in England, you can experience a virtual world in a totally new fashion (see Fig. 8-15). If you visited the house on the hill from chapter 5 wearing one of these gloves, a new dimension of the virtual world would appear.

Reaching out with your gloved hand, you might notice a slight pressure on your fingertips as you touched the surface of a virtual sofa. Nothing would stop you from inserting your hand into the sofa, but the deeper you sank, the more pressure you would feel. Removing your hand, the pressure would disappear.

This is one example of how tactile feedback might be used to help locate virtual surfaces. It's an important contribution because most virtual environments have a ghostly, insubstantial feel to them. Providing even a limited amount of tactile feedback greatly increases the ability to interact with objects. Two different approaches have evolved for tactile stimulation: air pressure and vibrations.

Figure 8-15

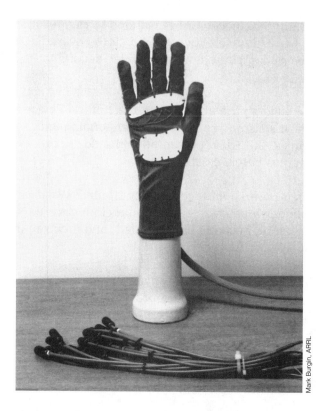

The Teletact I glove was the first device to provide tactile feedback for a virtual environment.

The use of small air bladders was pioneered in 1991 by Airmuscle Limited and the Advanced Robotics Research Center (ARRC) in England. By using a two-glove system, one to measure forces and the other to display them, ARRC created a tool for the simulation of tactile forces.

The input glove possessed 20 force-sensitive resistors (FSRs), distributed across the underside of the hand. The output glove had 20 correspondingly located air pockets that could be proportionally inflated up to 12 pounds-per-square-inch (psi). By using control electronics and a compressor, pressures could be quickly modulated based on real-time input.

Next, working with VPL Research, ARRC combined their glove with VPL's DataGlove. In doing so, they discovered problems with reliability from both a physical and calibration point of view (Stone,

1992). They found that the glove would lose calibration and become highly frustrating to use, and the fingers would exhibit sporadic movements and even bend in physically impossible shapes.

To eliminate these problems, they built a hand-held device called the Teletact Commander, using only three to five air bladders. After attaching a position and orientation sensor to it, they found it to be a successful method of controlling a robotic arm.

Another method of tactile stimulation uses small vibrating transducers. These can be as simple as a voice coil from a disassembled speaker, or as complex as esoteric shape-memory alloys. These special alloys change shape and flex when an electrical current is applied to them, as shown in Fig. 8-16. They can be made in just about any size (currently, they're about the size of a paper clip and ⅛ of an inch thick) and can be placed anywhere on the skin's surface.

Figure 8-16

These small transducers can create minute vibrations or momentary impulses and can be placed anywhere on the skin.

Unlike air bladders, transducers can respond almost instantly to a control signal. This makes them well suited to generating discrete sensations like moving a finger over a rough surface. However, air bladders generate larger forces than current shape-memory alloys, which makes them more useful for representing the gentle pressure of, say, holding an egg.

Both techniques are starting points in the development and refinement of tactile forces. They serve mostly as experimental tools in learning about the nature of this complicated sense.

Additional research into tactile displays has been pioneered by a small company, Begej Corp., based in Colorado. Since 1986 they have been working on creating tactile displays for JPL and Wright Patterson AFB, and they're currently working on one for the NASA Johnson Space Center. Their first project resulted in a glove device with about 50 *taxels* (a term coined by the founder to describe individual tactile input or output sensors) distributed across several fingers, joints, and the thumb. Each taxel output device measures about 3mm in diameter and is designed to connect to a taxel input sensor mounted on a robot hand. This would allow the operator of a remote robot arm some sense of touch as the robot hand encountered objects.

Begej Corp.'s latest project involves building a tactile display for the entire upper body. Up to 512 taxels are distributed across the forearms, upper torso, thighs, chest, stomach, and pelvic regions of the body. Taxels, 10mm in size, attach to a tight-fitting spandex suit and are capable of generating up to 3mm of vertical motion. Taxels are driven with a 10-Hz analog signal, with modulation of the signal's amplitude to convey the sense of touch. Again, the body suit is designed to be driven by duplicate sensors mounted on a dual-arm robot—though with suitable electronics this could be connected to a VR system.

Though Begej is still a couple years from commercializing their system (and even then it will be fairly expensive), they have demonstrated some of the intriguing possibilities for finally reaching out and touching someone in VR.

Force feedback

In chapter 3 you read about Frederick Brooks' attempts at the University of North Carolina to harness a remote manipulator to explore the use of force feedback in simulating molecular docking. While watching a stereoscopic display, chemists wrestled virtual molecules into appropriate docking sites. They actually "felt" the push and pull of simulated molecular forces transmitted through the robotic arm.

Now imagine feeling the weight of virtual objects, or squeezing a virtual ball to determine if it was a hard golf ball or a soft rubber ball. What if you could reach out with your hand and feel either the unyielding surface of a wall or the thick resistance of water?

At the University of Utah, where Sutherland pioneered his head-mounted display in 1968, a system capable of generating exactly these kinds of forces has been developed. It's based on an exoskeleton that fits closely around the arm and hand. At strategic locations on the upper arm and forearm, a metal collar is snugly attached—like a massive high-tech bracelet. Fingers slip into semirigid tubes connected to hydraulic lines or mechanical linkages.

All together, you can move your hand and arm in ten different directions simultaneously (10 degrees of freedom). A computer continuously monitors the precise location and position of all the joints. And despite the 50-odd pounds strapped to your arm, you don't feel more than a slight tug because the computer constantly adjusts the exoskeleton to appear weightless to you.

When you grasp a virtual object, precisely controlled hydraulic actuators allow you to actually feel its weight and stiffness. As you move your arm and bump into a virtual wall, the collars around your arm abruptly stop your movements. Suddenly the virtual world has gained mass and substance. Of course, the complexity and expense of using devices like this will restrict them to only the most exclusive VR labs, but it does demonstrate some intriguing possibilities.

In Michigan, Cybernet Systems is one of the few companies actually shipping a product for systems requiring force feedback. The PER-Force hand controller can be used to mimic forces acting on the operator's hand. Composed of a motorized joystick connected to a robotic arm and six small electric motors attached to various joints, the motors can be programmed to emulate various forces.

Using the PER-Force hand controller, operators controlling a robotic arm might encounter resistance if they moved the robot's arm towards a region that was either dangerous to them or to the robotic arm. Or someone using the hand controller to pilot a remote vehicle might encounter resistance to directing the vehicle in an impossible or hazardous direction. There are many possibilities for using this device.

VR systems that can simulate and generate tactile and force-feedback signals for general use are still a long way off. The most likely application of current haptic technology is to either specific training situations where the high cost of the system is offset by the benefits of improved training or to controlling remote robots and telepresence. This situation will improve as we better understand these haptic forces and incorporate that understanding into current VR tools.

 # Motion platforms

Anyone who saw the movie *Lawnmower Man* might remember a scene where two people were lying face down on a movable bed (known as a *flogiston chair*) and raced through a virtual world. As they maneuvered, their entire bodies pitched and rolled based on their actions.

Although the virtual worlds and movable beds were only special effects (they weren't connected to a real VR system), similar devices do exist. They're known as *motion platforms*, and are available in many different forms. Their use, however, has been limited to either arcade games or very expensive flight and motion simulators (see Fig. 8-17).

Because motion platforms can be easily controlled by a VR system's computer, it's just a matter of time before your sense of

Figure 8-17

CAE-Link Corp.

An example of a sophisticated motion platform built by CAE-Link for use with the Black Hawk flight simulator.

balance is one more perception stimulated by the computer. This is already happening in several recent entertainment systems, such as Magic Edge.

Taken together, all these various output sensors provide different methods of stepping through the new looking glass into various virtual worlds. Through the sensory experience of sight, sound, and touch, we can focus our minds on solving new and complex problems. And by focusing all our powers of perception on a single problem, we can gain new insights and a more intuitive understanding.

⇨ Input sensors

You gain entry to virtual worlds through sensory portals created by various output sensors. Input sensors, on the other hand, allow for movement and interaction once you enter the virtual world. They are key to unlocking the power of interaction. Without them, you can experience the virtual world only passively.

Most input sensors fall into one of two categories: interaction devices or tracking devices (a few devices fit into either category). Interaction devices provide access (the ability to move and manipulate objects at will), while tracking devices monitor various body parts to create a sense of presence, or *affordance* (the feeling of being physically present in the virtual world). Both types of devices are required for the well-dressed cybernaut, two of whom are shown in Fig. 8-18.

⇨ Interaction devices

Just as you use many different tools for different jobs, the same is true for virtual worlds. You wouldn't use a sledgehammer to open a can of soup, nor should you choose the wrong VR tool for a specific task. Fortunately, a virtual world designer has an increasingly large selection of tools to pick from. This rapid proliferation of devices signals the beginning of a very active VR tool-making business.

In chapter 5, we described four primary VR tasks: *navigation*, *selection*, *interaction*, and *command*. The virtual explorer wants to be able to move, or navigate, to a particular point in space, to select objects or other entities, to interact with objects, and to issue commands that control the simulation or interaction. In the same chapter we also discussed how different devices offer different levels of support for these different modes of interaction.

The most important thing to remember when using any of the following devices is that their effectiveness is determined by how well the software accesses the device's capabilities. In fact, many times the

Figure 8-18

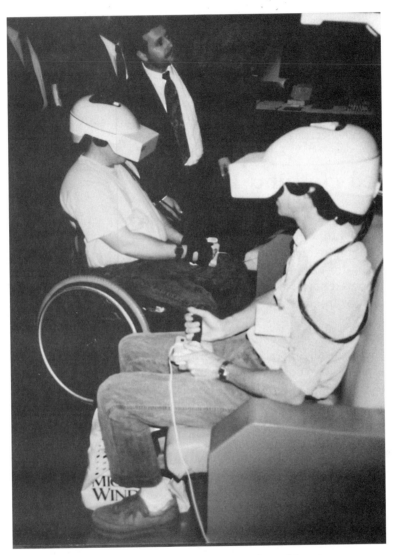

Two people interacting in the same virtual world, using joysticks for navigation. The person sitting in the chair isn't aware that the other person is in a wheelchair because physical limitations become less obvious in virtual environments.

software, more than the physical hardware, determines how these devices are used. This means that by modifying the software you can perform the equivalent of opening a can of soup with a sledgehammer.

Interaction devices can be grouped into several loose categories. There are wired-clothing devices that are worn like a glove or a suit. There are wand devices that you hold in your hand, much like a baton or hand grip. Devices that simultaneously measure six degrees of freedom (6 DOF) are used for navigation and object control. Even a 2-D mouse or a common joystick has its use in VR. Finally, there's a small class of devices that rely on biologic input like voice recognition or muscular-electrical signals.

⇨ Wired clothing

While VPL's DataGlove is one of the most recognized wired-clothing devices, several other approaches exist as well. The basic premise is to wear some external form of tracking device to monitor the position and orientation of key hand or body parts. While this would normally be considered solely a tracking function, wired clothing is usually intended for interaction.

In chapter 3 we described how NASA Ames used VPL's DataGlove device to naturally interact with virtual objects through various techniques. Users could communicate with the computer through simple gestures made with their hands while wearing the wired glove. They could grab virtual objects by sticking a gloved hand into the graphic representation of the object and making a fist.

The computer recognizes the gesture, and the graphic image of the object is attached to the graphic image of the user's hand. When he moves his hand, the object moves with it until he drops it by opening his hand. This is a simple and natural method for interacting with objects.

Wired clothing works by measuring bend angles of various body joints, like fingers, wrists, and elbows. Either mechanical, fiberoptic, or resistive sensors are used. Each approach offers different advantages and limitations.

Fiberoptic sensors are used in the two most popular versions of the wired glove and wired suit. These work by looping a single strand of fiberoptic cable across a joint, like a knuckle (see Fig. 8-19). As the

Figure 8-19

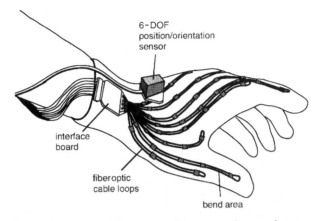

6-DOF
position/orientation
sensor

interface
board

fiberoptic
cable loops

bend area

*This illustration shows the fiberoptic loops that
measure the amount of bend or flex of a body
joint like a knuckle or a wrist. The 6-DOF sensor
keeps track of the position and orientation of the
hand in virtual space.*

knuckle moves, the cable bends, which causes a reduction in the
amount of light passing through it.

This effect is enhanced even more if minute scratches are placed
where the cable passes over the knuckle. The varying light output is
measured by a photodetector and then communicated to a controller,
which summarizes the current state of all the sensors and sends it on
to the computer.

A separate fiberoptic cable loop is needed for each joint, which
means as many as 22 sensors might be used in a single glove. The
simplicity of the design and its intriguing uses have made it a very
popular device, but early versions suffered from a variety of problems
that are still being addressed.

Glove users discovered that constant recalibration was necessary
because the sensor output was very sensitive to knuckle position.
Initial gloves were also very dependent on hand size and tended to be
overly fragile. Most of these problems have either been fixed or will
be soon. The same technology is used in complete body suits that
measure all the major body joint angles.

Electromechanical sensors can also measure bend angles, as shown in Fig. 8-20. These bulky devices are designed so that a direct linear relationship exists between the finger-joint angle and the sensor angle. This makes them less sensitive to different hand sizes and placement on the fingers.

Figure 8-20

This wired glove uses mechanical sensors instead of fiberoptics to precisely measure the amount of flex in the finger joints.

These different types of wired gloves can be used in different ways with a VR system. They can help establish a sense of presence (seeing your hand in the virtual world helps you believe you're really there), help you navigate around, and make it easy for you to manipulate objects.

One important consideration is minimizing the amount of lag between a person wiggling a gloved finger and seeing his virtual finger wiggle in the display. If this lag becomes too great, the glove becomes more difficult to use. Hygienic concerns can also be an issue if a single glove is to be used by dozens of people.

Wired gloves and devices like them offer an intriguing method of interacting in virtual worlds. It will be interesting to see how future applications make use of them.

⇨ Wands

Wands are the simplest VR device available. They're nothing more than a 6-DOF sensor with a couple of switches attached. Because of this simplicity, they're very easy to use in public demonstrations of VR.

One of the strengths of virtual environments is that the appearance of an object can be whatever the designer chooses—it need bear no resemblance to the object's physical appearance. At the click of a button, a device like a wand can look like a drill, paintbrush, spray gun, or sculpting tool.

Many computer paint programs allow you to do the same thing with a mouse. If you select the icon with a spray gun on it, the cursor will change into the shape of a tiny spray gun. Techniques like this allow plenty of freedom in creating a large virtual tool chest with just a single simple device like a wand.

Here are some other ways of using a wand. To select objects, users point the wand at an object and press a button. This causes a laser beam to shoot out, and the closest object intersecting the beam is selected. To navigate, they just point the wand in the appropriate direction and press another button. Wands, like gloves, lose

effectiveness if too much of a delay exists between physically moving the wand and seeing it move in the display.

⇨ 6-DOF devices

Objects, unless constrained, normally have six different directions or rotations they can move in. This is shown in the illustration in Fig. 8-21.

Figure 8-21

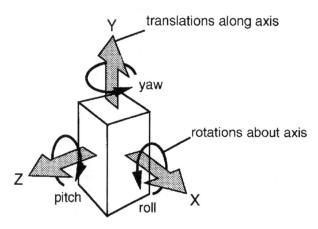

This illustrates the six different directions a 3-D object can move in. Three translations and three rotations are possible.

Objects can move forward or backward (X axis), up or down (Y axis), and left or right (Z axis)—these are known as *translations*. In addition, objects can rotate about any of these principal axes. Borrowing from flight terminology, these rotations are called *roll* (X axis), *yaw* (Y axis), and *pitch* (Z axis). All together, they add up to six different degrees of freedom in which the object can move.

In virtual environments, you typically want to move in any direction without being constrained. This might mean combining several translations and rotations all at once. 6-DOF devices support this by simultaneously measuring the three translations and rotations directly.

Even though it's possible to take a 2-DOF device, like a standard mouse, and use its buttons to move virtual objects in all six directions, this doesn't make it a 6-DOF device. Only by concurrently measuring all six parameters does a device warrant this label.

Two very different approaches provide a 6-DOF capability. Isometric devices use optomechanical methods to measure forces and torques applied to a stationary ball or puck. 6-DOF mice, on the other hand, use 6-DOF sensors to keep track of their position and orientation as they're moved around.

✳ Isometric devices

Although they look like someone stuck a baseball on a joystick or a hockey puck on a metal base, isometric devices differ from joysticks in one crucial respect—there's very little physical movement. Instead, they measure the amount of force or torque. To fly upwards using an isometric device, you simply pick up the ball or puck shape as if you were picking it off a table.

The ball sensor is attached to a base that's secured to a rigid surface, so you can't actually pick the ball up. Instead, the force you exert is measured by six LEDs and six optical sensors located at the center of the device.

A small microcontroller buried in the base interprets the electrical signal from each optical sensor. This is then translated into a set of six values (three translations and three orientations) that are communicated to the computer. These values are relative to the at-rest state of the isometric device. In other words, if no one is touching the ball, all the values should be zero.

A force as small as 0.1 lb. can cause the values to change. The simulation manager running on the computer receives these values and decides what to do with them. In this case, it moves the viewpoint by the relative amount specified by the transmitted record. The result is that you fly upwards. The illustration in Fig. 8-22 depicts the six forces measured by an isometric ball.

Figure 8-22

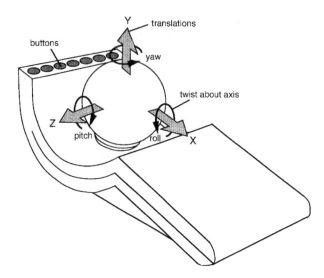

Isometric balls can be manipulated in up to six different directions simultaneously.

Although this method of navigating might seem a little unnatural at first, after 15 or 20 minutes it becomes more comfortable. To fly faster, you just push harder on the ball. Novice pilots can ignore some of the translations or rotations (or have the software constrain them). By turning off pitch and roll motions, they'll find it much easier to control just the three translations and yaw.

In addition to this feature, some isometric devices have up to nine software-programmable buttons for developers to configure. Typically, one of them is used as a "panic button"—which resets your viewpoint if you get completely lost.

Isometric devices work well for navigating or moving objects around. Just as the ball sensor can control your viewpoint, you can also attach it to virtual objects so that moving the ball moves the virtual object in a similar manner. These devices are durable and simple to use, and they're designed for stationary environments instead of ones where a participant might be physically walking about.

✳ 6-DOF mice

Several companies have taken a basic mouse design and modified it by adding some form of 6-DOF or 3-DOF tracking sensor. Either

ultrasonic, electromagnetic, or gyroscopic tracking is used. Some designs include the concept of a clutch that allows you to remain within a set physical volume of space, while moving beyond it in the virtual world.

You do the same thing when you pick up your mouse: it reaches the edge of your mouse pad, and you set it back down in the center. 6-DOF mice usually have two or three buttons, like a regular mouse, for user input.

These devices have many of the same capabilities and limitations as wand devices. Their effective use is primarily dependent on the qualities of their 6-DOF tracking system. These factors, more than anything else, determine how the 6-DOF mice are actually used.

2-DOF devices

Interaction in virtual environments doesn't require complicated and expensive devices. Many tasks can be accomplished with simple 2-DOF devices like mice and joysticks. Joysticks are particularly easy to work with. By limiting the degrees of freedom a new user has to deal with, you can reduce the amount of time and frustration in achieving a task.

For example, if the goal is to move a wall from one place to another—changing its position without affecting its orientation—it might be better to use a joystick because you could easily move the wall in one direction without moving it up and down or left and right at the same time. The other advantage of a joystick is that many people quickly adapt to them—an important issue if the participant has only a few minutes to use the system.

Biologic input sensors

Biologic input sensors, also called *biosensors*, process indirect activity, such as muscle electrical signals and the recognition of voice commands. They use correctly placed dermal electrodes to

detect certain muscle activity. If placed near the eyes, they can be used to navigate through virtual worlds by simple eye movement (see Fig. 8-23).

Figure 8-23

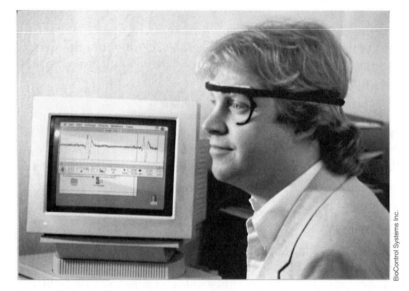

Dermal electrodes, contained in the eyeglass frame, track eye movements by measuring muscle electrical activity.

Squinting or blinking an eye could cause the color of an object to change, or some other action. Placed on the forearms, you could use them to navigate by clenching either the left or right fist.

Some day we might be sophisticated enough to be able to eliminate wired gloves. Instead of a glove, a simple tight-fitting bracelet might be able to distinguish individual finger movements. This kind of technology might also offer people with certain physical disabilities an opportunity to join the rest of us in virtual environments.

Voice recognition has been in development for over 20 years and has recently begun showing up on more and more desktops. Simple voice recognition, using trained voices and discrete commands, has been available for many years. This is a far easier problem than understanding continuous speech and untrained voices.

For virtual environments, the ability to give discrete voice commands, like "open door" or "reset view," is a powerful adjunct to controlling the environment. Voice recognition is useful when keyboard entry is difficult, or the person's hands are involved in some other task. This technology stands a good chance of becoming a standard feature in VR systems because it's well suited to providing hands-free control of the simulation.

⇨ Other interaction devices

On the far fringe of interaction devices are a couple of interesting approaches that don't really fall into any of the other categories. Earlier, we discussed how MIDI sequencers can be programmed to generate sounds. In an interesting twist, MIDI devices like keyboards or other electronic instruments can send signals to the VR system.

This means that you could create a virtual world where every note on a keyboard had a virtual representation. Not only could you hear the music, you could see it. This is an avenue that has yet to be fully explored, but as musicians and artists become familiar with the territory, you can expect some interesting applications.

Another device, recently introduced, solves the problem of bringing your keyboard with you into a virtual world. Based on keyboard-alternative technology (KAT), the single-handed KAT keyboard looks like a handgrip with five keyboard buttons (see Fig. 8-24). Each button has seven different positions, allowing all possible keyboard characters, including upper- and lowercase letters.

And it doesn't have to be used as a keyboard, either. You could create a very versatile device for general interaction by attaching it to a 6-DOF sensor. It would be much like a 6-DOF mouse or wand, but with more capabilities.

For every device we've talked about in this section, there are probably several other brand-new ones being worked on in garages and labs all over the world. You can already see that there are many different solutions to the problems of interaction in a virtual world. The fun part is picking the right one!

Figure 8-24

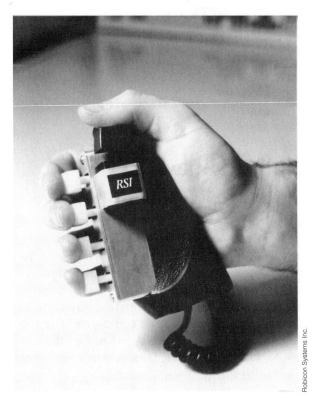

Prototype of a device that will allow keyboards to travel with you into a virtual world. Up to 144 characters can be generated with this one device.

Robicon Systems Inc.

⇨ Tracking devices

Many of the devices and capabilities previously mentioned, such as head-tracking, wands, and wired gloves, rely on the basic ability to detect an object's position and orientation at any instant. Whether you're moving your head or raising your hand, the computer needs to track these movements in real time so the virtual world remains synchronized to your actions.

In the previous section, we mentioned how tracking quality to a large degree determines the effectiveness of interaction. With better tracking, the wand, wired glove, and other devices will become easier to use. Several key parameters determine this effectiveness:

Lag or latency Lag is the delay between sensor movement and the resulting signal being processed for final use. This is one of the most important parameters, as lags above 50 milliseconds (msec) will affect human performance. Unfortunately, not all products specify this crucial parameter. Sensors vary from between 4 and 5 msec to over 100 msec.

Update rate The update rate is the speed at which measurements are made. You can have a lag of 100 msec, but still send 100 measurements per second. Update rate and lag are mostly independent of each other. Most sensors support at least 60 updates per second.

Interference Interference is defined as sensitivity to environmental factors. Sensors can be sensitive to various conditions, like large metal objects, radiation from display monitors, extraneous sounds, and objects coming between the source and the sensor. Problems can also occur when several sensors are used in close proximity to one another.

Accuracy Accuracy in tracking effectiveness is how accurate the position and orientation information is. This usually varies with distance from the source, or drifts over time. Translational values vary from about 0.01 to 0.25 inch, while rotational values vary from 0.1 to 1.0 degree.

Range The range is the maximum distance between the source and sensor, while retaining the specified accuracy. This varies greatly with different sensor types. It can range from a three- to eight-foot cube surrounding the source to an entire room.

All trackers work by measuring changes in position or orientation relative to some reference point or state. Typically there's a *source*, which generates a signal, a *sensor*, which receives the signal, and a *control box*, which processes the signal and communicates with the computer. Their relationship is illustrated in Fig. 8-25.

After the sensor is attached to an object and both the source and sensor are correctly oriented, the control box is sent an initialization signal from the computer. This establishes the current orientation and position as the reference point. If the source and sensor aren't correctly aligned at this stage, you might not know which way is up—up might be down and left might be right.

Figure 8-25

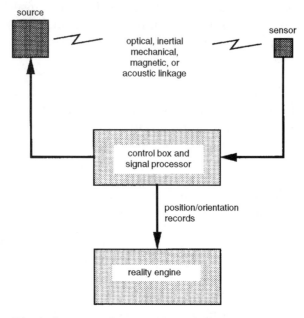

Block diagram of a typical tracking system. The source transmits a signal that's picked up by the sensor and converted to position and orientation information.

This is why you have to be careful to hold the HMD or wand in a particular position at startup (though it can be easily reset later on). After this initialization, or calibration, the tracker is ready to start sending values to the simulation manager.

⇨ Relative versus absolute tracking

Earlier, we discussed how isometric devices return relative values based on how hard they're pushed or pulled. If no forces are applied, they return zero values. 6-DOF trackers, on the other hand, return absolute values, which define exactly where objects are in space. It's important to understand this difference if you plan on using them.

Let's use the book you're currently reading as an example. If you pick a corner of the room as the origin of a coordinate system and lie the book flat in the corner, you can describe its location using Cartesian

coordinates (X, Y, and Z) and its orientation by using Euler angles (roll, pitch, and yaw). If the book is lying flat at the origin point, these values are all zero.

Now pick up the book and sit in a chair without changing the orientation of the book. Assume you have translated the book to a new position, for example, 10 feet from both walls and 4 feet up, or (10,4,10). Because you didn't change the orientation of the book, the Euler angles remain (0,0,0). If you now rotate the book 45 degrees around the Z axis, you've changed its pitch by 45 degrees and the new Euler angle is (0,0,45). See Fig. 8-26 for an illustration of these orientation values.

Figure 8-26

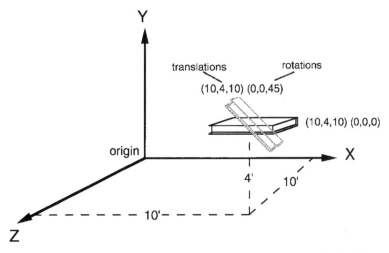

Any object's position and orientation in space can be defined by six values—three for its position and three for its orientation.

By using these six values, you can describe everything you need to know about an object's position and orientation. And, unlike a relative sensor that returns to zero if left alone, an absolute sensor continuously returns its position and orientation if stationary.

Once the sensor has made a measurement and the control box has processed it, the *record* must be passed to the computer. Most 6-DOF trackers provide two communications modes—streaming and polling—to do this.

In *streaming* mode, records are constantly generated by the tracker as fast as it can send them over the serial line (the same serial line you would use to hook up a modem). In *polling* (or demand) mode, records are sent only when requested by the simulation manager. This is how most sensors are controlled because it reduces the amount of effort required to communicate with the device.

Because most trackers communicate over an RS232, or serial, line, the size of the record being transmitted can become a factor in the overall lag or delay of the tracker. Even at 9,600 bps, sending six 16-bit words takes at least 13 msec. This is a big chunk of time when you're trying to stay under 50 msec overall.

⇨ Tracking technology

Several different approaches have evolved for detecting an object's position and orientation. Most of them require a transmitter and a small sensor device attached to either an object or body part. This approach is known as *active tracking* because it involves broadcasting a signal by a transmitter, which is picked up by a receiver or sensor on the tracked object. Active 6-DOF trackers use either electromagnetic, mechanical, optical, or ultrasonic techniques for making 6-DOF measurements.

The alternative, *passive tracking*, uses cameras, optical, or inertial sensors to "watch" an object and determine its position and orientation. Unlike active tracking, passive systems require only a sensor to track objects.

✴ Electromagnetic

This is the most popular method of active tracking because of the sensor's small size and freedom of movement. A low-frequency signal generated by a control box sequentially excites three small coils of wire in the source, creating three magnetic fields.

When a similar set of three coiled wires is positioned in range of the source, a small voltage is induced in each of the coils as the three fields are created. This yields a total of nine measurements that are then processed by the control box to yield six values for position and orientation.

This technique was first developed over ten years ago by a company called Polhemus, for military applications. (The Polhemus FASTRAK system is shown in Fig. 8-27.) The same device was used by NASA Ames and Tom Furness to perform head-tracking for their HMD prototypes.

Figure 8-27

The Polhemus FASTRAK is an example of an electromagnetic tracker that can simultaneously support up to four sensors with one source. The large cube is the source and the smaller cubes are sensors.

It has since evolved into a reliable and accurate method of tracking. Because the sensor is about the size of a dice cube and doesn't rely on line of sight, it can be buried inside other devices, like wands or wired gloves.

Its chief limitation has been lengthy lag times due to signal processing and filtering each set of nine measurements. However, improvements by manufacturers since 1992 have dramatically reduced this lag to less than 5 msec (unfiltered), greatly improving its usefulness. Its only other problem is a sensitivity to large metal objects and magnetic fields generated by nearby TVs and workstation monitors. Newer trackers provide a synchronization sensor that can be placed on a TV or display to reduce interference from these sources.

Many of these problems, however, are usually easy to avoid. From a performance and usability standpoint, this type of tracker is one of the easiest to work with. In addition, a special mode allows multiple sensors to work with a single control box, which lets several objects or body parts be tracked at once within the same control space.

✳ Ultrasonic

This approach typically uses three ultrasonic transducers and three small microphones (active tracking). The transducers are usually mounted in a triangular arrangement in a frame one to three feet in size. A much smaller sensor, containing three-pin microphones, is placed on the object to be tracked.

Using the same principle as before, each ultrasonic transducer emits a high-frequency sound pulse that's picked up by all three microphones. A signal processor measures the time delay (and therefore the distance) between each transducer and each set of microphones. Next, the nine distance measurements are processed to yield the required values.

A big advantage of most ultrasonic trackers is that sensor lag is typically much less than 25 msec, allowing rapid head movements with only a small detectable delay. Unfortunately, the tracking system suffers from several other deficiencies. For accurate readings, the transducers must remain in sight of the sensor microphones. If they're obstructed by some other object or are tilted away from the transducers, the signal can be lost. In addition, they're subject to external noise like keys jingling, glasses clinking, and other ultrasonic sensors used for light or security systems.

One interesting version of an ultrasonic system is manufactured by Transition State Corporation. This system uses four ultrasonic transmitters placed in the four corners of a room. A ten-inch-long, wireless wand picks up the ultrasonic tracking signals and uses radio frequencies to communicate the information to control electronics in a PC. Up to four wands can be tracked simultaneously in a 700-square-foot region. This is one of the few systems that can cover such a broad area.

✳ Mechanical

Less well known than the previous two techniques is the mechanical tracking system, which uses a direct mechanical connection between a reference point and the object to be tracked (active tracking). This is typically a mechanical arm with rotating joints, allowing for full 6-DOF tracking.

One version uses a lightweight arm connecting a control box to a simple headband. As the person moves his head, encoders placed at all six joints measure the change in position. This approach has the advantage of being very fast (lag time of less than 5 msecs), accurate, and relatively inexpensive. However, it suffers from a fairly restricted range of motion. This method of tracking is well suited to the head-coupled displays created by Fake Space Labs and LEEP Systems. One version of this approach from Shooting Star Technology is shown in Fig. 8-28.

Figure 8-28

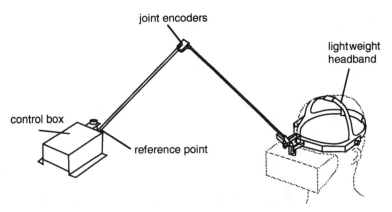

A mechanical arm can provide a simple and inexpensive method of head-tracking. Shooting Star Technology

✳ Inertial

A very different approach is to use a couple of miniature gyroscopes, or inclinometers, to measure yaw, pitch, and roll (passive tracking). These aren't true 6-DOF sensors because they typically measure only orientations and not translations, but they could be effective as head-tracking sensors where position information is rarely required.

Gyroscopic sensors rely on the principle of the conservation of angular momentum. Using a rapidly spinning wheel suspended in a gimballed housing, any change in orientation is resisted by the wheel. This same principle explains why a bicycle is difficult to keep upright when you first start to pedal it, but takes little or no effort to remain upright once you're up to speed. The resistance of the spinning wheel to changes in orientation can be measured several different ways and converted into values of yaw, pitch, and roll.

For head-tracking purposes, two miniature gyroscopes (no bigger than a film canister) could be mounted in an HMD. A tiny motor spins the inertial weight at 10,000 revolutions per minute (rpm). Changes in motion are reflected on a pattern illuminated by an LED. The reflected beam is picked up by an optical sensor and translated into an orientation angle. To get all three values of yaw, pitch, and roll, one gyroscope is mounted vertically and the other horizontally. An exploded view of a miniature gyroscope is illustrated in Fig. 8-29.

Figure 8-29

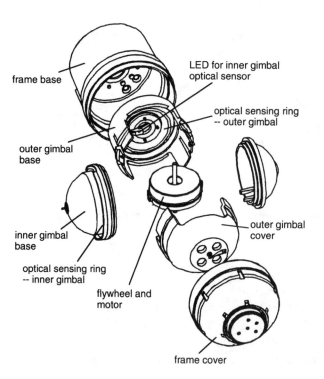

frame base

LED for inner gimbal optical sensor

optical sensing ring -- outer gimbal

outer gimbal base

inner gimbal base

optical sensing ring -- inner gimbal

flywheel and motor

outer gimbal cover

frame cover

Exploded diagram of a miniature gyroscope that can measure orientations. Gyration Inc.

Gyroscopes provide fast, accurate tracking in a compact package. They don't need a separate source or transmitter, so their range is determined only by the length of their cable. Though initially expensive, in volume they can be manufactured quite cheaply. Their biggest flaw is that they suffer from significant amounts of drift—up to ten degrees per minute. Improved versions will reduce this to two degrees per minute, but it still remains an important drawback to their use as 3-DOF sensors.

Flux-gate sensors are another form of inertial tracking commonly used by the military for various guiding purposes. They can track only orientation changes and are based on the principle of inducing a small voltage in a coil of wire based on changes in physical orientation. These types of sensors typically have low accuracy (± 1 degree) and a limited range of motion, and can track only a single degree of freedom.

✳ Optical

Several infrared trackers, based on principles already covered, are available or are being researched. One system, used in aircraft simulators, has three or four infrared LEDs mounted on top of an HMD. Sensors, mounted on a support above the HMD, perform line-of-sight tracking with imperceptible lag (active tracking). In fact, in one configuration, the system tracks accurately even at ranges of up to 30 feet. Unfortunately, it uses expensive signal-processing hardware that restricts its use to high-end simulators.

Another company, Origin, has created an "optical radar" tracking system that measures position information based on a small optical target placed on an object (passive tracking). Using image-processing techniques, a computer locks on to the small (7mm) target and maintains tracking as long as it is in direct view. This system works well when someone is facing a monitor and only head-position information is required (the current system doesn't perform orientation tracking).

At the University of North Carolina, they've experimented with mounting four cameras on top of an HMD—all pointed at the ceiling. In addition, they string about 1,000 infrared LEDs uniformly across the ceiling. A computer sequentially pulses the LEDs and

simultaneously processes the camera's image to detect a flash (active tracking). Based on this, it calculates the position and orientation.

Several universities have investigated using multiple video cameras and image extraction techniques to determine where someone is looking or to track body movements (passive tracking). The relative simplicity of this approach comes only at the expense of some very complex calculations in order to perform the tracking accurately. It will be several years before such a system makes it out of the lab.

Like head-mounted displays, most 6-DOF sensors are a forced compromise between cost and performance. The "perfect" low-cost tracker has yet to be developed. Until a large-volume VR application shows up, bringing low-cost, effective trackers to market, these devices will remain expensive.

Because tracking technology is at the heart of many VR devices, improvements in cost or performance have important repercussions. And like interaction devices, the technology behind tracking devices promises to constantly evolve and explore new solutions. More cost-effective solutions are out there; they just need to be brought to market.

Conclusion

The intent of this entire chapter was to communicate the richness of tools and technologies available for interacting with and exploring virtual worlds. We also wanted to show how the first steps have been made so you can understand the nature of this new man/machine interface.

By exploiting the innate capabilities of our senses, we can achieve insights not possible with other methods. But keeping current with the latest tools and techniques is a constant struggle in such a rapidly evolving field. In this chapter, we hope to have equipped you with a basic understanding of the technology, allowing you to follow the many developments yet to come.

Designing virtual worlds

"To see a World in a Grain of Sand
And a Heaven in a Wild Flower,
Hold Infinity in the palm of your hand
And Eternity in an hour."
William Blake, *Auguries of Innocence*

CREATING virtual worlds is a new field full of challenges and rewards. Largely unexplored, it beckons the adventurous, the curious, and the inventive mind with its flexibility and power. In a scientist's hands it becomes a tool as basic as a microscope. To a teacher it suggests new ways of educating children and adults. For many people it's simply a great new form of entertainment. And for artists it inspires new forms of art, ones in which there's no longer a separation between art and audience.

There are a handful of world builders who have already begun exploring some of this new territory where almost anything can be simulated or suggested. They find themselves studying perception and psychology, but also borrowing from the art world with its long traditions of creating virtual worlds inside people's imaginations. Theater, painting, music, and story-telling have lessons and insights for the world builder.

The first question is, what does the world builder want to achieve? How does he set parameters and limits when the dynamic laws of a virtual environment, the basic rules it runs on, can be as unreal as those in *Alice's Adventures in Wonderland?*

There was more to Wonderland than a white rabbit and a cheshire cat; Alice explored a world where distortions of space and time and the humanlike response of objects were integral parts of the story. In the playful way Lewis Carroll structured the reality of Wonderland, he inadvertently foreshadowed some of the scientific insights of quantum mechanics and Einstein's theory of relativity (40 years before Einstein published his theories and overhauled the paradigm of reality).

At the subatomic level and the speed of light, reality begins to behave in strange ways analogous to Lewis Carroll's Wonderland. For example, if you could travel fast enough you would find that, at the speed of light, there's no duration or movement—everything is stuck in one place, one moment. Alice learned the same to be true in Wonderland when she was unable to move forward no matter how fast she ran. "Now, here, you see," said the Red Queen to Alice, "it takes all the running you can do, to keep in the same place." Such a playful virtual world might be helpful today to teach Einstein's nonintuitive discoveries in grammar school or college.

More so than engineers and scientists, painters, musicians, playwrights, and storytellers have specialized in developing ways to enchant and engage the mind. They have used abstraction, perspective, plot, memory, ambiguity, mystery, suspense, and symbolism to communicate, educate, and inspire. These techniques are available to the world builder to create more useful and engaging virtual worlds.

Every element of a virtual world is a design decision. What colors, shapes, and sounds should you use? What effects will your choices have on the user? How do you make something appear realistic, and does that really serve your purposes? How do you structure an application when you can make it do anything you want? How do you guide users when they can do anything they want—or anything might happen?

None of these problems are definitely answered yet; the field is just too new. In the chapters ahead you'll read about the brave new worlds already being created and see how the creators of virtual worlds have tried to answer some of these questions. But first let's

look into how the mind works and plays to discover some of the insights of the early virtual world builders.

⇨ Software of the mind

"The virtual world is to the cognitive map as the ecosystem is to the biostructure."

Bob Jacobson, VR consultant

Building virtual environments requires some understanding of the patterns and behaviors of the mind. Working together, our senses and central nervous system create our own personal virtual reality—sensing *is* believing. Marshall McLuhan pointed out that an enhancement of any one sense alters the information reaching the brain, thereby changing the way we think, act, and perceive the world.

For example, the invention of the microscope and telescope extended our ability to *see*; they made us aware that our world contained forms of life smaller than we could see and planets floating far out in space.

The invention of the telephone and the radio extended our ears and gave us the ability to instantly communicate around the world, thereby changing our notions of time, distance, and community. Anyone who wears glasses or a hearing aid can testify how even these simple tools can change your sense of reality.

Computers designed for virtual reality are the first tools that act as an extension of the entire mind because they enhance all the senses to create environments. Just like the mind, these computers can create new realities.

As humans, we experience the world through the sensory portals of sight, hearing, kinesthesis, smell, and taste. These sensors impose limits on what we know and bias our understanding of the world. Many animals have seeing, hearing, or a sense of smell far more acute than our own, giving them a very different experience of their surroundings.

The brain takes in data from the senses and analyzes, filters, and abstracts it, thereby imposing limits on what we know. Consider the researcher who wore special glasses that made the world appear upside down—initially he couldn't make sense of anything or even walk around, but after a few days his brain adapted and the inverted view became "normal" to him. He was able to walk around without any assistance. In fact, without the glasses the world now appeared inverted. Without conscious effort the brain abstracted the sensory information and imposed its own interpretation.

Representational systems

One of the most important facts about how the brain creates individual experience is that each of us processes our experiences differently, in terms of *representational systems*. Representational systems are those internal sense media that we use to experience the world around us. These internal media channels mimic the brain's input sensors. Just as our eyes bring in outside images, our brains use internal pictures and movies to represent ideas and memories.

We have ears, and we can talk to ourselves and create or remember sounds and music. And we rely on internal sensations such as emotions and "gut feel" for guiding our decisions. While the "hardware" of the brain is chemically based, the "software" operates by using these internal representations of the five senses. Representational systems are the internal media that convey thoughts—the software of the mind.

Dr. John Grinder, a linguist and co-founder of the neurolinguistic programming field, has done extensive research into how people's representational thinking is reflected in their language, habits, beliefs, and behaviors. He found that, while everyone's representational systems are operating all the time, we each have a favorite—a learning bias. This favorite mode shapes our sense of reality by twisting and filtering our point of view.

Mathematicians, architects, and engineers tend to be visually oriented people who think in terms of images. Musicians obviously tend to

favor the auditory mode, while physical therapists, sculptors, and athletes are usually kinesthetically oriented thinkers.

This isn't to say that their other modes don't operate. Thinking is a combination of all the modes working together. But when visually oriented people try to understand something, they tend to focus on the visual portion of their experience—it's the mode they've specialized in to comprehend the world.

For example, decision-making is an imaginative trial-and-error process where many people compare images to other images while experiencing certain reactions to the options. However, for a more auditory-oriented person, images are accompanied by an internal conversation that's equal to or more significant than the imagery.

The crucial interactivity of all these thinking modes and the way they vary from person to person is why multisensory world building is vital for creating convincing, engaging environments.

When developing a virtual world, a developer's own biases can inadvertently cause him to favor one sensory mode over others. Much of the early world building has been done by engineers and scientists who have concentrated on visual experiences. Teachers will tell you that, while the visual mode is the strongest sense among humans, there are many people and cultures who pay more attention to the other channels.

The first lesson virtual world builders need to learn is to fully exploit all the sensory software channels available. Reality is a multisensory experience.

Submodalities

"There are children playing in the street who could solve some of my top problems in physics, because they have modes of sensory perception that I lost long ago."
J. Robert Oppenheimer, father of the atom bomb

Unlike the randomness of everyday reality, a virtual experience is a planned experience in which every sensory detail is a design decision. The usefulness of virtual environments is not that it duplicates all the details of reality (a feat technically impossible), but because it functions like our consciousness—as a filter and focus, presenting only those details essential for enhancing a specific experience or solving a given problem.

Story-telling is an auditory method of creating virtual worlds. Words evoke images, experiences, meaning, and when properly used they can vicariously give us powerful experiences. In his 1978 book, *Therapeutic Metaphors*, the research therapist David Gordon laid out a process for intentionally structuring stories he told to people to help them understand and resolve problems—personal or intellectual.

David Gordon went beyond the abstract study of story structure and delved into the individual's personal experience of the story. He approached his task as a developer of virtual worlds, exploring how the brain makes meaning and how it handles internal representations to create engagement with the listener. He discovered that the smallest elements of experience actually hold the most significance.

People divide sensory information into small, discrete units. These units are called *submodalities*. The submodalities of vision include color, brightness, form, movement, saturation, and pattern (among others). Auditory submodalities include pitch, intensity, pattern, location, and timbre.

Each type of submodality is responsible for encoding information along a particular dimension of an experience. Normally, as information is processed at increasingly complex levels, generalization is gained at the expense of detail. Submodalities are the way humans compress meaning and significance into the smallest details our minds can represent to us consciously.

When you ask people to describe their experience, they generally use words that stand for the whole experience: "I feel upset," "I smell flowers," "I hear music." These kinds of words describe the entire category of the experience. But if you ask them to specify what they're seeing, hearing, feeling, and smelling, they'll answer with

submodalities: "There's a pressure in my chest," "It smells light and kind of sweet," "The music is strong and quick."

What this suggests is that the smallest details of experience are understood at the submodal level. They are the quantum mechanics of experience, the smallest building blocks of thought to which people assign specific intellectual and emotional meaning.

Understanding submodalities can aid in the design of any virtual world, such as the design and testing of a jet wing created on a computer. Steve Bryson and Creon Levit at NASA Ames have developed a virtual wind tunnel to test computer-designed jets. The application runs on supercomputers and displays its output on a high-resolution Fake Space boom.

As the computer calculates the effects of wind passing over the virtual wing, Bryson and Levit have imitated the classic wind-tunnel techniques of smoke injection by creating streamers of color that pass over the wing, curling and rippling to reveal the shape of the wind's turbulence.

A designer who's conscious of submodalities could explore additional ways of adding meaningful feedback to the simulation. The smoke stream could be programmed to change color depending on variables like shifts in wind speed or reactions of the wing. Sounds could be added as a separate channel of information with various tones, notes, locations in space, words, and pitches to signify different data.

If we had the haptic technology, even the texture of the wind might be given various levels of meaning. In this way a designer could walk the wing of the virtual jet and each of his sensory channels would bring him specific data, revealing a variety of insights about his wing design.

Stretching this paradigm even further, it's possible to imagine a time in the next century when each sensory channel will acquire its own alphabet. The blind already have a touch-sensitive alphabet, Braille. Musicians have musical scales and notes. Individual professions might develop their own multisense languages for providing information for ear, eye, nose, and fingertip.

There's already an extensive array of medical and psychological research on how people categorize experience. Table 9-1 lists the relationships between various submodalities. Some of these equivalences have been established experimentally (particularly the relationships between color and pitch, color and temperature, and brightness and loudness). Others arise from David Gordon's work in creating auditory virtual realities for clients.

Table 9-1   **Equivalences between submodalities**

Vision	Audition	Kinesthesis	Olfaction
Color	Pitch	Temperature	Fragrance
Brightness	Loudness	Pressure	Concentration
Saturation	Timbre	Texture	Essence
Shape	Patterning	Form	- - - - -

The interplay of sensory submodalities affects our experience. For example, auditory stimulation affects color perception. "Low tones make colors darker, warmer, unclear, and dirty. With high tones colors usually become brighter, colder, sharply contoured, and more solid or surfacy." (Rayan, 1940 and London, 1954).

And seeing influences hearing; in a green-illuminated room auditory sensitivity is increased, and in a red-illuminated room sensitivity is reduced. When we're locked up in a dark room sensitivity decreases, but if we're bathed in a white light it increases. The length of a tone will be judged as lasting longer than that of a light stimulus even though they're presented for the same duration.

Blocks appear to be larger or smaller, depending on the color they've been painted. Going from largest apparent size to smallest apparent size, the subject ranking of colors is yellow, white, red, green, blue, and black.

Color exerts a similar and stronger effect on judgments of object weight (Payne, 1958 and 1961). Objects that are black, blue, or red tend to be judged heavier than identical objects that are green, yellow, or white. McCain and Karr (1970) found that an object's color

affects distance discrimination, so that red objects appear to be closer and blue objects further away than they really are.

One researcher, Birren (1950), speculated that different colors actually evoke or correspond to different geometric shapes. For example, orange supposedly evokes the image of a rectangle; yellow, a pyramid or inverted triangle; blue, a circle; and red, sharp angles, squares, or cubes. Designing a virtual world to test this idea wouldn't be too hard to do and could produce some interesting results.

There are also subtle physical limits to the senses. The eye can perceive blue and yellow farther out on the periphery of vision than red or green because of the distribution of retinal sensors. At its outer limits, only white light is recognizable. The optimal viewing area is a cone of perception stretching straight out in front of the eyes and arching 15 degrees to either side.

Developers of advanced fighter-pilot helmets have used auditory submodalities to improve the human-jet interface. They've learned that a woman's voice, preferably that of a relative or girlfriend, whispering right behind the pilot's ear that he is about to run out of fuel has more effect than any bells and whistles. The close location—inside the pilot's personal space, the low volume, and the use of a woman's voice are all submodalities they've exploited.

Representational systems and their submodalities are the building blocks of experience to which meaning is applied. They give us a language for categorizing the most basic elements of experience and talking about them in terms of a virtual environment. In a virtual world, nothing is taken for granted because everything is under the control of the developer. And every decision will affect the user who steps into the world.

⇨ Creating reality with illusion

Mark Bolas has dark hair and eyes and, like many small business owners, he has a hurried, intense nature. He is the President of Fake Space Labs and one of the earliest developers of virtual worlds. He

moves, talks, and gestures with quick, deliberate movements, giving you the feeling that somehow he's made the time to think out everything he wants to say and do.

Like the Soviet space station astronauts who hold records for time spent in space, he's a member of a select club of people who have spent the most time in virtual reality. He became hooked on virtual reality before it had a name, when it was still a scientist's toy at NASA Ames. At that time he was working on a degree in design at Stanford University, a special program between the Art and Computer Science departments (he now teaches in this same program).

After convincing the Stanford faculty to let him do his thesis on this strange new thing (the term *virtual reality* hadn't been coined yet), he made an important decision. He froze the system hardware where it was. He decided to focus on developing the experience—building and creating virtual worlds. Along the way he learned a lesson about creating realism with illusion.

"When people are in a virtual world and they tell me that they're afraid to look down because they're up too high, or they come out and act disoriented, I know I've succeeded. They've accepted the virtual world as if it is real," Bolas says, sitting on a park bench near his offices in Palo Alto, California. "But when I started out there was nothing to go by; I just experimented at building worlds."

No matter what improvements to the frame rate or resolution came along, he decided that his job was to push the technology as a medium as far as he could without improving it. He stuck to this religiously. Even if it meant taking 20 minutes to make a change in the software code, he left the machine alone. The temptation would be too great to go on tinkering with the equipment instead of with the worlds.

"The first thing I decided to do was to spend an hour a night for a week using the equipment. But after 20 minutes the first night I decided it was a big mistake—there was nothing to do after flying around but stare at my virtual hand. It was boring. So my goal became over the course of the year to create worlds that people would want to spend time in."

It was 1988 and Mark's previous experience had been studying computer music at the University of California, San Diego. He knew how captivating good music could be (and it didn't need goggles), and it seemed to him that virtual worlds could be equally captivating.

But he found that most people using the early virtual reality systems never lost a sense of the other people around them, the room, the line of people waiting to use the system. They rarely got caught up and taken away by the experience, something that music lovers are familiar with.

At that time, even with sophisticated workstations, all he could animate was simple wireframe outlines of shapes. So he designed a suite of offices from real blueprints. At first he constructed the world without coloring in the polygons so the walls were only outlined and transparent. You could get a sense of size but also see how each room affected the other rooms if you started moving walls around.

When he colored in the walls to make the rooms more realistic all he could see was the room he was in—and viewers enjoyed the experience less! This started him wondering about the usefulness of abstraction versus realism. The colored wall might be more realistic, but the see-through boundary lines were more useful and enjoyable for certain tasks. And by leaving the world more abstract, versus building in more realism, Mark could draw users deeper in.

Abstraction isn't a reason to reject VR worlds. Apple Computer's desktop metaphor for the interface software between person and computer was quickly rejected as a childish toy by many when it first appeared. Yet the use of icons and windows provides a better way of simplifying and focusing on a computer for many users. The graph in Fig. 9-1 describes Mark's results of trying to get people involved in virtual environments.

At first people start off *here*, in a room putting on a helmet, loading software, etc. Their orientation is to the room. As they enter the virtual world, their depth of engagement gradually meanders away from *here* until they cross the threshold of involvement. Now they've become absorbed in the virtual world, similar to becoming engrossed in a good book.

Figure 9-1

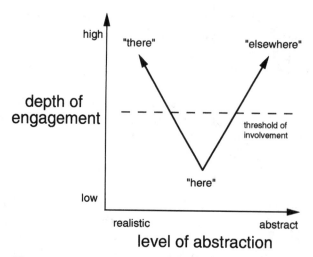

Illustration that depicts two different approaches to immersion. Both realistic and abstract environments can result in the same sense of being somewhere else.

The model or paradigm that most people use to construct virtual environments is based on flight simulators. Their goal is to bring the person to the building, to the wind tunnel, to the office. Flight simulators offer a very powerful illusion of being *there*, on the plane.

But most VR systems don't come with all the motion-control chairs and environmentally accurate plane cabins like flight simulators. Yet designers keep trying to build the software as if everything else was real. Mark Bolas found that by being more abstract he could pull people further into the environment.

"I don't know what to call it to differentiate it but *there* and *elsewhere*. I found that no matter how good the world, you could get only so far to *there*. The more abstract, the more *elsewhere* the world, the more people felt 'in there' than anything else. I feel that *elsewhere* represents the true nature of the VR medium."

Humans are spatial creatures; we're always aware of and scanning our environment. The most important and single most common piece of information all our senses provide us with is a sense of location. So

Mark started experimenting by building an entry world to quickly orientate people to the new environment.

He devised movements and events for the front end of the application that forced users to become involved "in there." Mark had people quickly fly around in a figure eight racecourse pattern before they entered the rest of the world. As they did this they saw themselves passing through a chain of open boxes.

Part Ferris wheel, part roller coaster, the image cognitively engaged people, forcing them to orient themselves to the new environment. It also effectively spun them around before they entered the intended world.

He didn't just design worlds and let people try them; he spent time watching them as they went through the experience. What sections did they spend a lot of time in? What maneuvers were the most attractive? Where did people like to go? He'd watch on a side monitor as people moved around with the goggles on so he could see what they were seeing.

By trial and error he discovered visual and spatial guides to draw people into and through virtual environments. Discoveries were accidental, hit and miss. One time he created a world that used a stairway and found that people loved to go up the stairway.

"You have to ask yourself why?" Mark says. "There was a white light at the top of the stairs and people are attracted to bright lights. But there's more to it than that—people love to go up in virtual worlds. I don't understand why. They also love to go down. If you tilt your head down you wind up flying down. People seem to love to do offsets, things they can't do in normal everyday modes."

By the end of the year he was able to build a couple of worlds that people would spend 40 minutes in, but 75 percent of the worlds he tried failed. He had no guides to go by; no one had ever created worlds before. By experimenting, he began to learn what the real power of the medium could be and the power of illusion in designing worlds.

He learned to use grid patterns on floors to create a railroad-track effect to enhance the sense of depth in the rooms (a lesson from the Renaissance). He began drawing white lines around the outside edges of polygon boundaries to make them punch out. It's a standard artist's trick to give shapes a border, because whenever there's a change in contrast the brain actually enhances the contrast.

One of his most successful worlds was based on a 1920s musical instrument called a Theremin (see Fig. 9-2). The project allowed him to mix his background in music with his desire for abstraction. Working with another engineer, Phil Stone, he created a world in which you could modify pitch and change the character of sound by using a wired glove to make sweeping gestures with your hands. It allowed them to compose soaring organ-like music.

Figure 9-2

A virtual Theremin, developed by Marc Bolas and Phil Stone while at NASA Ames.

There are many more sophisticated techniques for pictorial communications, depending on what the world builder is trying to design. Besides perspective, there's the use of shadows to aid in the illusion of depth, suggest a single light source, and also imply a time of day.

Cartoon animators have developed a visual language for characters that engages the viewer while replacing the subtle clues that real body language provides. Anticipation, for example, has its own motion characteristic in cartoons, which provides information and produces dramatic effects. By pulling backwards slightly just before they move, cartoon characters telegraph their intentions. Their movement adds visual continuity and a sense of realism that keep audiences involved with the character.

Sound can represent position, direction, and speed of motion in a character. Sound can be similarly applied to virtual worlds to establish continuity and provide information for the user. All these submodal elements are dynamic functions that can be built into objects or environments within virtual worlds.

One area awaiting experimentation is the use of standard film techniques. Film shots like fade-ins, fade-outs, close-ups, and continuity cuts are pictorial communication techniques we've already been trained to unconsciously understand. Some might work well in virtual realities; others will only be disruptive.

Just as D. W. Griffith imported literary story-telling techniques into his visual style, world builders must experiment to see what other fields have skills they can use. Movie editing and the camera's point of view make up a very effective language of the eye for influencing our emotions. If you doubt their effectiveness, just try recalling the face of someone very important to you and notice how you feel as you zoom in on their image or change it from color to black and white.

Full sensory stimulation isn't always useful or effective. In the 1920s, the theatrical producer David Belasco introduced aromas and fragrances into the production of his realistic plays. He wanted to increase the sense of realism.

He stopped the experiments when he noticed how the smell of bacon frying distracted his audience from the action on the stage. Perhaps it threw the audience into confusion because it blurred the lines between the designed experience and random everyday life. They were unprepared to deal with the information, to categorize it as part of the show. If frying bacon could unexpectedly appear, what other "real" events might threaten the audience?

217

There's a subtle agreement, a kind of social contract, between the audience and the experience designer. For a simulation to be believable and engaging, there needs to be roles and boundaries assigned to both sides of the curtain. Neither the designer nor the user actually believe that the actions on the stage or in the computer are real, but they agree to pretend as if they are real. There's safety in the knowledge that they can escape at any time by leaving the theater or turning off the computer.

This contract between the designer and the user is even more crucial in a virtual world because they need each other to complete the work. Sudden shifts in the boundaries and roles, and mistakes in continuity of design aren't just bothersome, they destroy the entire illusion of being "elsewhere."

When a world builder decides to construct an environment, before he decides on what objects to include or colors to use he needs to determine the goals of the application. What are the users of the experience supposed to learn or experience? What benefit are they going to get out of this simulation?

The next step is determining the associated tasks required to deliver the benefit. What tools, activities, and perceptions will allow the users to acquire the knowledge or produce the product they want? Once these activities are identified, it's important to decide how to represent them in a world and how to interact with that world.

Just as an icon designer for a Microsoft Windows' application must be sure the iconic symbol communicates its function clearly, the world builder must think about what his tools look like in the world and how well they work together with other tools to communicate function. Too much creativity and imagination can result in worlds that are annoying and unnecessarily difficult to use.

Many VR world designers are beginning to design wands as multifunctional hand tools, instead of using wired gloves. The wand can be programmed to function in a manner analogous to that of a mouse—you zap and click instead of pointing and clicking to activate objects and processes.

Always focus on ease of use. At the core of all virtual realities is the activity; the performance is the difference that sets VR apart from other computer applications. Most of today's world builders have focused on solving a particular problem. In the future, most virtual worlds will be designed in and of themselves to generate new discoveries, new insights, and new delights.

⇨ VR as theater

Virtual world travelers find themselves in environments with limitations and freedoms that aren't immediately apparent. Touch an object and it might tell you its name, crack open to reveal more detailed information, fall to the floor, or fly through the wall to fetch yesterday's mail. Each application will have its own images, metaphors, structure, and its own dynamic laws of interaction.

Virtual worlds operate in a more demanding realm than traditional computer applications; unlimited freedom is the ultimate responsibility. If the application is clumsy or confusing to use or if it doesn't engage the users, they'll simply abandon it. The world will fail and the marketplace will decide its fate.

A virtual world must not be merely functional or user-friendly. It has an absolute test to pass—it should be user-delightful. This isn't to say it must be a game (though computer games have valuable lessons to offer). Few people think of a spreadsheet program as fun to use, but the power it gives users over previous methods is decisive.

"Focus on designing the action. What do you want the user to do? The design of objects, environments, and characters are all subsidiary to this central goal," advises Brenda Laurel, author of *Computers as Theater* and editor of *The Art of Human-Computer Interface Design*.

Brenda Laurel has been a part of the personal computer industry since it began, first as a programmer and later as a software designer, marketeer, producer, and researcher. Her academic background in theater aided her in developing interactive fantasy architectures at Atari Research Lab in the early 1980s.

Since then she has worked as a consultant in interactive entertainment and human-computer interface design for Apple, LucasArts Entertainment, and the School of Computer Science at Carnegie Mellon University. In 1990, she joined Scott Fisher (fresh from his virtual reality work at NASA Ames) in founding Telepresence Research, but left in 1992 to resume her independent consulting career.

"A piece of computer software is a collaborative exercise between the imaginations of the program's creator and the people who use it," Laurel said while talking on the phone from her home in California. "It's never finished because it comes alive only when someone uses it and each use is slightly different. Designing human-computer experiences isn't about building a better electronic office. It's about creating imaginary worlds that have a special relationship to reality— worlds in which we can extend, amplify, and enrich our own capacities to think, feel, and act."

Virtual reality allows the user unique capabilities, such as the ability to fly, to occupy any object as a virtual body, to observe the world from multiple perspectives, and to be in places too small or far away for humans. It's a powerful setting in which you can control time, scale, and physics through the dynamic laws of the environment.

"I used to imagine that to design really great interactive software we'd require artificial intelligence (AI) behind the action," Laurel says. "We would script out these elaborate plots and the AI would shuffle events around, so as the users made choices they would still be invisibly guided toward the climax of the story. What I've come to realize is that my traditional ideas of authoring are heading toward a train crash.

"In interactive media, the author can't make the entire experience and give the user any choices! Our notions of traditional media can't come with us. We've limited the choices for users and all that is broken now. We are in a region where the authorship of the experience is about collaborating with users in real time. You don't want to force them to meekly go through the plot you've authored; you want to give them enough constraints and resources so the plot they invent by taking action in the world is an interesting one.

"To find precedents for what I'm talking about you have to go outside traditional Western ideas of authoring and art. The ideas we need aren't where you'd expect to find them. An architect authors a building, but he doesn't author what people will do inside the building. He knows how to design a space that provides materials for people doing certain things in that space.

"We need to ask different questions, such as 'How do people relate to landscapes?' When gardeners in Japan create landscapes designed for specific contemplative experiences, they are engineering experience. We're stuck with a top-down Western model of authoring. The use of VR is a new frontier closer to imaginative play than anything else, closer to playing cowboys and Indians as a child. The one traditional area we can look to is the stage."

Brenda Laurel suggests that the theater presents us with a powerful metaphor for creating virtual worlds. At the theater we relax our psychic boundaries to become engaged with the action, feel empathy with the characters, and struggle with the problems enacted on the stage. The action and the performance is what matters.

Theater allows us a safe place to experiment and explore various emotions, ideas, and situations. One of the great themes of Classical Greek theater was the debate over honor and revenge. In a society that prized both, how much revenge was enough when it required an endless cycle of murders? It was both a public and a personal debate, simultaneously carried on in the virtual world of the Greek theater.

At the theater, we agree to ignore that there's a backstage with ropes, risers, stage hands, costume makers, and a director making last-minute changes. With a computerized virtual world, the user enters into the same conspiracy and agrees to forget about the computer, the software, the head-tracker, the glove, and goggles. They're all "out of sight"—the performance is the thing.

"Now there's a rule to theater set-design: whatever is on the stage is there for a reason—you don't put random stuff around," Laurel says. "If there is a candelabra, it's there for light, to hit someone with, maybe it's connected to one character's past, but it has a purpose; everything has a purpose.

"The set is the visible aspect of a designed world all focused on aiding the action. If you don't have a script, the elements that guide the actor come from the lighting, the stage, the props, the clothing. Even on a bare stage with improvisational theater, the first thing the actors do is start to define the space. They begin describing where they are standing, what furniture is there, what food; they create boundaries for each other to work and create in.

"The well-designed world is, in a sense, the antithesis of realism—the antithesis of the chaos of everyday life. We get to play 'what if' in an organic world where everything is there for a purpose. This is what virtual world designers need to be investigating; this is what's new about this new media. We will have to design in cues, clues, and overviews to serve as advance organizers for travelers new to the territory. The key to a great experience is going to mean a well-designed setting."

 ## Coyote World

Brenda is testing her ideas by turning them into reality—that is, virtual realities. She and her partner Rachel Strickland are working with the Banff Center for the Arts on the Coyote World project. It's a virtual world for two people in which the environment is animistic and endowed with multisensory objects. In it, materials like trees, rocks, hills, and grass are conscious beings with the capacity for action.

The characters are derived from Native American fables: The Great Spirit, Coyote, Bear, Antelope, Quail, and Fox. Her goal is to create a world full of potential causes and potential effects that will act as catalysts for creative possibilities. Simply moving through this virtual environment will invite reactions.

"You need to give people enough constraints so the plot they create is an interesting one, but enough ambiguity so they have a variety of directions to go in. Ambiguity is not the absence of meaning, but the presence of more than one. If you give too much realism you cauterize imagination; it hasn't room to work.

"The theory behind the Coyote World project is that if you put people in a virtual world with enough enticing possibilities and things to play with and things that play with them, then the technology bumps us up into a new kind of media experience. It bumps us into a new place where our imaginations are heightened and emboldened, where we have confidence that we can take action in the world without falling off the edge," Laurel says.

Instead of Native American folk tales, the characters and objects of the Coyote World project could be replaced by molecules and atoms with their own particular dynamic properties and capabilities. A chemist let loose in such a world could bring to it a vast personal library of information, a personal history of what these elements are supposed to do, could do, and might do if combined. Most discoveries are the result of many failed attempts and experiments.

But for the first time he would be able to mix and match in real time as if assembling molecular building blocks on a workbench. What new life-saving drugs or chemical reagents might be created if molecular chemistry became a hands-on design process, a new kind of high-tech craftsmanship?

Questions that Laurel is currently exploring include: How do you develop guides and techniques to help people develop and conjure up the details of situations? How can people develop and keep track of (and maintain some control over) their ideas in a world that's constantly changing in response to ideas? What methods might an artist employ, either in real time or through program design, to introduce new situations for moving the action along?

Laurel and Strickland have spent the past two years working with children in schools to research this approach. The children were told Native American folk tales by their teachers for several months. The themes were used in drawing exercises and games. After several months, when the children had clearly absorbed the mythos and its characters, they were given paints, paper, bits of walnuts, and wool and encouraged to work up their own versions of the stories.

As the groups of children created their own stories, and stepped into the roles of various characters or created new ones, Laurel and

Strickland changed the collection of tools the children were using to see which ones contributed the most as creative catalysts, and to understand how the narrative process changed. Then they were ready to use what they learned to create worlds for grown-ups, a new kind of narrative and a foundation for other virtual world builders.

"It's a chance to enter into a fully formulated world of the imagination, but one that will truly be new to most people," Laurel says. "You discover all this stuff about yourself you didn't know. And you are free to try things you might not feel comfortable doing in public.

"Nobody hasn't had the fantasy of being an actor, of thinking what it would be like to be that character, what it would be like to be in that world. What we have with VR is the possibility to walk into the world of Hamlet or Wile E. Coyote. But you don't have the problem of being watched, you are not performing; you are stepping into the world."

Laurel's plan is ambitious. The use of structured plots has been refined over hundreds of years by playwrights and authors to guide us through experiences in a set amount of time. They play on our emotions, values, and assumptions about life to create catharsis.

The characters and parameters of a Coyote World, or any other dynamic mythic world, will need to be familiar to the users—whether from Shakespeare or Road Runner cartoons—so they can relax and participate, not stand around and puzzle out what they're supposed to do. Then users can bring to the world a sense of what their roles could be and more readily grasp what the connections between the various pieces suggest.

The schoolchildren Laurel worked with had several months to absorb the new characters, myths, and magic. If the parameters aren't understood by the users, entering such a world could be like visiting an interactive house of mirrors. Users would wander around amazed and delighted at the strange effects, altering mirrors as they went, playing in the maze, chasing each other into strange new experiences, but never achieving more than a great thrill.

The challenge Laurel has set for herself is to create a new kind of story-telling. She might be ahead of her time. It might be that the children of today's baby boomers, the schoolchildren she worked with who are growing up with computers, are the ones who will one day fully appreciate virtual worlds.

 Invisible Site

In the multimedia theatrical drama, *Invisible Site*, George Coates and his company of actors explore a host of ideas by imagining what could happen during a visit to a future virtual reality store. Because computers as powerful as the show supposes don't exist yet and because they couldn't afford to give everyone a pair of VR goggles anyway, the company turns the entire theater into a single, giant VR helmet. They immerse the audience in the performance by using 3-D slide projectors and 3-D glasses, film, trick lighting, sounds, and images projected throughout the theater, while actors float in mid-air—and much more.

"The job of artists, whatever the medium, is to direct attention. But when the user is directing his own attention, the user becomes the artist," George Coates said while sitting in the middle of his theater in San Francisco, a stylishly decayed cathedral, abandoned for over 30 years until his company took it over. Packed with computers, projectors, lights, cables, wireless mikes, hidden speakers, and other pieces of high-tech equipment, the place has a post-apocalyptic *Blade Runner* feel perfectly matching the show.

"Developing *Invisible Site* made me realize how wide a range of creative possibilities the designers of virtual worlds will have," Coates says. "It's different from a film or theatric experience, or even an author writing a novel. The designer will have to take into account all the options a participant might want to avail himself of in a given world.

"The designers of virtual worlds create complete sensory environments which the participant will be navigating through and interacting with. And not just strange or magical or peculiar or ordinary environments, but different eras, different times, different cultural places. They will be able to create situations where characters from different time frames can meet. Elizabethan England can collide with 18th-century China."

The characters in *Invisible Site* come to the store to change identities, take on the image of their heroes, switch their sex, visit exotic locations, and have adventures in cyberspace. They shift from city to city with the speed of film, reverse time, repeat time, fly, crawl, and meet their double when a software hacker breaks into the network and takes on the same identities they have (see Fig. 9-3).

Figure 9-3

In this scene from Invisible Site, an actor becomes trapped in a projection of a broken TV set while a large eye looks on.

George Coates Performance Works, 1991, photo by Jennifer Sauer

"Like talking on the phone, but disguising your voice, users of virtual worlds will eventually create digital identities—digidentities," Coates suggests. "Someday in the future, instead of watching a film of Shakespeare's *Tempest*, you'll go to an island in a virtual world and become Prospero. And if the network is big enough you are bound to find someone who wants to be your Caliban. You'll enter into the *Tempest* as a performer instead of a spectator."

The play explores the dynamic possibilities of a future virtual reality era. It also mirrors VR's structure within its own theatrical model of hidden backstage tricks used to create on-stage magic.

Whether in reference to design techniques or the resulting virtual experience, a discussion about creating virtual worlds often leads to that of art because they both share many of the same concerns. Dr. William Bricken of Washington State University's HIT Lab (and a former co-founder of Autodesk's VR program) has addressed these issues by summing up his years of VR design experience in a short manifesto:

Psychology is the physics of VR.
Our body is our interface.
Knowledge is in experience.
Data is in the environment.
Scale and time are explorable dimensions.
One experience is worth a trillion bits.
Realism is not necessary.

VR designers borrow from every field and discipline of thought. Along the way they're creating a new tool more flexible than anything mankind has previously invented. Historically, tools have been good for some single purpose. Computers and virtual reality are flexible tools that can serve a wide range of applications.

The remainder of this book will show how people are already taking this new tool and putting it to a wide range of uses. Along the way they're also redefining what it means to be a tool builder.

"It's a new creative form we don't have a language for yet," Coates concludes. "The designer will need to be conversant in a vocabulary that treats all the languages of experience equally: verbal language, visual language, musical language, textural languages, languages of graphics and animation. A virtual designer is going to become a kind of theater impresario, someone who is going to be able to develop the art of the mix."

Education as simulation

"What computers had offered me was exactly what they should offer children! They should serve children as instruments to work with and to think with, as the means to carry out projects, the source of concepts to think new ideas. The last thing in the world I wanted or needed was a drill and practice program telling me to do this sum next or spell that word!"

Seymour Papert, *The Children's Machine: Rethinking School in the Age of the Computer*

FOR most of human history, learning a trade, art, or profession was not something found in books. People learned by doing; young men and women became apprentices. Beginning in childhood with toys, we all imitate adult behavior to acquire the skills we need to survive and thrive in society.

Today you can watch this process in every schoolyard as children play doctor, soldier, carpenter, and movie star. You can also find it in the most advanced medical schools where interns follow older doctors as they visit patients, to learn the healing art first-hand.

Every virtual environment is a learning experience. It steps users through a series of activities, with rewards and penalties of various degrees along with opportunities to apply what they've learned.

Virtual reality technology was first used to train pilots. The military then took this lesson and applied it to the entire battlefield. One of the reasons that U.S. tank battalions were able to perform so brilliantly in the Gulf War was that they had already fought there in cyberspace.

In two huge warehouses, one in Kentucky and the other in Germany, over 250 military tank simulators train personnel (see Fig. 10-1). The job there isn't to learn how to drive tanks, but how to fight, win, and survive in them. The two centers can be networked over satellite so different numbers of tanks can fight with or against each other.

Figure 10-1

Institute for Simulation and Training

Developed by BBN, the U.S. Army's highly successful SIMNET program allows up to 250 networked players in a virtual tank-training environment.

These training centers were built during the 1980s to prepare soldiers to fight a land war in Europe. Not only can the computers be networked together, but they can perfectly simulate the appearance and fighting style of tanks and helicopters from other countries. The tank drivers are never certain whether they're engaged against the computer or other people.

During the buildup to the Gulf War, computer programmers were kept busy creating a virtual Kuwait City so that the retaking of that city could be choreographed and rehearsed by the generals and soldiers who had to do it. VR will take this method of training and spread it throughout our economy and culture.

In the previous chapter, virtual worlds were compared to theater with the user becoming an actor in an ever-evolving performance. The user's decisions and actions become input the computer uses to alter the virtual world. Our own process of learning can be described in a similar way as *the use of experience to create new experience.*

Every virtual reality application described in the rest of this book introduces the user to a new way of viewing, learning, and thinking. VR's most profound impact on our culture will occur when it becomes a common classroom tool. The generation of children about to grow up will truly see the world differently from their parents—in 3-D and interactively.

⇨ Learning by doing

At The Computer Museum in Boston, part of the exhibit space has been turned into an open lab to explore the educational potential of VR. Museum visitors are invited to explore the microscopic world of cell biology by building a human cell, blown up millions of times in size (see Fig. 10-2).

Figure 10-2

Scene from Virtual Adventure: Explore a Human Cell, created by ERG Engineering and The Boston Computer Museum. The user grabs elements of a cell and attempts to correctly assemble them.

C-1 *Silicon Graphic's Reality Engine2 represents the new wave of high-performance scene generators available for under $100,000. With machines like this, developers can create fully textured, real-time virtual worlds, like these two: the art gallery (above) and the space station (below). Within the next three to four years, this level of performance will become possible on powerful desktop systems.*

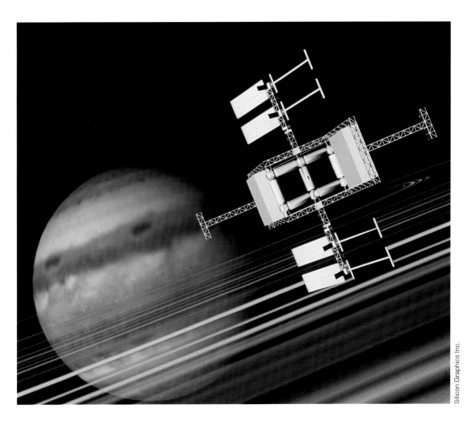

C-2
Worldesign, in Seattle, created a virtual balloon ride that allows participants to visit the Pyramids, the Sphinx, and other ancient Egyptian wonders.

C-3
Using the most sophisticated head-mounted display available, a pilot prepares to enter a virtual world created by powerful image generators. State-of-the-art equipment like this is capable of blurring the line between reality and simulation.

C-4
A participant tries on a VPL DataSuit for complete immersion in a virtual world. Sensors lining the outside of the suit detect body movements that are then transmitted to a computer. Wearing the suit, the participant can see his virtual body in the simulation.

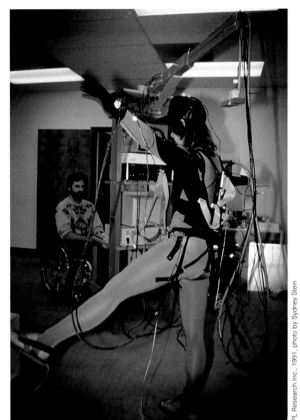

C-5 Example of a force-feedback hand and arm system built by the SARCOS Research Corporation. The operator "feels" the weight and handle of the hammer, while the robotic arm performs the same action with a real hammer.

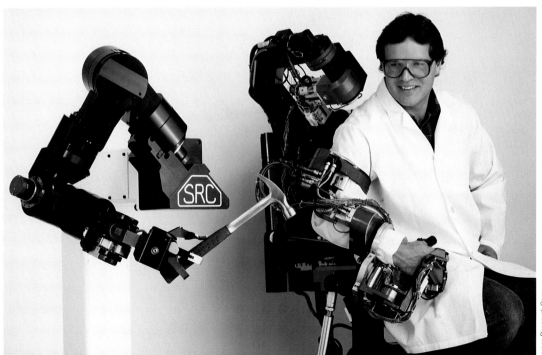

C-6 *In The Architecture of Catastrophic Change, George Coates uses powerful projection systems to create dramatic environments that appear to surround the actors.*

C-7
In the Virtual String Quartet, by Thomas Dolby and Eric Gullichsen, participants can "tickle" members of a virtual string quartet, thus prompting them to improvise unconventional solos. This was one of the works presented at the Guggenheim Museum, SoHo, in New York City.

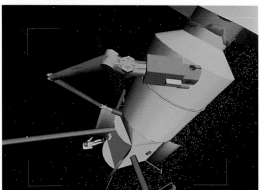

C-8
Fokker created a training system based on virtual reality technology for the shuttle's European-designed remote-arm manipulator.

C-9

The level of realism achievable in today's top-of-the-line image generators will eventually make it to the desktop in ten years or so. This image was captured on a Compu-scene V while performing a 60-fps simulation of an MH-53J helicopter. The visual database was modeled using DMA (Defense Mapping Agency) terrain elevation data and photographs (satellite, aerial, and hand-held camera) of a 60-square-mile area in Nevada.

C-10

Real-time texture mapping is the key to enhanced realism in this ship simulator based on a sophisticated ESIG-2000 image generator. Specialized hardware permits scenes like this to be rendered at 30 frames per second.

C-11

Participants of The Computer Museum's Virtual Adventure: Explore a Human Cell can wander around a virtual room, assembling various cell types by hand. This was part of a larger experiment to determine the effectiveness of VR in educational situations.

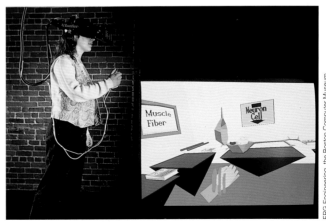

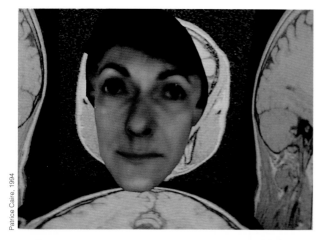

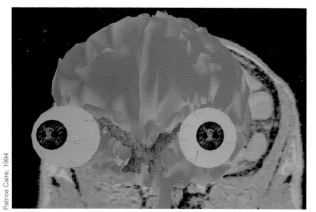

C-12
Designed by modern artist Patrice Caire and based on actual MRI data, the Cyberhead: Am I Really Existing? project takes viewers on a convoluted trip inside the brain, traveling through the visual and auditory systems.

C-13 *In a scene from Peter Gabriel's Mind Blender sim ride, Gabriel (the frog) leads a princess on a fanciful underwater exploration of a pond.*

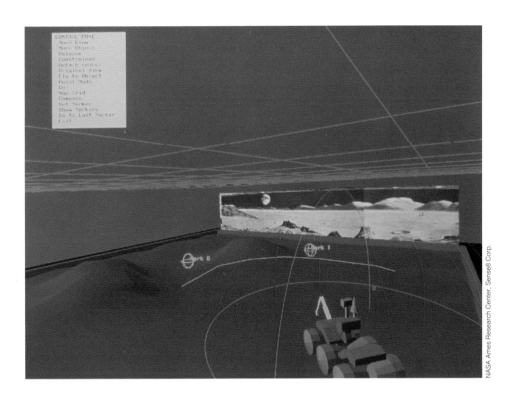

C-14 *NASA Ames uses a virtual environment to visualize and control the operation of both undersea (top) and extraterrestrial rovers (bottom).*

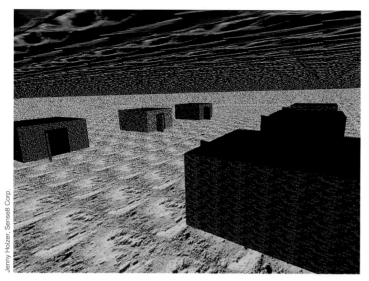

C-15

Jenny Holzer's Bosnian Virtual Experience was first shown at the Guggenheim Museum. It combines images of desolate villages and endless landscapes with the voices of victims, perpetrators, and witnesses of the violence in Bosnia.

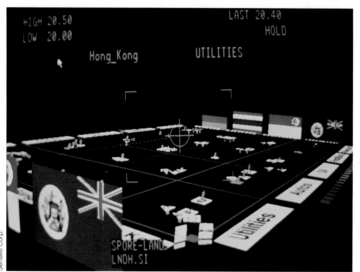

C-16

The Metaphor Mixer, designed by Maxus Systems and Sense8, is one of the first virtual environments where real-time stock information is presented in an interactive 3-D environment. Up to seven variables of financial information are presented simultaneously.

C-17

Virtual World Entertainment uses a Victorian parlor theme for their entertainment centers. Each center is an outpost of the mythical Virtual Geographic League (VGL). Founded by Nikola Tesla and Alexander Graham Bell, VGL is a secret society that developed UPT pods to transport pilots to different dimensions or virtual worlds.

Programmer Eben Gay and Director of Exhibits David Greschler are the principal developers of the cell world. With funding from the National Science Foundation, they've used Sense8's WorldToolKit running on a personal computer from DEC to create their experiment.

"One of the original reasons for the project was to see if we could simulate the thinking style of Barbara McClintock, a pioneering cytogenetic," said Greschler. "Not everyone can visualize ideas the way she could. She could get inside a cell and look around, and get a feel for the organism, its structure and system, by exploring it in her mind. I think VR could give us a way to help others understand cell biology the way she did."

The first version of the cell world was tested on over 80 visitors to the museum who spent an average of 20 to 30 minutes in the world. Unless these users asked for help, they were given very little instruction beyond what was in the world.

When they entered the virtual world, they found themselves looking at a young woman sitting in a chair. By touching her head, arm or stomach, they were immediately transported inside a room containing an empty six-foot neuron, muscle, or intestinal cell.

The cell was surrounded in the room by organelles (the different elements of a cell). There was a lid on top of the cell. When visitors placed the right organelles in the cell, they closed the lid and an animation showed the cell in action. If they didn't choose the right elements, the cell didn't work.

Instead of sitting in a chair like most VR experiences, users were free to stand and move about while wearing VR goggles. The virtual room they entered was sized and mapped to the actual room they were standing in. The position of their body and head was monitored by motion sensors in the ceiling.

Users interacted with objects in the virtual room by using a hand-held mouse that activated a virtual hand. The developers found that the natural behaviors of walking, grabbing, and pushing objects greatly increased the user's sense of "being there."

"Even though the graphics of the cell world are pretty simple, giving people a construction project, getting them involved with the living dynamics of the world, really engages them," says Eben Gay.

In each room there was a virtual book containing information about that particular cell. Surprisingly, many users never took advantage of this resource. "We learned fairly quickly that if information is not presented as a natural part of the whole experience, and is instead included as an add-on help option (such as books), many people do not use them," says Greschler. "I've also seen this happen with other interactive exhibits around the museum."

Visitors were more likely to learn from their experience if it came about as part of the general attributes of the world. Closing the lid on the cell to see if it ran didn't make sense given the context.

"If the activity had been for people to build a ball with a lot of bounce in it (instead of a human cell), the test should be to throw the ball against a wall and see how well it bounces. The test shouldn't be to put the ball in a 'testing box' and see if it works," Gay notes.

The test phase of the program has resulted in a redesign of the application. Gay and Greschler realized that the first model was "information poor." Not only was the topic unfamiliar to most people, so was VR. It took users 5–10 minutes just to get used to navigating in the virtual world. And at the same time they were trying to figure out what they were supposed to do there. So the first change was to add a simple tutorial to the beginning of the cell world that made the activities very clear.

The developers then applied the dynamic qualities of VR to help people learn more. Now, upon entering the redesigned cell worlds (intestine, neuron, and muscle), the purpose of the world is described both aurally, with a small model of a completed cell placed next to the large empty cell.

Each time an organelle is touched, the user hears information about it. When the wrong organelle is put into the cell, it's "spit" out and the user learns why it isn't needed. This way the cell becomes a living test environment.

"There are no wrong answers," Greschler says. "The user is encouraged with immediate feedback to keep testing the system until it works, just as a scientist would. Each test teaches you something immediately and increases the amount you learn. The repetition— hearing a description of an organelle each time you touch one—will make it more likely that users develop a mental model of the cell and where the organelle fits into the larger context."

The second phase of the program will be to test three groups of people on the redesigned application. One group of 200 will experience full, immersive VR, as described previously; a second group of 100 will learn in a nonimmersive, desktop-VR format. They will view the application on a computer monitor and interact using a spaceball. A third group of 100 will simply view the material in a video presentation.

"Not only will we test the level and type of cognitive information gained in the world, we want to test the effectiveness of simulation as a teaching medium vs. other media," Greschler says. "We will also test for changes in attitudes about cell biology. Does 'being there' increase the user's interest in the topic?"

Gay and Greschler are learning how to take complex information and teach it as experience. They're also redefining how the museum is used. Instead of simply acting as a warehouse to display a record of past events, it's helping to invent the future.

Can the same tool that trains tank commanders really teach biology students about human cells? Another group of researchers in the Boston area want to teach high-school students about the human immune system using VR. They're developing a course curriculum mixing classroom lecture time with a VR simulation lab on personal computers. Students will learn to fight and survive as T-cells in the human body. To do this they'll need to understand how the body responds to diet, disease, and other cells.

VR can be a valuable teaching aid for many kinds of practical and scientific skills. Whether practicing repairing the Hubble telescope or learning to drive a car, simulations engage users with immediate feedback by involving their primary senses. Just as we learn about the world as children by interacting with it, so we do with VR. But what about more abstract topics? Can VR help us learn about art, language, or even history?

⇨ Simulated history

The first thing you see when you put on the head-mounted display is the front facade of the ancient Egyptian Temple of Horus. It sits in a large field surrounded by an enclosing stone wall. The sky is a bright blue and animal sounds can be heard outside the enclosure.

The front wall of the temple rises in two massive pylons that are covered with beautiful murals. Flagpoles fly colored streamers atop the front of the temple. In the middle, between the two pylons, is a great processional doorway over 60 feet high. On either side of the door are huge hawk statues representing the god Horus (see Fig. 10-3).

Figure 10-3

Carl Loeffler, Carnegie Mellon University

Image from Virtual Ancient Egypt, created by Carnegie Mellon University. This is the front view of the Egyptian Temple of Horus.

"I wanted to explore new technologies for impacting the interaction between students and teachers," says Lynn Holden, Egyptologist and co-developer of the virtual temple with Carl Loeffler at Carnegie Mellon.

"I started with a CD-ROM interactive program to see how I could offer a variety of experiences to the student to bring ancient cultures to life. The program covers ancient Egyptian art, language, architecture, customs, religion, and more. It is designed in a modular form so other ancient cultures can be added to the program and all the information interconnected."

After he had started this project, he showed it to Carl Loeffler, head of the Studio for Creative Inquiry at CMU. Carl had come to CMU with a background in networked education. Carl saw the potential for expanding the information in the CD-ROM into a virtual temple experience.

As you walk up and approach the temple, you see a mural of the king defeating the traditional enemies of Egypt. He's shown holding a sword. There is lesser god standing in front of him holding out the sword of victory and giving a blessing to his activities. Moving closer, you step on an invisible pad in the ground that activates animation in the mural. The king's sword arm comes down and strikes his captives.

If you move over to the doorway, your presence awakens the hawk statue, which addresses you. It informs you that this is the temple of the god Horus and that the reason he is in the form of a hawk is that the king was identified with the most powerful creatures in nature: hawk, bull, lion, and mythical creatures.

Inside the first room is a courtyard. It's open to the sky with a ring of columns around the edges. You hear the sounds of pious Egyptians praying in the background. You are joined by a virtual guide, an animated priest figure, someone who would have worked in this temple around 500 B.C.

The virtual priest explains how the temple acted as an interface between mortal humans and the divine Egyptian gods and goddesses. There are murals you can walk up to that have animations showing the king being purified for his rituals receiving the blessings of the gods. A small cat, representative of one of the sacred animals, comes scurrying by your feet.

"I foresee that we will eventually have educational computers not unlike the holodeck on Star Trek," says Lynn Holden. "You will be

surrounded by a total environment that will take you to places that are distant in terms of time and space. You will meet guides and intelligent objects able to recontextualize for you the available knowledge about that particular time and place. Each one will offer a different point of view, such as a slave, a farmer, a merchant, a warrior, or a member of the royal family.

"Rare art and artifacts that are scattered around the world in museums will be virtually replaced in their appropriate location and position. Each mural and statue in an Egyptian temple had meaning not only by itself but in its relationship to other pieces around it and even its placement in the temple."

You enter the inner sanctuary of the temple. It's raised up to represent the original act of creation when the first piece of land arose out of the primordial flood waters. It holds a shrine made of stone or gilded wood, protecting a statue of the god made out of gold, silver, or precious stone.

Here another agent in the image of the king explains the purpose of the room. There's a priest kneeling in front of the shrine offering food to the god. On the walls, there are more murals that animate to show the king worshiping the god for all Egyptians.

"For each historic culture of the world—India, China, Africa—all the phases of culture could be represented and shared on a network among many classrooms," says Carl Loeffler. "You could have a database of all the background reference information connected to a virtual experience of that culture. Murals and statues will come alive to teach you. And you won't just visit a temple, but also an ordinary person's house, a palace, a tomb, a fort. When you go into these environments you will be able to access additional information by interacting with the surroundings."

Loeffler and Holden also see an "edutainment" side to these virtual environments. They want to add a gamelike experience where you demonstrate what you've learned about a culture. In Egypt, you might play a game called Dynasty, where your goal is to assemble the pieces of the story that lead to the fall of a particular royal family.

"I am taking the lessons I've learned with the temple and developing a virtual Viking village with Ola Odegard at University Norwegian Telecom Research," Loeffler says. "They want to experiment with distributed virtual education because the towns and schools in their country are isolated by tremendous fjords and mountains.

"Theirs is a culture without any major ruins from the past—the Vikings didn't build stone temples. The simulated village will give students a way to connect with this lost history. All cultures, past and present, function out of a need to answer the same basic questions: who are we, why are we here, and where do we come from? Historical simulations are a new way for students to explore these questions for themselves."

Loeffler and Holden have developed a rich environment with significant historical accuracy and depth. In its initial incarnation, the temple is more like visiting an extraordinary museum than the kind of interactive learning lab the cell world represents. Yet between the two projects, an entirely new paradigm in learning is emerging—one where the student is empowered to learn by direct experience.

⇨ Reinventing school

". . . computer education was a failure in the 1980s. One reason dispersal of personal computers to schoolrooms failed to check the deterioration of traditional public education in the media age was that the computers were so often seen as just another channel for transferring knowledge from the teachers to the students (broadcast paradigm) rather than providing an environment in which the students can explore and learn together (network paradigm)."

Howard Rheingold, *The Virtual Community: Homesteading on the Electronic Frontier*

There are many problems facing the use of VR in schools. Besides the obvious problems of maintaining and purchasing the equipment, there are many additional questions. How effective are these environments with children? Whose viewpoints would be represented

in these virtual experiences? Can you customize a query so the answer you get back is tailored to your needs?

Perhaps the biggest challenge is transforming the traditional roles of student and teacher. If a time traveler from 1776 arrived in 1994, only the way we teach our children would be completely familiar to him. Just as computers are restructuring the workplace, they will soon change the way we and our children learn.

David Fox expresses a vision shared by many in the VR community. Fox is an independent consultant in the development of interactive worlds. Along with Adam Grosser, he was formerly at the heart of Rebel Arts & Technology, a new media research program (since disbanded) within Lucasfilm. Grosser and Fox developed the prototype of a major VR attraction based on the film *Star Wars*. They put you at the controls of a starfighter (using jet-fighter simulation technology) so you can battle the forces of the evil Empire on a distant planet.

"There's a couple of science-fiction books that can give you a sense of my philosophy of experience development. *Dream Park* is one, but *Ender's Game* is closer. It's by Orson Scott Card and the lead character, named Ender, is living on a space station in some distant future where he is training to be a warrior. He's learning to grow up with a powerful simulation computer as a teacher and mentor.

"The computer is powerful enough and knows him well enough that it can design problems for him that he will have a hard time solving because of his own mind-set. The problems the computer develops for him are linked to his personal blind spots. The way he solves them is that he has to alter his way of thinking, his point of view, or his personality in some way to see the world differently."

The idea that someone can grow and learn by solving computer games is Fox's hope for virtual reality. He's just not sure how to do it yet, and neither is anyone else.

It might take a hundred years before there are computers as powerful as the one in *Ender's Game*. However, it's not too soon to think

about how to design applications in which people learn, and learn about themselves, while they're having fun.

The rest of the chapters in this section will lead you into a new kind of information age, one in which the information comes alive. You'll discover over and over that the most powerful thing VR is doing is teaching us to see, think, and learn in new ways.

Business enters the cyberage

"... unlike a lot of people who think the computer industry's maturing, I think it's in its infancy. I think there are technological breakthroughs that happen once every ten years, maybe ... And that those technological breakthroughs have the force to reshape the tools that we build, and to reshape the industry along with them, as certain companies pay attention to them earlier and certain companies wake up fairly late."

Steve Jobs, *MicroTimes*, 1992

FEW technologists understand better than Steve Jobs the dynamics of turning a new technology into a successful industry. It not only requires good workers and good products with customer solutions, it requires that trends be nurtured when customers find a feature or solution that works especially well for them. Sometimes a single application can become the key trend that allows a product to stand out. Is there such an application for virtual reality?

The visual emphasis of the Apple Macintosh computer's design made it ideal for automating the typesetter's job of page layout and text integration. For the first time, what users saw on the screen was what came out of the printer. The job of activating commands was simplified with the innovation of the mouse; on-screen windows and graphical icons made accessing and organizing information much easier.

But it wasn't typesetters or graphic artists who first jumped to the Mac; they were already comfortable with the tools they had. It was their customers. Hundreds of small businesses and private individuals saw a

way of reducing their costs, increasing control, and becoming more directly involved in the creative effort of communicating with others.

As the word spread, these users were joined by more and more small desktop publishers. Brochures, fliers, and newsletters by the thousands sprang forth as people found a new way of communicating. No one forecasted desktop publishing, but it became the key application that drew many people's attention to the Macintosh, allowing them to discover all the other great things a computer could do.

There are a wide range of applications under development for virtual reality, tools like 3-D product prototyping, air-traffic control, molecular modeling, spreadsheets you can walk inside of, and trips into space without leaving earth or into the chambers of a beating heart.

Hollywood is working on virtual movies where the audience participates in its own entertainment. And artists are building experiences in which the user becomes both co-artist and a part of the art itself. No one knows which one of these ideas could be the "killer application" that pulls the VR industry forward. Perhaps virtual reality has such broad application that its widespread use will eventually pull the computer industry forward into the next century.

⇨ VR's unique benefits

It isn't enough to just do a job better; a new technology needs to provide distinctive benefits. A rule of thumb is that it must deliver a ten-to-one improvement over existing solutions before people will adopt it. Can it help us learn faster, more easily, and more accurately? Will it reveal insights we wouldn't discover otherwise? Can we use it to improve or speed up the invention and production of new products? Can it make our jobs easier and more enjoyable? How can it help us enjoy the time we have with our families in new ways?

There are two major benefits to using virtual reality. First, it gives us a new way to explore reality. Like the microscope and telescope, it extends our senses so we can learn or do something with reality we couldn't do before.

For example, chemists have traditionally built stick figures to visualize the molecular structure of the chemicals they design. With VR they can perceive the molecule at any size, distance, and color, as shown in Fig. 11-1. They can animate it to study how it moves and affects other molecules.

Figure 11-1

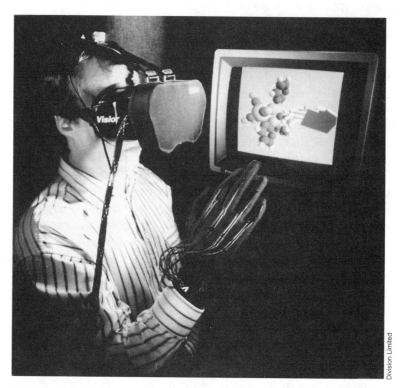

Using a wired glove, humans can "shrink" themselves and enter a world where they can manipulate virtual molecules. The picture on the monitor shows the image the participant sees in the VR goggles.

Today, you can't touch and hold a virtual molecule with the same physical satisfaction that a stick figure provides. But both the stick-figure model and the VR model communicate certain aspects of the same idea equally well. However, simulating reality is something the computer does especially well. While you can hold a stick figure in your hands, you can't fly inside it or watch it vibrate as it interacts

with other molecules. Virtual reality allows you to experience and manipulate reality in new and productive ways.

The second thing virtual reality allows us to do is perceive abstract ideas and processes for which there are no physical models or representations. VR acts as a translator, converting concepts into experiences our senses and mind can appreciate and analyze.

For example, utilities use massive software programs to coordinate and maintain huge power grids in which electricity generated by power plants is distributed to industries and homes as needed. These systems rely on software programs that have become very large and complex.

Tokyo Electric Power (TEPCO) is developing a VR application to visualize large abstract software programs that control their systems. The TEPCO program is aimed at creating visualizations of the total structure of the program (and therefore the power grid) to manage problems of data flow and message paths on a time axis.

In the application, the software program appears as a huge, transparent, multistoried building, interlaced with rooms representing sections of the program, which are connected by piping to represent data flows. The visualization will be connected to the actual operating software to provide a real-time, online method of managing local problems while still displaying the overall program.

Spreadsheets are a more familiar way in which computers allow us to represent and work with abstract data and ideas. It's often said in Silicon Valley that the VisiCALC spreadsheet program created Apple Computer and that Lotus 1-2-3 is responsible for the success of the Intel-based personal computer. Neither hardware platform would have enjoyed the early surge of success it did without these killer applications.

The demand for financial software tools, therefore, created a demand for the hardware systems they ran on. Despite the more than 50,000 applications that run on personal computers today, financial applications continue to make up one of the largest and most

demanding segments of computer use and are a likely area where VR's first killer applications might emerge.

➡ Cyberspace meets Wall Street

The world's financial markets are irrevocably speeding toward a single, 24-hour-a-day, totally computerized market. The chaotic image of the floor pits of different countries' stock and commodities exchanges are fast becoming an old-fashioned anachronism.

Today's money manager sits with several computer screens in front of him and watches data come in from a wide variety of sources in real time. While mentally juggling the movements of the markets and other influences on his portfolio, he needs to make quick decisions that might result in thousands, even millions of dollars in profits or losses.

On Wall Street, information is wealth and virtual reality offers a way to increase the effectiveness of money managers by condensing and streamlining the way abstract information reaches them so they can make faster, more effective decisions.

"VR allows me to create a single interface within which I can share data live with other programs and keep track of many variables. It allows me to integrate the abstract information coming from many different programs and sources and express it in a single graphical language. I can also pull in data from international boards, back-room databases, and keep track of it all in three dimensions," says Paul Marshall, President of Maxus Systems International.

Maxus creates international portfolio management systems for pension funds and money managers, specializing in global securities and derivative products. Maxus' software allows a portfolio manager to integrate data from existing external sources, such as Reuters or Knight-Ridder, with in-house and proprietary databases, including links to back office systems.

"With the downsizing of Wall Street all the business is being done by the numbers now," Marshall says. "Today's portfolio manager has more information to swim through, a complex sea of variables involved in trading strategies. And the people making money are the pure arbitrageurs who are dealing with low-risk strategies, working much more quantitatively on risk management. There is a lot of hedging of options and managers want to play out a lot of 'what-if' scenarios. They are asking themselves, 'do I buy the stock, the option on the stock, the convertible bond, or can I synthetically create the same security for less?' They want a more complete risk profile and by dealing in three dimensions are able to map in all the variables. We can make the data come alive."

Paul Marshall, along with his partner Sean Manefield, got into the international arbitrage field in the mid-1980s. They developed 3-D surface maps (see Fig. 11-2), and visual metaphors of positions and risks associated with those positions. Both have extensive backgrounds in money management as well as computers. Manefield formerly worked for the Reserve Bank of Australia (the equivalent of the U.S. Federal Reserve).

"In doing these kinds of trades, the way you beat your competitors is by having better software that signals movements in the market to you," Marshall says. "With virtual reality I can take a quantum leap in representing data. There are so many different variables I can monitor, different attributes of different stocks, abnormal volume or occurrences, fundamental inefficiencies. The output of 45 different reports could be summed up in the behavior of a polygon that changes color, blinks or spins, behaves in a preset way to instantly communicate with the manager what has happened to that security."

Using Sense8's WorldToolKit on an Intel Pentium Processor-based computer, Marshall has created a vast ocean of data on which securities rise and fall on the tides of the market. The area can be interactively divided into any combination of subregions on a grid. You can pick a single industry and look at it across all markets, or look at all industries across a single market. He calls it the Metaphor Mixer.

A grid can be broken out based on the American stock exchange: transportation, health care, pharmaceutical, computers, and retail subregions. A segment like automotive could be organized across categories such as trucking, passenger cars, farm machinery, and

Figure 11-2

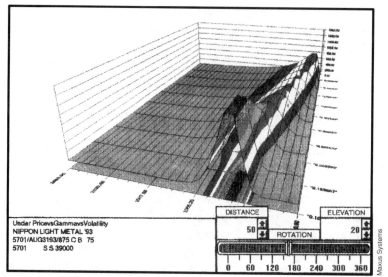

This 3-D surface map is one way of representing complex stock-market data in a more understandable form.

heavy equipment, or it could be divided by international regions: America, Japan, Germany, England, Sweden, etc.

The viewer can fly down into each subregion and move among the stocks and bonds, each of which is represented by a flat polygon that's rising or falling among an undulating sea of similar panels. The stock's shape, position, behavior, and color are dependent on conditions in the market. Each panel can have a company's logo (which is itself an informational icon) texture-mapped onto it for faster recognition.

ABD Securities Corp., the New York-based securities trading arm of Germany's Dresdner Bank, has begun using the Metaphor Mixer. With $235 million in assets, they're using the system to compress large amounts of real-time data into a computer interface any trader could use. The bank serves as a broker-dealer in numerous equity markets around the world and provides trading, execution, and clearance functions for global institutional and private clients.

Decision support systems

Paul Marshall's ocean of securities represents a new way for professionals to "get inside the numbers." The possibilities for representing information are greatly expanded when you move from the flat 2-D world of screen and paper into a dynamic 3-D world.

Traditional spreadsheets can be viewed as replacements for accounting ledgers, but their real value is in allowing business people to simulate the behavior of their markets, products, and companies. A spreadsheet program is a simulator—a symbolic metaphor for the behavior of a business, the life of a product, or the behavior of stocks.

The fundamental characteristic of the spreadsheet metaphor is that the events (represented as monetary figures or measurements) input into the spreadsheet are equivalent, or *isomorphic*, to the real events and transactions within the situation. As a metaphor, the spreadsheet simplifies and condenses a lot of complex data without losing the essential structure of the activities. It allows businesspeople to track the health of a product (or their own lifestyle) and explore "what if" scenarios, such as the cost of offering a discount to spur sales or the personal impact of buying a new house.

The Metaphor Mixer and other reality-based graphical computer simulations work the same way, with several important additions: real-time data feeds, networked communications, and informational depth. This kind of data visualization can model the flow of energy through a living creature or ecological system—or the accumulation, distribution, and use of dollars within a company or business.

Real-time data feeds mean that the decisions reached from viewing the simulation can respond to and influence situations in real time. This means an increased speed of response to financial situations or changing business conditions.

Because the same ocean of icons can be shared on a network, decision-making can be shared with everyone viewing the same situation. More important, a "what-if" scenario can be quickly run on the simulation and evaluated by a team in widely separated locations, and comments shared before a final decision is made.

The other important difference is depth of information. Because each icon can have multiple attributes—such as position (x, y, z), size, orientation (roll, pitch, yaw), color, shape, and behaviors (spin, vibration, sound)—they can quickly communicate many different kinds of information. The Metaphor Mixer has indicator arrows, either blue or red, above each logo to show trends. A logo might be a triangle, square, or pentagon, depending on the company's capitalization size.

In addition, you can use software agents to presort information or execute multiple tasks at the same time. Brenda Laurel defines *agents* as "a character, enacted by the computer, who acts on behalf of the user in a virtual (computer-based) environment."

The computer enacts a specific software function for the user, and the way the user interacts with this function is through a cartoonlike character. The character could be an animal, machine, person, whatever. The Metaphor Mixer has a voice-activated, star-shaped agent that searches through the database for good stock picks, reports on its findings in a female voice, and leaves a visual trail of its hunt to find the stock. "For some traders, we've considered redesigning the look of the agent to be a 'profit-seeking missile,'" says Paul Marshall.

Virtual reality simulations represent the next step in the evolution of database interfaces. Each virtual interface will be customized to the content or purpose of the database and allow the user to obtain a much greater amount of information than has previously been possible.

Several large department stores, including one in Australia, are working at creating their own version of the Metaphor Mixer. Instead of a vast field of corporate logos, the icons would represent different products and departments within the store. Washing machines, beds, TVs, stereos, shoes, books, suits, shirts, jackets, jeans, china, crystal, various sports equipment—the hundreds of items in the store will each have their own icon. This living, interactive, graphic image will be the interface to a huge database for real-time inventory control and management of the entire store.

Getting low on a particular brand of washing machine? The icon might spin, flash, or rise up above the other icons to get your

attention. Click on it and you're sucked inside the icon, where text-based data, digitized photos of potential new products, voice-mail, or a video message from the company president awaits your attention.

A transportation company could take the Metaphor Mixer concept and turn it into a shipment scheduler. The grid would be changed into a map of the entire country. Icons representing various trucks, trains, boats, or planes carrying different kinds of cargo would be moving across the map. Real-time data from the street (the kind United Parcel Service already collects) would allow schedulers all around the country to keep track of every shipment, when it was delivered, and who signed for it. A helpful software agent would find alternate routes for trucks when a major accident ties up a freeway. Perhaps the character would be designed to look and sound like an old truck who knows all the short-cuts.

If keeping track of and managing companies with this kind of real-time information sounds like a military campaign, you'd be right. The military is very interested in the Metaphor Mixer concept, too.

Remember the old World War II movies where the generals stand around a giant map while assistants push toy ships and tanks around to track the progress of a battle? The information these generals were viewing was hours, even days old. Change the icons on the Metaphor Mixer to tanks, cannons, ships, and soldiers. Let each icon represent the position and movement of a squadron of planes, division of tanks, even an individual man. The possibility exists now to visually direct the flow of battle in real time.

For the military, not only is it about tracking and managing a battlefield situation, it's about planning, practicing, and understanding the art of war. With these kinds of computer simulations, a student of war could fast-forward, rewind, freeze frame, change variables, and play out dozens of "what if" scenarios.

The design of new weapons and the improvement of old ones will be enhanced as these simulations are shared with developers. Just like the department stores mentioned above, the military is also looking to use VR as an interface to their databases in order to track their vast inventory of supplies.

In the same way VR is changing how the military studies and fights wars, it will change the way businesses are run. The owner of a company will create an abstract "war game" of his business to explore different financial decisions, restructuring options, or how competitive developments might affect the entire organization. Bradford Smith, Director of Research for the Institute for Nonprofit Organization Management, has been working on the design of just such a program to monitor the health of a company.

 # Flowsheets

"On the nightly news we see complex weather patterns moving over the earth's surface," says Smith. "Like slow-motion photography, the display compresses 12 to 24 hours of data into a period of a few seconds, allowing the viewer to gain an understanding of the weather that no numerical presentation of the data could possibly convey— even to an expert. The same kind of information compression can be done for a business with a flowsheet."

A company is a living thing made up of dozens, hundreds, even thousands of people. And a single day in the life of a company can be expressed in the hundreds of complex variables contained or derived from its profit and loss ledgers, balance sheets, and cash-flow statements.

In many large-scale companies, spreadsheets reside on mainframes or personal-computer networks. They automatically monitor and store financial data from various locations in and outside a company. Using the concept of the Metaphor Mixer as inspiration, it's possible to design a system to monitor the health of a company: parts in storage, shipments and deliveries, outstanding debt, utility costs, overtime paid, orders coming in, new product-design schedules, stock prices, competitive information—the entire life of the company.

Smith has created his own icons and metaphors that are isomorphic to a business' own environment, that condense data while preserving the structure, and that could accurately help people visualize the

outcome of their work. Smith's flowsheet has three underlying concepts:

> ➤ A boundary between the system to be described (the company) and the environment (market, government, competitors, etc.)

> ➤ Flows of value (like rivers) measured over some span of time

> ➤ Reservoirs where value accumulates measured at any instant in time

Openings in the boundary around the company represent the flow of value (represented by dollars) in and out of the system. The size of these flows can change depending on the amount of value entering or leaving the system. Icons represent various services, departments, and product groups.

Reservoirs (cash, debt, fixed assets, etc.) are depicted by a stepped icon that easily conveys a range of several orders of magnitude. A general funds reservoir might swell with value from an increase in sales and then decrease as a particular debt is paid off or its funds are diverted into research and development. Research and development is a separate reservoir that feeds value into various product groups as new products are invented and commercialized.

The flow of resources in and out of the organization acts as a framework for the collection and assimilation of other information about the organization, e.g., personnel, the physical plant, and inventories. The display can be run at different rates, stopped, run backwards, and shifted to reflect particular time periods—monthly, quarterly, or yearly. The flows and icons can then be integrated into a display, shown in Fig. 11-3, that fosters contemplation and discussion about the performance of the company and the possible future results of specific decisions.

The advantage of VR is that it can creatively represent vast amounts of abstract data in new and interactive ways. And it can do it in real time. This combination allows users to organize information in new ways and find relationships that previously lay buried in the numbers.

Figure 11-3

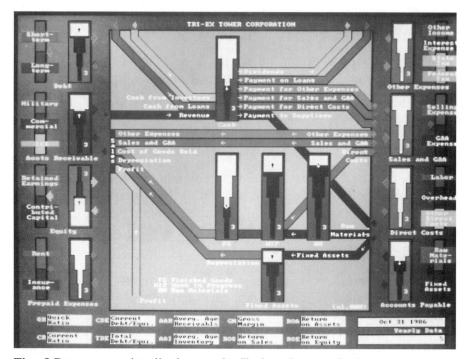

This 2-D image graphically depicts the "holistic" state of a business or institution at any moment in time. By animating parts of the image based on changing financial conditions, you can cause various aspects to grow or shrink.

Information management magic

"This is a whole new paradigm shift," suggests Jerry Slambrook of Sandia Labs. "Artificial intelligence software fell short of people's expectations because we found out how hard it is to duplicate how the human mind analyzes and does pattern recognition. The tack we are taking now is that our job with the computer is to present the data to the senses in the most natural way possible and put the knowledge and skills of the human to work."

Sandia Labs started off in the nuclear weapons business, building safety devices and developing weapons. Their labs are a Department of Energy engineering house for doing extensive research in robotics and nuclear-waste dump clean-up.

Slambrook is working on several VR application design projects. Instead of creating artificial worlds to manipulate abstract ideas, he's looking to represent reality more usefully and interactively than was previously possible. One long-term project is a satellite command and control system in which the earth and the satellites orbiting it will appear in their natural relationships to each other (see Figs. 11-4 and 11-5).

Figure 11-4

At Sandia Labs, Jerry Van Slambrook uses the BOOM from Fake Space Labs to research the use of VR to perform satellite-tracking visualization.

Figure 11-5

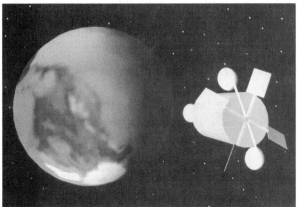

By using a powerful graphics workstation, you can generate this image in real time, allowing the operator to "fly" up to the satellite or to visualize the section of the Earth that it covers.

253

Slambrook's first step was to map the earth and several satellites with the dynamics of their orbits. The idea is for the operator to be able to move around in space among the satellites and see how the orbits overlap, what the satellite's footprint on the earth covers (how much it can see or broadcast to), and what happens with adjustments in its position relative to the earth, sun, and magnetic belt.

If satellite designers can actually "sit" in orbit, then they can do a better job in placing solar panels and robotic devices. By simulating the orbit and its view of the earth, weather patterns and solar position information can be added to the orbital simulation to enhance the planning phase for satellite command and control.

A variety of orbit patterns can be quickly evaluated before making emergency changes, such as monitoring a sudden volcanic eruption or a regional war. Eventually, it might be possible for an operator to adjust virtual satellites on the ground and have the vehicles up in space automatically respond.

In a similar fashion, the Air Force is investigating the possibility of using VR to ease the job of air-traffic controllers. From movies and TV, many people are familiar with the image of air-traffic controllers hunched over their screens, monitoring the movement of commercial jets through the sky. At Brooks Air Force Base, they're exploring how virtual reality can put air-traffic controllers up in the air with the planes.

Imagine you're an air-traffic controller. Instead of watching a screen while sitting at your desk, you're above the entire airport with everything important within your view, as shown in Fig. 11-6. You can monitor and communicate with planes in the sky based on their positions in 3-D space.

Below, you see a model of the airfield and the planes that are your responsibility are clearly marked, but you can also see other activities around the airfield. You can quickly evaluate an object's distance and altitude just by looking at it, and additional information is just a command word away.

Figure 11-6

Evans and Sutherland, Inc.

Simulated airports like this can be used to train air-traffic controllers and pilots in order to avoid costly and dangerous mistakes. This image was rendered at greater than 30 fps on an Evans and Sutherland image generator.

Imagine you're sitting at your station when suddenly you realize that there's a danger situation; a plane is moving onto a runway for take-off just as another jet is beginning its landing run towards the same runway.

Wouldn't it be nice to have everything not essential to the situation disappear? The computer can not only display what's important, but it can also remove things that are in your way; everything potentially distracting disappears from the air and the airport visualization. Escape routes both on the ground and in the air become highlighted, and any trucks or planes in the vicinity remain visible.

All this would be possible if the airfield was represented by a graphical computer model. It's what sets VR apart from other communications channels; you can decide what to display, where to display it, and what not to display. This same ability to customize information in command and control situations can extend to communicating through partially overlapping or partially shared VR displays.

With virtual reality, the air-traffic controller can be sitting almost anywhere wearing a set of goggles (on a plane, in a closet) and everywhere he looks can be a display space. Instead of a model of the airfield, he would be surrounded by windows of information. If he wants something in particular, he gestures with a wave of his hand, or verbally requests that a screen be moved. He can put various display spaces together as the need arises and organize incoming information in the best way to suit his needs, moment to moment.

Add to this that the control panel he's working with can be adjusted as well (like a music synthesizer keyboard that can become a piano, a flute, an organ, or a cello with the flick of a switch). Reconfigurable virtual control panels like the one in Fig. 11-7 will allow a worker's station to become many stations. The operator will either use a physical control panel whose functions are changeable, or wear a wired glove for touching completely virtual controls (the glove's functions will be instantly reconfigured depending on the virtual display it's touching).

Figure 11-7

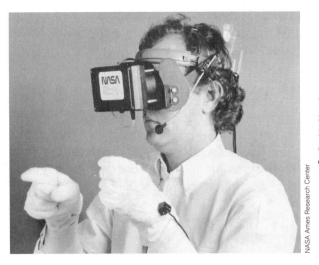

This NASA researcher appears to be pressing a button on a virtual control panel.

NASA Ames Research Center

It's not only possible to use virtual reality to put people inside abstract data or to manage real information to suit them, but the same equipment can be hooked up to other sensory devices instead of a computer. The goggles can be connected to video cameras. The movement of a wired glove can be mirrored by a robot arm.

Virtual reality can project your presence inside of computer-generated worlds. It can also project you around the world to places you can't reach or into environments too dangerous to visit.

⇨ Telepresence

NASA Ames is investigating the interface between man and machine in which virtual reality equipment is used to extend a man's body into a robot. If all goes as planned, in 1996 camera eyes on both NASA and Russian Mars-roving robots will display data back to earth, allowing a researcher to plot the robots' course and see what they see of the terrain. Figure 11-8 shows a remote-control video setup.

Figure 11-8

In this interactive simulation of a proposed Mars rover vehicle, scientists can plan possible exploration routes. The vehicle is based on a Russian design, while the landscape and terrain images come from actual Mars data.

257

Because the time lag between Mars and earth is so long (30 minutes), a virtual environment will be created that incorporates all the data accumulated by the rover. This virtual model of Mars can then be shared in real time with hundreds of researchers; Mars will come to them rather than their having to travel to a special satellite ground station.

This concept was successfully tested in 1993 with a science mission in the Antarctic where the sea floor and ocean organisms were being studied. A submarine called a TROV (a small robotic unit mounted with cameras and other sensors and linked to a support ship via cables) substituted for the Mars rover. Using a satellite uplink, the submarine's mission in Antarctica was run from NASA Ames in California. The submarine was controlled via telepresence and sensors, and its information was digitized and modeled in real time to provide a virtual view of the undersea environment. Not only were scientists around the country able to share the same virtual world view, they could interact with each other in the virtual world and discuss the data as if they were sitting together.

At Sandia Labs, a team of robotic specialists is exploring the use of VR to help clean up toxic-waste dumps. They've already developed a robot that can enter and clean storage tanks at nuclear-waste dumps. Using VR, they plan to overlay video from the robot with computer-generated graphics to outline what the robot can't see.

The operator can guide the robot through the tank with the computer overlay representing hidden problems that are there but out of sight, while revealing additional information to the controller, such as fluctuating radiation levels. Rather than trying to make the robot smart enough to think like a person, the human controller stays a safe distance away and works as if right inside the tank.

Fujita, a Japanese construction company, is developing remote-controlled robots for inspection of construction projects. With a worldwide portfolio of construction projects and limited human resources, Fujita is trying to see if robot-mounted cameras can be used to allow an inspector in Japan to review work in progress in Saudi Arabia. The system would also be useful for inspecting underground work such as tunnels and storage tanks that might be difficult to reach.

Not only does VR allow you to extend the reach of your eyes and hands into dangerous situations, but it allows designers and dreamers to put their hands on their ideas before a single item has been built. Designers are already able to draw and simulate their ideas on 2-D computer screens. The next step is to "put their hands through the screen" and take hold of their ideas in a virtual design space.

⇨ Virtual design

We live in a designed world. Not just houses and space shuttles, but doorknobs, toothbrushes, floor mats, clothing, ball bearings, hammers, jewelry, food, pots and pans, egg beaters, saws, carburetors, clocks—the list goes on and on because everything we use has been designed. Design is the first step in the process of building a product. It's the blueprint of a house, the schematic of an electronic toy, and the 3-D computer visualization of a jet engine.

Computer-aided design (CAD) is an area where computers have already contributed to tremendous leaps in productivity. Products like Autodesk's AutoCAD allow designers to quickly create and edit complex designs on personal computers for all kinds of products.

Photo-realistic images of products can be created from these computer blueprints with the aid of additional software programs. Computers can animate and simulate how the product will perform when actually built, how light will reflect off a surface, and how sound will bounce around a room. Simultaneously, the computer can automatically check through a parts inventory to see if the components a designer has selected for assembly are available.

Already, many companies have teams of designers working together over networks of computers, sharing files, working on common projects, and collaborating together. Combining these systems with a virtual reality interface is the next leap forward in computer-aided design.

"Boeing has made a major commitment to entirely design its next generation of commercial aircraft, the 777, on computers. We can see a big pay-off if we can learn how to integrate virtual reality throughout the process," Chris Esposito, the head of Boeing Computer Services, Advanced Technology Center, says.

Boeing has a company-wide steering council with people from each division to evaluate what applications will benefit most from applying VR. After looking into what Boeing needs to develop in-house, and what it can go outside for (like wired gloves and knowledge from the external VR market), they have set a mission agenda for what in-house research to do first.

Boeing's virtual reality work is divided into three major programs. One group is researching the application of 3-D sound for pilots and AWACS operators who need to have multiple radio channels coming into their headsets at once. Right now the sounds are all right in their ears, mixed together. But if each input could be made to sound like it was coming from a separate and distinct point in space, it would be possible to separately attend to them.

It's the same skill we all use at cocktail parties to pay attention to more than one conversation at a time, except for the pilot each location would have its own designated meaning. For example, priority levels could be set by how far away a sound seems to be from the listener. The more urgent the information, the closer it would be.

The second group at Boeing is researching transparent, or augmented reality. This is being developed primarily for manufacturing. The goal is to improve the productivity of workers by getting them the information they need when they need it.

Imagine a machinist with a metal form in front of him in which he needs to drill holes. By wearing see-through VR glasses, he could see images and data instructing him how and where to drill the holes projected on the lenses. A certain sequence of dots could appear that remain stable to the steel's shape and form no matter how the machinist moves his head. Or the dots might light up in sequence. An actual shop-floor test of this concept is in the works using Virtual I/O Corporation's special head-mounted displays.

The graphic requirements of such a display system are simple, but the head-tracking requirements are extensive. To place the information accurately means monitoring not just the positioning of the VR glasses (which is done today), but of the rest of the environment as well.

For maintenance personnel, see-through VR glasses hold the promise of bringing data to them without requiring them to take their hands off their work. In situations where a mechanic doesn't have as much training as his boss would like, or the plane is an unfamiliar model, VR can make a good mechanic wonderful by putting all the information he needs right at his retina.

Such transparent glasses might one day even provide a kind of x-ray vision. In many jet-engine repairs, the mechanic can't see his hands because they're inside the engine. By tracking the positions of the hands in terms of where the parts are inside the engine, he could effectively "see through" the machinery to where his hands are working, as shown in the illustration in Fig. 11-9.

Figure 11-9

Illustration of how an aircraft mechanic could use a VR system to view virtual information panels that overlay the real image of the jet engine. This is known as augmented reality. University of North Carolina at Chapel Hill, Dept. of Computer Science

The third group is investigating fully immersive VR with the goal of integrating it into the design, testing, and mock-up process. Traditionally, when blueprints were drawn-up (by hand or computer) the design wasn't finished until after a series of life-sized wooden mock-ups were built and reviewed.

These full-scale models of the 727, the 747, and other aircraft were tremendously expensive, but it was the only way to put together such a large and complex creation. Engineering a plane is different than a lot of other design work—a wrong answer here can kill people. Engineers test their designs over and over because there's no room for error.

The Boeing 747 has hundreds of thousands of parts. Versions of the 777 will be flying for the next 50 to 70 years, well into the middle of the 21st century. It will be upgraded and stretched, the avionics will be replaced, and new replacement parts will be designed.

It's a product whose life will span decades and outlast the life of its original developers. There's no way for a single designer or group of designers to keep the entire design of the 777 in their heads when it's finished, let alone as the design goes through evolution and change.

Boeing's Chris Esposito had the challenge of demonstrating the potential and selling the idea of virtual reality inside the company. In October of 1991, his group began showing off a reconstruction of a V-22 aircraft, a tilt-rotor vertical take-off and landing craft. A 3-D model of the plane was designed with all the functional behaviors built-in. This initial project allowed the team to develop new processes for engineers to utilize the new VR technology.

"The demo allowed us to work directly with our customers, Boeing's design engineers, and get input from them about what problems they had in the 3-D design of aircraft that the CAD systems didn't help them find. What issues would they like to learn more about in terms of maintainability and human factors?" Esposito says.

For the designers at Boeing, realism means using the real product data. The VR team discovered that there was an acceptable trade-off between design realism and design usefulness in the VR simulation.

The computational fluid dynamics that affect the surface of a wing are very complex. In the computer model, they found they could replace the design details by a ratio of 20 to 1—that is, reduce the need to draw and animate 500,000 triangles down to 15,000 triangles.

What was important was maintaining the integrity of the design structure and function, keeping the metaphor isomorphic so the simulation would reflect accurate behavior. At this level they were able to animate the design in real time so the designers could step inside the V-22 and give it a test flight.

"We gave that demo until we were sick of it and then we gave it six more months. As we did we turned the table on the engineers we showed it to. We asked *them* to tell *us* what it would be good for. We ended up with a list of some three dozen things that range across all the various points of the product's life cycle, from early concept design to training, education of maintenance engineers for specific procedures and tasks, and even ways of using it when the aircraft is up in the air," Esposito says. See Fig. 11-10 for this list of possible applications.

Figure 11-10

	3-D sound ▽	CATIA compatibility ▽	See-through display headset ▽	Rendering engine ▽	Dynamic interaction ▽	Extended position tracking ▽	Collision detection ▽	Graphics optimizing ▽	Precision movement ▽
Defense & Space Aerospace & Electronics AWACS Workstation		Multi radio channel tracking							
Eng. Design & Test		RFP oral presentations			Astronaut operations evaluation				
ASW Battle Management Workstation					3-D display				
Auto. & Robt.							Remote assembly control		
Military Airplane Cockpit					Digital cockpit design evaluation			Exocentric situation awareness display	
Mat. & Processes					3-D Materials destruction analysis				
Helicopters Manufacturing		Electronic mockup	Wire harness formboarding; Connector & electrical panel assembly		Digital product definition			Digital component installation testing	
Human Factors					Digital cockpit evaluation		Digital crew - chief ops. eval.		
Commercial Airplanes Eng. Computing/Fabrication		Electronic mockup; Pre-assembly			Remote concurrent engineering			Eliminate physical mock-up	
Operations			Wire harness formboarding; Connector & electrical panel assembly			Strut assembly; riveting; Kevlar duct layup			
Maintainability Methods								Digital maintenance demo/evaluation	
Flight Deck						Human model control		Testing of digital airplane cockpit	

A10239.08

Boeing's analysis of where VR could be effectively applied in their business.

It won't replace traditional CAD tools. Traditional CAD will maintain a big lead in usefulness because of the maturity of its functionality and the fact that it's been around longer with more time invested in refining its usefulness. There's also the lack of affordable high-resolution display goggles. At least for the foreseeable future, wide-screen monitors will continue to lead VR goggles in terms of resolution.

Eventually, VR tools will become a natural part of CAD. The early CAD adopters of virtual reality design tools are going to be people doing 3-D modeling and 3-D positioning. This is a skill that's useful across many industries, from mechanics to architecture, jewelry to automotive design.

In particular, 3-D positioning and modeling are important in ergonomics, the design of environments in which people have to fit into and function. Designing a space or product for a person to use requires a 3-D perspective and interactivity that traditional 2-D design tools don't deliver.

⇨ Human factors

"Anytime you have a human who has to do something with a product, you are in the realm of human factors," says Pete Tinker, Research Engineer at Rockwell International. Like Chris Esposito, Pete is exploring how virtual reality can help his company produce better products and increase design efficiency.

"Whether they're jet engines or truck axles, there has to be a 'reach envelope' or a 'viewing cone' built into the design for repair work to be effective," says Tinker. "How far can someone reach from a certain position with certain constraints? Such as, he can't bend forward beyond a certain amount, or move something with just the strength in his fingers.

"If you can be sure something is maintainable up front in the design, then a lot of trouble can be saved. Traditionally, once you've reached a certain point in the design process it is going to cost you more money to redesign than to fix it, even if you know that to repair a truck axle will require you to pull out the engine and disassemble it. One of the worst examples I know of is a certain aircraft for which it takes eight hours to repair a simple problem: four hours to get to the area of the engine where the problem occurs, a few minutes to change the parts, and then four more hours to reassemble the engine. The engine works fine, but the human factors for repair were not well designed."

Virtual reality will change the way designers work by placing them inside the design and reducing, even eliminating, the need for mock-ups. Alias Research of Canada is exploring how virtual design can shorten the design process, reduce errors, and eliminate redundant steps, such as repeated creations of product mock-ups.

Originally developed to serve the needs of computer animators, the company's software products are used by designers at companies like Honda, General Motors, BMW, Sony, Industrial Light and Magic, and hundreds of others.

Alias Research's automotive customers have already asked for life-sized, real-time ray tracing in virtual worlds (a computer graphics process for creating accurate reflections on surfaces, such as the reflection on a chrome bumper). Even with today's supercomputers, however, this isn't possible. The reflective realism of images in such scenes is so complex to compute that it's in conflict with producing smooth motion. The computer spends so much time recalculating the images, frame by frame, that it's impossible to redraw them fast enough to maintain the illusion of reality.

The first stage in enhancing the automotive design process has been to incorporate a high-resolution boom-mounted VR, made by Fake Space Labs. Using the boom like a periscope, designers can climb inside a proposed design and experience it more fully than on a flat display.

Alias' designers find that filling the field of view gives them a better sense of the scale of large objects and of surrounding space in interior designs, such as the front seat of a car. They find that the freedom of the boom, the ease with which they can step up to it or walk away

and get in and out of virtual reality, is a plus. Future innovations in VR goggles will need to address this ease of use to succeed.

Designers who use CAD software are always looking to work faster, with more complex designs, and to integrate their models into one faithful representation instead of having to work on 30 different subassemblies. Such advances will require new kinds of software and enormous computing power, beyond even today's supercomputers.

Boeing's designers would like to be able to simulate a working jet-engine design so they could literally stick their hands into the engine and test repair practices along with performance before the engine is built. To do this will require software that can create objects (engine parts) that can recognize the boundaries or edges of other parts.

Boeing's designers want the spinning virtual turbine blades to be able to tell them if they're too close to the side walls of the engine housing. They want more than simulation; they want intelligent objects. But to get what they want could be a ten-year wait; the challenge is that big. Figure 11-11 shows a NASA wind tunnel, where results of a flow simulation can be interacted with in real time.

To simulate jet engines today takes supercomputers; to interact with tomorrow's designs will require massively paralleled supercomputers and distributed processing. To create a functionally accurate, working jet engine, each part of the engine will require its own piece of software and its own computer to exist. Massively parallel supercomputers do just that because they're made up of hundreds, even thousands of microprocessors.

The software that runs on such supercomputers divides up a task and assigns pieces of it to an individual computer chip within the system. This means each moving part of the engine would have its own microprocessor to draw its image and compute its relationships to all the other moving parts in the engine. The engine wouldn't have to look real (with shiny chrome and paint), but it would have to function realistically.

These kinds of supercomputers are being built today, but the software to create the simulations has yet to be written. And the software won't be easy to design.

Figure 11-11

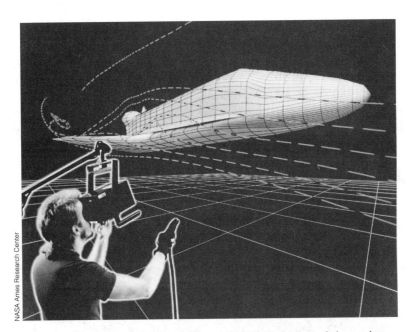

NASA Ames Research Center

At NASA Ames, engineers use a BOOM and powerful graphics workstations to experience a virtual wind tunnel, where results of a flow simulation can be interacted with in real time.

In addition to the problem of creating simulations that can re-create the look and function of a very complex jet engine, there will still be the difficulty of re-creating the *feel*. As of today, the wired glove has no way of physically signaling to the user that his hand is stuck. And there are even more subtle issues, such as figuring out how to simulate what is just enough space for a hand to wiggle into a tight opening.

There are software design programs that can calculate, based on real-world examples, how much space is enough for a hand, but just as a stick figure molecule is better at representing the tactile shape of a molecule than a VR simulation, there will continue to be limitations and trade-offs to balance the amazing capabilities of virtual reality for a long time to come.

Virtual prototyping

Once upon a time, people designed a part and then went over to the forge and started hammering it out. There was an intimate, inherent

bonding between design and manufacture because the designer really understood how the thing was made.

Virtual prototyping promises to turn the engineer back into an artisan. He will be able to work with the design as if it were a malleable yet solid object, be able to move and handle the product as if he were crafting it in a workshop, and then produce it himself without leaving his office.

When the design is ready, the parts can be "printed out" directly from the computer screen. Designers will eliminate weeks, even months from the process of making prototypes. And eventually they'll be able to fabricate real parts for short production runs with the ease of printing out an engineering diagram. The increase in engagement and personal involvement with the work will go up, along with a sense of realism in the work.

"Virtual prototyping is one area where I think we are going to see good uses of VR," says Pete Tinker of Rockwell. "You can make sweeping changes to a new jet, can change the physical characteristics to something new without having craftspeople tear out everything and destroy the original. It means you'll be able to change the entire design much further along in the process than ever before."

From a wireframe skeleton that a designer can stretch and bend, twist and shape, a rough form is crafted. Then the part can be given a skin and smoothed with a surface modeler, or converted to a solid with more traditional 3-D CAD tools. These tools will eventually be available by speech command or whatever interface the designer wants.

Many companies already have advanced 3-D CAD systems coupled to databases of basic parts. As designers develop products on the computer, they check their selection of components against the database. This not only tells them if the parts they need already exist, but also provides background data on strength, size, amount in stock, etc.

In the future, design analysis and verification will be performed on the computer in real time (it currently can take hours), with interactive finite element modeling so that the stress level in the part will also be modeled as the designer works.

Plastic prototyping is already available on PC-based systems. 3-D Systems, a Valencia, California company (which is 37% owned by the pharmaceutical and chemical company Ciba-Geigy), has sold hundreds of systems to produce prototypes with a process known as *stereolithography*. In this process, the computer takes a set of coordinates from the computer model of the part and uses it to control the movement of an ultraviolet laser. The laser traces cross-sections of the part onto the surface of a liquid polymer solution, causing it to solidify. The pattern builds up the part in layers of plastic a few thousandths of an inch at a time. The process can produce prototypes of engine blocks or diseased hip bones patterned from the data from a medical scanner. Figure 11-12 shows a component that was created using stereolithography.

Figure 11-12

DTM Corp.

Using stereolithography, this part was fabricated out of loose powder with the aid of a laser beam. With virtual prototyping, objects created in the virtual world can be converted into something you can hold in your hand.

This is fine for prototypes, but a plastic jet-engine block will never stand up to temperature tests. Research is under way at M.I.T. on three-dimensional printing. Researchers take a 3-D computer design and slice it into minute slices. Instead of a laser, a small nozzle (like on some computer printers) squirts a binding chemical onto a bed of powdered ceramic, stainless steel, or another metal. After this process is repeated for hundreds of layers, the semisolidified part is then fired in a furnace.

This method is already being used to develop ceramic molds for metal casting. Called *CAD casting*, it bypasses having to make metal dies to create wax patterns that are dipped in a ceramic slurry to create such a mold.

There are technical problems yet to be overcome before companies can make metal parts with nearly the same density as those produced through conventional casting and milling. Yet casting and prototyping is already possible for a wide range of products to be produced by "desktop manufacturing."

A new kind of computer network will appear, one built around "product servers," the manufacturing version of an office automation server. Instead of information on marketing, finance, and research, however, it will transmit data on product design from the design department right out to the factory floor. The entire manufacturing process will be transparent to everyone on the product network. Manufacturing management will be able to monitor the development of products and anticipate retooling needs while having some control over the parts database from which the designers can draw. Product marketing input on customer reactions to products in development will be fed directly into the network.

NEC is already installing their first experimental virtual design network on which engineers can work together to create products, as shown in Fig. 11-13. They're going to study the effectiveness of real-time manipulation of 3-D objects in the design process and how engineers, distributed over many sites, can work together.

This evolving process of computer-aided design and computer-aided manufacturing will contribute to further flattening out organizations

Figure 11-13

In this picture, a designer uses VPL DataGloves to collaboratively design a new car with the help of another designer located in a building hundreds of miles away. This project is part of NEC's investigation of the uses of VR.

and breaking down institutional walls. Nearly all the information product designers need will reside on the network. This will make it more likely that a designer could work at home rather than traveling to an office. It also means that a factory might not be a dedicated facility. The product server might be down the hall, across town, or in a vendor's office—a service bureau that specializes in producing quick, short runs of customized parts.

Along the way the designer's role will begin to resemble that of the traditional craftsman or artisan who both designed and built his creations. Large production runs of fixed designs can be replaced by large, medium, and small runs of custom designs. Not only will manufacturing and design teams be more closely integrated, the customer will become part of the design process.

In his book *Future Shock*, Alvin Toffler prophesied a future production environment where the power of the computer coupled with telecommunications would allow many items, such as clothing, appliances, and furniture, to be produced in a semicustomized manufacturing process.

A businessman could go to buy a suit and, instead of picking one off a rack, would select a basic design. His measurements would then be taken with microlaser exactness; buttons, collar style, and fabric would be selected and all the data sent off to a computer-controlled tailoring factory. A week later the customer would return to pick up his finished tailored suit with its perfect custom fit.

While this tailor shop is still somewhere off in the future, its forerunner already exists for more expensive, large-scale products. Matsushita has installed a Virtual Space Decision Support System (VSDSS) at its Shinjuku showroom in Tokyo. The system has been designed to allow customers to design a kitchen, based on over 30,000 products manufactured by Matsushita for the home.

Virtual marketing and sales

Imagine you've returned to the Shinjuku showroom after your first visit last week. You're planning to remodel your kitchen. Matsushita will manufacture the entire kitchen, ship it to your door, and install it. But first you have to design it.

The Shinjuku staff takes you back into the design room, which is empty except for a table with a few chairs and a computer sitting on it. Last week you sat at that computer with an operator and sketched out the shape, size, and structure of your present kitchen. Then you selected the new appliances, floor tile, shelving and cabinets, colors, and curtains you wanted for your remodeled kitchen. You experimented with dozens of floor plans and countertops. Today you've returned to visit your future kitchen for a final inspection. The completed computer-simulated kitchen is waiting for you to inspect (see Fig. 11-14).

When you put on the gloves and goggles, the empty display room is suddenly replaced with the simulated animation of your new kitchen. Reaching out with your virtual hands, you begin to walk around the room. You study the placement of the new cabinets, the way morning sunlight comes in through the new window. Your virtual hand slips through the wood panel of a drawer, and by curling your fingers you're able to pull it open.

Figure 11-14

Matsushita Electric Works Ltd.

A Japanese woman's view of her kitchen as rendered by a graphics workstation in real time. Water "flows" from the faucet she just turned on.

Reaching towards the sink, you turn the cold-water handle and bright blue water starts to pour from the faucet. You can hear birds outside and the sound of water pouring down the drain. You decide that the dark granite you selected for the countertop is too dark and there isn't enough room between the counter and the sink to work comfortably. You take off the goggles; it's time to redesign. Figure 11-15 is the finished kitchen design.

In the case of traditional products, it's been possible for a customer to decide on a purchase only after looking and touching the parts in a showroom. With a virtual showroom, customers can experience their custom-designed product before it's built. How well is a room lit after changing lighting equipment, or how much is the car noise decreased after inserting sound-proofing material in a wall?

Reading specifications off a brochure can never replace experience. No one except a specialist can appreciate a brochure that states, "outside noise is reduced by 10 decibels when upgrading to new insulation."

Figure 11-15

Matsushita Electric Works Ltd.

After the design has been approved, in just five days a custom-designed kitchen will be installed.

The showroom now takes on an entirely new function. It's not simply a display center; it has become a design center where the customer comes into direct contact with the manufacturing process. Using the telepresence aspects of VR, it's possible to present many more products than a showroom could possibly hold.

Matsushita has over 30,000 different products. It could never display all of them nor could they easily be combined with a large-scale product such as the system kitchen, for customer inspection. The virtual showroom is a display without a display space or geographic limitations, which allows for an unlimited combination of ideas and products.

With the development of such hands-on design systems for customers to interface with, it's possible to envision a total production system that translates a customer's experience directly into a manufactured product. Architects already use computers to provide limited 3-D walk-throughs inside new building designs. But peering through the window of a computer screen is a very different experience than actually walking around inside the proposed room and making changes as you go.

In presenting a virtual-building walk-through, the architect can be sure to add features and colors the customer is fond of, emphasize the customer's most important design ideas in the simulation, and give the customer a feel for what the real building will be like. Working together with the customer, the architect can design a floor plan and move walls around, change the landscaping, and even complete the interior design of a house. The customer then gets to visit, step into, and walk around the home before a dime has been spent physically building it.

This kind of decision support will help eliminate the chance of errors or misunderstanding in the production of a new kitchen or home. It draws the customer into the development cycle, making him a partner in the process and helping to close the sale.

There's less of a chance for "buyer's remorse" because the customer has been intimately involved every step of the way. If and when complaints arise with a finished product, both parties will have fully detailed simulations, along with a parts list and blueprints, to use in resolving misunderstandings.

Virtual reality also gives retail stores a new way of testing out a variety of store layouts and aisle-display strategies before committing to remodeling a store. The ways in which products are displayed within a supermarket or department store are crucial to the success of the store. Customers can be invited in to see their reactions to new designs.

Warehousing duplicate sample products at each showroom can also be cut back. Products displayed in Shinjuku, Tokyo can be seen by a customer using the desktop showroom at Takamatsu as if he was walking through the remote showroom. This reduces the need for redundant display space, and the expense of maintaining multiple showrooms can be kept at a minimum.

Of course, these savings need to be balanced against the cost of the computer equipment, its upkeep, and the training of the operators. The trade-off is cost-effective only with large purchases today, such

as the designer kitchen described previously, but once the system is in place, adding products and services is easy.

Matsushita claims that customers feel a sense of increased control and satisfaction over their purchases by "visiting" their kitchen before purchasing it. Meanwhile, factories await producing certain products until specified customer orders arrive. Just-in-time manufacturing becomes only-when-ordered manufacturing.

Not only can customer involvement help with current products, it can help design products that are years, even decades away. Mercedes Benz is using a simulation to test and evaluate new car designs. Unlike Matsushita, Mercedes' manufacturing depends on large-scale production runs of essentially the same car. However, customer input on the ergonomics and handling of the product are being incorporated into the design process.

They're bringing potential customers and designers to a driving simulator that contains the finished car (see Fig. 11-16). The car is set inside a dome and is wired with an extensive array of sensors. Somewhat like a flight simulator, a driver gets inside the car and goes for a virtual ride. The designers can then simulate all sorts of weather and road conditions. Sound effects add rain, and a motion-control platform supporting the car accurately re-creates road conditions. With this simulator, designers can evaluate the effect of altering the dashboard, or learn how the driver's experience changes as they change shock absorbers and other equipment to build safer cars.

Unfortunately, safety can't compete against performance on an automotive trade-show floor. Surrounded by the glitzy booths of performance cars like Porsche and BMW, Volvo has a hard time pulling in show attendees. People wait in a long line for a change to sit in a Porsche racecar simulation. Volvo turned to Division Ltd. in the United Kingdom to develop a fully immersive crash simulator to dramatically demonstrate Volvo's key benefit. The five-minute crash sequence provides the experience of a 25-mph side impact without the reality of physical harm. The system debut at last year's London Motor Show was so successful in drawing crowds and communicating Volvo's benefits that it has been used throughout Europe.

Figure 11-16

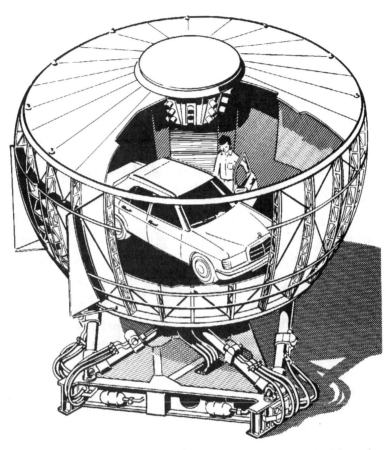

Illustration of sophisticated driving simulator built by Mercedes Benz. Mercedes Benz

The marketing department of a cruise-ship line is planning to test a projected reality-type system in shopping malls. One of the ways they typically reach new customers is by setting up information booths inside shopping malls. A large-screen system showing the deck of a cruise ship with the sun going down over a tropical sea as music plays would be a real attention-grabber. Then when potential customers walk up, they'd be surprised to see their own mirror image projected into the scene. It's a dramatic and very literal way to get potential customers to "picture" themselves on a cruise.

And what about architectural walk-throughs? They were the first simple demo just about every VR lab ran out and created as an example of a

277

practical application. At the Siggraph '93 trade show, The Institute for Simulation and Training at the University of Central Florida demonstrated a virtual version of a real four-story, 300-room office building. Fully texture-mapped, the lobby had paintings and carpets, the cubicles had furniture, and the lunch rooms had vending machines.

In the north of England, near Newcastle, the Tyne and Wear Development Corporation is using VR to showcase a 25-acre redevelopment project. The Quayside development, along the banks of the Tyne river, has an estimated budget of 180 million pounds. The finished site will incorporate offices, shops, housing, leisure and cultural facilities, and parking.

A more conventional approach to representing the development site would have been paper-based designs and handmade models. While some models are still being used, a VR version of the site was constructed with the help of Dimension International.

Already existing buildings are shown alongside proposed additions. As the design for additional buildings is completed, they're added. The ease and speed at which the virtual site can be updated is impressing the architects, civil engineers, planners, and members of the corporation. The general public and likely customers can tour the site to inspect potential rental space, the furniture, the even take in the view through a virtual window.

⇨ Is it too good to be true?

Virtual reality is already beginning to change the way business works. It provides new ways to represent and communicate reality and abstract data by customizing it for our senses. It allows people to use their natural human talents for analysis and pattern recognition in areas from finance to information management, product design, manufacturing, and sales. There's the danger, however, that it will become too good to be true.

Literacy is important in a modern society because language shapes the way we think and also determines what we can think about. This is equally true if you substitute the word *visualization* for *language*.

There's no such thing as the "last word in data representation" in virtual reality. Lotus-style spreadsheets have been the financial simulator of choice for over a dozen years. Something like Bradford Smith's flowsheet might be the equivalent for the 1990s.

The danger with this new medium is our own unfamiliarity with it. Solutions might arise too swiftly with too much success. A stale set of visual metaphors creates a more subtle and profound problem than wrong data. By restricting the set of available images, we limit the ways we think about computer-generated models and thereby limit potential insights. In a recent article entitled "Computer Graphics as Allegorical Knowledge: Electronic Imagery in the Sciences," R. Wright noted that "There is a danger that once programming solutions to visualization problems have been satisfactorily implemented, they might become entrenched in methodological frameworks difficult to escape from, static interpretations restricting the innovations necessary for the unbounded growth of knowledge."

The long-term problem with virtual reality might not be the question of "what can we do with it?" but rather that we can do too much with it and become seduced by the engaging dynamics of interactive reality. It's important to never forget that these are computer-generated models.

Building and managing computer-generated realities for accuracy and honesty is important. The output is only as good as the data fed into the system. Constantly questioning the usefulness of the metaphors that are developed will keep VR applications fresh and productive.

This is important in business, but it's vital in medical research and practice. The American practice of medicine is already big business, infused with high-technology products like CAT scans, MRI, x-rays, endoscopic surgery that puts tiny fiberoptic cameras inside patients, laser surgery, genetic engineering, and much more.

Just as virtual reality is changing the nature of research and work in business, it will provide doctors with new tools for education, investigation, and healing of the human body.

Medical applications

MEDICINE in America has been a high-tech industry for some time. The image of the family practitioner has been replaced by specialists with strange new tools and technologies. Twenty-five years ago the first heart transplant operations made headlines around the world. Today, not only are organ transplants common, but doctors are attempting to transplant baboon hearts and livers into people to find a way to alleviate the short supply of organs.

The grandfather of high-tech medical sensors, the x-ray machine, is joined today by ultrasound, computer-aided tomography (CAT) and magnetic resonance imaging (MRI) machines. These devices create volumetric images of internal organs, or cross-sectional images of the body's interior. They've revolutionized neurosurgery by providing a window into the structure of the brain, revealing tumors, malformations, hemorrhages, lesions, and a variety of pathologies without the need for a surgeon to go in.

The medical community and its institutions are careful about adopting new technologies, and with good reason. History shows that many new wonder drugs, techniques, and methods demonstrate unexpected complications over time. For every new technique that succeeds, many others fail. Because of this, the U.S. Food and Drug Administration (FDA) can take up to ten years to approve a new medical technology as it's studied for side effects and usefulness in long-term clinical trials.

This conservatism has its own side effects. Over 15 years ago, CAT-scan manufacturers offered doctors color monitors for improving the way they studied the interior of the body. Most doctors, familiar with

the shades of gray found in x-ray images and the early CAT scanners, turned down the enhancement. One of the few doctors who bought a color monitor placed it where his patients could see it, set the controls so that the brain would appear purple and the surrounding flesh green, and continued to use his black-and-white monitor for diagnostic work.

But times are changing in the medical community. Reform of the health-care industry is on the national agenda and everyone is looking to high-tech solutions to help make medicine more efficient and affordable. A generation of doctors are emerging who have been raised on computers and trained on high-tech equipment. Medical schools are beginning to incorporate multimedia training programs, and course work is being distributed over local-area networks for access by individual dorm-room computers. The tools of virtual reality are poised to contribute to saving lives in several ways.

In research, virtual reality is helping to design new drugs. Biochemists are using it to better understand the structure and properties of large organic molecules, while working with these molecules as if they were physically on a workbench in front of them.

Virtual methods are also being tested as an aid in diagnostics. At the University of North Carolina, Chapel Hill, they're developing a set of VR goggles that will hook up to an ultrasound scanner. The ultrasound image will be overlaid on transparent goggles (the same way Boeing hopes to provide jet mechanics with information).

When these methods are implemented, an obstetrician will be able to use see-through VR goggles while examining a pregnant woman, as shown in the illustration in Fig. 12-1. He will be able to see the woman and talk with her while watching her fetus as if with x-ray eyes. Even the individual components of VR are proving useful in medicine. Wired gloves are being used to aid in the rehabilitation of injuries and as a new kind of prosthesis.

Developing medical VR applications is going to take longer than industrial ones because the need for accuracy is higher and harder to produce. It's much easier to test an engine design than an artificial heart.

Figure 12-1

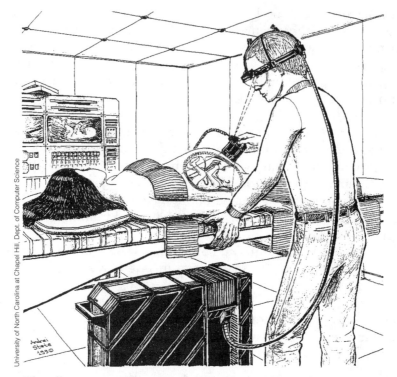

University of North Carolina at Chapel Hill, Dept. of Computer Science

This illustration is one way future physicians might use virtual reality technology to provide an augmented view of an unborn child using ultrasonic imaging.

The largest and most immediate potential benefit from virtual reality systems might be in improving teaching and training procedures for doctors. Medicine is changing and advancing as fast as computer technology, maybe even faster. New procedures and techniques appear every year.

At the same time, patients are becoming more informed and aggressive as they learn to shop for medical treatment just as they would for other services. Established doctors are being pressured to pick up new procedures faster than ever. Virtual reality's biggest contribution to medicine might be in improving doctors' learning curve.

⇨ The learning curve

There are two kinds of learning curves in surgery. One is when an experienced surgeon first performs a new operation. The other is when a young doctor first performs an established operation. New doctors gets their chance only after much study, and after assisting a doctor who already knows the procedure. Usually the initial practice is done on animals and cadavers, but eventually the new doctors make the jump to real patients.

Surgeons have long accepted the inevitability that some patients will be injured from the learning curve. But in 1992, New York health officials stepped in and established ground rules for a new laparoscopic gallbladder procedure, insisting that surgeons not be allowed to perform it until they've shown adequate skill in at least 15 supervised cases.

Laparoscopic and endoscopic methods are part of a family of new surgical procedures that avoid cutting open major portions of the patient in favor of cutting several small holes. Instead of opening up the patient to reach the work site, a laparoscope, a device with a fiberoptic light and a tiny camera on the end of a thin cable, is inserted and carefully maneuvered through the body for a close-up view of organs and tissues. The images from the camera are displayed on a video monitor in the operating room and instruments are inserted through the other holes and manipulated from outside the body.

The surgeon, then, is actually performing a kind of telepresence, watching on the television the work he's doing while pivoting long-handled instruments through a hole. This method cuts down on the chances for infection and the amount of damage done to the body to simply reach the work site.

For the first time a doctor doesn't have his hands inside his patient where he can touch and see all the organs. Doctors familiar with traditional surgical methods have had to relearn the feel for the tissues and instruments. How much pressure is enough as they find pathways and cut through the body?

Over 500,000 gallbladder operations are performed each year in the U.S. The new laparoscopic method of doing gallbladder surgery promises patients less pain and a shorter stay in the hospital.

The demand for this new procedure has been so dramatic that it has forced doctors familiar with the older method to quickly learn the new technique rather than risk losing patients to competitors who offer the new method. The unprecedented demand for the new procedure highlights an old concern in medical circles surrounding the learning curve.

Most medical complications in surgery occur with doctors who are new or who are performing a new procedure. While doctors are put through lengthy apprenticeships, their chances to observe and assist on actual patients is limited.

In a typical college situation, six or seven young doctors walk through a ward with an older teaching doctor. Surrounding a bed in a ward (or in a surgical theater), there is room for only one or two doctors to actually be at the teacher's side. The other students are listening, taking notes, and scanning through textbooks for back-up information on the disease or procedure.

Unlike airline pilots who are trained on flight simulators, there hasn't been a way until now to even consider developing a surgical simulator to help bridge the gap between practicing on cadavers and working with a real patient.

Surgical simulator

Cine'-Med, of Woodbury, Connecticut, is developing a surgical simulation system to train doctors in laparoscopic cholecystectomy. Their system, the Virtual Clinic, is focused primarily on television-controlled endosurgical procedures since this mimics the real-life operating-room environment.

Development of the Virtual Clinic began with the creation of an accurate anatomic landscape: three-dimensional representations of

the liver, the gallbladder, and related structures. Programming free and occupied space, collision detection, and spontaneous objects gave the simulation its realism.

The rules of free and occupied space allow each simulated organ, or piece of an organ, to have its own dedicated space. Collision detection algorithms define when a virtual organ is touched by a virtual surgical tool. As organs are dissected, spontaneous objects are created that are subject to the same rules as the other objects.

Actual surgical instruments are used for the system I/O, and are inserted into a fiberglass replica of a human torso. The instruments have been retrofitted with switching devices to relay the opening and closing of the tips, and position trackers are located within the fiberglass torso.

On the video monitor, graphic images of the organs and instruments appear. An inset window relays monitoring information: blood pressure, heart rate, and other vital signs. The patient's physiological reactions during the procedure are simulated by the Triage Knowledge System.

The Triage Knowledge System is an expert system built on artificial intelligence programming. It allows for realistic patient reactions derived from surgical stimuli, including death, if bleeding isn't controlled, or if the heart rate fails.

The Virtual Clinic allows a professor to adjust the difficulty of the simulation to match the expertise of individual students. Surgical anomalies and emergency situations can be replicated so students can experiment and gain expertise on a wide range of problems before moving on from computer simulations to animals.

Procedural steps can be repeated and recorded for review at a later time. There's no other type of training situation in medicine that allows such a degree of personal feedback and performance evaluation. Surgeons can repeat particular steps many times without having to perform the entire operation. They can replay their efforts many times in order to study areas in need of improvement.

The Virtual Clinic is just the first step. Cine'-Med plans to develop other modules for the Virtual Clinic, including the Virtual Abdomen, the Virtual Thorax, the Virtual Pelvis, and the Virtual Heart. Developing individual simulations of different areas of the human body is the difficult first step. Developing a complete body simulation will be a tremendous task. Unlike a flight simulator, where the pilot's point of view passes over an essentially static landscape, the interior landscape of the human body is alive in thousands of ways.

⇨ Full-body simulations

Joseph Rosen of Dartmouth Medical School in Hanover, New Hampshire, has a team working on a computer graphics-based patient model of skeletal muscle. The team's goal is that this virtual patient will accurately reflect the geometry of the body and the biomechanical behavior of the physiological systems under study.

A fully authentic software reproduction of the human skeletal muscle system will require a clear understanding of the structure and function of muscle cells. Rosen's team is investigating how best to represent and re-create them in a computer graphics model. Once they can faithfully represent the muscles and their performance and interaction, the simulation could help plan operations.

For example, large wounds require surgical reconstruction. The best option is often a muscle transfer, in which an insertion point is shifted so that a healthy muscle covers the affected area. Surgeons typically rely on experience to judge which muscle is appropriate in terms of shape and to save as much overall body functionality as possible.

Think of the body's system of muscles as an interdependent series of springs and pulleys. The repositioning of a muscle will reduce the strength available for coordinating certain body functions. One muscle's gain is another's loss; there's always a trade-off. An accurate computer model of the body could assist in understanding the biomechanical results of reconstructive surgery and help the surgeon make the best choice.

Rosen's group has developed the software models they believe will allow them to construct a complete body. They've developed computational models of several parts of the body (skeletal muscle, skin, and an articulated skeleton) that need to be integrated into a more complete model.

The generic design will eventually be able to accept MRI, CAT-scan, and other data to customize for a particular patient's physical condition. It will allow for preoperative planning, training, and perhaps even surgical assistance during the actual operation. This is an incredibly challenging task, one that will require years of work.

Parts or all of this virtual body could be viewed on a surgical workstation. A more useful simulation would involve the use of transparent high-resolution goggles. Putting on the goggles, the doctor would see a virtual body on the table in front of him while still being able to see his hands, tools, and assistants. The body would be transparent in order to reveal the important organs or biological systems he wants to study. Through the goggles he would have a virtual display of vital information, visible wherever he wants it, containing a wide variety of patient data.

For teaching purposes, a group of students could all be wearing similar goggles or viewing online simulations from their dorm-room computers. Because this would be entirely generated out of a computer model, the students could choose to have a point of view from anywhere in the operating room, even mimicking the doctor's point of view, directly over the patient.

Information screens and the ability to zoom in on various details would be user-specific. The doctor could demonstrate procedures, such as administering a particular drug, and the effects of the drug on various organs and systems could be illuminated as it spreads through the body.

⇨ Simulations as teachers

Computer simulations aren't new to the medical field, but the ability of computer graphics to create virtual organs and bodies is. For

many years there have been computer-based text-only simulations for new procedures and medications. Pharmaceutical companies often support the production of these programs so that doctors can keep up on new products.

A text-based simulation describes a series of symptoms and then offers a choice of options for the doctor to select from. Depending on his selection, the reaction, side effects, or necessary intervention appears on the computer screen.

Many universities are already developing their own multimedia simulations and databases for eventual sale to other colleges. The medical school at Washington State University has spent over ten years gradually developing a complete digitized catalog of the human body.

They've already released a laser disc containing 54,000 microscopic photographs of the human heart. And they're mapping the entire human body with the goal that, by the time they're done in the late 1990s, there will be computer technology capable of taking their images and creating an animated virtual body for medical simulations.

Working with a team of medical illustrators, ADAM Software Inc. of Marietta, Georgia has built an interactive multimedia reference guide to the human body, Animated Dissection of Anatomy for Medicine (ADAM). It offers an anatomical database with high-resolution illustrations coupled with detailed medical information.

ADAM lets the user peel away the skin and dig into the body one tissue layer at a time, to as many as 40 layers, revealing every bone, muscle, and nerve. Each area of the body can be viewed from the front, side, back, or by cross-section. In side windows, users can consult x-rays, CAT scans, and tissue studies, and even view typical pathology progression on the displayed section.

The software has authoring tools so that instructors can organize material for training by attaching notes in side screens, animation, and video. Students can be guided through simulated surgery and doctors can use it to brush up on procedures.

ADAM (soon to be followed by a female version, EVE) can provide a more realistic experience of studying the body. For example, a professor at the University of Arkansas School of Medicine is developing course material that will reinforce understanding of the relationship between layers of the body by taking students on a journey through the skin and asking them to identify vessels and muscles and note the nerve supply for each muscle. He will be able to construct animation to illustrate the consequences of injuries, such as a knee's reduced range of motion because of ligament damage.

James Black, Ph.D., uses ADAM to train and test residents at the James A. Haley Veteran's Hospital in Tampa, Florida. He rehearses surgical procedures with his students and then tests them on the system before they actually step into the surgical arena.

Systems like ADAM are the forerunners to fully interactive virtual surgical simulators. Students coming out of the training colleges will be ready to accept the new virtual methods now under development. Even medical researchers are getting involved. They're taking the same techniques used in virtual design and prototyping and making them available to doctors.

⇨ Computer-aided surgery

The advent of telepresence interfaces such as the endoscope and intelligent tools like a force-sensitive scalpel are leading some researchers to envision a form of telesurgery.

Early in the next century, surgeons might be able to choose to work from surgical workstations for some procedures. These stations will sit in a special room or right inside the operating theater. The doctor and his assistants will prepare the patient, correctly placing the endoscope and tools into the operation site and hooking them up to a bilateral robotic system that can control their movement in any direction the doctor requires.

Retreating to the surgical workstation, the doctor will see a 3-D view from the endoscope on his monitor that will let him know exactly

where it is in the patient's body. A separate monitor (or a window within a larger screen) will provide a view from a different angle, a computer-generated image of the body for guided positioning of the endoscope's placement.

Assured of the instrument's location, he will take up the interface tools that provide feedback to his hands. These special joysticks (or some other new devices) will provide position scaling and force scaling so that the movements of his hands are carefully transferred down to the micron-level movements of the tools at the operating site.

Important medical information will be overlaid on the monitor for easy access or conveyed by speech synthesis, depending on the doctor's choice (foot pedals might offer another form of physical interface).

Such a surgical workstation would also provide a collection point for the integration of other medical information. For example, previously processed MRI or CAT-scan data on the patient, along with his medical record, could be downloaded to the workstation from the hospital's computer network. Or the data might come from an out-sourced MRI clinic's image-processing databank.

The surgical workstation would also allow the surgeon to plan several moves and simulate them on the monitor before actually doing them. By rehearsing his efforts on the computer before instructing the system to automatically carry them out, the doctor could find the best solution before making his move. The uses for a surgical workstation aren't limited to human bodies. When used with an electron microscope, it will allow microbiologists and genetic engineers to work directly inside cells.

➡ Fantastic voyage

In the classic science-fiction movie, *Fantastic Voyage*, a team of scientists and their medical submarine are shrunk down to cell size and injected into the body of a political leader to do emergency repair work deep inside his brain. Along the way they travel through the swirling currents of his blood system.

In the real world of the 1990s, researchers are using computers today not only to teach and heal, but to go on fantastic voyages to study biological processes. They're studying the composition of the body in a similar way to NASA engineers studying the flow of wind across a wing.

A team in Germany is using a supercomputer to realistically simulate the functioning of the heart. They want to download the results of their computations to a system using Silicon Graphics hardware so they can tour the interior of the heart as it pumps. Like the NASA Ames team who's developing a virtual wind tunnel, these German researchers want to take the computational skills developed by material researchers to study fluid dynamics and apply it to the interior of the heart.

How does blood flow through the heart? What happens to the swirl of blood during a heart attack? Virtual reality will allow the German team to stand inside the ventricles of the heart and watch the blood swirl around them.

The fantastic voyage takes on even smaller dimensions as another group of medical researchers are shrinking down to the size of atoms. In a dimly lit room in Chapel Hill, North Carolina, a pair of molecules float in space. DHFR (dihydrofolate reductase) is a protein molecule; its partner is methotrexate, a drug molecule used in cancer treatment. Both appear as collections of different colored spheres, where the colors represent the drug's individual atoms.

A research chemist sitting in this room watches a large molecule, his hand holding the pistol grip of a GROPE-III. Developed by Frederick Brooks over many years, it's a mechanical navigation device that transfers the chemist's hand movements into the behavior of the atoms.

He's been trying to dock the two molecules and find the right spot that will allow them to link up. Molecules not only have shape, they have regions of varying electronic force depending on the placement of their atoms. From every position they shake, and attract and repel different points at the same time. The researcher has been unable to get the two molecules to link up simply by using visual cues.

Stepping on a floor pedal, the researcher activates the force feedback in the maneuvering arm. The bar he's holding begins to shudder and pull as a motor hooked up to the grip translates the electric behavior of the atoms into his hands. Now he can judge the structure of the atoms and their physical and atomic forces.

This system gives chemists the ability to physically experience how drug molecules dock. Chemists report that they have a new understanding of the details of the receptor site and its force fields, and of why a particular drug docks well or poorly. The chemists who've used the system can quickly reproduce the true docking positions for drugs whose positions are known. They also can find very good docking spots for drugs whose true dockings are unknown.

These haptic displays provide an important design bridge between the stick-figure models chemists have traditionally used to help them visualize molecules and computer graphics. Scientists can acquire a feel for the forces that link and bond atoms into molecules, both the kinds of fields and the distribution of forces within a single molecule. It helps them understand why each particular candidate docks poorly or well, leading to ideas for new candidate drugs.

The molecules are modeled using several feature sets. CPK models are spheres representing individual atoms colored according to type. Sticks represent the bonds between the atoms, and a ribbon is the amino-acid chain backbone of the molecule. Depending on the power of the supercomputer that does the initial computations for the simulation, very complex molecules can be created.

The National Supercomputing Center is working on extremely complex simulations of molecules, with thousands of atoms. The researchers want to simulate them in real time with the correct representations of their bonding force fields so they can reach in with a wired glove, tug on the atom, and study how it retains its integrity. Being able to watch this behavior will give chemists a more intuitive understanding of the nature and construction of molecules.

It's not only atoms that researchers want to position. Treatment procedures can be simulated and run with the same kind of control as a research chemist juggling molecules. Radiation planning, for

instance, is one of the most difficult parts of cancer treatment. Doctors try to position the gamma-ray beams to irradiate a tumor with a high enough dosage to kill the malignant cells without damaging the tissues around it. Doctors study 2-D x-ray films of the body to try to plot the 3-D trajectories of the energy beams.

By incorporating actual 3-D data of the patient's body, doctors could run trials of various beam therapies by hand and see immediately how well they'd work. A hand-held wand or other pointing device could be used to angle and control the beam.

Putting on a set of goggles, the doctor could see the patient's body in 3-D as he worked on a tumor. He'd position beams, lock in their positions, and then move around to review his own work from a different position. Several beams could be lined up and their configuration adjusted for the best possible effect. A low-frequency hum could be used to give real-time feedback on how far off target the beam was from the tumor. The color of the beam could shift as the doctor moved off target or when his approach touched too much healthy tissue.

Rehabilitation

Most of the attention in virtual reality goes to the immersive experience of putting on goggles and glove and going into another world. In the medical field, however, there's as much interest in using the separate elements of VR equipment as there is for the total experience.

Walter Greenleaf, co-founder and chief executive officer of Greenleaf Medical Systems (GMS), has licensed exclusive medical rights to VPL's DataGlove and DataSuit technology. He sees a range of applications where the pieces of VR can be as useful as the 3-D worlds.

The GloveTalker is GMS's first VR-based product. It uses the hand-gesture recognition capability of the glove to translate gestures into spoken words (or text on a screen) so patients who can't talk can communicate. Using a Macintosh computer and proprietary software, specific phrases and words can be assigned to individual hand positions.

The product is designed primarily for use in hospital settings and has been tested at Loma Linda University Medical Center in San Diego, California, and Cal State Northridge. Stroke victims, someone whose larynx has been removed, or people with cerebral palsy who have both motion and vocal impairment but can still use their hands can use it to communicate with their caregivers. The glove can be programmed with several hundred phrases.

This kind of gesture recognition offers the possibility not only of aiding hospital patients, but also of serving as a new kind of prosthesis in the outside world. Because the DataGlove can translate gestures into computer commands and spoken words, it's possible for someone with very restrictive limitations to control preprogrammed equipment.

For example, there's an application where a DataGlove and a Macintosh II computer are hooked up to a receptionist's PBX telephone workstation. Using hand gestures, the receptionist can instruct the computer to answer and route telephone calls, or to activate prerecorded messages for callers.

Because only two degrees of freedom are necessary to reproduce the position of a cursor on the screen, a user of the glove can control the positioning of a mouse with just his fingers or by the movement of his wrist. In this way he can select icons off a screen to control the equipment.

With a change of software and the addition of an analog-to-digital converter card in the computer, the same glove can be used to measure the freedom of movement for the wrist and hand. In real time, a computer is able to calibrate the glove's position and range of motion at 14 different joints: finger and thumb, wrist extension, flexion, and radial/ulnar deviation.

This information can be useful for worksite ergonomic analysis for computer operators, assembly-line workers, and other people with Repetitive Strain Injury (RSI). RSI occurs from performing tasks that require limited and repetitive hand movements and is one of the more crippling and prevalent injuries of the modern workplace. The glove can also assist in tracking patient rehabilitation and therapy.

The interactive ability of the computer to manage and display information and control devices to suit an individual's needs opens up new ways for handicapped workers to participate in society. Computers are already being used to help severely handicapped individuals function in society.

The great physicist, Dr. Stephen Hawking, most widely known for his bestselling *A Brief History of Time*, is a victim of ALS (amyotrophic lateral sclerosis), or Lou Gehrig's disease. Hawking is often referred to as a successor to Einstein, but his body has gradually deteriorated over 30 years and his mind has remained unaffected. He has almost no control over his body and must be propped up in a wheelchair. He is unable to feed himself and needs nursing 24 hours a day.

Dr. Hawking communicates with the world by selecting words on a computer with one finger, which are then converted by a speech synthesizer. In this difficult and limited way he has managed to convey the solutions to some of the great physics problems of our time and write several books. Not only could a VR system with goggles provide him with a sense of openness and escape from the limitations of his body, it could revolutionize his ability to work and communicate his ideas.

Besides the GloveTalker, there are already sensitive control mechanisms for tracking eye movement that could be coupled with button or joystick controls to serve as an interface to a custom VR information-management system.

In this way, people who are physically impaired could use their minds to the fullest extent possible. Instead of having to conform to their handicap, the handicap could, in a sense, conform to fit them. And very weak physical movements could be augmented by equipment that amplifies the user's body.

Another way that VR equipment could aid in healing is by tracking and recording very small improvements in a patient's physical condition. The DataGlove and the DataSuit can collect data about a body's position and freedom of movement dynamically in three-dimensional space. This allows a level of accurate motion analysis that was previously unavailable.

For example, the progress of stroke patients is made up of small improvements; the biggest problem can be keeping their spirits up when they have no way of judging their own progress. As patients gradually recover control over their bodies, accurate tracking of small but increasing freedom of movement and control can provide a way for the patients, care providers, insurers, and family members to monitor the progress.

Besides directly assisting people with disabilities, virtual reality is being used to help redesign the buildings they have to move around in. In Chicago, at the Hines Rehabilitation and R&D Center, Dr. John Trimble and Ted Morris have developed a wheelchair simulator using Sense8 software to test the accessibility of building designs to be sure they meet government standards.

The Americans with Disabilities Act passed by Congress includes legislation designed to ensure that public buildings and spaces accommodate the needs of the physically disabled. Until now it was difficult to test designs, and doing so involved either building large cardboard models of the space in order to simulate what it would be like to navigate through it in a wheelchair or asking a wheelchair user to provide input based on written documents and blueprints.

Now architects can download the computer-designed floorplans of their buildings into the system and then test out the building. The system uses a real wheelchair installed on a platform that transfers the movements of the wheels into navigation information for the Intel Pentium Processor-based personal computer.

Putting on Virtual Research goggles and a glove, anyone can travel around the building, reach out to shelves, drawers, and doors, and tour virtual buildings from the perspective of someone in a wheelchair. Corresponding views of someone using the system and his virtual reality viewpoint are shown in Figs. 12-2 and 12-3.

The system is set with width parameters so if a doorway is too small the software won't allow the virtual wheelchair to get through. Not only is the simulation a powerful way to test new buildings for accessibility, it simultaneously educates architects on what life is like when you can't stand up and walk through a building.

Figure 12-2

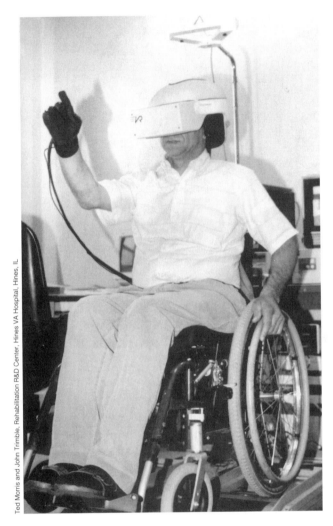

Ted Morris and John Trimble, Rehabilitation R&D Center, Hines VA Hospital, Hines, IL.

By hooking up a wheelchair to a VR system, architects can design buildings to be more accessible to the physically disabled. Rollers underneath the wheelchair feed information to the computer controlling the simulation.

⇨ Medical wonders

By the turn of the century, the "graying of America" will be a major social trend. We're going to see a restructuring of health care in the U.S. as new technologies enter the field and public pressure to reduce costs increases. Computer networks will allow many hospitals to out-source services they once brought in-house.

Figure 12-3

An example of the kinds of images seen by the wheelchair VR user. Access to cupboards can be measured with a wired glove.

Hospitals often acquired MRI scanning equipment as a way to attract high-quality doctors who would refer patients to them and as a way of generating extra revenue. These services are going to either be localized at a few hospitals in a region or spun-off into small independent business units as a way to lower costs and increase efficiency.

Research laboratories are going to go online as advanced electronic microscopes and scanning tunnel microscopes become accessible by distant medical researchers via telepresence. The results will be greater access to technology for researchers, and lower cost as the equipment is spread out and shared by many more people.

Computer-aided imaging technologies will be an online resource to every doctor. Doctors will share services over networks of workstations within hospitals or from private clinics.

More and more computer-aided imagery will be used to explain and educate patients about what is happening to them. In the next century we'll very likely see the emergence of home imaging systems in which patients can monitor and keep track of developments inside their own bodies (much as diabetics already track their own blood pressure and blood sugar levels).

Many of the real rewards from the integration of virtual reality technology and medical technology, however, won't begin to appear until the late 1990s. Luckily, the underlying technology is common across many different fields and industries. As Boeing, Rockwell, NASA, and other companies figure out what it takes to create industrial simulations as rich as a fully functioning virtual jet engine, the same information will become available to medical software developers working on living virtual bodies.

The new entertainment economy

"The entertainment industry is now the driving force for new technology, as defense used to be."

Edward R. McCracken, CEO of Silicon Graphics, Inc.,
***Business Week*, March 14, 1994**

ON February 25, 1993, over 28 million viewers in Europe, the U.S., and Japan watched virtual reality on the Oprah Winfrey show. Oprah had dedicated the day to showcasing new technologies that promise to change the way we live, work, play, and think. She seated herself in a Visions of Reality game pod, put on the HMD, and entered cyberspace.

She flew through a galaxy of stars, shot at enemy spacecraft, and got sucked through a wormhole that tossed her out on the other side of the sky. When she took off the HMD, her eyes sparkled and the "Wow" that escaped from her lips said it all—that virtual reality entertainment had arrived.

The entertainment industry is going to be the vehicle that turns VR into big business. At a conference in Japan, the chairman of Sony was heard to say, ". . . after the camcorder, the next big thing is going to be virtual reality."

How big is the entertainment industry? From toys to cable TV, movies to sports, entertainment is the fastest growing sector of the

U.S. economy. Using data from the Bureau of Labor Statistics, *Business Week* calculated that the entertainment and recreation industries added 200,000 workers in 1993—a stunning 12 percent of all new employment. That's more workers than were hired by the health-care industry, the preeminent job creator of the 1980s.

Movies already allow us to vicariously step into other worlds. Museums use giant IMAX movie theaters and amusement parks use simulation rides like Disney's Star Tours to thrill visitors with an even greater sense of sensory immersion and physical participation. Entertainment and virtual reality seem made for each other.

In *The Psychology of Optimal Experience*, Mihalyi Czikszentmihalyi describes six criteria that most often characterize experiences individuals consider optimal. The experience must:

➤ Require the learning of skills

➤ Have concrete goals

➤ Provide feedback

➤ Let the person feel in control

➤ Facilitate concentration and involvement

➤ Be distinct from the everyday world

Virtual reality entertainment clearly meets these criteria. The difficulty can be increased with usage in order to challenge the improving user's skill. The goals are concrete whether it's dodging hockey pucks, making music, or blowing up tanks. Virtual reality stands out with its potential for extensive feedback in real time and its unique ability to give players a sense of being in worlds very different from the one they live in.

Many entertainment companies (with the exception of Lucas Arts) sat out the emergence of the computer-game industry. Like the old railroad companies that didn't initially perceive airplane transportation as competition, the Hollywood studios initially disdained the computer-game craze.

While regular software applications are considered successful if they achieve sales in the tens of thousands, computer-game titles regularly sell in the hundreds of thousands. Characters like Sega's Sonic Hedgehog have become cultural icons to millions of young boys. The BattleTech computer game has given birth to clubs, books, and now even a virtual-reality arcade business.

From big screen racecar simulators, like Sega's Test Run, to Visions of Reality theme centers and Sega's Home VR game system, everyone is betting that virtual reality will be the television or computer-game innovation of the 1990s.

Sim rides

Just as flight simulators were the forerunners of today's virtual reality systems, simulation rides are the vanguard of the new immersion entertainment industry. The evolution of sim rides holds lessons for the future of VR entertainment.

Lucasfilm's Industrial Light & Magic (ILM) has created several of these rides for amusement parks around the world. In one, SpaceRace, the riders are loaded into a space shuttle (a long room) for a ride up to NASA's orbiting space station. There are rows of airplane seats all facing a big screen at the end of the room. The roar of the rockets fills the riders' ears as the cabin shakes with the lift-off and clouds fly by, thinning out into darkness, until the stars of space appear in the windows.

Over the intercom, their friendly space-shuttle pilot narrates the trip with a John Wayne drawl. As the shuttle nears the space station, it passes by a black-hole generator. The device inadvertently turns on and sucks the shuttle down a swirling wormhole and ejects it in a distant section of the galaxy.

In the far reaches of space, the riders find themselves caught up in a Star Wars-type stockcar race. The captain aggressively pilots the craft around a racecourse littered with traps and obstacles, all the while dodging competitors who try and crash each other's hotrod spaceship.

The ride's most powerful effect is the invisible motion-control platform beneath the cabin that tilts and tosses the whole room. It's very effectively timed to work with the visual cues happening on the screen to manipulate riders' sense of gravity. It's relatively limited, but sharp motions are all that's required to create vertigo and draw screams from the riders as they see themselves crashing into walls and swerving around obstacles.

Neither big budgets nor big-name talent assures a winning sim ride. Universal's Back to the Future: The Ride cost well over $15 million dollars to create and is a major success. But the far more expensive Secrets of the Luxor Pyramid, at the Luxor hotel in Las Vegas, has not done as well.

Both were developed by special-effects wizard Doug Trumbull. But where Back to the Future has a familiar ride and story that's easy to follow—flying through a brief history of time—Secrets of the Luxor Pyramid has an original but overly contrived story you have to follow through three separate theater experiences. The first theater is a wide-screen movie about an archaeology adventure. Customers are then ushered into a virtual talk show with the same characters from the first movie chatting away. Part Three, the Theater of Time, is a seven-story theater with sim-ride seats. The audience is taken on a gently rocking journey through mankind's potential futures. The technology is impressive; the story isn't.

Reviewing the experience for *Wired* magazine, Michael Krantz writes, ". . . I can't help but think that, despite all this new movie tech, I would have been more lost in the experience—more immersed, if you will—watching *Terms of Endearment* on a six-inch black-and-white screen. Sorry, fans. The Trumbull attractions had boring and barely coherent stories."

Star Tours and Back to the Future: The Ride succeed because the ride is based on popular movies—meaning the stories are well known—and the ride is used as the climax of an entire entertainment experience. These rides employ elaborate preshows consisting of video presentations, actors, and a holding area designed to complement the story. In Star Tours, you meet the Star Wars

characters while waiting in line and the holding area is designed to look like a launch center for spaceships.

In these settings, the public arrives already understanding the environment, premise, and characters. Very little plot development is necessary; instead the customer just enjoys the ride, which is about all you can do when your seat is tossing you about. Trumbull's attempt at innovation with Luxor, pulling the preshow into the ride, might have worked if he had put as much energy into the story as he did the technology.

Sim rides go interactive

Even though these rides can create a powerful illusion of going to another world, they lack VR's key ingredient—interactivity. Essentially, viewers are taken on a roller-coaster ride with special effects.

Learning from the success of the sim-ride industry, a new generation of interactive sim rides are beginning to appear at centers like Fightertown (Irvine, CA) and The Magic Edge Entertainment Center (Mountain View, CA). These centers use flight simulators to let customers experience the same thrill of air combat that Air Force pilots have experienced for years.

Kenney Areo's Fightertown offers players a choice of F-104 Tomcat, F-16 Falcon, F-111 Aardvark, or F-104 Star Fighters with full-motion simulation. All pods are networked so players can participate in multiaircraft strikes and play against each other. Each aircraft is supported by an Intel-based personal computer and a Tellurian AT200 Image Generator, which produce 8,000 flat-shaded polygons per frame at a 30-Hz frame rate.

The Magic Edge Entertainment Center houses 12 two-ton interactive fantasy flight simulators called Hornet-1s. The interior of the single-passenger fiberglass cockpit has all the trappings of an F/A-18 fighter plane—flight harness, joystick, and throttle (see Fig. 13-1).

Figure 13-1

Magic Edge
*Magic Edge
Entertainment Center
in full motion.
Occupants are treated
to a thrilling ride in an
F/A-18 fighter plane.*

The motion-control system can pitch the nose of the capsule up at a 45-degree angle, roll it plus or minus 60 degrees, and pitch the nose down at 25 degrees. The system can move the pod so quickly that the designer claims it will give people a sensation of pulling 2.5 Gs for half a second. Up to six units can be networked together so players can fly missions and dogfight with one another.

The 12,000-square-foot center is the first of many planned for construction in the U.S. and Japan. It combines briefing and training areas to boost the overall experience. Customers are treated as fighter pilots from the moment they enter the center. Clearly, Magic Edge has learned from the older sim-ride industry.

New themes and games will be introduced regularly at the center to provide a variety of experiences. Of course, a cafe and gift shop will round out the facility so excited customers can relax after a ride and select a souvenir to take home.

In a development that's becoming common throughout the VR industry, Magic Edge has signed a multimillion-dollar joint deal with an established entertainment company, Namco Operations, Inc., that will allow Magic Edge to expand rapidly and refine its technology while acquiring management skills from one of the largest commercial game equipment makers. Established over 35 years ago, Namco operates more than 700 amusement centers and amusement parks worldwide. It's one of the world's foremost designers of electronic games, including such well-known titles as Pacman, Wacky Gator, Final Lap, and Galaxian.

Like most other new technologies, these sim rides take existing products—flight simulators—and enhance them just enough for the public to enjoy. The true creative potential of the technology is still in the hands of technologists, and just like the early film industry it remains a genie locked inside a bottle.

⇨ Virtual rock 'n roll

In 1993, a new direction in sim-ride software was pioneered by Danny Socolof and Peter Gabriel. Socolof is a producer whose work ranges from staging rock-concert stadium tours to creating traveling interactive events for companies like MTV, Nintendo, and Pepsi. His company MEGA is staging the Blockbuster Video championship video-game playoffs, as well as the interactive high-tech showcase at the 25th-anniversary Woodstock concert.

Socolof toured the sim-ride and VR industries in the early 1990s, visiting all the major players. He was searching for a new kind of interactive experience he could bring to the public via a touring exhibit. While the quality of most VR systems he saw would disappoint the public, traditional sim rides seemed to hold untapped potential.

Sim rides had traditionally required fixed installations, but a new mobile breed of ride was just beginning to appear. Mounted on large trucks, they could easily tour the country. In some cases, instead of the entire cabin moving, just the individual seats moved. Socolof's inspiration was to marry the exciting software of music videos with sim-ride technology.

To bring his vision to fruition, he enlisted the aid of rock musician Peter Gabriel, himself famous for his innovative music and use of technology. Based on Gabriel's song, Kiss that Frog (from the Us CD), a surreal and impressionistic retelling of the classic frog/prince fairytale was created. They called the ride The Mind Blender to express their ambition to creatively shake people up.

Brett Leonard, the director of *Lawnmower Man*, and Angel Studios, one of Hollywood's hottest computer graphics houses, were brought into the project. Using one of the first all-digital, high-definition video cameras, Gabriel and an actress were first filmed dancing, singing, and flying in the air against a giant blue backdrop.

The digital video was then transferred to workstations where computer graphics and fine-art illustrations were substituted for the blue background. The frog first entices the princess into his surreal pond and then chases after her through the water, a forest, even underground, changing into Gabriel only after she finally kisses him (see Fig. 13-2).

Figure 13-2

Peter Gabriel, 1993, Angel Studios

Scene from Peter Gabriel's Mind Blender sim ride.

Gabriel himself took a hand in programming the movement of the sim-ride seats. He wanted the chairs to do more than bounce, pitch, and rock as the music and visuals played; he wanted the riders to "get funky" and feel like they were dancing.

The combination of great music with a familiar story and dazzling visuals made for one of the best sim rides ever. It also awakened the medium to a whole new marketing and creative direction—people who would never bother with a roller-coaster sim ride want to ride the music video-driven Mind Blender. Socolof and Gabriel demonstrated what can happen when artists get hold of a new technology and reinvent it.

The only problem with the Mind Blender is that the audience is still stuck on the other side of the screen as passengers. Many people don't want more than that, but what about the rest of us who don't want to be simply passengers on a wild ride. What if we want to be the driver?

Virtual reality arcades are arriving at a shopping mall, amusement park, and soon a home computer near you. Arcade simulation rides with limited interactivity, single- and dual-person cabs, and free-standing units are the first VR systems reaching the public. They come with names like BattleTech, Dactyl Nightmare, and Cybergate, and they're showing up all around the country, in Europe, and in Japan.

⇨ VRcades

> "Well, what if you had a game with the addictive nature of Tetris together with strong character development and a compelling plot? What would happen if you backed up these terrifically visual games with great themes and great characters? You'd be in a whole other stratosphere."
>
> **Jeff Berg, head of International Creative Management (ICM), *Wired*, March 1994**

Virtual reality gaming parlors are at the center of an explosion in location-based entertainment (LBE) centers. For many years there were a set number of alternatives for entertainment away from the

home: movie theaters, amusement parks, music and sporting events, concerts, clubs, dramatic theaters, and museums. New technologies are reshaping this mix, blending together traditional destinations, formats, and media to create completely new kinds of entertainment.

Commercially oriented IMAX theaters are being built to rival the traditional museum-based network of theaters. These giant-screen high-resolution theaters provide an almost immersive experience of being in the action. Mainstream-style movies are now being created to supply the newer theaters with more exciting fare than traditional museum-dictated space and nature documentaries.

Interactive adventure centers with names like Big Future and Kids' Place are coming to cities around the U.S. They're commercializing the playful hands-on approach to science and learning pioneered by places such as San Francisco's Exploratorium.

Amusement parks build new roller coasters to attract more customers. They can cost up to $7 million (or more) and have at least a ten-year lifespan. Roller coasters are proven winners for amusement parks, and a new roller coaster almost always boosts park attendance.

Virtual reality rides don't have the proven track record of roller coasters yet. But unlike roller coasters, virtual reality rides are programmable. With a change of software, dueling spaceships can become a journey into a haunted castle, a hovercraft race, or a time-machine ride. The hardware stays the same but the ride can be anything the fickle public wants.

Virtual reality arcade centers combine the thrill of sim rides with the interactivity of video games to produce a new kind of suburban entertainment destination. These centers are being conceived and designed with complete theme environments and role-playing personnel. The ambition of their owners is to create theme parks inside shopping malls—a single store housing more rides than Disneyland.

There are already a handful of success stories in the VR entertainment industry, role models being closely watched and

emulated by the newest start-ups. Though more elaborate competitors are chasing them, the originators have the advantage of being first to market.

The most successful product to date has been Virtuality from W Industries. For $60,000, you can purchase either a sit-down or stand-up game. In the sit-down game, players use joysticks to fly a simulated Harrier jump-jet on various missions and dogfight with other networked players. Accelerated Amiga computers generate the real-time stereoscopic images and quadraphonic sound, and interface with the various sensors and trackers. A six-pound custom head-mounted display called a Visette (based on LCDs and an electromagnetic tracker) is clamped to the participant's head.

In the stand-up game, shown in Fig. 13-3, you move about on a platform that houses the equipment and are surrounded by a circular railing that keeps you from having an inadvertent collision with a reality called the floor. Putting on the helmet, you see a fairly simple world called Dactyl Nightmare, where one or more players are represented by a humanoid, cartoon form.

You stalk and pursue each other around a multilayered set of chess boards, like the 3-D chess set on "Star Trek." The idea is to kill or be killed in this shoot-'em-up game. And if battling other people isn't thrilling enough, there's a giant green pterodactyl swooping about the world looking to turn you into its lunch. *Newsweek* called it a video game on steroids. Think of Virtuality as the pinball machine of VR entertainment. Because of its convenient size, it can be set up almost anywhere or added to an existing arcade location (a number of nightclubs have ordered one).

Virtual World centers represent the next level: a complete VR entertainment center. The technology was inspired by the idea of networked military-tank simulators. The original, and most popular game, BattleTech, is configured for two teams of four people who play against each other. The players sit inside ten-foot-long cabs (see Fig. 13-4) called Battlemechs that are made of metal and plastic and are supposed to be the command cockpits of giant robot warriors.

Figure 13-3

W Industries Ltd. UK, 1992

The Virtuality VR game system from W-Industries Ltd. Participants use pistol-gripped devices to shoot each other in the game Dactyl Nightmare.

Each cockpit holds one player who watches the action unfold over two monitors. One is a 25-inch color monitor showing the "outside" virtual world. A smaller secondary screen below the main monitor shows radar and other detection systems to let you know if there are any other mechs around and whether they're friend or foe (see Fig. 13-5). Microphones let team members communicate with each other. The second screen also shows real-time information about the Battlemech's condition: sustained damage, heat buildup, etc. There's a joystick with triggers and buttons for controlling different weapon systems, and there are panels of switches for configuring which weapons are fired by which buttons. You don't have to understand all these controls to get in and immediately have fun.

Figure 13-4

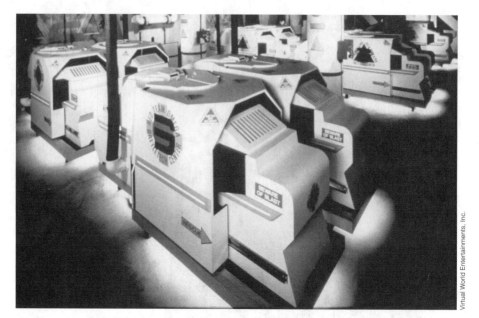

Virtual World Entertainments, Inc.

View of BattleTech control pods. Groups of players battle one another in a simulated future war zone.

After signing in at the front desk in the Explorer's Lounge, visitors are matched up with other people to create teams. The teams are taken into the Containment Bay to prepare for their trip. A uniformed officer instructs the players on their mission, the enemy, and how to use the pods. Veteran pilots huddle around interactive kiosks to learn about advanced controls or access to up-to-the minute vehicle, map, weather, and terrain conditions. The center staff matches the simulation's difficulty to the expertise of the teams. The officer also gives each player a choice of Battlemech to fight in so his cabin can be programmed accordingly. There are Lokis, Vultures and Thors, with various combinations of armor, weapons, and speed for each.

You steer a pod like a battle tank, with two floor pedals for turning left and right and a forward/reverse throttle. You're surrounded by speakers, which heighten the sense of realism by supplying the sounds of machinery and battle. There's also a subwoofer in the seat, and though it doesn't sit on a motion-control platform the entire pod seems to shake when the Battlemech is hit.

Figure 13-5

Virtual World Entertainments, Inc.

BattleTech control console. The top monitor displays the view outside the vehicle and the bottom screen shows current operating status.

The game starts. You and your Battlemech are released on the surface of a stark, empty landscape. Almost immediately you're in a fire-fight, with lasers and bombs from other Battlemechs going off all around you. Your pod is rocked by an explosion. You've lost an arm. You turn around and blast away at the nearest Battlemech—regardless if it's on your team or not. Its like being dropped into the middle of an old Western shoot-out. You're inside a giant video game where the whole point is shoot up the landscape and each other.

The first Center opened August 1, 1990 at Chicago's North Pier and was entirely designed around the BattleTech game with a military,

postnuclear-war look. Three additional BattleTech-styled centers successfully opened in Japan, two in Tokyo and one in Yokohama.

The newest U.S. centers are in Walnut Creek and San Diego, California. They've reconceived the look and idea of the business as a new kind of theater that will host various games that change the same way movie theaters change products. To do this, the "story" of the center has been expanded.

The new look is Victorian and each center is now an outpost of the Virtual Geographic League (VGL). Founded in 1895 by Nikola Tesla and Alexander Graham Bell, VGL is a secret society that developed the UPT pods to transport pilots to different dimensions, or virtual worlds. From the 19th-century furniture and VGL archival photos to the riveted steel walls of the Containment Bay, the theme is best described by VWE president Jordan Weisman as "Jules Verne meets Blade Runner." The new theme of the centers allows them to easily introduce new games, and therefore attract repeat customers.

Visions of Reality

Following in the same mold and chasing the same market, Visions of Reality (VOR) seeks to out-do Virtual Worlds on every front, including marketing, game development, design, and technology.

Instead of simple graphics created with inexpensive hardware, VOR drives each game pod with a powerful graphics workstation to create truly interactive VR. Each pod has its own 3-D graphics workstation by Kubota Graphics, Inc. (KGI was formerly the graphics supercomputer maker Stardent). The stations can manage worlds up to 10,000 textured polygons, at 20 frames per second or better. With this kind of graphics performance, complex and realistic environments can be easily created.

The workstations are networked via Ethernet, allowing for up to 36 players on the same network. Because the system is a distributed architecture, if one pod fails the others can keep playing. And adding more pods doesn't slow down the entire game because each pod's

experience is rendered by its own workstation. Positioning information is shared between pods, so each player's point of view accurately reflects the group activities.

VOR's adventures are presented to players in a 7×8-foot spaceshiplike pod that incorporates controls for playing the game and multiphonic sound. An HMD by Kaiser Electro-Optics, Inc. provides fully immersive viewing of the game's real-time, 3-D graphics.

Where the Virtual Worlds experience is based on a tank-simulator format (the image is displayed on a monitor), VOR is more like flying around in an open-cockpit WWI biplane. You see the virtual world no matter which direction you look as you fly among the stars and starships.

Instead of trying to keep track of the action on two screens (front view and radar), VOR's tracking radar is an optional transparent map you can project over your view of the action. This re-creates the heads-up display found on modern jet fighters. Players find they can keep track of multiple information variables more easily because they don't have to keep moving their eyes between two screens.

Like the movie industry, the cost of introducing virtual reality arcade centers will depend on amortizing the installation costs over time, using new titles and updated releases of old games to bring in new customers and sustain repeat business. The parent company of each competing center talks of opening dozens of sites (as many as 150), but virtual entertainment is a risky business; millions of dollars are riding on the success or failure of just these two companies.

Whether there's a market for multiple chains of equal size will depend on their ability to differentiate themselves from each other and attract a loyal audience. Yet each chain is going to require a large number of sites to bring in enough money to fund the annual development of new games and destinations. The creation of a top-rate video game routinely costs several million dollars.

Already one VR center might close without ever having opened its doors: Star Trek: The Next Generation. Paramount Communications signed up Spectrum Holobyte, a computer game firm, to develop the

software for the new virtual reality theme centers. Plans for the centers called for re-creating the sets of the popular television series, including the bridge, holodeck, transporter room, and engineering. The concept of the role-playing centers called for teams of players to stand-in for some of the various TV characters and essentially act out a 20-minute episode of the show.

Early software prototypes used simulated actors, computer graphics versions of the show's real actors. Texture-mapped images of the actors' and actresses' faces were attached to a programmable wireframe skeleton. These synthetic people were so realistic that Paramount executives were reportedly shocked.

Who owns the rights to an actor's face in a digital re-creation, when that face is associated with a character created in another format? Hollywood has never had to tackle this issue before. What rights do actors have when a synthetic version of themselves can be made to say lines they never spoke, or appear in a film (or a game) they never agreed to do?

Escalating costs, concerns over the marketability of such a complex role-playing scenario, and internal company politics has led to repeated delays. Now it seems that the project might be shut down or changed entirely.

Home systems

Where are the home VR systems? What are Sega and Nintendo up to? They both have research projects. Nintendo is working with Silicon Graphics and Sega has shown off a system, but repeatedly delayed the date of an actual product introduction. Difficulties in developing a low-cost (under $500) head-mounted display have been partially the problem.

Sega is still struggling to develop an inexpensive HMD with enough resolution to satisfy customers. Their first attempt was showcased at a large trade show, but never made it to market. They have since completely reengineered the product and it's rumored to be released in time for Christmas '94.

The gradual trend towards home VR is already apparent as companies lay the foundation for the kind of high-performance systems needed for home VR. As computing power gets better and cheaper, we'll see a dramatic change in the entertainment industry as Hollywood software is married to Silicon Valley hardware. It has already started to happen on sound stages around the world.

Inside a converted office building next to Highway 101, Sega engineers Spencer Nilsen and David Javelosa translated the actual movie footage from *Jurassic Park* into a computer game that put users face to face with a rampaging Tyrannosaurus Rex.

For the game, Sega had a team of writers, artists, and composers combine actual film footage with animation and sound. It follows the movie, where genetically engineered dinosaurs created by a fictional Palo Alto research firm run amok on an island off the coast of Costa Rica, terrorizing a half-dozen hapless humans (sort of an updated Lost World).

Sega of America built its own multimedia production studio, so they were able to release the game at the same time the movie debuted. To bring film-quality images and sounds to a video game, Sega (as well as Nintendo) have both developed custom CD-ROM drives to attach to their systems, the same kind now becoming standard on personal computers.

CD-ROM, short for *compact disc, read-only memory*, is exactly the same size and design as the audio CDs that now dominate the music industry. And they can hold 100 times more information—including video and sound—than the traditional game cartridges used by Sega's Genesis system and the Super NES from Nintendo.

This kind of storage capacity will give the game makers a foothold in the home for the emerging world of multimedia computing. And it's the same kind of data storage device that will help bring VR into the home. Sega's plans, however, don't stop with Jurassic Park; they're also planning games based on the Looney Toons characters, including Bugs Bunny and Daffy Duck.

The D. W. Griffiths, Orson Welles, and Alfred Hitchcocks of VR haven't appeared yet. But some artists are already experimenting with interactive worlds.

⇨ Interactive movies

While arcade experiences will be the initial offering to the public, creators are already looking beyond these forms of enhanced video games. Just as radio incorporated vaudeville before finding its own entertainment forms, and TV incorporated radio variety shows before finding its own way, virtual reality entertainment will use video games as a stepping stone to something new and original.

Thomas Dolby has been making innovative music and videos since the early 1980s. Best known for such songs as "She Blinded Me with Science" and "Hyperactive," he is also well known among recording artists for his role in championing new technologies.

"When the first synthesizers came out, I did everything I could to get hold of one," says the composer and rock star. "They were expensive, but they allowed you to make completely new kinds of music. I knew that eventually everyone would be able to afford one, but I'd be ahead of the game. That's why I'm jumping into VR now; I want to learn how to create and compose in 3-D because I think it's where entertainment is going."

In 1993, Dolby formed Headspace, a company dedicated to being a leader in the emerging world of three-dimensional, interactive music. Dolby wants to pioneer the new musical landscape of virtual reality. Besides several CD-ROM projects, he has contributed to scores for several VR game attractions.

"You can either use music linearly to drive the pace and shape the experience, as is done in music videos, or it becomes its own unique creation within the world," Dolby says. "In a fully interactive VR world, you can't write a traditional score because you can never know what's going to happen next. Instead you give each object or character its own musical signature. For example, in an underwater adventure the deeper you go in the water the darker and more foreboding the tones become. Little fish have small, chime-like notes to them, which become louder the closer and more of them there are. A shark or octopus entering your vision has its own unique sinister refrain. The challenge is to create sparse little arrangements that will work together in whatever combination they might occur in. It is very easy to create cacophony."

Working with VR pioneer Eric Gullichsen, with support from the Intel Digital Education & Arts program, Thomas created the first interactive music world that synchronized animated figures with 3-D sound. Along the way Gullichsen and Dolby created what could be considered the first short virtual movie, the *Virtual String Quartet*.

In the very early days of film, very short subjects were created to give people a taste of the new experience. The *Virtual String Quartet* provides an immersive, interactive experience with characters who don't talk, but express their moods through their music.

"For most people VR is strange enough as it is with all the equipment you have to wear," Dolby says. "So my idea was to reach out to the rest of the public who normally wouldn't have anything to do with it by enticing them with a string quartet. Your granny wouldn't do VR, but she might like to sit in with a professional string quartet and listen to Mozart. And what if she had the chance to direct them?"

The Turtle Island String Quartet went into a recording studio with Dolby and Gullichsen. Dolby directed the recording of the music, first the complete piece and then individual improvisations. Gullichsen strapped sensors to the musicians' wrists and arms. He digitally recorded their movements so that he could use them to program the animation of their computer-graphic alter egos.

In the *Virtual String Quartet*, viewers find themselves in a rehearsal space where a string quartet is playing Mozart's Quartet no. 21 in D Major. Moving to a different location in the room shifts the sound accordingly, so that the cello sound always appears to be coming from the cello, the viola sound from the viola, and so on. You can even stick your head inside the violins.

Adventurous users can approach the musicians and, by tickling them, send them into an improvised jazz or bluegrass solo. Only one solo can be discovered at a time, allowing the user to create distinctly different pieces of music or just enjoy the Mozart. The solos represent each character's mood and personal musical taste, which doesn't always blend into the classical accompaniment of the group.

The first public display of the *Virtual String Quartet* was part of a show entitled Virtual Reality: An Emerging Medium, presented by Intel and the Guggenheim Museum in New York. At that show, the quartet was displayed in an augmented reality format using transparent VR goggles from Virtual I/O. Users could see the museum gallery and other visitors through the glasses while also seeing the computer graphic characters of the quartet seated around them playing. This mixing of "real" and "virtual" realities made for a unique presentation.

"I can see this going two ways in the future," Dolby says. "One way will be toward more complex experiences that users will explore or view as they choose. The characters will do more than play music; they'll re-create scenes out of movies, or create entirely new dramatic scenes. The other direction will be to create unique virtual places in cyberspace for people to meet, play, and create in."

Dolby's long-range vision for VR reflects his musical tastes, and he wants to see the creation of a networked virtual musical conservatory. The virtual rooms of the conservatory would each house a limitless supply of musical instruments. There would be a room with every kind of drum, bell, chime, cymbal, rattle, and other percussion instrument. There would be a brass room filled with horns, a woodwind room, and a room for string instruments. There could even be rooms for sampled sounds, voices, and synthesized noises, each sound represented by its own unique icon.

"The exciting thing is that all this would incorporate the latest synthesizer technology, which can create every conceivable sound, even sounds we've never heard before," Dolby says. "You could combine virtual objects and the synthesizer would create its corresponding sound.

"You also wouldn't be limited to expressing your musical interests in sound alone. Part of the artistic possibilities would be creating instruments that generated colors, shapes, and objects while you played. I've thought of staging a concert tour in which I play all the instruments by manipulating objects in virtual reality that relate to various synthesizers. The objects would be projected by a 3-D video projector so the audience could watch the movement and interaction as a light show. We'd start to have a visual language of music."

Looking across the entertainment landscape, there's one industry that has been going through dramatic changes due to technology—the music industry. From CDs to music videos to multisite global concerts with satellite hook-ups, technology continues to change the shape and nature of the music business.

Just as Danny Socolof and Peter Gabriel re-created sim rides, Thomas Dolby is pushing the boundaries of virtual entertainment in original directions. While most digital futurists look to Hollywood for inspiration and the virtual entertainment revolution, it might well be that the music industry is where the revolution will take place. Even jerky, 15-fps video on a PC can appear very acceptable when accompanied by high-quality audio. Virtual music-worlds are in everyone's future.

⇨ The optimal entertainment experience?

In a survey of BattleTech players by Michigan State University students, players rated the game nearly off the scale as challenging, fun, exciting, unique, and very high as creative, competitive, intense, and absorbing. Rather than being a system of alienation, where people are drawn away from social activities, virtual reality can be a very social technology.

The Michigan State study consistently identified a strong desire for interaction with real people in addition to virtual beings and environments. Just two percent would prefer to play only against the

computer, while 71 percent prefer to play on teams and the remainder want to play individually against everyone else.

Entertainment like BattleTech and Cybergate will appeal to audiences seeking intense experiences within a small social community, which is just what these companies need to survive—dedicated, loyal, repeat customers. It's precisely this kind of group experience that no amount of interactive TV (or VR) can provide at home. A big part of a BattleTech visit is the socializing around the game.

Music, and eventually theatrical and movie features, will find a way to translate their products into virtual experiences—just as they convert them into games and laser discs today. At Siggraph '94 in Orlando, Fla., the Walt Disney company demonstrated the future of the new entertainment industry by translating the animated movie *Aladdin* into a VR experience. Called the Magic Carpet Ride, it's not a sim ride like Star Tours, with one preordained flight path; instead, you're free to fly where you will in the cartoon Arabian city from *Aladdin*. You can zoom down alleys, across streets, from rooftop to rooftop. Along the way you meet actual characters from the movie who interact and talk with you. Best of all, the graphics are as good as the movie! You can expect to see other animators take the plunge soon, first with location-based theme-park attractions and eventually with at-home experiences.

How will the frequent use of designed virtual experiences alter our perception of the world? How will meeting and playing with people in virtual worlds change our relationship to the world and each other? These are the kinds of questions that artists have been asking for hundreds of years. At what point does virtual entertainment cross over into art, and is there a boundary?

In the hands of the first virtual artists, we can begin to see where virtual reality will take us and what kind of experiences it will be. And perhaps the same way the works of Van Gogh, Picasso, and Matisse changed the world, we can learn how VR might alter our way of thinking, our point of view, and perhaps even our personalities by changing the way we see the world.

Art in VR

"If men were able to be convinced that art is precise advance knowledge of how to cope with the psychic and social consequences of the next technology, would they all become artists? Or would they begin a careful translation of new art forms into social navigation charts?"

Marshall McLuhan, *Understanding Media*

IN ancient Greece the patron goddess of both science and art was Techne. In Greece, her name means "to create." From her name the words *technique* and *technology* were derived. Over the last 2,000 years science and art have gradually gone their separate ways, but once they both looked to the same source for inspiration—the will to create and understand the world. Today, art and science are coming back together again.

In his recent book, *Art & Physics*, Leonard Shlain builds a compelling case for the idea that the effect of artists' work in changing the attitudes and perceptual filters of a culture makes way for the insights and discoveries of its scientists.

Shlain suggests that a way to understand Einstein's revolution in physics is to juxtapose it with radical breakthroughs in modern art. The artist and scientist each strive to perceive and interpret the world, yet seem completely opposed to each other in spirit. Shlain builds his case by tracing insights and discoveries in both fields over the last 2,000 years.

"In the case of the visual arts, in addition to illuminating, imitating, and interpreting reality, a few artists create a language of symbols for things which there are yet to be words . . . the radical innovations of art embody the pre-verbal stages of new concepts that will eventually change civilization . . .. This collation leads to abstract ideas that only later give rise to descriptive language."

Leonard Shlain, *Art & Physics*

Computers and virtual reality are seminal inventions whose future impact we can barely guess at. How many people watching the first steam engines 300 years ago could foresee the Industrial Revolution and the changes to the world that would come?

Only as artists explore the new electronic media will we get clues to the long-range potential for the changes it will bring to our lives. We're entering an age in which everything can be digitized and expressed in a computer as an object or environment with which we can interact.

By the last half of the 19th century, the techniques of representational painting had all been pioneered. Not only had traditional still life and portrait painting been done to death, but a new technology had appeared that was quickly displacing them—photography. Not only was it faster and easier to do, but reproductions of the original work could be done quickly, in large quantities, with little or no degradation in quality.

Beginning with the impressionists (and followed by the surrealists, futurists, etc.), artists turned their attention from the outer world to their own inner world of thought and perception to find new artistic challenges. They used art as a mirror of the mind. This modern art of concepts and ideas frequently rejected Giotto's 3-D perspective techniques and was so different from the representational art that came before it that the general public still hasn't acclimated to the shift, 100 years later.

Marcel Duchamp was one of the first to create this art of the mind. But even as he tried to suggest and express concepts, he felt confined using the traditional material media that artists had always used (paint, canvas, and stone). He knew he needed to break free, so he shattered forms to create mobiles, turned sheets of glass into canvas, and used found objects and motors instead of stone for sculptures. He did all he could to suggest unseeable ideas.

This century has seen a creative explosion of styles and methods for representing and expressing concepts, and exploring perception with nontraditional and unusual materials. Now it appears that almost all methods of artistic expression have been pioneered.

Virtual reality, however, represents an entirely new and unexplored universe for creation. It's an art form in which shape, space, and time

can be bent, and in which viewers can participate. Take, for example, the unusual series of virtual compositions shown in Fig.
14-1. The first expressions of virtual art worlds evoke the emotional wizardry of the surrealists such as Dali, with barren lonely landscapes where anything can happen. Here at last is an art medium as fluid as the mind itself.g

Figure 14-1

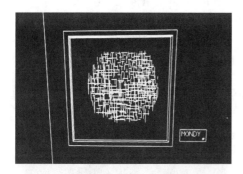

The first picture in this sequence shows a virtual art gallery with a painting that appears identical to one by Piet Mondrian, entitled Composition with Line. *As the user flies around the painting, it falls apart into a 3-D sculpture (second and third pictures in sequence).*

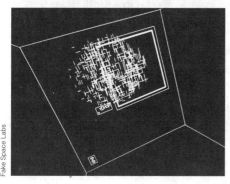

Fake Space Labs

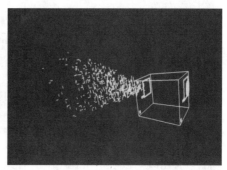

Throughout the fall and winter of 1991, there was a unique gathering of artists and technologists at the Banff Center for the Arts in Calgary, Canada. As part of a special program run by Doug MacCloud, for the first time ever artists were given the opportunity to work with Sense8 VR tools to explore the power of this new medium. Several fascinating virtual experiences combining sound and images resulted from this collaboration.

The Ottawa-based artist, Robert McFadden, created a piece called *Picture Yourself In Fiction*. In a vast, empty void, a box without a

top or bottom floats. The inner and outer panels of the cube are covered with scanned photographs of the artist's body. As you pass near panels, digitized samples of his poetry are triggered and audibly played. The very nature of space itself distorts and loops back on itself as you move about.

Virtual art is a technology, media, and concept. It's not three different things, but three different aspects of the same idea—the ability to control and create experiences. It's:

➤ A magic cauldron for integrating the techniques of painting, film, sculpture, and literature with the dynamic structures of music, theater, and even dreaming.

➤ A meta-medium that can encompass all art styles simultaneously: cubist, religious, realistic, abstract, primitive, postmodern, etc.

➤ An experience in which art viewers are transformed from vicarious voyeurs into co-creators of their own experiences.

The computer's ability to store and retrieve events could allow us to explore our notions of time, space, and memory. After spending time in a world, the virtual traveler could be confronted by virtual memories of his own virtual experiences. Key incidents and phrases seen and heard could come tumbling back. Some day he might even be able to reexperience episodes from his own life.

Places can be constructed that don't physically exist in real life, for example, the worlds of M. C. Escher and Magritte, Mobius strips and convoluted stairways, the geometry of mysterious spaces where people and creatures blend back and forth into each other or a train floats out of a fireplace.

Virtual travelers might find that, depending on the direction they move in an Escher art world, they could have the form and capabilities of either a fish or bird, but not both. Virtual travelers returning again and again to a virtual world, trying to achieve a goal so they can get into another world—isn't this a metaphor for reincarnation? Are these travellers working through their virtual karma, unable to advance into another reality before completing certain tasks in the current one?

Art isn't just a way of observing, a way of doing; it's fundamentally a way of knowing. Virtual art can be used as a new kind of mirror to explore and challenge ideas, experiences, and states of mind in the real world. Visits to virtual worlds will undoubtedly change the way we think about ourselves and the world, and will ultimately alter our understanding of reality.

⇨ Becoming the art

Two women dance in front of a screen. A camcorder above the screen picks up their image and feeds it into a computer that projects them into a graphical 3-D world. As they dance, they see themselves weightless on the screen: moving mirror reflections, puppet-selves playing amid planets and space—musical refrains triggered as their hands brush against the stars. On separate screens, people interact with poems such as *Risk My Shadow Kissing Yours* and *The Geisha Snail and the Phosphorescent Samurai*, which offer eight possible endings, depending on the choices you, as the viewer, make.

All great works of art have one thing in common, the German philosopher Arthur Schopenhauer maintained: they have the power to pull viewers out of themselves and into the work of art. They suspend the division between inner and outer, self and other, and usher you—if only for a moment—into the realm of the timeless. You momentarily become the art. This description captures the essence of what makes virtual reality such a special medium. The viewer is no longer a passive observer, but becomes an active insider "doing" the art.

The immersive/interactive quality of VR removes the traditional chasm between art viewer and art object, pointing the way to a new kind of awareness as the viewer becomes a participant "inside" the art. Virtual travelers who experience several points of view or reside inside several different personalities will become confronted by questions of identity and the social masks they wear.

As VR concepts and technology develop, VR art creations will be able not only to suggest insights and altered states of consciousness, but to actually simulate them the way the artist experiences them. The inner

327

experience of an artist will become as portrayable as a still life in the material world. Virtual art spectators won't look through windows that contain static or moving objects (as in paintings or film); they will step through into the various points of view the artist creates.

Will virtual realities eventually replace reality? No. The feel and taste of a carrot, the look and smell of a rose, the robust richness of the world we live in will never be completely representable (unless in some far-off future we can only dream about).

And we don't need virtual reality to be a substitute for reality—we have the fresh, vivid reality of our everyday experiences already. Instead, VR offers a way to experience life in a way that adds to our everyday experiences. For example, when we see a play or movie, read a book, or stand before a great painting, we give ourselves up to its special reality for a purpose. Our surrender to these guided intentional experiences allows us to feel and learn more than we normally would from the capricious occurrences of everyday reality.

When the creation is effective, it produces a very special reaction. Aristotle called this experience *catharsis*, or the pleasurable release of emotion—specifically those emotions evoked by art. He didn't mean that the emotions were necessarily pleasurable, but that the release of the emotions was pleasurable (the popularity of slasher, horror, and thriller movies attests to the variety of pleasure people find in the release of unpleasant emotions).

The multisensory symphony of virtual reality worlds offers a new and very powerful way of delivering catharsis; the freedom of the medium is a challenge to both the linear tradition of story-telling and the structured methods and media traditionally used to deliver tales.

Will the VR artist's role be subverted by the VR audience in this new media? Will the audience get into the art and make a mess of it? If the world isn't carefully constructed, most certainly. But the rewards available to an artist can be greater, too. The virtual artist will need to use *all* of the skills and lessons artists have struggled to amass over the last two thousand years. This new art media combines the power of the eye and ear, and the lessons of the musician, painter, film maker, sculptor, and playwright.

Our great-grandchildren will lack our generation's close attachment to the impressionists because their appreciation of art will have evolved far beyond them. They themselves will want to be creators and doers, not simply the viewers of art. They might look to Jackson Pollock's abstracts and intense form of creation as their foundation for appreciating art:

> "My painting does not come from the easel . . .. On the floor I am more at ease. I feel nearer, more a part of the painting, since this way I can walk around it, work from the four sides and literally be in the painting . . ."
> **Jackson Pollock, in Jose Arguelles's _The Transformative Vision_**

Future artists will know of Pollock not from copying him but from being immersed in his simulations. Artists will step into Pollock's point of view, he will whisper his ideas in their ears, and his insights will be synchronized to the fling and swing of virtual paint on virtual canvas. They will learn from his spirit as they learn from the canvas. In the process, tomorrow's artists will leave Duchamp and Matisse behind.

The material techniques of conceptual art have all been well developed. New generations will pioneer nonmaterial, audience-inclusive creations, where the dynamic laws of reality depend on their own creative, intellectual, and spiritual maturity. As these creations appear, they will blaze a way to a new kind of conceptual and spiritual art.

Spiritual art

The crescent moon is high in the Canadian night sky. You cross the green forest floor to the red walls of a spirit lodge. As you draw closer, you begin to hear the drum beat coming from within the lodge. A coyote howls in the distance.

Passing through the open door, the drumming grows louder. There's a fire burning in the center of the lodge. Smoke escapes through the hole in the roof. You can hear soft, hypnotic chanting in time to the drum, but no one is here, just the totem obelisks, great blocks

standing tall along the red walls, traditional spirit paintings sketched in vibrant Van Gogh colors.

You move down the long room under the watchful eyes of the totems. The music stays by the door. You pass the fire and the moon peeks in through the hole in the roof. You come up to the great eagle totem. It reaches over your head up to the roof, beak pointed at the moon. Suddenly the lodge shakes with the cry of an eagle. The drumming and chanting continue by the door (see Fig. 14-2).

Figure 14-2

A view from inside the lodge, this scene is taken from Inherent Vision, Inherent Rights, created by Lawrence Paul Yuxweluptun at the Banff Center for the Arts in Calgary.

Lawrence Paul Yuxweluptun, a native Canadian of the Salish tribe, created this virtual environment using WorldToolKit software and calls it *Inherent Vision, Inherent Rights*. It's the first virtual-art world to be selected for exhibition at the National Gallery of Canada in Ottawa. As the only modern art piece of its kind, and a very high-tech one at that, it will have a unique place among the traditional Native American arts in an exhibition entitled *Land, Spirit, and Power*.

Lawrence Paul is the first artist to use VR for the purpose of crossing cultural and religious divides to immerse other Canadians in the

spiritual world in which he was raised. This is the great artistic and social potential of virtual reality—to take us into the artist's mind, into another culture, and into possible higher realms of the spirit.

The philosopher Ken Wilber notes that ". . . men and women possess at least three different modes of knowing: the eye of the Flesh, which discloses the material, concrete, and sensual world; the eye of Mind, which discloses the symbolic, conceptual, and linguistic world; and the eye of Contemplation, which discloses the spiritual, transcendental, and transpersonal world. These are not three different worlds, but three different aspects of our one world, disclosed by different modes of knowing and perceiving."

From the Renaissance to the impressionist period, art was mainly concerned with the eye of the Flesh, representing the real world. Modern art has focused on the eye of the Mind, using physical materials to convey nonmaterial ideas and concepts to teach people new ways to think about the world. Virtual reality provides the artist with the first purely conceptual medium for exploring not only the eye of the Mind, but evoking the spirit world as well.

The traditional painter's canvas is a two-dimensional medium: length and width. To suggest a third dimension of depth using traditional painting methods, you must use Giotto's tricks of perspective, yet the result is still only two-dimensional lines on a flat page. Modern art has been limited by a constraint on expression.

Four-, five-, and six-dimensional ideas have had to suggest, hint, and inspire within the limits of two- and three-dimensional art media to create full experiences. Some have succeeded very well. Duchamp's *Nude Descending The Staircase* is both a cubist view of form, a futurist commentary on time, a study in shattered perspective, and a statement on the use of the nude in art.

To understand the great works of conceptual art requires the viewer to expand beyond his accustomed habits of perceiving the world. You have to struggle to see what isn't there, to make a mental leap with a limited number of physical clues.

Dali's painting *Abraham Lincoln* reveals one image from far away—the dead president's outline appears in the picture's blurred colors. From ten feet away, details emerge and it's clear that the painting is a nude woman with her back to the viewer looking out a window at the sea. As you step closer, still more details emerge until finally with your nose to the canvas you can see that Dali has embossed religious and spiritual symbols and figures into the fabric of the painting.

The more dimensions there are in art, the harder it is for people to make an essential initial connection to change their mind's eye so they can step into the art and let it carry them away. In its multisensory and therefore multichannel modes of communication, VR allows for art environments that ask us to see the world through a new pair of eyes.

By putting us into total experience, it provides multiple ways to actively discover the many possible meanings of both virtual worlds and the real world. Rather than being an electronic cocoon that insulates people even further from the real world, carefully crafted virtual experiences could provide a way to reconnect us to each other in profound ways.

⇨ At the Guggenheim Museum

On the morning of October 26, 1993, the doors to the Guggenheim Museum opened and crowds streamed in to see the first art museum installation dedicated entirely to VR. The presentation *Virtual Reality: An Emerging Medium* was developed by the Guggenheim in conjunction with the Intel Digital Education and Arts program.

The installation explored the unique characteristics of VR, compared to other media, and suggested a number of future directions. Five worlds were featured, three of which made their public debut at the show: The Virtual String Quartet by Thomas Dolby, the networked Virtual Museum featuring the re-creation of an ancient Egyptian Temple, The Metaphor Mixer from Maxus Systems International, and two art worlds by Jenny Holzer. Dolby and Holzer's worlds were on public display for the first time.

"The Guggenheim has a 70-year tradition of supporting new trends in contemporary art," says John Ippolioto, the presentation's curator. "If we had been around when man first began to use paint on cave walls to represent ideas and the world around him, we would have wanted to stage a similar presentation to try to understand its implications."

The inspiration for the show started when the museum's director of computer services, Rich Roller, contacted Intel's virtual reality program. Intel was in the middle of a research project to explore the potential of VR by putting the technology in the hands of artists and educators. These projects (the Egyptian Temple, the String Quartet, and Holzer's art worlds) formed the core of the show.

Intel realized that for VR to be taken seriously it needed to demonstrate original content the average person could appreciate. A focus on content led Intel to seek out artists and educators, society's content experts. Working with Sense8, small teams were assembled to bring the artists' visions to life. The first of these teams was led by the contemporary artist, Jenny Holzer. She has a unique talent for using language and environments to frame ideas and emotions.

In 1990, Holzer represented the United States at the Venice Biennale, one of the most prestigious international art events, where she was awarded one of three grand prizes, the Leone d'Oro (golden lion). She became the first woman to ever receive this award. Holzer communicates her ideas through phrases delivered in unconventional environments, such as:

➤ Abuse Of Power Comes As No Surprise

➤ Protect Me From What I Want

➤ Murder Has Its Sexual Side

➤ In A Dream You Saw A Way To Survive, And You Were Full Of Joy

These statements catch viewers by surprise as they flash across the baseball scoreboard at San Francisco's Candlestick Park, loom from a roadside billboard (see Fig. 14-3), peek out from a bus stand, or show up on the back of a cash-register receipt. Her work uses surprising and startling statements to break through viewers' informational filters.

333

Figure 14-3

Jenny Holzer uses provocative messages to break through the perceptual filters of passers-by, as seen by this spectacolor board in Times Square, New York (The Survival Series, 1985-1986).

One of her most famous installations was staged inside the spiral rotunda of New York's Guggenheim Museum. Designed by Frank Lloyd Wright, the central stairway of the museum spirals up several floors to the skylight, like the interior of a sea shell. She lined the wall with LED signs and programmed them so that the text silently swirled from bottom to top, up to the skylight. Previously, other artists had hung giant mobiles in the rotunda, but no one had ever incorporated the entire rotunda in an installation before; she incorporated the building's architecture into her work of art.

Ken Pimentel of Sense8 worked with Holzer to create her first virtual art world. An untitled piece, it was inspired by one of Samuel Beckett's short stories, *The Lost Ones*. It features a cavernous world in which souls alternately flee from and engage the viewer. The souls are

represented as cubes with animated faces texture-mapped on them. If you catch them they speak one of Holzer's phrases (see Fig. 14-4).

Jeff Donovan of Inworld also worked on Holzer's second art world. Based on completely new writings, it offered a response to the violence against women in the Bosnian war.

Figure 14-4

Jenny Holzer's first experiment with virtual art led her to create an environment based on Beckett's short story The Lost Ones.

You enter the world and find a vast patterned desert of striking color: bright orange earth and deep blue sky. As you travel across the landscape, a circle of buildings appears on the horizon. When you reach the village you see that each building is an identical cinder-block hut. Where the door should be is a black curtain or shroud (see Fig. 14-5).

Everything is quiet. You enter a hut to discover a barren room. Where is everyone? Then a voice comes to you out of the air—simple, undramatic, almost flat in its unemotional tone. It is a woman speaking about birds and light. There is something disturbing in the flat tone of her speech.

335

Figure 14-5

Jenny Holzer, Sense8 Corp.

Jenny Holzer's second experiment with virtual art was based on the stories of rape and violence emerging from the Bosnian conflict.

You go back outside. The world has changed; the earth is brown and the sky green. You enter another hut in the circle. It too is empty except for a voice, which speaks of pain and sexual violence. You leave the hut to find that the earth and sky have changed color again. You hurry away across the desert leaving the strange village behind.

Soon you reach another village. Again the same square, block huts, but these are lined up in double rows like barracks. The voices here have the same simple, flat tone, but the words are violent. Each hut harbors a different voice. Each village has a different story to tell. The silence of the desert seems to be watching you.

Somehow this simple landscape is forcing home an emotional truth that the nightly news has numbed us to by the way it reports facts and figures. The barren huts are the homes emptied by "ethnic cleansing." The voices are the actual words of the perpetrators, victims, and witnesses of rape and murder in Bosnia. You are not watching this on TV; you are there. You are a silent witness to the devastation.

Now the silence of the desert suggests all the other observers who do not speak out; the barren landscape suggests the emotional price everyone pays. You come to another village with huts arranged in a square. You stand in the empty space between them, all the dark doors staring at you, and you hesitate to go inside. It occurs to you that these haunted villages could easily be from the killing fields of Cambodia or World War II concentration camps; the voices could be speaking the words of soldiers, workers, gypsies, Jews, and others who suffered and died while the world looked on.

Reviewing the work in *Virtual Realty World*, Dan Duncan writes, ". . . what Jenny Holzer's brilliantly disturbing work proves once again is that immediacy is more than immersion. And that VR technology, like paint in a tube, can be validated only by an artist whose vision is beyond the technology she is using."

The Bosnia world, with its simple use of sound and landscapes, shows the power of VR to put you inside an experience. There are seven different villages: from a single lonely hut to villages with 20 or more huts. Each hut has its own ghostly voice and each village emphasizes either the victims, perpetrators, or observers. While the overall message and theme is the same, there are hundreds of different experiences to be had depending on the huts you enter and the words you hear.

"We reviewed a number of additional art worlds for possible inclusion in the show," says John Ippolioto. "None of them had the power of Jenny Holzer's work, but more significantly almost all of them were simple fly-throughs of visually interesting landscapes with some music or poetry. No matter how many times you entered them you would get the same experience, like using a video game. All the works that made it into the show emphasized the dynamic quality of VR instead of the immersiveness. The user was a co-creator of the experience. You had the ability to enter a world many times and have different experiences each time."

Jenny Holzer's Bosnia world shows the emotional and spiritual potential of virtual reality when it's used for art. It's also a powerful political statement. Hachivi Edgar Heap of Birds, a Native American artist, could be speaking for all of us when he wrote, "The white

man shall always project himself into our lives using information that is provided by learning institutions and the electronic and print media . . .. Therefore we find that the survival of our people is based upon our use of expressive forms of modern communication. The insurgent messages within these forms must serve as our present-day combative tactics."

Virtual reality represents a fundamental shift in art, a new kind of 3-D environment through which any content can be expressed, and space and time can be bent. It's a medium for which every expression has multiple perspectives, where media is content, content is media, and viewing becomes doing.

The term *virtual reality* doesn't do justice to what this art form can accomplish. Perhaps a new word, like *visualmusic*, is a more appropriate, creative name for virtual art experiences. It suggests the blending of the senses, fluidness of forms, and mixing of all the arts.

Conclusion

Einstein taught us that our experience of reality was relative, that what we know depends on our point of view, our position in time. All our experiences are designed and shaped first by the circumstances of the moment, secondly by our senses, and thirdly by the filters and attitudes of our minds.

Virtual reality drives this point home again and again. Each world is a designed experience and each experience is a learning situation. VR will change the way we think as it turns our thoughts into commodities and artifacts we can copy, share, or sell to others. It will transform our notions of originality, presence, and ownership.

Just as the alphabet and printing press changed the way people thought, virtual reality will shape our notions of community, self, space, and time. The future is arriving; it's happening at computer arcades and shopping malls, inside software and hardware companies, and in artists' lofts.

By using a full spectrum of artistic techniques, including painting, theater, film, and music, VR artists will merge together all art forms. They'll simulate as well as stimulate mental and emotional states and experiences and make possible the emergence of a new holistic art experience of the mind.

The next generation

JUST like the Wright Brothers' airplanes, today's VR technology is crude compared to the imaginings of the media, but it's good enough to get us off the ground and into the air for an exciting experience. To try and predict the future trends of virtual reality, you must first put it in context; we're in the barnstorming days of VR when it's possible for almost anyone to jump in and make a contribution.

The next few years are going to see rapid growth and development in virtual reality applications and hardware. This growth will be fed by the rapid improvement in graphics hardware and the reduced cost of these systems. Business and medical-related applications will slowly begin appearing in the marketplace.

Various companies are already beginning to experiment with coupling 3-D interfaces to communication networks, a natural evolution of the online interface. Today, several services like American Online and Prodigy are combining 2-D graphics with their text-based interface. Within several years, 3-D interfaces or virtual worlds should begin appearing on these same services. By the year 2000, internationally networked VR, or *cyberspace*, should be common. Already, the United States Department of Defense is working to integrate VR technology into its global computer network.

But as VR becomes a part of our culture, there are serious questions we need to ask about the consequences of turning experience into a commodity. We need a new literacy for this new age of experiential information.

VR is being championed by a small group of inventors, artists, and software programmers who enjoy using their inventions and enjoy improving them. Unlike artificial intelligence (AI), which also received a lot of public attention early in its life, VR's limitations are bound more by computing power than by a lack of technical understanding.

This is the key difference between AI and VR. Early AI developers assumed that what was easy for a human to do would also be easy for a computer. But it turned out to be the opposite. A computer can do things that are very hard for people, such as complex mathematics. But skills a two-year-old has mastered, such as recognizing a face or an object on a plate, has been a 40-year struggle for AI systems.

VR doesn't require a major breakthrough in software or in our understanding of how the brain works. Like the dynamics of the Wright Brothers' plane—the wings, motor, and steering—all the major components of VR already work. Continuing the industry's growth is mostly an issue of delivering graphics at higher resolution for less money. Where we go with VR is more important than how we build it, and our lack of understanding about how it will affect us and our civilization is the bigger mystery.

⇨ The experience industry

The invention of the phonograph and its mass distribution created a means of reproducing music that had never existed before. Previously, each community had its own bands and orchestras that reproduced the music of the leading composers of the day.

Phonographs allowed bands, composers, and singers to create copies of their own work for sale. They could now sell their talents directly to a mass audience. This allowed lovers of music to create and control their own private worlds of music in the same fashion that books allow readers to create their own private world of ideas.

Today, the music industry is one of the biggest forms of entertainment in the world, providing a common link among diverse people through the shared experience of music. This same type of

"commoditization" occurred with the visual experience as photography evolved into movies, which were followed by TV and VCRs. Sales of cameras, camcorders, video tapes, and VCRs have led to personal libraries of movies and still images.

Over 140 million personal computers have been built and distributed in the just over 15 years of their existence. More than 40 million are built each year now. And the technology trends of the computer, broadcast, and telecommunications industries are converging. In the course of the 1990s, all forms of media are going to become available on PC-based knowledge stations: video, digital photography, text, and audio.

Think of the personal computer as the phonograph of the 21st century. By combining it with telecommunications, broadcast, and compact-disc digital technology, the stage is set for the creation of a new kind of home theater—a personal library of experience.

In the near future, artists will create virtual art, education, and entertainment worlds for public consumption. These experiences will range from very linear, passive experiences (immersive movies delivered like a Disney Star Tours ride) to nonlinear worlds alive with interactive insights and delights. These will be worlds you can return to again and again for new surprises and discoveries—games of complexity and challenge that will be played by hundreds of people.

These experiences might be delivered over fiberoptic phone lines or conveyed on compact disc and artwork will be replayed in a digital format that faithfully re-creates it as it was intended. This will provide artists with a level of public acceptance and financial reward historically unavailable.

There are implications in the idea of an "industry of experience" that suggest a major shift in our culture. Five hundred years ago Giotto changed the way we looked at the world by creating a 3-D point of view in static paintings. Five hundred years ago books began to make ideas a widely available commodity.

VR will make experience a commodity and an artifact we can buy and sell, preserve and share. Rather than leading to a homogenized culture, we might be heading for an even more fragmented and

individualist society, as people go beyond championing their own
particular point of view to emphasizing their particular experience.

Within 50 years, virtual reality will become an accepted, semi-
invisible service in society, like telephones, books, and television—a
tool for communication, work, and pleasure that we use without
thinking about it. We need to know what we're reaching for before it
becomes so commonplace that we relate to it unconsciously.

⇨ Near-term growth

The VR industry is set to experience a period of rapid growth and
innovation over the next 30 to 40 years. But in the near term, VR
firms still struggle to exist in a small but growing market. As of mid-
1994, we estimate that about 1,500 head-tracked, fully immersive
VR systems exist in the world, as shown in Fig. 15-1. About 60% of
these are entertainment systems.

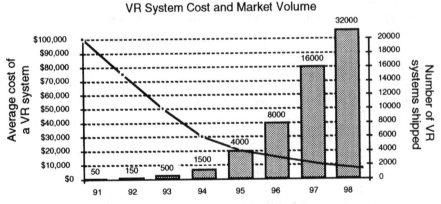

Figure 15-1

*Estimated growth in number of VR systems sold each year and the
declining cost of the systems.*

This estimate is based on conversations with other industry watchers
and sales analyses of key VR companies. Of course, the overall
market for VR is much larger than just the sales of head-tracked
immersive systems. The market appears to be more than doubling in
size each year, which bodes well for the industry. And if companies

like Sega and Nintendo enter the market, there will be a period of explosive growth. Today, almost all VR companies have 15 or fewer employees—still very much a pioneering industry.

As mentioned previously, the entertainment industry is the driving force behind VR's introduction to the public. The limitation of today's low-end technology isn't a factor for VR game systems. They're selling the excitement of the experience.

On the other hand, acceptance of VR in the workplace will require at least a magnitude increase in both graphics performance and HMD resolution. This should occur by 1995 as color VGA-quality goggles become available for around $2,500, and Power PC or Pentium processor-based PCs become common and inexpensive.

What we can't foresee is what the Japanese are going to do; they're the wild card in the forecast. The large Japanese corporations (Sharp, NEC, Toshiba, etc.) are driving screen technology towards higher resolution and improved color. Palmtops or the new PDAs (personal data assistants) might provide a volume market for LCD screens of the appropriate size and resolution to make personal data goggles affordable for the home market.

Any number of technologies could lead to the introduction of goggles with acceptable resolution that would cost only a few hundred dollars by 1996. We don't expect this to be an isolated offering, but rather part of a packaged home-entertainment system, as shown in Fig. 15-2. The first company to market a system that offers compelling, interactive experiences will potentially reap big rewards—but, as always, it will be the software that sells the system.

Virtual reality software might provide the consumer demand to create a new computer platform. The first systems that sell will create the crucial mass volume to drive prices down and make the goggles and hardware widely affordable. The late 1990s will see a battle for the home VR market similar to the VCR battles of the early 1980s. At that point, composers of virtual experiences and applications will begin to work out of their homes developing applications, just like the early software program developers did for the Apple I.

Figure 15-2

Intel Corp.

From NEC's Advanced Design group comes this futuristic version of a wearable VR system that could be used as a portable data terminal.

The big news by 1995 will be in entertainment arcades. VR arcades are going to blow away the 2-D computer-arcade game business in much the same way that Pong and Pacman displaced pinball machines. This process will familiarize thousands of people with virtual reality so that, as home systems appear in the second half of the 1990s, consumers will eagerly await them.

Computational demands of VR

Virtual reality is a power-hungry proposition. Today, it runs on systems that cost from $10,000 to $200,000 and beyond. At a minimum, powerful desktop computers are required for even low-end VR systems. For example, using a 100-MHz Pentium processor-based PC and a special graphics board, textured worlds of 2,000 to 3,000

polygons can be displayed at 10 to 20 frames per second. Even with this power, the world appears cartoonish with a hint of visual lag as you move your head about.

At the high end of the VR business, Silicon Graphics Inc. (SGI) has a $100,000 RealityEngine2, which has become the platform of choice for VR developers. In introducing the system, SGI became the first billion-dollar company to market a product emphasizing its use for virtual environments. SGI claims that RealityEngine2 went from a $100-million-a-year to a $1-billion-a-year business in just one year.

RealityEngine2 is designed to create fully textured worlds at 30 frames per second. The fully configured system is capable of 600,000 textured polygons per second. This impressive performance requires eight Intel i860 RISC CPUs, four raster processors, and 20 low-level graphics processors. To achieve the utmost sophistication in representing colors, 36 bits per pixel are used instead of the 24 normally associated with high-quality "true-color" displays (a standard PC rarely has more than 8 bits per pixel, allowing it to display 256 different colors).

It also includes other features, like a staggering 160 megabytes of video RAM, compared with one to two megabytes on many desktop PCs. With technology like this, the distinction between what's real and what's virtual begins to blur just slightly.

Other companies, such as Kubota Pacific and Evans and Sutherland, have also introduced hardware in the $40,000 to $100,000 range that's capable of generating complex, textured worlds at 20–30 frames per second. These machines represent the leading edge of the level of performance necessary for delivering practical business and scientific uses of VR. Every year graphics hardware costs half as much for the same level of performance. This trend is a crucial force behind the growth of VR systems.

What will VR be able to do in 2001? Will we provide the power of the SGI RealityEngine2 at home? That will depend on what kind of microprocessors are at the heart of affordable computers.

Intel's plans are driven by an internal vision of what the microprocessor of the year 2000 can be (see Fig. 15-3). Called the Micro 2000 project, it envisions a microprocessor with 80–100 million transistors on a single piece of silicon. It will have four processing units on the same chip running like parallel supercomputers. The speed of this chip will be 250 MHz and, with complex circuitry and four processors on board, it will execute over two billion instructions per second!

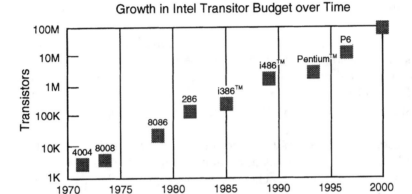

Growth in Intel Transitor Budget over Time

Figure 15-3

Moore's law states that the technology on which microprocessors are developed doubles in complexity (as measured in transistors) every couple of years. Intel's series of microprocessors demonstrate this trend. W Industries Ltd. UK, 1992

These performance numbers might be hard to believe, but chip technology is already taking us there. In 1993, the first version of the Pentium processor delivered 100 million instructions per second (new, faster versions are delivering more power). The next-generation Intel processor, codenamed P6, will deliver 300 million instructions per second when it's introduced in 1995.

Besides processing units, the Micro 2000 chip will very likely have special circuitry for graphics and digital video. Virtual reality simulations that run on this kind of chip will be unlike anything in today's applications. Photorealistic imagery in VR worlds will be possible. Speech recognition will be widely used to input and receive information and commands. New devices and modes of interaction

will be available. It's even possible that your gestures will be monitored by a pair of small TV cameras and converted into meaningful signals to the computer and the VR system.

The display system of choice in the 21st century might not be a pair of lightweight VR "sunglasses." Instead, homes might have their own media room. The first media-room prototype has been developed at the Electronic Visualization Lab of the University of Illinois in Chicago. In research papers it's known as the Audio-Visual Experience Automatic Virtual Environment, but the team calls it the CAVE.

The CAVE is a cube with display screens on all six sides. Stereo images are displayed by six Silicon Graphics VGX workstations that drive individual rear-projection displays. Everything is controlled over an Ethernet network with an SGI Personal Iris system acting as a master controller.

The user of this system wears liquid-crystal glasses that shutter at a rapid rate to trick the eyes into seeing the 3-D stereo worlds. The user's head position is tracked by a Polhemus ISOTRAK sensor mounted on the glasses.

There are already several worlds you can literally walk into with the CAVE and explore. The Cosmic Explorer is a combination of stored database images and real-time Cray computations, allowing a viewer to fly through and explore the Great Wall (a supercluster of galaxies over 500 million light years in length). Like Carl Sagan in his PBS series "Cosmos," the viewer is able to travel the length of the Great Wall and zoom in on individual galaxies.

Another application allows a user to create a weather system over part of North America and be inside the storm to study it. Yet another application developed by the University's Biomedical Visualization Lab is a trip through a human fetus via simulation.

The quality of simulation available on systems 30 years from now will allow the types of special effects used in *Terminator 2* to be performed in real time on hand-held computers. Today, Hollywood stars like Elizabeth Taylor license their name and photographic image

to clothing and perfume merchandisers. In the next century, they'll license their face, body, and voice—their digitized persona.

Artists like Peter Gabriel, Led Zeppelin, and the Grateful Dead will continue to perform in VR simulations. New music, new movies, new simulations will be created that incorporate their digital images. Fifty to 100 years from now virtual realty users worldwide might be communicating over vast networks. At that point, William Gibson's cyberspace will stop being science fiction and will become reality.

⇨ Cyberspace

> "Cyberspace: The tablet become a page become a screen become a world, a virtual world . . .. A new universe, a parallel universe created and sustained by the world's computers and communications lines. A world in which global traffic of knowledge, secrets, measurements, indicators, entertainments, and alter-human agency takes on form: sights, sounds, presences never seen on the surface of the earth . . ."
> **Michael Benedikt, *Cyberspace: First Steps*, 1992**

Cyberspace, a term coined in the novel *Neuromancer* by William Gibson, is an imaginary computer world and a word that stands for a kind of computer network that doesn't yet exist. Cyberspace has been envisioned as the fully accessible sum total of all the interconnected computer networks spanning the globe.

It's a word with mythic power. It's a global computer network with the completeness and openness of the telephone system, but instead of just an auditory experience it's multisensory. Instead of listening on the phone, you fly into the network. In Gibson's vision, it's an alternate universe, a computer dimension of reality you can enter via special virtual reality machines.

Already the first experimental cyberspace villages are being settled. In 1993, Carl Loeffler's team at the Studio for Creative Inquiry demonstrated the first internationally networked virtual city. At VR Vienna '93, participants in Tokyo, Japan, Vienna, Austria, and the

U.S. (Pittsburgh) donned HMDs and were able to meet on a street in the "Virtual Polis."

"Like the birth of the first cities, the Virtual Polis was motivated by commerce," says Carl Loeffler. "It is a complete three-dimensional inhabitable environment with people, private homes, museums, parks, stores, and entertainment centers. Participants are able to go to the park or go shopping to obtain virtual objects to bring back 'home.' The city is presented as a contemporary, western-style, urban center. Some buildings are new, bright, and shiny; others are tattered with the appearance of plaster falling off the walls. The goods and services offered are extremely varied, including clothing, an auto showroom, furniture, and items for home decoration, digital media, leisure, and travel. We even provide journeys to distant times. The travel store can set you up for a visit to a virtual Ancient Egyptian Temple of Horus. There are intelligent agents, presented as people or animals, who lend elements of surprise to the city. Future development will explore more deeply the notions of virtual work, play, and consumption."

Loeffler finds that his city-building efforts in cyberspace have raised ethical and moral issues about what kind of society we're creating. The artist Nam June Paik describes this crisis in detail: "If you want naked economic truth in Europe, America, and Japan . . . people have already bought everything. They have every kind of hardware, from washing machines to VCRs. There is nothing more to buy." This makes it necessary, he continues, to "invent new software [to] stimulate [the] economy."

"What this points towards is the virtual domain," says Loeffler. "Virtual beings, manufacturing virtual things, for virtual people."

As we rush in and colonize cyberspace, we must move cautiously. The artist, composer, and programmer David Rokeby cautioned about this in *Evolution and the Bioapparataus*. "There is a kind of colonialism implicit in western approaches to the unexplored territories of virtual realities. We seem to assume that virtual space is ours for the taking and that we can colonize this space, imbuing it with our own notions. I believe that we will spend more and more time living in virtual spaces, in virtual relationships, even perhaps virtual time. It would seem that, if general trends continue, we will be spending this time living within our own models. We are already capable of ignoring perceptions that run counter to our conceptions. We will have to take care to avoid massive, collective self-delusion with these self-constructed models."

The day when thousands of people will hook up to and enter a globally networked virtual reality universe is at least 50 to 100 years away—but a limited version might be available in just 5 to 10 years. William Gibson's vision of people directly plugging their central nervous systems into a computer might always remain a fantasy. It's just too complex and runs counter to the neurological structure of human bodies. Our five senses already provide a natural connection into our brains.

Just as television and video games have raised a generation of children ready to adopt computer technology, a generation that seems to feel instantly at home with virtual reality, it might take several generations before the general public is ready for cyberspace.

⇨ A new literacy

The alphabet was created as a coding system to allow people to share their internal thoughts and realities without having to meet. Reading and writing created a form of external, nonperishable memory, one that retains its original information despite additional events. It became much easier to go back and compare new ideas to previous ones, to shape and refine an idea over time. Ideas could be quickly communicated and copies could be made and distributed across boundaries, time zones, and cultures.

What we don't have from the early days of writing, however, is much of a record of the resistance or the social upheaval caused by the appearance of this new technology. How did Homer and the other Greek bards feel about having their stories written down? They depended on memory to store their sagas, and interaction with the audience to influence the telling. Plato argued that writing was a threat to the culture and inferior to oral-based memorization.

What about merchants—did it change the way they did business? It took many generations for the use of writing to spread, and even in modern times there are vast numbers of people who never learn to read or write. But it has changed the world by changing the way people think even without everyone using it. What will VR's impact be?

Literacy means more than the ability to read and write, though these are its most basic requirements. Reading allows for reflection and contemplation about the ideas on a page. What does the writer mean? What is he trying to convince me of? What are the implications of these ideas to other ideas, institutions, and people—to me and my life? Do I agree or disagree?

Meredith Bricken, a research scientist with the HIT lab in Seattle, Washington, points out that reading and writing are basically cognitive functions, but virtual reality is both cognitive and behavioral. The act of participating in a simulated world involves us physically, visually, emotionally, magically, and rationally in organized and spontaneous events.

Someday teachers will be able to take students to the bottom of the ocean without leaving their classroom. Students will play with atoms and make their own molecules in VR to experience chemistry, instead of just reading about it. The development and widespread use of VR raises valid concerns about what we will teach ourselves and our children in these simulations. Optimistically, it will lead to a revolution in teaching and learning. Students will acquire a sense of control over knowledge.

But what about the violence of video games? Will home VR systems teach children to all be Mutant Ninja Turtles? There's a striking difference between the passive viewing of violence on television and being invited to spend hours hunting and shooting opponents in a virtual game.

Adults might be able to make the moral distinction between reality and fantasy in a simulation, but what about children? How old is old enough to appreciate the difference when you're immersed in a world of 3-D sound and color and the enemy is attacking? Ray Bradbury

asked this question allegorically over 30 years ago in his horror tale of a future virtual-reality-like media room, *The Veldt*.

Will the military's use of VR lead to desensitized soldiers who fight video-game wars, never seeing the enemy? The use of VR, computers, and telepresence in war could shield people from the disturbing consequences of their actions. It could also save lives by removing people from the battlefield.

It's dangerous, of course, to jump to conclusions too quickly, to look at individuals isolated from home, family, society, and work as if they were devoid of free will and easily influenced by *every* media message. More study and debate is needed in this area.

Some critics are ready to denounce virtual reality as a mind-numbing, brainwashing technology that will homogenize culture. The same fears were raised 40 years ago with the emergence of television. These are valid concerns—even after 40 years the public debate continues over the numbing and conditioning effects of violence on television—but this is a debate over content, not technology.

As the debate on TV focuses on the negative, the global impact of television is often overlooked. TV has also lived up to its early promise of linking and communicating with vast areas of the world formerly isolated from each other. Just as reading and writing can be used for propaganda, pleasure, or critical analysis, so too can VR. VR can be used to educate, train, and make us more aware of our own behavior. The alphabet allows writers and readers to carefully study thoughts and ideas, and virtual reality will allow the same critical analysis of behavior.

Virtual reality, however, will bring about the need for a new kind of literacy, one that's behaviorally as well as cognitively based. When designers construct a world, they'll be forced to consider the actions they're taking a user through.

The implications are that it might force society and culture as a whole to become aware of the messages and meanings in behavior as well as words. Worlds will be designed (probably first by artists) that attack

353

the potential of virtual reality for abuse and make us aware of our own unconscious habits and behaviors.

Like the holodeck on "Star Trek: The Next Generation," future VR might become vast libraries of experience that will be as accessible as opening a door. We'll shift through different points of view, considering ideas and events from several vantage points and personalities.

The founding fathers of the United States had very different points of view about what course the country's development should take. How would it be to study American history first from John Adams' point of view, then Thomas Jefferson and George Washington, before switching to King George for the English side of the story? Then you could examine the insights of Native Americans, indentured servants, merchants, and slaves.

Twenty years ago, Alan Kay developed a singular vision of what computers could contribute. He was inspired by the insights of Marshal McLuhan. It was the sum total of McLuhan's writings that changed the way Kay looked at computers from a tool into a medium. Out of this came his inspiration for the Dynabook:

> "The intensely interactive and involving nature of the personal computer seemed an antiparticle that could annihilate the passive boredom invoked by television. What kind of thinker would you become if you grew up with an active simulator connected, not just to one point of view, but to all the points of view of the ages, represented so they could be dynamically tried out and compared? I named the notebook sized computer idea the Dynabook to capture McLuhan's metaphor in the silicon to come."
> **Alan Kay, *User Interface: A Personal View*, 1991**

Virtual-reality-based computers are laying the foundation to finally deliver on Kay's vision. They're part of a paradigm shift as our civilization comes to terms with the powerful new information tools it has developed. As we learn to harness the power of virtual reality, we'll be moving from an information-based age to a simulation age in which the information serves us.

Like a child with a new toy at Christmas, who runs excitedly around the house imagining all the different things the toy can do, we too are trying to figure out what to do with our bright, shiny, new toy. Though virtual reality has many potential uses, it will take innovation, dedication, and a little bit of imagination to change the toy into a variety of useful tools.

VR is off the ground and flying at last, but the journey has just begun.

A

Resource guide

There are many different methods, tools, and hardware for building virtual environments. In chapter 5, *Reality simulators*, you learned about the basic components of a VR system and how, working in concert, they can create simulated 3-D worlds. In chapter 8, *Gloves, goggles, and wands*, you learned how dozens of different devices and sensors function and are used in these same simulations. In this appendix, pictures and specifications provide interesting details of many of the products and prototypes developed for virtual reality. By looking through these pictures, you might be amazed at the variety of methods that already have evolved. If you're interested in applying virtual-environment technology, then this guide can be an invaluable resource in learning about the state of the current technology.

In several cases, we've estimated specifications due to a lack of information from the manufacturer. Also, don't take any of these specifications too literally because there's a lack of standardization in how the parameters are measured. For up-to-date information, including the latest pricing, contact the manufacturers listed in appendix B.

This guide is organized the same way the book is. The first part is a summary of available VR systems or software packages. Then the second and third parts cover most of the output and input sensors currently available.

⇨ VR systems

Instead of a list of all products that claim to be virtual reality, we will once again impose the description of VR used at the beginning of chapter 5. We'll stick to describing products that support head-tracked, head-mounted displays and stereo views, and are commercially available as of mid-1994. In addition, we'll limit the list to products that are based on real-time 3-D renderers and exclude systems that are used only for entertainment. This narrows the field to the major VR companies, which account for 95% of the systems installed in labs and businesses all across the world. You can expect this list to grow quite a bit longer in the next couple of years. Many of the manufacturers listed here offer many more products and features than there is space to describe, so please contact them for up-to-date prices and information.

Autodesk
Product: CDK (Cyberspace Development Kit) v1.0
Platform: DOS
Graphics hardware: VGA, SPEA Fireboard, Future Vision
Cost: $2,500
Comments: A C++ programmer's toolkit. It contains drivers for many of the common VR interface devices, reads Autodesk DXF and 3DS files, and generates stereo images.

Division
Product: PROvision
Platforms: SGI, Custom system, Unix PC
Graphics hardware: SGI, Custom
Cost: $55,000–200,000
Comments: Options include VPL DataGlove, stereo HMD, and stereo audio imaging of the virtual world. Provides a C language toolkit (dVS) for creating custom virtual worlds. Another tool, Dvise, is available for nonprogrammers. It reads Autodesk DXF and 3DS files, and generates stereo images.

Sense8
Product: WorldToolKit v2.1
Platforms: DOS, Windows, Sun, SGI, DEC, HP
Graphics hardware: VGA (Windows), SPEA Fireboard, Future Vision, SGI, DEC/Kubota, Sun ZX, Evans & Sutherland Freedom, HP
Cost: $795–$10,000

357

Comments: A C library of 400 functions that supports interfacing to many of the common VR devices such as HMDs, 3-D and MIDI sound, force balls, networking, etc. Reads Autodesk DXF and 3DS files along with Wavefront OBJ and ProEngineer files. Most hardware platforms support real-time texture-mapping.

Superscape
Product: Superscape VRT (Virtual Reality Toolkit)
Platform: DOS
Graphics hardware: VGA, SPEA HiLite (TIGA)
Cost: $5,000
Comments: Designed for end users, this DOS product includes modeling and simulation scripting tools. It supports MIDI sound, force balls, and analog joysticks, reads Autodesk DXF files, and supports real-time texture-mapping.

VREAM
Product: VREAM v1.0
Platform: DOS
Graphics hardware: VGA, Windows
Cost: $595
Comments: Designed for end users, this product includes modeling and simulation scripting tools. It supports many of the common VR devices such as HMDs, MIDI sound, force balls, networking, etc. It reads Autodesk DXF files and supports real-time texture-mapping.

⇨ Other tools

Several companies have products that can be used for real-time display of 3-D objects, but they don't always support head-mounted displays or the other tools of the VR trade. Some of these products are simply real-time 3-D renderers that run on computers with limited support for VR devices. This lists a few of the more common products.

Domark
Product: Virtual Reality Studio
Platform: DOS, Amiga
Graphics hardware: VGA
Cost: $100
Comments: Designed for end users, this product includes simple modeling and simulation scripting tools. It's an entry-level tool, with no support for VR devices.

REND386
Product: REND386/VR386
Platform: DOS
Graphics hardware: VGA
Cost: freeware
Comments: This is a popular tool with hobbyists. It reads script files for both modeling and simulation descriptions. It supports some sound and interface devices such as joysticks and the Logitech head-tracker.

Virtus
Product: Virtus Walkthrough
Platforms: Macintosh, Windows
Graphics hardware: VGA
Cost: $400
Comments: Designed for end users, this product is principally a walk-through tool. There's no support for moving objects or simulation dynamics, and no support for VR devices.

Output

These devices provide either sight, sound, or haptic sensory output. They're intended to provide participants with particular sensory cues regarding the virtual world.

Head-mounted displays

Note that display resolution is measured in either triads or by individual color elements. It takes three color elements (RGB) to make up a single triad. The resolution of CRT-based designs is given in pixels, which is similar to that of triads. LCD display resolutions are typically given as color elements instead of as triads. The important thing to remember is that one pixel does not equal one color element. An LCD display with 400×200 elements might have 80,000 elements but only 26,700 triads or pixels.

CAE-Electronics
Model: FOHMD
Display: Fiberoptic, two-color light-valves, 1,000×1,000 pixels
Weight: 5–6 lbs.

Field of view: Up to 127H×66V, Pancake Windows optics
Video in: NTSC or RGB
Cost: $250,000–$1,000,000
Comments: Top-of-the-line HMD, high resolution and wide field of view with higher resolution insert at center of view. Designed for simulator use only, it uses 4,000,000-element fiberoptic bundles. Four overhead sensors are directed at six helmet-mounted LEDs to determine head position and orientation (see Fig. A-1).

Figure A-1

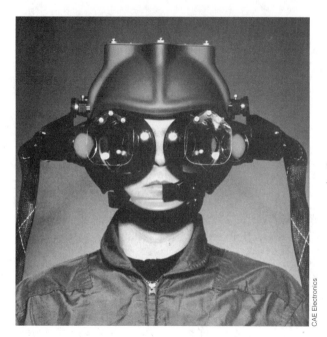

CAE-Electronics FOHMD.

CyberSense
Model: Renegade Stereo
Display: Two color AM LCDs, 428×244 elements
Weight: 3.5 lbs.
Field of view: 100H×60V
Video in: NTSC
Cost: $7,500
Comments: Includes stereo headphones.

Division
Model: dVISOR
Display: Two color AM LCDs, 345×259 elements
Weight: 4.75 lbs. (estimated)

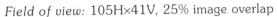
Field of view: 105H×41V, 25% image overlap
Video in: NTSC or PAL
Cost: $5,000
Comments: Special depixelation technology from MicroSharp reduces pixelation problems without blurring the image. Helmet-like design is fully immersive and comes with stereo headphones and an integrated Polhemus FASTRAK sensor (see Fig. A-2).

Figure A-2

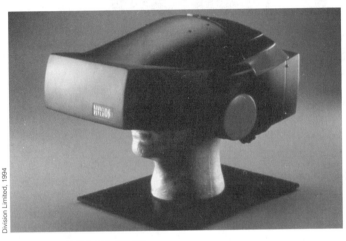

Division Limited, 1994

Division dVISOR HMD.

FORTE Technologies Inc.
Model: VFX1
Display: Two color AM LCDs, 428×244 elements
Weight: 1.5 lbs. (projected)
Field of view: 46H×35V, 100% image overlap
Video in: VGA, NTSC, or PAL
Cost: $800 (projected)
Comments: Includes passive 3-DOF head-tracker integrated into HMD housing and stereo headphones. Head-tracking system requires ISA PC add-in board. Includes IPD adjustment, and display can be flipped up if needed. The display connects to VGA boards through a VGA feature connector (see Fig. A-3). Available January 1995.

General Reality Company
Model: CyberEye
Display: Two color AM LCDs, 420×230 elements
Weight: .88 lb.
Field of view: 22.5H×17V, 100% image overlap

Figure A-3

Forte VFX1 HMD.
Forte Inc.

Video in: NTSC
Cost: $2,000 (mono) and $2,500 (stereo)
Comments: Lightweight HMD with IPD and focus adjustments. Available as either a stereoscopic or monoscopic version, it has stereo headphones and a portable control box. The design allows you to easily flip up the display in order to use your keyboard.

IMP ART
Model: SenseCover cx2
Display: Two color LCDs, 400×300 elements
Weight: 1.75 lbs.
Field of view: 120H×90V, 60% image overlap
Video in: PAL
Cost: $8,700
Comments: Includes headphones. The product is made in Germany and distributed by VRT GmbH.

Kaiser Electro-optics
Model: Sim Eye 60
Display: Two monochrome CRTs with color filters, 640×480 pixels (noninterlaced) and up to 1280×1024 pixels (interlaced)
Weight: 5.2 lbs.
Field of view: 60 diagonal, 100% image overlap
Video in: RGB (field sequential)
Cost: $50,000

Comments: Monochrome CRTs are used with an LCD-based switchable color filter. It requires a field-sequential RGB signal (an RGB converter is an available option). The same HMD is available with an FOV of 40 degrees.

Model: Vim 1000pv
Display: Four color AM LCDs, 505×230 elements each
Weight: 1.7 lbs.
Field of view: 100H×30V, 100% image overlap on two center LCDs
Video in: VGA, RGB
Cost: $10,000
Comments: Biocular system based on four LCD panels. The two center LCDs have 100% image overlap and the effective resolution is three times that of a single LCD. It contains built-in microphone and stereo headphones, as well as an integrated Polhemus sensor. Adjustments for IPD, head size, and fore/aft position are available. Requires special video converter unit to display image across multiple LCD panels. Future versions will support stereoscopic display (see Fig. A-4).

Figure A-4

Kaiser Electro-Optic Vim HMD.

Model: Vim 500pv
Display: Two color AM LCDs, 505×230 elements each
Weight: 1.5 lbs.
Field of view: 50H×30V, 100% image overlap
Video in: NTSC
Cost: $3,000

Comments: Contains a built-in microphone, stereo headphones, and integrated Polhemus sensor. Adjustments for IPD, head size and fore/aft position are available.

LEEP
Model: Cyberface 2
Display: Two color LCDs, 479×234 elements
Weight: 4.25 lbs.
Field of view: 140H, 100% image overlap
Video in: NTSC, PAL, or RGB
Cost: $8,100
Comments: The counterbalance is worn on the front, like a bib. This has the largest field of view of any HMD, and requires image correction to use it properly.

Liquid Image
Model: MRG2
Display: One color LCD, 720×240 elements
Weight: 5 lbs. (estimated)
Field of view: 84H×65V, 100% image overlap
Video in: NTSC, PAL (optional)
Cost: $3,500
Comments: Biocular system based on a single LCD panel. It cannot be used for stereoscopic display, and includes stereo headphone. Robust construction makes it popular with gaming systems (see Fig. 1-6).

Model: MRG4
Display: One color LCD, 720×240 elements
Weight: 2.5 lbs.
Field of view: 60H, 100% image overlap
Video in: NTSC, PAL (optional)
Cost: $2,200
Comments: See MRG2.

n-Vision
Model: Datavisor 9c
Display: Tektronix NuColor CRTs, from 640×480 to 1280×960 pixels
Weight: 3.2 lbs.
Field of view: 50H, 100% image overlap
Video in: VGA, RGB
Cost: $56,000
Comments: Has IPD adjustment, infinity focus, and optional headphones and microphone additions. Supports 100% image overlap.

Polhemus Labs
Model: Looking Glass
Display: 4- to 8-foot fiberoptic cables, 500×500 pixels
Weight: .88 lb.
Field of view: 40H, 100% image overlap
Video in: NTSC or RGB
Cost: $35,000–50,000
Comments: Requires optical interface to a 200–300 foot-lambert image source (very bright). Note that Polhemus Labs is not related to Polhemus Inc, though they were started by the same person (see Fig. 8-12).

RPI
Model: HMSI Model 1000
Display: Two color LCDs, 450×240 elements
Weight: .3 lb.
Field of view: 45H×32V, 100% image overlap
Video in: RGB, NTSC
Cost: $5,000
Comments: Has IPD adjustment, depixelator, and headphone, and is a very small and compact HMD. Many other options are available, including wireless operation (see Fig. A-5).

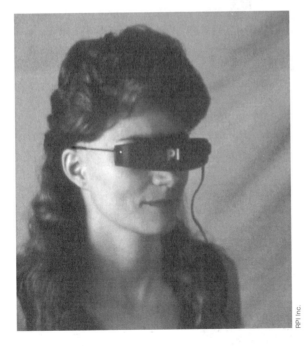

Figure A-5

RPI HMSI Model 1000 HMD.

VictorMaxx

Model: CyberMaxx
Display: Two color AM LCDs, 505×240 elements
Weight: .95 lb.
Field of view: 62H, 100% image overlap
Video in: VGA, RGB, NTSC, PAL
Cost: $700
Comments: Has IPD adjustment, individual focus controls, headphones, and built-in sourceless tracking system. Stereopsis is achieved by using alternating video scan-lines. Can also be used in monoscopic mode. Tracking system is 3 DOF with .75 msec lag and serial-port interface (see Fig. A-6).

Figure A-6

VictorMaxx CyberMaxx HMD.

Victormaxx Inc.

Virtual I/O

Model: VIO UltraView
Display: Tektronix NuColor CRTs, from 640×480 to 1280×960 pixels
Weight: 2 lbs.
Field of view: 55D, 100% image overlap
Video in: dual VGA-frame sequential inputs
Cost: $75,000

Comments: Containing optics based on holographic lenses that support a "see-through" design, this is one of a few HMDs with this capability. Large-exit pupil eliminates the need for IPD adjustment. Includes stereo sound (see Fig. A-7).

Figure A-7

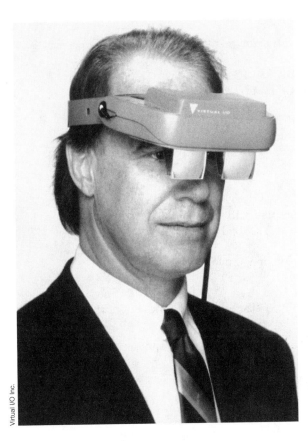

Virtual I/O Inc.

Virtual I/O VioMan HMD.

Model: VioMan 2000M or 2000S
Display: Two color AM LCDs, 505×240 elements
Weight: .7 lb.
Field of view: 34D, 100% image overlap
Video in: NTSC, S-Video
Cost: $1,650 (mono), $2,250 (stereo)
Comments: see entry for VIO UltraView. (See Fig. A-7)

Virtual Reality Inc.

Model: Personal Immersive Display P1
Display: Two color LCDs, 479×234 elements
Weight: 5 lbs.
Field of view: 63H, 100% image overlap
Video in: NTSC
Cost: $5,000
Comments: Helmet design with adjustment for fit. Includes headphones.

Model: Personal Immersive Display 131
Display: Two monochrome CRTs, up to 1,280×1,024 elements
Weight: 3 lbs.
Field of view: 40H×30V, 100% image overlap
Video in: NTSC, RGB
Cost: $56,000
Comments: Adjustments for head size and IPD. The optics support see-through and opaque mode.

Model: Personal Immersive Display 133
Display: Two color CRTs, up to 1,280×1,024 elements
Weight: 3 lbs.
Field of view: 40H×30V, 100% image overlap
Video in: NTSC, RGB
Cost: $87,000
Comments: Adjustments for head size and IPD. Optics support see-through and opaque mode.

Virtual Research

Model: VR Flight Helmet
Display: Color LCD, 360×240 elements
Weight: 3.7 lbs.
Field of view: 100D, 50% image overlap
Video in: NTSC
Cost: discontinued
Comments: Though no longer in production, this HMD is included due to its widespread use.

Model: Eyegen3
Display: Two monochrome CRTs with RGB color wheels, 493×250 pixels
Weight: 1.75 lbs.
Field of view: 40D, 100% image overlap
Video in: NTSC
Cost: $7,900

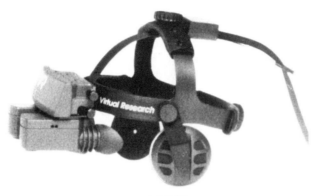

Virtual Research Eyegen3 HMD. <small>Virtual Research Inc.</small>

Comments: Has focus, IPD adjustment, and integrated headphones. Displays flip-up or moves in-out (*see* Fig. A-8).

Model: VR4
Display: Two color LCDs, 742×230 elements
Weight: 2 lbs.
Field of view: 60D, 100% image overlap
Video in: S-Video, NTSC (RS-170)
Cost: $7,900
Comments: Has focus, IPD adjustment, and integrated headphones. Display accommodates glasses, and has fore/aft adjustment and a separate control box.

Virtual Vision
Model: DK210
Display: Two color AM LCDs, 300×200 elements
Weight: .5 lb.
Field of view: 60H, 100% image overlap
Video in: NTSC, PAL
Cost: $2,900
Comments: Lightweight HMD with IPD and focus adjustments. One of the few HMDs that support a nonoccluded or "see-through" view of the physical world. Options include a remote transmitter/receiver for cableless operation.

W-Industries
Model: Visette2
Display: Two color LCDs, 756×244 elements
Weight: 1.4 lbs.
Field of view: 60H×47V, 100% image overlap

Video in: PAL
Cost: not sold separately
Comments: Designed for arcade use. The new design is considerably improved over the previous Visette.

⇨ Related display technologies

Fake Space Labs
Model: BOOM-2C
Display: Dual two color CRTs, 1,280×1,024 pixels
Weight: NA
Field of view: 90–100H, 100% image overlap
Cost: $74,000
Comments: Provides simplified access to the virtual world. Uses CRT monitors for high resolution, and has limited color space due to the use of only two primary colors instead of three. Counterbalanced design eliminates the weight of the displays. Control buttons on handles allow control of movement along the view direction (see Fig. 5-9).

Model: BOOM-3C
Display: Two color CRTs, 1,280×1,024 pixels
Weight: NA
Field of view: 90–100H, 100% image overlap
Cost: $74,000
Comments: Provides simplified access to the virtual world. Uses CRT monitors for high resolution. Limited color space due to the use of only two primary colors instead of three. Counterbalanced design eliminates the weight of the displays. Control buttons on handles allow control of movement along the view direction.

LEEP
Model: Cyberface3
Display: One color LCD, 720×240 elements
Weight: NA
Field of view: 70H
Video in: NTSC, RGB
Cost: $15,000
Comments: Biocular display uses a single LCD screen for both eyes. Though not capable of stereo, Cyberface 3 is designed to be attached to a desktop and is intended for uses where color and resolution are important. The price doesn't include a tracking system. Head-tracking is accomplished with either a standard 6-DOF sensor or a custom mechanical design (see Fig. A-9).

Figure A-9

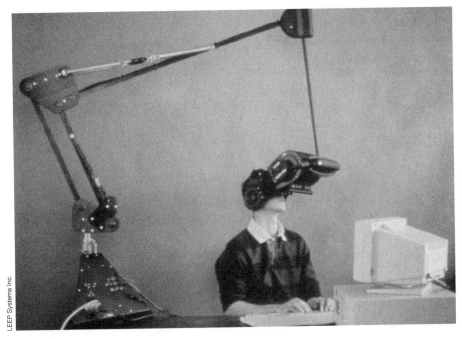

LEEP Systems Inc.

LEEP Systems Cyberface3.

Reflection Technology
Model: Private Eye
Display: Monochrome (red) LEDs, 720×280 pixels
Weight: .12 lb.
Field of view: 22H×14V
Video in: Custom PC board
Cost: $500
Comments: Specs are for a single-eye setup. The company is working on a 1,000×1,000 monochrome display with Sun Microsystems (see Fig. A-10).

Simsalabim
Model: Cyberscope
Display: Any monitor from 14" to 17"
Weight: 2.1 lbs.
Field of view: 47H×35V, 100% image overlap
Cost: $199
Comments: Lightweight plastic hood fits over monitor screen. Left- and right-eye images are rotated 90 degrees on the screen to maximize horizontal resolution and field of view.

Figure A-10

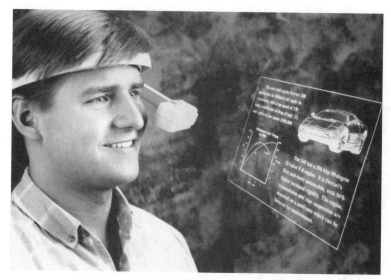

Reflection Technology Private Eye display.

StereoGraphics

Model: CrystalEyes-PC
Display: Active LCD shutters mounted on glasses
Weight: .19 lb.
Field of view: NA
Cost: $985
Comments: Requires a 120-Hz monitor and must be viewed within a 12-foot radius of the monitor. Another version, called CrystalEyes-VR, includes a Logitech ultrasonic head-tracking sensor integrated into the frame of the shutter glasses. Projection display systems are also available from StereoGraphics (see Fig. A-11).

Tektronix

Model: SGS
Display: Passive glasses, active LCD shutter placed in front of monitor
Weight: NA
Field of view: NA
Cost: $1,500–8,000
Comments: Requires a 90- to 150-Hz monitor. The system is based on polarized sunglasses and an LCD shutter that's placed in front of the monitor. Versions are available that integrate the LCD shutter into a multisync monitor.

Figure A-11

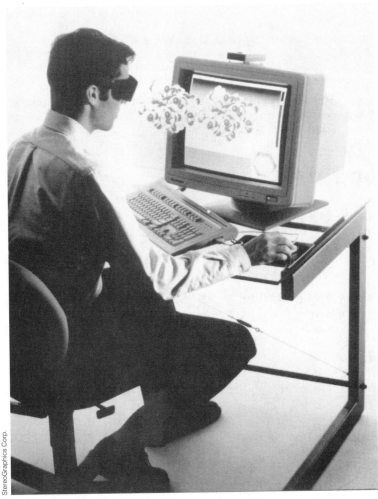

StereoGraphics Corp.

StereoGraphics CrystalEyes LCD flicker glasses.

Virtual Vision
Model: RSP110 or LSP120
Display: One color AM LCD, 300×200 elements
Weight: .25 lb.
Field of view: 20H
Video in: NTSC, PAL
Cost: $700
Comments: Designed for a single-eye display. The image is projected onto a mirror in the bottom part of a see-through visor.

VRex
Model: VR1000
Display: Passive glasses, active LCD shutter, 640×480 pixels
Weight: NA
Field of view: NA
Cost: $7,925
Comments: This is a 3-D LCD display panel that can be placed on top of an overhead projector. Inexpensive passive 3-D glasses are used to view the image. Also available is a 3-D video camera and other 3-D projection systems.

 # Sound

All these devices can produce realistic 3-D sound effects, and most of them can perform this operation in real time. Some products require preprocessing of the sound files in order to simulate 3-D sound.

Crystal River Engineering
Model: Acoustetron Audio Server
Input: 16 channels
A/D: 16-bit samples at 50 kHz
Cost: $50,000
Comments: Includes a 486 33-MHz PC and four Convolvotrons (see following). This system is configured to perform as an audio server for other computing platforms.

Model: Convolvotron
Input: 4 channels
A/D: 16-bit samples at 50 kHz
Cost: $15,000
Comments: Two-board set designed for the IBM PC. Up to four independent sound sources can be convolved at once. A second set of boards can be cascaded to create a simple reflective model of an environment. Requires a separate sound source or MIDI sequencer.

Model: Beachtron
Input: 2 channels
A/D: 16-bit samples at 44.1 kHz
Cost: $1,495
Comments: This is based on Turtle Beach's digital signal processing board, and up to two audio sources can be convolved. It also has an on-board programmable sound synthesizer and sequencer.

Model: Alphatron
Input: 2 channels
A/D: 16-bit samples at up to 44.2 kHz
Cost: $495
Comments: Some features as the Beachtron, except no on-board synthesizer.

Focal Point 3D Audio
Model: Focal Point
Input: 2 channels
A/D: 16-bit samples at 44.1 kHz
Cost: $1,500
Comments: A single board for the Macintosh or the PC. It has on-board synthesizer capabilities.

Gravis
Model: UltraSound
Input: 2 to 4 channels
A/D: 16-bit samples at 44.1 kHz
Cost: $200
Comments: Though this board cannot convolve real-time sounds like the more expensive products, it can produce realistic 3-D effects using preprocessed sound samples.

Visual Synthesis Inc.
Model: Audio Architect
Input: 2 channels
A/D: Selectable, 8-bit to 16-bit samples, from 8 to 44 kHz
Cost: $500–$995
Comments: A full development system, it uses "native" audio capability on the host system. Multiple file formats; prototyping for SoundCube; speech capability; and SGI, Sun, and DEC versions are supported.

Model: Audio Image Sonic Architect
Input: 2 channels
A/D: Selectable, 8-bit to 16-bit samples, from 8 to 44 kHz
Cost: $1,500–$2,500
Comments: Same as Audio Architect, plus absorption and reflection modelers.

Model: Audio Image Sound Cube
Input: 2–8 channels
A/D: Selectable, 16-bit samples, at 20–39 kHz
Cost: $8,000–$15,000

Comments: Sound channels can be independently manipulated in real time with special hardware and function libraries. It supports absorption, reflection, Doppler modeling, and up to 32 independent audio sources from up to 8 channels. It's supported on SGI, Sun, and DEC platforms.

 Haptic

Research in this field has resulted in a limited number of commercial devices. Much work still needs to be done from both the software and hardware standpoint before these devices become widely accepted.

✳ Tactile feedback devices

Aura Systems
Model: Interactor
Type: Tactile display for chest
Sensors: Single voice-coil mounted on vest
Cost: $89
Comments: A voice-coil mounted on a plastic vest is driven by an audio system. Volume and filtering controls are provided. Intended for game use.

Begej
Model: Research projects
Type: Tactile display for hands or body suit
Sensors: 40 to 50 analog "texels" on glove, 512 on body suit
Cost: NA
Comments: Begej has both tactile gloves and a full-body tactile design under research. Both designs combine tactile sensors mounted on a robot as input to the tactile display devices mounted on the glove or body suit.

CM Research
Model: DTSS X/10
Type: Temperature display for skin surface
Channels: 8 (input or output)
Cost: $10,000
Comments: This device provides temperature feedback with thermodes. A solid-state heat pump moves heat into or out of a heat sink based on signals from a controller. Each thermode can generate hot or cold sensations, and measure them. Their small size allows them to be placed directly on the fingertip.

Exos

Model: TouchMaster
Type: Tactile display for fingers
Sensors: Voice-coils
Cost: Contact vendor
Comments: Up to 10 channels can be driven. The standard version uses a fixed frequency of 210 Hz and constant amplitude.

Xtensory Inc.

Model: Tactools XTT1
Type: Tactile display for skin surface
Sensors: 1 channel
Output force: 30 grams
Cost: $1,500 (with 1 tactor)
Comments: Uses a controller that can support up to 10 tactors, and communicates over serial or MIDI ports (see Fig. 8-16).

✳ Force feedback devices

ARRC/Airmuscle Ltd.

Model: Teletact II
Type: Force display for fingers and hand
Sensors: 30 air pockets
Output force: 12 psi
Cost: $4,900
Comments: Improved version has 30 pockets instead of the original 20. In addition, it has a large palm pocket than can be inflated up to 30 psi. Teletact II control system is an additional $13,400 (see Fig. A-12).

Figure A-12

Teletact II force-feedback glove.

Model: Teletact Commander
Type: Force display for fingers and hand
Sensors: 3 to 5 air pockets
Output force: 12 psi
Cost: Prototype
Comments: Simple hand-held device has five control buttons. Either a Polhemus or Ascension 6D sensor is mounted internally. Uses a low-cost airbrush compressor.

Cybernet Systems
Model: PER-Force Handcontroller
Type: Force display for fingers and hand
DOF: 6 or 3
Range: 4-inch travel, 90-degree rotation
Output force: 2 lbs. (peak) and .3 lb. (avg.)
Cost: Contact vendor
Comments: Robot-like arm that supports a motorized joystick. Small electrical motors generate resistance to motion. The device has a limited mechanical range, but is fully programmable for different situations. Available with either 6-DOF or 3-DOF motion. A finger-forcer option that provides up to 2 lbs. of force and 11 DOF (two for each finger and three for the thumb) is also available.

Exos
Model: Force ArmMaster
Type: Force display for shoulder and arm
DOF: 5
Range: 100–120 degrees of rotation
Output force: 31 lbs. (peak)
Cost: Contact vendor
Comments: Provides joint torque feedback to the shoulder and arm. System weight is distributed around waist using a harness. Can also be used to measure shoulder and arm rotations.

Model: SAFIRE
Type: Force display for fingers and wrist
DOF: 11
Range: 30 to 90 degrees of rotation
Output force: 50–100 ozs.
Cost: Contact vendor
Comments: Provides joint torque feedback to the fingers and wrist. Can also be used to measure finger and wrist rotation.

Sarcos and the Center for Engineering Design
Model: Exoskelatal Master
DOF: 10
Cost: $100,000 (prototype)
Comments: Can also be used with the Sarcos Dexterous Arm for teleoperation. This was developed at the University of Utah and is the leading system of its type in the world. High-pressure hydraulic lines precisely control the forces being applied to the operator's arms and hands.

 Input

These are the various devices you wear or manipulate in order to interact with a virtual world. Together, they represent many different approaches to establishing a dialog between man and machine.

Wired clothing

Exos
Model: Dexterous Hand Master
Type: Mechanical Hall-Effect sensors
Sensors: 20
Cost: $15,000
Comments: Mechanical design allows for accurate (.5 degree) and repeatable measurements. Bulkiness limits its use for some applications (see Fig. 8-20).

Mattel
Model: PowerGlove
Type: Resistive sensors
Cost: Discontinued (originally $89)
Comments: Developed in cooperation with VPL, Abrams-Gentile Entertainment, and Mattel. Based on conductive ink deposited on a strip of plastic inside each gloved finger. Low-cost ultrasonic sensors were used to detect glove position and orientation. First available in late 1989, and discontinued in late 1991. Available from 3DTV Corp.

Sarcos and the Center for Engineering Design
Model: Exoskelatal Hand Master
Type: Mechanical sensors
Sensors: 16

Cost: Prototype
Comments: Mechanical design allows for accurate and repeatable measurements. Bulkiness limits its use for some applications (see Fig. A-13).

Figure A-13

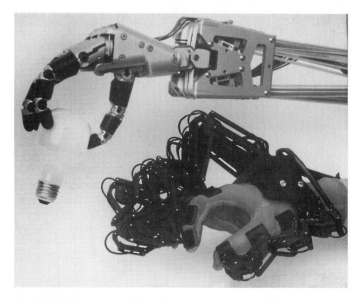

Utah/MIT Dextrous Hand with Sarcos Exoskelatal Hand Master.

Virtual Technologies (Virtex)
Model: CyberGlove CG1801
Type: Fiberoptic sensors
Sensors: 18 (up to 22)
Cost: $6,500
Comments: Designed to fit all sizes of hands and to be less sensitive to joint positioning. Virtex also supplies CyberForce, a force-feedback system, and various cyberwear such as a CyberSuit for measuring other body motions. Comes with software for visualizing motions on a computer screen (see Fig. A-14).

Greenleaf Medical Systems
Model: DataGlove
Type: Fiberoptic sensors
Sensors: 10 (more available as an option)
Cost: Contact vendor
Comments: Includes Polhemus ISOTRAK position and orientation tracking system. Gloves come in different sizes (see Fig. A-15).

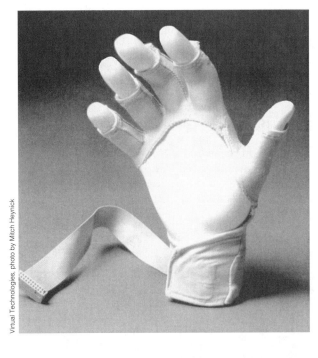

Virtual Technologies, photo by Mitch Heynick

*Virtual Technologies
CyberGlove.*

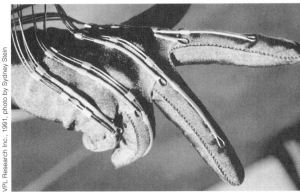

VPL Research Inc., 1991, photo by Sydney Stein

*Greenleaf Medical
Systems DataGlove.*

⇨ **Isometric devices**

GLOBAL Devices
Model: GLOBAL 3D Controller
DOF: 6
Measurement method: On/off values returned in all six directions

Cost: $250
Comments: Switch-based device returns on and off values for all six degrees of freedom. Supports 16 levels of tactile feedback.

Logitech
Model: Magellan (Space Control Mouse)
DOF: 6
Measurement method: 256 values returned in all six directions
Cost: $900
Comments: Compact device based on measuring forces and torques via LED sensors. Nine user-definable buttons are provided (see Fig. A-16).

Figure A-16

Logitech Magellan.
Logitech Inc.

Model: Cyberman
DOF: 6
Measurement method: 200 dpi in X-Y plane. On/off returned for all other directions.
Cost: $129
Comments: Device can mimic a standard mouse. A range of values are returned for only two of the six degrees of freedom. The other four simply return on/off values. A tactile display can be programmed to generate different durations and intensities of pulses.

Spaceball Technologies
Model: Spaceball 2003
DOF: 6
Measurement method: 256 values returned in all six directions
Cost: $1,600
Comments: Based on the same technology as the Geometry Ball. Nine user-definable buttons are provided (see Fig. 5-7).

Model: SpaceController
DOF: 6
Measurement method: 256 values returned in all six directions
Cost: $800
Comments: Based on the same technology as the Spaceball. Two user-definable buttons are provided (see Fig. A-17).

Figure A-17

*Spaceball
Technologies
SpaceController.* Spaceball
Technologies Inc.

 # 6-DOF mice and wands

Ascension
Model: The Ascension Bird
Type: Electromagnetic tracking
DOF: 6
Accuracy: .1-inch position and .5-degree orientation
Effective range: up to 3 feet (8 feet is optional)
Lag: < 15 msecs (unfiltered) and 30–90 msecs (filtered)
Update rate: 144 Hz
Cost: $3,000
Comments: An electromagnetic 6-DOF sensor buried inside a mouse-like device. Three user-programmable buttons are available, and the angular range for elevation is less than 360 degrees. It uses a pulsed dc method, which is intended to be less sensitive to metallic interference.

Digital Image Design
Model: The Cricket
Type: Multiple methods of tracking supported

DOF: 6
Specs: Can use Logitech, Polhemus, and Ascension trackers
Cost: $3,200
Comments: A hand-held device with trigger, grip, thumb, and suspend buttons. A programmable vibration transducer is also incorporated into the design. Variable pressure is measured on trigger and grip buttons, and the thumb button measures direction. The cost doesn't include a tracker.

Forte Technologies
Model: CYBERBAT
Type: Inertial tracking
DOF: 3
Accuracy: .1- to .25-degree orientation
Effective range: Vertical ± 70 degrees, horizontal 360 degrees
Lag: < 25 msecs (estimated)
Update rate: 30 Hz or better
Cost: Contact vendor
Comments: Has two sets of five programmable buttons. Uses a sourceless tracking system and communicates over RS232.

Gyration Inc.
Model: GyroPoint
Type: Inertial tracking
DOF: 3
Accuracy: .1-degree orientation
Lag: < 4 msecs (unfiltered)
Update rate: 100 Hz or better
Cost: $500
Comments: Mouse device with two micro-gyroscopes mounted inside. The mouse also has five programmable button controls. It's a completely integrated sensor, and doesn't require a source transmitter. The biggest problem is an accuracy drift of up to 10 degrees per minute.

InWorld VR
Model: CyberWand
Type: Multiple methods of tracking supported
Specs: Uses Polhemus tracker
Cost: $100
Comments: Hand-held joystick contains a 2-DOF thumb control and four programmable finger buttons. An optional Polhemus sensor can be installed inside the device. Includes a PC game-port board, and an optional serial port version is also available.

Logitech
Model: 3D Mouse
DOF: 2/6
Accuracy: 2 percent of distance from source, and .1-degree orientation
Range: Up to 2-foot, 8-inch fringe area
Lag: < 20 msecs (filtered)
Update rate: 50 Hz
Cost: $1,400
Comments: Uses ultrasonic tracking. Mouse can operate in normal 2-D desktop mode, and automatically switches to 3-D when picked up from the desk. Five user-programmable switches are available (see Fig. 5-8).

MULTIPOINT Technology Corp.
Model: Z Mouse
DOF: 5
Accuracy: 300 dpi (estimated)
Range: NA
Lag: < 10 ms (estimated)
Update rate: > 60 Hz (estimated)
Cost: $250
Comments: This device is the result of combining a 2-D mouse with a 2-D trackball. A thumb wheel on the side provides an additional degree of freedom. No external form of position or orientation tracking is used.

 Biologic

BioControl Systems
Model: BioMuse
Channels: 8 (independent)
Cost: $25,000
Comments: Multiple dermal electrodes can track muscle activity or brain waves. Electrical signals can be processed to control other devices such as MIDI sound hardware or a video game. Each channel can support multiple sensors and can run an independent processing algorithm (see Fig. 8-23).

Dragon Systems
Model: DragonVoiceTools
Cost: $1,000+
Comments: PC-based voice-recognition software. Capable of discrete or continuous voice recognition, and runs under DOS or Windows. Requires an audio capture board.

AICOM Corp.
Model: Accent SA
Cost: $500 and up
Comments: PC-based text-to-speech synthesis board.

Voice Connexion
Model: Micro IntroVoice
Cost: $1,600
Comments: Provides voice recognition of up to 1,000 words and text-to-speech synthesis. Independent serial port device works with any computer.

Covox Inc.
Model: SoundMaster II
Cost: $230
Comments: Supports audio, music, and voice recognition. PC-based.

Other interaction devices

KATrix
Model: CyberKAT
Device: Hand-held nonchorded keyboard emulator
Lag: < 2 msecs
Update rate: > 100 Hz
Cost: $2,500
Comments: A molded hand-grip contains five special switches (one per finger). Each finger switch can produce seven unique values, and the thumb key is used to choose one of five character sets. Up to 141 characters can be generated this way (see Fig. 8-24).

Handkey
Model: Twiddler
Device: Hand-held chorded keyboard/mouse emulator
Lag: < 2 msecs
Update rate: > 100 Hz
Cost: $195
Comments: This device combines both a mouse and 101-keyboard functionality into a small hand-held device. Twelve finger keys and 6 thumb keys provide "chord" keying.

Immersion
Model: Interface Box
Device: Serial port interface to foot pedals, knobs, sliders, and hand controllers

Inputs: Four 8-bit analog and four digital
Update rate: Sampling rates up to 14.4 kHz
Baud rate: Up to 115 kbps
Cost: $1,000
Comments: General-purpose interface box for connecting to various analog devices such as foot pedals and joysticks. Provides A/D conversion. Supports up to 8 devices on a single serial port.

 6-DOF sensors

These are devices used to track either various body parts or other physical objects. Many of these devices are integrated into other VR tools.

✳ Electromagnetic

Ascension
Model: Flock of Birds
DOF: 6
Accuracy: .1-inch position and .5-degree orientation
Effective range: Up to 3 feet (8 feet is optional)
Lag: < 15 msecs (unfiltered) and 30 to 90 msecs (filtered)
Update rate: 144 Hz
Cost: $2,800
Comments: Up to 30 control boxes can be daisy-chained together to track 30 independent items using a single transmitter, while maintaining a 144-Hz update rate. It uses a pulsed dc method, which is intended to be less sensitive to metallic interference. Also available in an extended-range version that tracks up to eight feet (see Fig. A-18).

Polhemus
Model: ISOTRAK II
DOF: 6
Accuracy: .1-inch position and .75-degree orientation
Effective range: Accurate up to 3 feet, tracks up to 5 feet
Lag: < 20 msec (unfiltered) and 50 to 150 msec (filtered)
Update rate: 60 Hz
Cost: $2,875
Comments: Supports unrestricted angular motion. The sensor cube is about .5 cubic inch. The sensor is subject to interference from large metal objects or nearby TVs or monitors. It includes synchronization hardware for multiple units, and the control unit supports up to two sensors.

Figure A-18

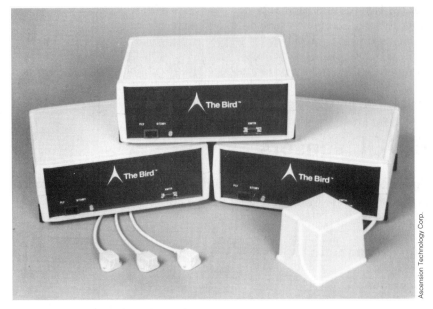

Ascension Flock of Birds tracker.

Model: InsideTRAK
DOF: 6
Accuracy: .5-inch position and 2-degree orientation
Effective range: Accurate up to 30 inches, tracks up to 5 feet
Lag: < 12 msec (unfiltered) and 50 to 150 msec (filtered)
Update rate: 60 Hz
Cost: $2,250
Comments: This model is designed as an ISA PC board. See comments for
ISOTRAK II.

Model: FASTRAK
DOF: 6
Accuracy: .03-inch position and .15-degree orientation
Effective range: Accurate up to 30 inches, tracks up to 10 feet
Lag: < 4 msecs (unfiltered)
Update rate: 120 Hz
Cost: $5,750
Comments: Supports up to four sensors with one source. Multiple control
boxes can be multiplexed without impact to update rate (see Fig. 8-27).

❋ Ultrasonic

Logitech
Model: Head-tracker
DOF: 6
Accuracy: 2 percent of distance from source, and .1-degree orientation
Effective range: Up to 7 feet
Lag: < 20 msecs (filtered)
Update rate: 50 Hz
Cost: $1,000
Comments: Low-cost method of head-tracking. Limited to line-of-sight tracking, so therefore has reduced angular range. Subject to interference from other high-frequency sounds.

Transition State Corp.
Model: GAMS
DOF: 3
Accuracy: ± 1-inch effective range
Effective range: 700-square-foot region
Lag: 75 msecs
Update rate: 32 Hz
Cost: $8,500
Comments: System uses four ultrasonic transmitters stationed in corners of a room. 10-inch-long wand is tracked within a large region. The measurement includes position, velocity, and acceleration. Requires a PC AT or better (not included in cost). There is an upgrade option that allows tracking of up to four wands simultaneously.

❋ Mechanical

Gyration Inc.
Model: GyroEngine
Type: Gyroscopic
DOF: 3
Accuracy: .1-degree orientation
Effective range: Limited by cable length
Lag: < 4 msecs
Update rate: > 1,000 Hz (depends on interface)
Cost: $700
Comments: Single miniature gyroscope. Suffers from same drift problem as GyroPoint. Available as a Directional Gyro or as Vertical Gyro. Each one has some limitation on the range of angular motion. A cableless version is also available (see Fig. A-19).

Figure A-19

GyroEngine's size, compared to a film canister.
Gyration Inc.

Precision Navigation
Model: NA
Type: Inertial
DOF: 3
Accuracy: .2 to .5 degrees
Effective range: ± 25-degree tilt, 360 degrees horizontal
Lag: < 150 msec
Update rate: 8+ Hz
Cost: $550
Comments: The current design is a 2-inch cube containing an electronic compass and tilt sensor. Improvements in the update rate and latency are expected by the fall of 1994. The design is sourceless (doesn't require a transmitter).

Shooting Star Technology
Model: ADL-1
Type: Mechanical linkage
DOF: 6
Accuracy: .2-inch position and .3-degree orientation
Effective range: 18 inches high, and 30-inch-diameter half-cylinder
Lag: < 2 msecs
Update rate: 300 Hz
Cost: $1,500
Comments: Uses shaft encoders and lightweight mechanical arms to measure positions and orientations. It isn't subject to interference, but is limited by the mechanical arm (see Fig. 8-28).

Vidtronics
Model: WrighTRAC
Type: Mechanical linkage
DOF: 6
Accuracy: .1-inch position overall and 1-degree maximum accuracy per axis
Effective range: ¼ sphere about 40 inches in diameter
Lag: NA
Update rate: 300 Hz
Cost: $800
Comments: Not subject to interference, but also limited by the mechanical arm.

✴ Optical

GEC Ferranti (Gaertner Research Division)
Model: GRD-1010
Type: Infrared LEDs and optical sensing
DOF: 6
Accuracy: .1-inch position and .6-degree orientation
Effective range: About 2 feet
Lag: 4 msecs (filtered)
Update rate: 240 Hz (RS-422)
Cost: $50,000
Comments: Based on three infrared LEDs that must be mounted on an HMD or glove. An optical sensor, pointed at the glove or HMD, tracks its movements. Requires that line of sight be maintained between LEDs and optical sensor.

Origin Instruments
Model: DynaSight
Type: Infrared LEDs and passive target sensing
DOF: 3
Accuracy: .16-inch position (down-range)
Effective range: 3 to 18 feet (target is size-dependent)
Lag: 15 msecs (unfiltered)
Update rate: 64 Hz
Cost: $2,195
Comments: Tracker contains two infrared emitters mounted in a control box that sits on top of a display monitor. A disposable target (7mm in size) is placed on the item to be tracked. It requires that line of sight be maintained between target and optical sensor (see Fig. A-20).

Spatial Positioning Systems, Inc.
Model: RtPM
Type: Laser transmitters and optical sensing

Figure A-20

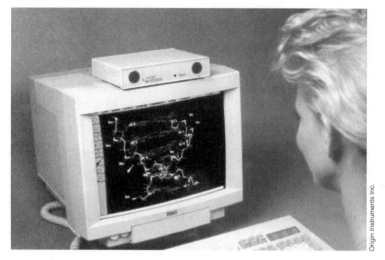

Origin Instruments DynaSight optical tracker.

DOF: 3 or 6
Accuracy: 1 part in 100,000 (.01 inch at 100-foot range)
Effective range: 3 to 800 feet
Lag: Unknown
Update rate: 100 Hz
Cost: $50,000–70,000
Comments: The system is based on the use of several lasers to accurately detect the location of either a passive sensor or an active optical sensor. It operates in either a passive mode using retroreflectors or in active mode using an optical sensor connected to a portable Macintosh computer. In the active mode, multiple sensors can be tracked without additional laser transceivers. Three laser transceivers are required to measure both object position and orientation. This system is based on line-of-sight tracking and therefore has some inherent limitations.

 # 3-D object scanners and digitizers

Cyberware
Model: Cyberware scanner
Type: Laser transmitters and optical sensing
DOF: 3
Accuracy: Varies
Effective range: Varies
Cost: $36,000–88,000

Comments: This system is typically used to scan real objects to extract a 3-D model. A low-power laser projects a vertical or horizontal line on the target. A special camera calculates the X, Y, and Z values of 500 points along the line. Either the object or the laser then rotates for another scan line. Different systems are available to scan either small objects or the entire human body. Various precision levels are available.

Immersion

Model: Immersion Probe (IC, IX, MD)
Type: Mechanical linkage
DOF: 6
Resolution: .1-inch position and .7-degree orientation (IC model)
Effective range: 34×15×17 inches
Lag: 1 msec
Update rate: 300+ Hz
Cost: $1,000
Comments: Uses shaft encoders and lightweight mechanical arms to measure positions and orientations. Not subject to interference, but also limited by the mechanical arm. More expensive versions are available with higher resolution (see Fig. A-21).

Figure A-21

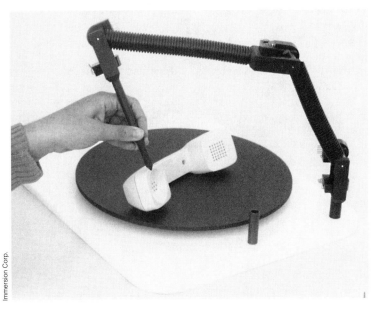

Immersion Corp.

Immersion Probe.

Mira Imaging
Model: Hyperspace
Type: Mechanical and electromagnetic tracking systems
DOF: 3
Accuracy: Varies
Effective range: Varies
Cost: Contact vendor
Comments: This system is typically used to digitize objects to create a 3-D model.

Science Accessories Corp.
Model: GP-12
Type: Ultrasonic transmitter
DOF: 3
Accuracy: Varies
Effective range: Varies
Cost: Contact vendor
Comments: This system is typically used to digitize objects to create a 3-D model. A large (3-foot or so) transmitter triangle is placed near the object to be digitized. Can capture data within an 8-foot cube.

B

Company and institution guide

This lists, in alphabetical order, the many companies who produce various types of products for constructing virtual environments. Included are also a few of the university research groups and other sources of information focused on VR. This is by no means a complete list of all companies and institutions working with VR. It is intended only to help you gain additional information about technologies mentioned in this book.

Companies

3DTV Corp.
P.O. Box Q
San Francisco, CA 94913-4316
U.S.A.
ph: 415-479-3516
fx: 415-479-3316

Advanced Robotics Research Centre
University Rd.
Salford M5 4PP
UK
ph: 44-617-457384
fx: 44-617-458264

Advanced Gravis
111,7400 MacPherson Ave.
Burnaby, B.C. V5J 5B6
Canada
ph: 604-431-5020
fx: 604-431-5155

AICOM Corp.
1590 Oakland Rd., Suite B112
San Jose, CA 95131
U.S.A.
ph: 408-453-8251
fx: 408-453-8255

Airmuscle, Ltd.
Unit 12 Orchard Close
Cranfield, Bedford MK4 3OHX
UK
ph: 44-234-750791

Artificial Reality Corp.
Box 786
Vernon, CT 06066
U.S.A.
ph: 203-871-1375

Ascension Technology Corp.
P.O. Box 527
Burlington, VT 05402
U.S.A.
ph: 802-655-7879
fx: 802-655-5904

Aura Systems
2335 Alaska Ave.
El Segundo, CA 90245
U.S.A.
ph: 310-643-5300
fx: 310-643-8719

Avatar Partners
13090 Central Ave., Suite 3
Boulder Creek, CA 95006
U.S.A.
ph: 408-338-6640
fx: 408-338-6462

AutoDesk
Advanced Technology Dept.
2320 Marinship Way
Sausalito, CA 94965
U.S.A.
ph: 415-332-2344

Battletech Centers Inc.
(see Virtual Worlds Entertainment)

Begej Corp.
5 Claret Ash Rd.
Littleton, CO 80127
U.S.A.
ph/fx: 303-932-2186

BioControl Systems
2555 Park Blvd.
Palo Alto, CA 94306
U.S.A.
ph: 415-329-8494
fx: 415-329-8498

CAE-Electronics Ltd.
8585 Cote De Liesse
Saint-Laurent, Quebec H4L 4X4
Canada
ph: 514-341-6780
fx: 514-341-7699

CM Research
2815 Forest Hill
League City, TX 77573
U.S.A.
ph: 713-334-4661
fx: 713-334-4860

Covox Inc.
675 Conger St.
Eugene, OR 97402
U.S.A.
ph: 503-342-1271
fx: 503-342-1283

Crystal River Engineering
12350 Wards Ferry Rd.
Groveland, CA 95321
U.S.A.
ph: 209-962-6382
fx: 209-962-4873

Cybernet Systems
1919 Green Rd.
Ann Arbor, MI 48105
U.S.A.
ph: 313-668-2567
fx: 313-668-8780

Cyberscan Inc.
2444 Honolulu Ave.
Montrose, CA 91020
U.S.A.
ph: 818-248-3279
fx: 818-248-6756

Cybersense
169 S. Main St.
Oregon, WI 53575
U.S.A.
ph: 608-835-2115
fx: 608-835-9482

Cyberware
8 Harris Ct., #3D
Monterey, CA 93940
U.S.A.
ph: 408-373-1441
fx: 408-373-3582

Digital Image Design Inc.
170 Claremont Ave.
New York, NY 10027
U.S.A.
ph: 212-222-5236
fx: 212-864-1189

Dimension International
See Superscape Ltd.

Division Ltd.
Quarry Road, Chipping
Sodbury, Bristol BS17 6AX
UK
ph: 44-454-324527
fx: 44-454-323059

Domark
1900 S. Norfolk St., Suite 202
San Mateo, CA 94403
U.S.A.
ph: 415-513-8929

Dragon Systems Inc.
320 Nevada St.
Newton, MA 02158
U.S.A.
ph: 617-965-5200
fx: 617-527-0372

DTM Corp.
1611 Headway Cir., Bldg. 2
P.O. Box 141069
Austin, TX 78754
U.S.A.
ph: 512-339-2922

Evans & Sutherland
Simulation Division
600 Komas Dr.
Salt Lake City, UT 84108
U.S.A.
ph: 801-582-5847
fx: 801-582-5848

EXOS Inc.
2A Gill St.
Woburn, MA 01801
U.S.A.
ph: 617-933-0022
fx: 617-933-0303

Forte Technologies
1057 E. Henrietta
Rochester, NY 14623
U.S.A.
ph: 716-427-8595
fx: 716-292-6353

Fake Space Labs
935 Hamilton Ave.
Menlo Park, CA 94025
U.S.A.
ph: 415-688-1940
fx: 415-688-1949

Flogiston Corp.
16701 Westview Tr.
Austin, TX 78731
U.S.A.
ph: 512-323-2083
fx: 512-323-9564

Focal Point 3-D Audio
1402 Pine Ave., Suite 127
Niagara Falls, NY 14301
U.S.A.
ph/fx: 416-963-9188

Future Vision Technologies
701 Devonshire Dr.
Champaign, IL 61820
U.S.A.
ph: 217-355-3030
fx: 217-355-3031

Gaertner Research Division
GEC Ferranti
140 Water St.
Norwalk, CT 06854
U.S.A.
ph: 203-866-3200
fx: 203-838-5026

General Electric
Simulation and Control Systems Dept.
P.O. Box 2825
Daytona Beach, FL 32115
U.S.A.
ph: 904-239-2906

GLOBAL Devices
6630 Arabian Cir.
Granite Bay, CA 95661
U.S.A.
ph: 916-791-3533
fx: 916-791-4358

Greenleaf Medical Systems
2248 Park Blvd.
Palo Alto, CA 94306
U.S.A.
ph: 415-321-6135
fx: 415-321-0419

Gyration Inc.
12930 Saratoga Ave., Bldg. C
Saratoga, CA 95070
U.S.A.
ph: 408-255-3016
fx: 408-255-9075

Immersion Human Interface Corp.
P.O. Box 8669
Palo Alto, CA 94309-8669
U.S.A.
ph: 415-960-6882
fx: 415-960-6977

International Telepresence Corp.
655 West 7th Ave.
Vancouver, B.C. V5Z 186
Canada
ph: 604-873-3300
fx: 604-275-2233

InWorld VR, Inc.
144 Buchanan Ct.
Sausalito, CA 94965
U.S.A.
ph: 415-331-5004
fx: 415-331-5010

Kaiser Electro-optics
2752 Loker Ave. West
Carlsbad, CA 92008
U.S.A.
ph: 619-438-9255
fx: 619-438-6875

KATrix Inc.
330 Alexander St., Suite 205
Princeton, NJ 08540
U.S.A.
ph: 908-329-9578

Lepton Graphics System
2118 Central Ave. SE, Suite 45
Albuquerque, NM 87106
U.S.A.
ph: 505-843-6719
fx: 505-843-9394

LEEP Systems
241 Crescent St.
Waltham, MA 02154
U.S.A.
ph: 617-647-1395
fx: 617-899-9602

Liquid Mirage
582 King Edward St.
Winnipeg, MB R3H 0PI
Canada
ph: 204-772-0137
fx: 204-772-0239

Logitech Inc.
6505 Kaiser Dr.
Fremont, CA 94555
U.S.A.
ph: 510-795-8500
fx: 510-792-8901

Mira Imaging Inc.
2257 South 1100 East, Suite 1A
Salt Lake City, UT 84106
U.S.A.
ph: 801-466-4641
fx: 801-466-4699

Multipoint Technology Corp.
319 Littleton Rd., Suite 201
Westford, MA 01886
U.S.A.
ph: 508-692-0689
fx: 508-692-2653

n-Vision Inc.
800 Follin Ln., Suite 270
Vienna, VA 22180
U.S.A.
ph: 703-242-0030
fx: 703-242-5220

Origin Instruments
854 Greenview Dr.
Grand Prairie, TX 75050-2438
U.S.A.
ph: 214-606-8740
fx: 214-606-8741

Optics1
3050 Hillcrest Dr., Suite 100
Westlake Village, CA 91362
U.S.A.
ph: 805-373-9340
fx: 805-373-8966

Polhemus Laboratories
P.O. Box 5
Cambridge, VT 05444
U.S.A.
ph: 802-644-5569
fx: 802-644-2943

Polhemus
P.O. Box 560
Colchester, VT 05446
U.S.A.
ph: 802-655-3159
fx: 802-655-1439

Precision Navigation
1350A Pear Ave.
Mountain View, CA 94043
U.S.A.
ph: 415-962-8777

Reflection Technology
230 Second Ave.
Waltham, MA 02154
U.S.A.
ph: 617-890-5905
fx: 617-890-5918

Robicon Systems
see KATrix Inc.

RPI Advanced Technology Group
P.O. Box 14607
San Francisco, CA 94114
U.S.A.
ph: 415-495-5671
fx: 415-495-5124

SARCOS
261 East 300 South, Suite 150
Salt Lake City, UT 84111
U.S.A.
ph: 801-531-0559
fx: 801-531-0315

Science Accessories Corp.
200 Watson Blvd.
P.O. Box 587
Stratford, CT 06497
U.S.A.
ph: 203-386-9978
fx: 203-381-9270

Sega of America
255 Shoreline Dr., Suite 200
Redwood City, CA 94065
U.S.A.
ph: 415-508-2800

Sense8
4000 Bridgeway, Suite 104
Sausalito, CA 94965
U.S.A.
ph: 415-331-6318
fx: 415-331-9148

Shooting Star Technology
1921 Holdom Ave.
Burnaby, B.C. V5B 3W4
Canada
ph: 604-298-8574
fx: 604-298-8580

SimGraphics Engineering Corp.
1137 Huntington Dr.
South Pasadena, CA 91030-4563
U.S.A.
ph: 213-255-0900
fx: 213-255-0987

Simsalabim
P.O. Box 4446
Berkeley, CA 94704-0446
U.S.A.
ph: 510-528-2021
fx: 510-528-9499

Software Systems
1884 The Alameda
San Jose, CA 95126
U.S.A.
ph: 408-247-4326

Spaceball Technologies
600 Suffolk Street
Lowell, MA 01854
U.S.A.
ph: 508-970-0330

Spatial Positioning Systems, Inc.
Innovation Center
1800 Kraft Dr.
Blacksburg, VA 24060
U.S.A.
ph: 703-231-3145
fx: 703-231-3568

StereoGraphics Corp.
2171-H East Francisco Blvd.
San Rafael, CA 94901
U.S.A.
ph: 415-459-4500
fx: 415-459-3020

StrayLight
150 Mount Bethel Rd.
Warren, NJ 07059
U.S.A.
ph: 908-580-0086
fx: 908-580-0092

Superscape Ltd.
Zephyr One, Calleva Park
Aldermaston, Berkshire RG7 4QW
UK
ph: 44-734-810077
fx: 44-734-816940

Telepresence Research
635 High St.
Palo Alto, CA 94301
U.S.A.
ph: 415-325 8951
fx: 415-325-8952

Textronix
Display Products
P.O. Box 500, M/S 46-943
Beaverton, OR 97077-0001
U.S.A.
ph: 503-627-6499

The Computer Museum
300 Congress St.
Boston, MA 02210
U.S.A.
ph: 617-426-2800

Transition State
11514-77 Ave.
Edmonton, Alberta T6G OM1
Canada
ph: 403-438-5810
fx: 403-436-0963

VictorMaxx Technologies, Inc.
510 Lake Cook Rd., Suite 100
Deerfield, IL 60015
U.S.A.
ph: 708-267-0007
fx: 708-267-0037

Vidtronics
65 Woodside Dr.
Oakland, MI 48363
U.S.A.
ph: 313-488-0330
fx: 313-488-0337

Virtual Images
2676 Billingsley Rd.
Columbus, OH 43235
U.S.A.
ph: 614-459-1232
fx: 614-764-7852

Virtual I/O
1000 Second Ave., Suite 3710
Seattle, WA 98104
U.S.A.
ph: 206-382-7410
fx: 206-382-8810

Virtual Research
3193 Belick St., Suite #2
Santa Clara, CA 95054
U.S.A.
ph: 408-748-8712
fx: 408-748-8714

Virtual Reality Inc.
485 Washington Ave.
Pleasantville, NY 10570
U.S.A.
ph: 914-769-0900
fx: 914-769-7106

Virtual Technologies (Virtex)
P.O. Box 5984
Stanford, CA 94309
U.S.A.
ph: 415-599-2331

Virtual Vision, Inc.
7659 178th Place NE
Redmond, WA 98052
U.S.A.
ph: 206-882-7878
fx: 206-882-7373

Virtual World Entertainment
1100 W. Cermak, Suite B404
Chicago, IL 60608
U.S.A.
ph: 312-243-6515
fx: 312-243-7818

Virtus Corp.
117 Edinburgh South
Cary, NC 27511
U.S.A.
ph: 919-467-9700
fx: 919-460-4530

Visual Synthesis, Inc.
4126 Addison Rd.
Fairfax, VA 22030
U.S.A.
ph: 703-352-0258

Vivid Effects Group
317 Adelaide St. W., Studio 302
Toronto, Ontario M5V 1P9
Canada
ph: 416-340-9290
fx: 416-348-9809

Voice Connexion
17835 Skypark Cir., Suite C
Irvine, CA 92714
U.S.A.
ph: 714-261-2366
fx: 714-261-8563

VoR (Visions of Reality)
15540 Rockfield Blvd., Suite B
Irvine, CA 92718
U.S.A.
ph: 714-587-1950
fx: 714-587-1954

VPL Research Inc.
3977 East Bayshore Rd.
Palo Alto, CA 94303
U.S.A.
ph: 415-988-2550
fx: 415-988-2557

VREAM
2568 N. Clark St., #250
Chicago, IL 60614
U.S.A.
ph: 312-477-0425
fx: 312-477-9702

VRex
8 Skyline Dr.
Hawthorne, NY 10532
U.S.A.
ph: 914-345-8877
fx: 914-345-8772

VRT GmbH
Am Gewerbepark 1
64823 Gross-Umstadt
Germany
ph: 06-078-74467-8
fx: 06-078-74458

W Industries Ltd.
Virtuality House
3 Oswin Road
Brailsford Industrial Park
Leicester LE3 1HR
UK
ph/fx: 44-533-542127

Xtensory
140 Sunridge Dr.
Scotts Valley, CA 95066
U.S.A.
ph: 408-439-0600
fx: 408-439-9709

 # Schools and research efforts

Advanced Robotics Research Centre
University Rd.
Salford M5 4PP
UK
ph: 44-617-457384
fx: 44-617-458264

CAD Institute
4100 E. Broadway Rd.
Phoenix, AZ 85040
U.S.A.
ph: 800-658-5744
fx: 602-437-5695

Human Interface Technology Lab
Washington Technology Center
University of Washington, FJ-15
Seattle, WA 98195
U.S.A.
ph: 206-543-5075

Institute for Simulation and Training
University of Central Florida
12424 Research Pkwy., Suite 300
Orlando, FL 32826
U.S.A.
ph: 407-658-5074
fx: 407-658-5059

NASA Ames Research Center
Moffett Field, CA 94035
U.S.A.
ph: 415-604-3937
fx: 415-604-3953

University of Nottingham
Dept. of Computer Science
University Park
Nottingham NG7 2RD
UK
ph: 44-602-514226
fx: 44-602-514254

SRI International
Virtual Perception Center
333 Ravenswood Ave.
Menlo Park, CA 97025
U.S.A.

The Media Lab
Massachusetts Institute of Technology
20 Ames St.
Cambridge, MA 02159
U.S.A.

University of North Carolina
Dept. of Computer Science
Chapel Hill, NC 27599
U.S.A.
ph: 919-962-1700

 # Newsletters and other resources

CyberEdge Journal
#1 Gate Six Rd., Suite G
Sausalito, CA 94965
U.S.A.
ph: 415-331-3343
fx: 415-331-3643

PCVR Magazine
P.O. Box 475
Stoughton, WI 53589
U.S.A.
ph/fax: 608-877-0909

Pix-Elation (VRASP)
P.O. Box 4139
Highland Park, NJ 08904
U.S.A.
ph: 908-463-VRVR

Real Time Graphics
Computer Graphics Systems
  Development
2483 Old Middlefield Way, #140
Mountain View, CA 94043
U.S.A.
ph: 415-903-4920
fx: 415-967-5252

VR News
Cydata Limited
P.O. Box 2515
London N4 4JW
UK
ph/fx: 44-812-921498

Virtual Reality Report
Meckler Corp.
11 Ferry Lane W.
Westport, CT 06880
U.S.A.
ph: 203-226-6967
fx: 203-454-5840

C

Sample source code

This is an example of a program written using Sense8's WorldToolKit C libraries. This program reads in a 3-D model called HOUSE.DXF, which was previously built using Autodesk's AutoCAD or some other 3-D modeller. Once the file is loaded, you can fly around and inspect the model from any angle.

Attached to the PC's COM1 serial port is a special device called a Geoball. This is a type of forceball that simplifies navigating in the virtual world. WorldToolKit supports many different types of device drivers. The two buttons on the Geoball are programmed to either end the simulation or reset your viewpoint back to your original view if you get lost.

```
/*   This program loads in a model stored in the file HOUSE.DXF, and lets
you navigate your viewpoint using a Geometry Ball device.
*/

#include <stdio.h>
#include "wt.h"

static WTsensor *sensor;      /* the Geometry ball */
static WTpq initial_view;     /* stores initial viewpoint */

/*   The user's action function is called once each time through the
simulation loop. This particular action function looks for and acts upon
Geometry Ball button presses. A left button press ends the program by
calling WTuniverse_stop(). A right button press resets the viewpoint to
its original position and orientation by calling WTviewpoint_moveto().  */
```

```
static void user_actionfn();

main()
{
    /*    Initialize the universe. (This must be the 1st WorldToolKit
          call.)
    */
    WTuniverse_new(WTDISPLAY_DEFAULT, WTWINDOW_DEFAULT);

    /*    This loads the graphical information from the 3-D model
          called HOUSE.DXF. The house is loaded as a "stationary
          backdrop."
    */
    WTuniverse_load("house.dxf", &initial_view, 1.0);

    /*    Move the viewpoint to the position read from the model.
          This provides the initial view upon entering the world.
    */
    WTviewpoint_moveto(WTuniverse_getviewpoint(), &initial_view);

    /*    Initialize a Geometry Ball sensor on serial port COM1. This
          "wakes up" the Geoball device and establishes communication
          with it.
    */
    sensor = WTgeoball_new(COM1);

    /*    Attach the sensor to the viewpoint. By doing this, the
          Geoball will now control where you're looking and the
          direction you travel in.
    */
    WTviewpoint_addsensor(WTuniverse_getviewpoint(), sensor);

    /*    Prepare the universe for start of the simulation.
    */
    WTuniverse_ready();

    /*    Scale sensor sensitivity with the size of the universe.
    */
    WTsensor_setsensitivity(sensor, 0.01 * WTuniverse_getradius());

    /*    Set the action function so that button presses will be acted
          on. This tells the simulation manager that a particular
          user-supplied function needs to be executed once per "tick."
    */
    WTuniverse_setactions(user_actionfn);

    /*    Enter the main simulation loop. Once this is called, the
          program will begin rendering the world, and will not return
          from here until it is told to stop.
    */
    WTuniverse_go();
```

```
    /*   All done; clean everything up. (This must be the last
         WorldToolKit call.)
    */
    WTuniverse_delete();
    return 0;
}

/*   This is the user's action function. The user can define whatever he
wants to occur, and WorldToolKit will execute this function once per
simulation loop. In the case of this example, the user wants the
following to occur:
         Check for button presses on the Geometry Ball.
         Exit the simulation loop if the left button is pressed.
         Restore the original viewpoint if the right button is
         pressed.
*/
static void user_actionfn()
{
    short buttons;

    /* get button press data from ball */
       buttons = WTsensor_getmiscdata(sensor);
       if ( buttons & WTGEOBALL_LEFTBUTTON ) {
    /* quit the simulation */
       WTuniverse_stop();
       }
       else if ( buttons & GEOBALL_RIGHTBUTTON ) {
    /* reset the view to the original viewpoint */
       WTviewpoint_move(WTuniverse_getviewpoint(), &initial_view);
    }
}
```

Glossary

3-D Three-dimensional; refers to the visual display that exhibits breadth, height, and thickness or depth (standard 2-D computer images and television displays create a flat image with only height and breadth).

3-D sound Filtered sound that appears to emanate from locations in front of, below, above, behind, and to either side of the listener. Any sound, such as a jet plane taking off, can be convolved or filtered so that it's spatially located. Listeners can seem to hear the plane approach from the front, pass over, and then continue on behind them.

6 DOF Six degrees of freedom; refers to the number of simultaneous directions or inputs a sensor can measure. Typically used to describe the combination of spatial position (X, Y, and Z) and orientation (roll, pitch, and yaw) measured by many tracking sensors.

application Software that describes the context of the simulation, its dynamics, structure, and the rules of interaction between objects and the user—for example, how doors open, where sunlight falls, and which way gravity works.

artificial intelligence (AI) The effort to build computers that mimic and automate human cognitive skills (e.g., understanding visual images, recognizing speech and written text, solving problems, and making medical diagnoses).

artificial reality Introduced by art and computer visualization scholar Myron Krueger in the mid-1970s to describe his computer-generated responsive environments. As realized in his VIDEOPLACE and the Vivid Group's Mandala system, it's a

computer display system that perceives and captures "a participant's action in terms of the body's relationship to a graphic world and generates responses [usually images] that maintain the illusion that his actions are taking place within that world." (M. Krueger, *Artificial Reality II*).

augmented reality This is the use of transparent glasses on which data can be projected. This allows users to work on a car, for example, and have the data they need displayed on the glasses while still seeing the car.

biosensors Special glasses or bracelets containing electrodes to monitor muscle electrical activity. Potentially capable of tracking eye movements by measuring muscle movements.

bus A means of distributing a set of electronic signals so the microprocessor at the heart of a computer can be connected with memory, external devices, and the display screen.

CAT scans Computer-aided tomography; the use of x-ray scanning devices to map cross-sections of the human body without damaging it or having to surgically enter it.

CD/CD-ROM The abbreviation for *compact disc, read-only memory*. Familiar to most people as the new standard for storing digital music. ROM means that the information stored on the disc cannot be rewritten or rerecorded over during use. Seen as the next standard for storage of music, text, and video for reproduction by computers.

cathode-ray tube (CRT) A vacuum tube like the one in a television set, a computer monitor, or an oscilloscope.

central processing unit (CPU) The part of the computer that controls the fetching of instructions from memory, the interpretation of those instructions, and their execution. This "computer inside the computer" is responsible for initiating and coordinating all activities of the computer.

Cinematographe The first true motion-picture system, the one today's technology is descended from. Developed in Paris in 1895 by the brothers Auguste and Louis Lumiere.

Cinerama A motion-picture technique for delivering a highly realistic visual image. It used a screen four times larger than traditional screens to provide an enhanced field of view.

compiler A software program that translates a program written in a human-readable programming language into a binary form (ones and zeros) that can be read by the computer.

conceptual art A recent movement in art where a work is intended to be appreciated for its ideas and its conceptual qualities as well as, or in lieu of, its perceptual ones.

convergence In stereoscopic viewing, this is when the left- and right-eye images become fused into a single image.

convolve The process of filtering sounds so that they can be spatially placed. *See also* 3-D sound.

CAD The abbreviation for *computer-aided design*. A CAD software package is a precision drawing tool that speeds up the design process by automating the work of the architect and engineer (editing, printing, plotting, and data import and export functions).

CPU *See* central processing unit.

CRT *See* cathode-ray tube.

cyberspace Coined by science-fiction author William Gibson in his book *Neuromancer* to describe a shared virtual universe operating within the sum total of all the world's computer networks. A global computer network that's allegorical to the current phone system, but provides a multisensory experience of "being there," not just an auditory experience.

DataGlove A glove wired with sensors and connected to a computer system for gesture recognition. Also known generically

as a *wired glove*. It enables navigation through a virtual environment and interaction with 3-D objects within it. DataGlove is a trademark of VPL Research.

DataSuit Same as a DataGlove, but designed for the entire body. DataSuit is a trademark of VPL Research.

digital Having discrete, as opposed to continuously varying, values. The difference can be illustrated by comparing the surfaces of an analog record and a compact disc. The record's grooves are long-playing wavy lines, while the much smaller tracks on a compact disc are a series of very distinct pits. With a compact disc, digital information is broken up into small packets and then reassembled into a whole.

driver A low-level routine of software instructions for controlling the interaction between the computer and a hardware device.

dynamics The dynamics of a virtual world are the laws that govern all actions and behaviors within the environment. A real-world example of such a dynamic is gravity. However, in a virtual world many nontraditional dynamics are possible, such as the dynamics of the interior of the human body or laws of reality that governed Alice's Wonderland.

effectors The input and output sensors that either communicate a user's movements or commands to the computer or provide sensory stimulation from the computer to the user.

endoscopic Part of a family of new surgical procedures that avoid cutting open major portions of the patient in favor of making small holes through which tools and a tiny camera are inserted and the surgery performed. The surgeon manipulates the tools by observing the surgery site on a monitor via the tiny video camera.

environment In VR terms, this is a computer-generated model that can be experienced from the "inside" as if it were a place.

event loop The sequence of events the computer loops through to maintain a simulation. Each pass of the event loop checks all the input devices for viewpoint positioning and command changes

before instructing the computer to re-create the environment. This needs to happen at least 16 to 20 times a second to create a sense of realism.

force feedback An output device that transmits pressure, force, or vibration to provide the VR participant with the sense of touch. Tactile feedback simulates sensation applied to the skin. Force feedback simulates weight or resistance to motion.

fractal A pattern generated by using the same rules at various levels of detail.

geometry Information stored and processed by the software application that describes the physical attributes of objects or worlds.

gesture A hand or body movement that conveys information.

haptic Refers to all the physical sensors that generate a sense of touch at the skin level and force feedback information for our muscles and joints.

HMD (head-mounted display) A set of goggles or a helmet with tiny monitors in front of each eye that generate images, seen by the wearer as being three-dimensional. VPL Research refers to the HMDs they sell as EyePhones.

immersion As applied to virtual reality, this is when one or more of a user's sensors (eyes and ears, generally) are isolated from the surrounding environment and fed only information coming from the computer.

impressionists A group of painters of the late nineteenth century who sought to capture the dynamic art of perception, as opposed to the static photographic recording of a scene.

interface The interconnection between two pieces of equipment, hardware or software, in which information or energy is transferred. By this definition, the transmission in a car is the energy interface between the wheels and the engine. And the wheel, clutch, and brake are the information interface with the engine.

isometric balls Electromechanical means are used to measure 6-DOF forces or torques applied to a ball-shaped device. Used as a navigational device for many VR systems.

Kinetoscope Invented by Thomas Edison, it was the first personal viewer for motion pictures. It consisted of a three- to five-minute long loop of film, powered by a hand crank and viewed through a small window on the top of the device.

LCD Liquid-crystal display, used in products like portable computers and wristwatches.

LED Light-emitting diode.

MRI Magnetic resonance imaging, a nonintrusive method for mapping the interior of the body by using magnetic energy.

megabyte (MB) A million bytes.

microprocessor Invented in 1971 by Ted Hoff of Intel Corporation, a computer implemented as a tiny integrated circuit smaller than a fingernail. The small size, low-power requirement, and low cost of microprocessors have revolutionized computer applications. Microprocessors are being used to put intelligence in everyday appliances, power virtual reality systems, and (when hundreds are strung together) build the world's most powerful supercomputers.

model Construction of the physical representation of a computer-generated world and all its objects.

monitor A video display that has no tuner and can't receive broadcast signals on its own. It can receive signals that are generated locally by a camera, computer, or videotape recorder.

MIDI Musical instrument digital interface, a standard that many electronic musical instruments support. Provides a simple method of controlling various devices through a single computer.

motion parallax The way the eyes can judge distance by noticing how closer objects move more than distant ones when you move your head about.

motion platforms These are mechanical platforms originally developed for flight simulation to provide pilot trainees with the correct physical sensations when they turn the plane or enter rough weather. These platforms are now commonly found in amusement park rides such as Disney's Star Tours.

NASA National Aeronautic & Space Administration.

network A way of connecting computers so that software and information can be transmitted among them as if on a highway. A local-area network (LAN) might link up a couple hundred computers within a building. The Internet is a global network that encompasses thousands of smaller computer networks.

NTSC National Television Standards Convention, the television standard used in the United States and other parts of the world. An interlaced signal displays two fields of information in $\frac{1}{30}$ of a second. A total of 525 horizontal lines of resolution is possible. There are several other standards in use around the world.

objects Discrete 3-D shapes within the virtual world that you can interact with.

occlusion You can judge how close objects are to you because the closer ones overlap and occlude objects in the background.

operating system A master software control program that allows other programs to run by acting as a translator and interface between them and the microprocessor. It also provides them with utility services as they're running.

parallax Refers to the difference in viewing angle created by having two eyes looking at the same scene from slightly different positions. The combined input to your brain helps create a sense of depth.

pixel A contraction of *picture element*, it refers to one point in a graphic image on a computer display. A standard VGA display might have 640×480 pixels. The number of bits per pixel determines how many colors can be represented on the image. VGA displays typically have eight bits per pixel. True-color displays typically use 24 bits per pixel.

polygon A flat-plane figure with multiple sides, the basic building block of virtual reality worlds. Think of them as sheets of wood that can be cut in any shape and size and linked together, colored, and texture-mapped with additional images. Virtual worlds are constructed from hundreds of thousands of colored polygons displayed on monitors or stereoscopic displays. The more polygons a computer can display and manipulate per second, the more realistic the virtual world will appear. "Alvy Ray Smith of Pixar has estimated that we perceive the equivalent of 80 million polygons at 30+ frames per second when we look at a view of the real world" (M. Bricken, 1991).

projected reality Using a computer with a camcorder attached. The video camera captures your picture and mixes it into a computer-generated graphical world, which is then projected on a wide screen. As you move, your figure on the screen moves with you.

real time The definition varies with use. In computer simulations, it means that the computer responds to inputs in a time frame that a human would perceive as instantaneous. Typically, this means a response less than 50–100 milliseconds.

reality simulator Any computer system specifically designed to generate virtual reality worlds.

rendering The computer process of calculating and then drawing images on a screen.

representational systems This is the mind's different ways of representing the outside world and its own internally generated worlds. They are a reflection of the input senses (vision, auditory, kinesthetic).

RS232 *See* serial line.

scan conversion This is the process of taking video signals from one format to another. It's typically used to convert noninterlaced computer video signals to the interlaced video signal needed for many head-mounted displays.

scripted languages A more natural language-styled software programming language that even nonprogrammers are able to pick up in a short amount of time. It translates the user's instructions into the complex code a simulation manager can understand.

Sensorama Invented by Mort Heilig, it was the first completely immersive entertainment experience, consisting of a simulated motorcycle ride that provided visual, kinesthetic, auditory, and even olfactory sensations.

serial line Also known as an RS232 line. Most PCs and workstations have ports or connections that allow serial communications between the computer and another device like a modem. Communication speed is measured in bits per second (bps), which is often referred to as the baud rate. Most modems and devices communicate anywhere between 2,400 and 9,600 bps.

server A computer dedicated to providing shared resources, such as files and printers, to a computer network. A product server is a special server tailored to support the manufacturing process, such as support for 3-D graphics and product-testing simulations.

shutter glasses Wireless, battery-operated, stereo-viewing glasses used to view 3-D computer-generated graphics.

simulation manager This is the core software program that organizes and manages the resources and devices available to a VR application to create its world.

spatial Refers to space (region, area, void) in all directions.

submodalities These are the smallest categories into which your senses can divide experience. For example, visual information can be broken down into brightness, saturation, location, and hue. The ears can differentiate sounds by their frequency, rhythm, tone, and duration.

suspended displays A 3-D display device suspended from a weighted boom that can swivel freely about so the viewer doesn't have to wear an HMD; instead, it steps up to the viewer like a pair of binoculars. The display's position communicates the user's point of view to the computer.

tactile Refers to your sense of touch, or pressure applied to your skin.

telepresence The experience of being in another location. Usually accomplished by transmitting the user's view through the eyes of a camera. This can include the operation of remote machinery through the computer translation of human movements into equipment commands.

texture-mapping The process of displaying a single digitized image on a polygon or structure that's made out of polygons. This display technique saves computing power because the image is stored in memory and displayed, as opposed to being recalculated and redrawn.

toolkit This is a compiled library of software commands and instructions for developing applications. While it provides the most flexibility and control, you generally have to be a programmer to use it.

universe This refers to the active environment of a simulation: all the objects, sensors, viewpoints, etc. being operated on. Only those elements present in the simulation's universe are drawn by the computer.

viewpoint This represents the point of view of an observer in a virtual world.

virtual Refers to the essence or effect of something, not the fact. IBM started using the word in the late 1960s to refer to any nonphysical link between processes or machines, such as virtual memory (random-access memory being simulated with disk drives).

virtual reality As a guideline, a virtual reality system should have the three following characteristics: response to user actions, real-time 3-D graphics, and a sense of immersion. It isn't enough to have just one or two of these properties; all three should be present. Typically, these characteristics are achieved using visually coupled displays and powerful graphics hardware.

visualization Formation of an image that can't be seen. The ability to graphically represent abstract data on a computer that would normally appear as text and numbers.

wired glove *See* DataGlove.

workstation Traditionally, this has referred to a specialized stand-alone computer with enough computational and graphical human-interface power to serve design engineers. With the increased power of personal computers, the distinction has become very fuzzy.

References and recommended reading

⇨ References

* **Title page**

  Carroll, Lewis. *Through the Looking-Glass*. New York, NY: Exeter Books. 1865.

* **Introduction**

  Gibson, William. *Neuromancer*. New York, NY: ACE Books. 1984.

  Electronic Frontier Interview with Barlow and Kapor. *Mondo 2000*. 1991.

* **Chapter 1**

  Bricklin, William. "Definitions." *Virtual Reality Report*. Westport, CT: Meckler Corporation. September, 1991.

  Ellis, S. R. "Nature and Origins of Virtual Environments: A Bibliographical Essay." *Computer Systems in Engineering*. UK: Pergamon Press. 1991.

  Ellis, S. R. (editor). *Pictorial communication in virtual and real environments*. NY: Taylor & Francis. 1991.

  Ellis, Stephen R. "Pictorial Communication: Pictures and the Synthetic Universe." *Leonardo*. Great Britain: Pergamon Press. 81–86. 1990.

Kay, Alan. "User Interface: A Personal View." *The Art of Human-Computer Interface Design*. Cupertino, CA: Apple Computer and Menlo Park, CA: Addison-Wesley Publishing Company. 1990.

Laurel, Brenda (editor). *The Art of Human-Computer Interface Design*. Cupertino, CA: Apple Computer and Menlo Park, CA: Addison-Wesley Publishing Company. 1990.

McLuhan, Marshall and Fiore, Quentin. *The Medium Is the Message*. Bantam Books. 1967.

Ofeisch, Gabriel. *Virtual Reality Report*. Westport, CT: Meckler. 1991.

Rheingold, Howard. *Virtual Reality*. New York, NY: Summit Books. 1991.

Walker, John. "Through The Looking Glass: Beyond 'User Interfaces.'" Autodesk whitepaper. 1988.

❋ Chapter 2

Cook, David A. *A History Of Narrative Film*. New York, NY: W. W. Norton. 1981.

Griffith, Linda A. *When the Movies Were Young*. New York, NY: Dover Books. 1969.

Laurel, Brenda. *Computers as Theater*. Menlo Park, CA: Addison-Wesley Publishing Company. 1991.

Rheingold, Howard. *Virtual Reality*. New York, NY: Summit Books. 1991.

Shlain, Leonard. *Art & Physics: Parallel Visions in Space, Time & Light*. NY: Morrow Williams and Company. 1991.

❋ Chapter 3

Brooks, Frederick P., Jr. et. al. "Using a Manipulator for Force Display in Molecular Docking." *IEEE pub*. CH2555-1, 1824–1829. 1988.

Brooks, Frederick P. "Walkthrough—A Dynamic Graphics System for Simulating Virtual Buildings." *ACM Workshop on Interactive 3D Graphics*. Chapel Hill, NC. Oct. 23–24, 1986.

Fisher, Scott S. "Virtual Interface Environments." *The Art of Human-Computer Interface Design*. Menlo Park, CA: Addison-Wesley Publishing Company. 423–438. 1991.

Fisher, Scott S. et. al. "Virtual Environment Display System." *ACM Workshop on Interactive 3D Graphics*. Chapel Hill, NC. Oct. 23–24, 1986.

Foley, James D. "Interfaces for Advanced Computing." *Scientific American*. Vol. 257(4), 126–135. October, 1987.

Krueger, Myron W. "VIDEOPLACE and the Interface of the Future." *The Art of Human-Computer Interface Design*, ed. Brenda Laurel. Menlo Park, CA: Addison-Wesley Publishing Company. 417–422. 1991.

Palfreman, Jon and Swade, Doron. *The Dream Machine: Exploring the Computer Age*. London, UK: BBC Books. 99. 1991.

Schmandt, Christover. "Interactive Three-Dimensional Computer Space: Processing and Display of Three-Dimensional Data." *SPIE*. Vol. 367, 155–159. 1982.

Sutherland, Ivan E. "The Ultimate Display." *Proceedings of the IFIP Congress*. 506–508. 1965.

Sutherland, Ivan E. "Head-Mounted Three-Dimensional Display." *Proceedings of the Fall Joint Computer Conference*. Vol. 33, 757–64. 1968.

Thompson, Steven L. "The Big Picture." *Air & Space*. 75–83. April/May 1987.

✳ Chapter 4

Barlow, John P. "Being in Nothingness." *Mondo 2000*. 44–51. Summer 1990.

Brand, Stewart. *The Media Lab*. New York, NY: Penguin Books. 1988.

Rheingold, Howard. *Virtual Reality*. New York, NY: Summit Books. 1991.

Walker, John. *Through the Looking Glass*. Internal Autodesk memo. Sausalito, CA: Autodesk. 1988.

✳ **Chapter 5**

Huxley, Aldous. *Music at Night*. 17. 1931.

✳ **Chapter 7**

Luther, A. *Digital Video in the PC Environment*. New York, NY: McGraw Hill. 1989.

✳ **Chapter 8**

Begault, D. R. "Control of Auditory Distance." Dissertation, University of California, San Diego, CA. 1987.

Gyration. "Gyration Overview." Company handout. 1992.

Howlett, Eric. "Product Information, Doc. #11540." LEEP Systems/Pop-Optix Labs. 1991.

Foster, S. H., E. M. Wenzel, and R. M. Taylor. *Real Time Synthesis of Complex Acoustic Environments*. Crystal River Engineering Literature. 1991.

Friedhoff, R. M. *The Second Computer Revolution Visualization*. New York, NY: W. T. Freeman and Company. 1989.

Greuel, Christian. "Simulation of Three-Dimensional Audio." Internal document. May, 1991.

Rebo, Robert K. and Amburn, Phil. "A Helmet-Mounted Virtual Environment Display System." *SPIE*. Vol. 1116, 80–83. 1989.

Stone, Robert. *Virtual Reality: A Tool for Telepresence & Human Factors Research*. UK Advanced Robotics Research Center. 1992.

Wenzel, E. M., F. L. Wightman, and S. H. Foster. "A virtual display system for conveying three-dimensional acoustic information." *Proc. Human Factors Society*. Vol. 32, 86–90. 1988.

✳ **Chapter 9**

Birren, F. *Color Psychology and Color Therapy*. New York, NY: McGraw-Hill, Inc. 1950.

Bryson, Steve and Levit, Creon. *The Virtual Windtunnel: An Environment for the Exploration of Three-Dimensional Unsteady Flows*. NASA Ames Research Center, Mountain View, CA: Applied Research Office, Numerical Aerodynamics Simulation Division. 1992.

Gordon, David. *Therapeutic Metaphors*. Cupertino, CA: META Publications. 1978.

Grinder, John et. al. *Neuro-Linguistic Programming: The Study of the Structure of Subjective Experience*. Cupertino, CA: Meta Publications. 1980.

Laurel, Brenda (editor). *The Art of Human-Computer Interface Design*. Cupertino, CA: Apple Computer and Menlo Park, CA: Addison-Wesley Publishing Company. 1990.

Laurel, Brenda. *Computers as Theater*. Menlo Park, CA: Addison-Wesley Publishing Company. 1991.

London, I. D. "Research on sensory interaction in the Soviet Union." Psychological bulletin. 531–568. 1954.

McLuhan, Marshall and Fiore, Quentin. *The Medium is the Message*. Bantam Books. 1967.

McLuhan, Marshall. *Understanding Media: The Extensions of Man*. New York, NY: McGraw-Hill, Inc. 1967–70.

Payne, M. "Apparent weight as a function of color." *American Journal of Psychology*. Vol. 74, 724–730. 1958.

Payne, M. "Apparent weight as a function of hue." *American Journal of Psychology*. Vol. 74, 104–105. 1961.

Ryan, T. A. "Interrelations of sensory systems in perception." Psychological Bulletin. 659–698. 1940.

Wallis, W. A. "The influence of color on apparent size." *Journal of General Psychology*. Vol. 13, 193–199. 1935.

✳ Chapter 10

Gay, Eben and Greschler, David. "Researching the Effectiveness of Virtual Reality as a Tool for Informal Science Education." White paper. January, 1994.

NASA, David Sarnoff Research Center and SRI International. "Next Generation Virtual Reality Research Workshop." Collected conference papers. June, 1993.

Papert, Seymour. *The Children's Machine: Rethinking School In The Age of the Computer*. New York, NY: Basic Books. 1993.

Papert, Seymour. *Mindstorms: Children, Computers, and Powerful Ideas*. New York, NY: Basic Books. 1980.

Rheingold, Howard. *The Virtual Community*. Addison Wesley Publishing Company. 1993.

✳ Chapter 11

Esposito, Chris, Meredith Bricken, and Keith Butler. "Building the VSX Demonstration: Operations with Virtual Aircraft in Virtual Space." White paper. Seattle, WA: Boeing. 1991.

Nomura, Junji et. al. "Virtual Space Decision Support System and Its Application to Consumer Showrooms." Matsushita white paper. 1992.

Smith, Bradford. "The Flowsheet: Animation Used to Analyze and Present Information About Complex Systems." Presentation at EFDPMA Virtual Reality Conference. Arlington, VA. 1992.

Stix, Gary. "Desktop Artisans." *Scientific American*. 141–142. April, 1992.

Tuori, Martin. "Immersive Simulation-Applications in Design." Presentation to The International Virtual Reality Symposium, Nagoya, Japan. November, 1991.

Wright, R. "Computer Graphics as Allegorical Knowledge: Electronic Imagery in the Sciences," *Leonardo*, supplemental issue. Pergamon Press. 65–67. 1991.

❊ **Chapter 12**

Altman, Lawrence K., M.D. "When Patient's Life Is Price of Learning New Kind of Surgery." *The New York Times*. June 23, 1992.

Brooks, Frederick P. et. al. *Project GROPE—Haptic Displays for Scientific Visualization*. Dept. of Computer Science, University of North Carolina at Chapel Hill. 1990.

Charles, Steve and Williams, Roy. "Dexterity Enhancement in Microsurgery Using Telemicrorobotics." Presentation at Medicine Meets Virtual Reality Conference. San Diego, CA. June, 1992.

Chung, James. et. al. "Radiation Therapy Treatment Planning." Siggraph handout. Dept. of Computer Science, University of North Carolina at Chapel Hill. August, 1991.

Holloway, Richard and Robinett, Warren. "Molecule Museum." Siggraph handout. Dept. of Computer Science, University of North Carolina at Chapel Hill. August, 1991.

Holloway, Richard. Robinett, Warren. "Flying Through Molecules." Siggraph handout. Dept. of Computer Science, University of North Carolina at Chapel Hill. August, 1991.

Mercurio, Philip J. et. al. "The Distributed Laboratory." *Communications of the ACM*. Volume 35, Number 6, 54–63. June, 1992.

Rosen, Joseph, David Chen, and David Zeltzer. "Surgical Simulation Models: From Body Parts to Artificial Person." Presentation at the Medicine Meets Virtual Reality Conference. San Diego, CA. 1992.

Shtern, Faina. "Imaging-guided Stereostactic Tumor Diagnosis and Treatment." Presentation at the Medicine Meets Virtual Reality Conference. San Diego, CA. June, 1992.

Stewart, Doug. "Through the looking glass into an artificial world— via computer." *Smithsonian*. 36–45. January, 1991.

Todd, Daniel. "ADAM Makes Anatomy Come Alive." *New Media*. 20–21. July, 1992.

❊ **Chapter 13**

Bricken, Meredith. *Virtual Reality Learning Environments: Potentials and Challenges*. Seattle, WA: Human Interface Technology Laboratory. 1991.

Carrie, Heeter. "BattleTech demographics." *IEEE Computer Graphics and Applications*. 4–7. March, 1992.

Grimes, Jack. "Virtual reality goes commercial with a blast." *IEEE Computer Graphics and Applications*. 4–7. March, 1992.

Helsel, Sandra. "BattleTech Center." *Virtual Reality Report*. Westport, CT: Meckler. 1991.

Ohbuchi, Ryutarou et. al. "Mountain Bike." Siggraph handout. Dept. of Computer Science, University of North Carolina at Chapel Hill. August, 1991.

Smith, Dawn. "The Practical Side of Virtual Reality." *Marketing Communications*. December, 1991.

Langberg, Mike. "The Multimedia Game Plan." *Mercury News*, May 25, 1992.

❊ **Chapter 14**

Arguelles, Jose. *The Transformative Process*. Berkeley, CA: Shambala. 1975.

Haggerty, Michael. "Serious Lunacy: Art in Virtual Worlds." *IEEE Computer Graphics and Applications*. 4–7. March, 1992.

McLuhan, Marshall. *Understanding Media: The Extensions of Man*. NY: McGraw-Hill, Inc. 1967–70.

Shlain, Leonard. *Art & Physics: Parallel Visions in Space, Time & Light*. NY: Morrow Williams and Company. 1991.

✳ **Chapter 15**

Benedikt, Michael. *Cyberspace: First Steps*. Cambridge, MA: The MIT Press. 1992.

Bricken, Meredith. "Virtual Reality Learning Environments: Potentials and Challenges." Siggraph presentation at the Human Interface Technology Laboratory. Seattle, WA. 1991.

Crua-Neira, Carolina et. al. "The CAVE: Audio Visual Experience Automatic Virtual Environment.." *Communications of the ACM*. Volume 35, Number 6, 64–72. June, 1992.

Kay, Alan. *User Interface: A Personal View. The Art of Human-Computer Interface Design*. Cupertino, CA: Apple Computer. Menlo Park, CA: Addison-Wesley Publishing Company. 1990.

Papert, S. *Mindstorms*. NY: Basic Books. 1980.

Smarr, Larry and Catiett, Charles E. "Metacomputing." *Communications of the ACM*, Volume 35, Number 6, 44–52. June, 1992.

✳ **Glossary**

M. Bricken. *Cyberspace: First Steps*. Cambridge, MA: The MIT Press. 1991.

⇨ Recommended reading

Brand, Stewart. *The Media Lab: Inventing the Future at MIT*. Viking Penguin, Inc. 1987.

Friedhoff, Richard Mark and Benzon, William. *Visualization: The Second Computer Revolution*. Harry N. Abrams, Inc. 1989.

Gibson, William. *Neuromancer*. New York, NY: ACE Books. 1984.

Jacobson, Linda. *Garage Virtual Reality: The Affordable Way to Explore Virtual Worlds*. Sams/Prentice Hall Computer Books. 1993.

Kalawsky, Roy. *The Science of Virtual Reality and Virtual Environments. Addison-Wesley*. 1993.

Laurel, Brenda (editor). *The Art of Human-Computer Interface Design*. Reading, MA: Addison-Wesley. 1990.

Rheingold, Howard, *Virtual Reality: Exploring the Brave New Technologies*. New York, NY: Simon & Schuster. 1991.

Stampe, Dave, Bernie Roehl, and John Eagan. *Virtual Reality Creations*. Waite Group Press. 1993.

Index

Illustration page numbers are in **boldface.**

About the authors

Kevin Teixeira is Intel's Virtual Reality Program Manager and co-founder of the Intel Digital Education & Art (IDEA) program. The goal of the IDEA program is to inspire new users and uses of computer technology. He has worked with the modern artist Jenny Holzer, the composer Thomas Dolby, and Carnegie Mellon University, among others, to explore the use of virtual reality in art, entertainment, education, and business. For the IDEA program, he developed an exhibit called Virtual Reality: an Emerging Medium with the Solomon R. Guggenheim Museum of New York in October of 1993. For this project he received a special industry award at the Meckler VR conference in the spring of 1994.

In addition to his work in VR, Kevin has also been the creative manager for the Intel Inside program and managed production of Intel's award-winning TV commercials created by George Lucas' Industrial Light & Magic.

Most recently, he played a major role in creating Intel's IMAX film, *The Journey Inside*. This is the first IMAX film explicitly developed for kids and their families. Conceived as a form of "edutainment," it's an exciting use of the science-fiction film genre to educate the general public on microprocessors. It includes a special computer graphics sequence where a young boy uses VR to fly inside a microprocessor, shrinking all the way down to the atomic level.

In conjunction with the release of *The Journey Inside*, Kevin is working on a national educational program. Its purpose is to translate the excitement of the film into in-class activities that teach young people about high-technology.

Kenneth Pimentel has many years of experience in dealing with technical issues related to virtual environments. He has spent the last

several years working at Sense8 as Product Manager and Vice President. Through his work at Sense8, Kenneth has helped create the industry's leading software tool for the development of virtual environments and has been intimately involved in the creation of various complex virtual worlds. Kenneth has also written several articles and has had many opportunities to speak on the subject of virtual environments and related issues.

Prior to joining Sense8, Kenneth worked at Intel in the Advanced Human Interface Group. He was awarded one of Intel's first Intel Fellowship grants to pursue research in virtual reality, where he pioneered the use of real-time texture mapping for virtual worlds using low-cost PC hardware. In his ten years at Intel, Ken also worked in the internal CAD group, developing user interfaces and tools for the manufacturing of Intel's chip technology. Ken has a BS in ECE from the University of California at Davis.